Pizz

Pizz

ALAN HOVHANESS

UNVEILING ONE OF THE GREAT COMPOSERS OF THE 20TH CENTURY

HINAKO FUJIHARA HOVHANESS

FOREWORD BY GERARD SCHWARZ

ISBN: 978-1-59849-381-8 (regular edition)
ISBN: 978-1-59849-385-6 (special edition)

Library of Congress Control Number: 2025904998

BISAC Codes:
BIO004000 BIOGRAPHY & AUTOBIOGRAPHY / Music
MUS006000 MUSIC / Genres & Styles / Classical
MUS050000 MUSIC / Individual Composer & Musician

Printed in China

Editor: Danielle Harvey
Design: Soundview Design

alanhovhanessmusic.com

Classic Day Publishing
206-860-4900
info@classicdaypub.com
www.classicdaypub.com

To Dan Shelhamer, for his commitment and countless hours documenting the important musical events in this book.

Acknowledgments

Written by William Holst

I would like to express my greatest gratitude to my family and very close friends of the Hovhaness family for their inspirational support in making Alan's music and my mother's stories available to the world.

Joni Holst – My sister spent many late evenings dictating and correcting my mother's stories. She was also a big part of my mother's life, as you can see from the many entries about her in this book.

Tracy Holst – My daughter and major book contributor. She has spent countless hours gathering information, pictures, and providing editing and proofreading to support this book.

Coleen Holst – My wife and partner in making book decisions. She spent large amounts of time investigating, locating pictures, proofreading, and editing. She also made sure the cats didn't jump on the desk and hit the delete key.

Sunako Hata – My mother's sister. She has been very supportive of my family and this book since my mother's passing. Investigating and writing her life story has opened my eyes to what great things she has accomplished, and she has been an inspiration.

Marco Shirodkar – A special thanks to Marco, the designer and manager of Hovhaness.com. He is probably the most knowledgeable person pertaining to Alan's music history. Many of the dates, individuals, and occurrences in this book were verified through Marco. He was always available to provide information, and all his great work was volunteered for his love of classical music and Alan's work.

Gerard Schwarz – One of Alan and my mother's great friends and musical associate. One of the great musical performers and champion of Hovhaness music. He is always available and provided significant support for this book.

Michal Ter-Minasian – A photographer, poet, and great friend of Alan and my mother. He provided several essential pictures and information to support this book.

Father Dennis O'Neill – A great supporter of Alan's music and had a fantastic spiritual friendship with my mother. I will always remember the trip he made to Seattle where we took turns caring for Alan.

Ara Ghazarians – An absolute pillar of integrity and well respected. Ara has dedicated so many hours to the Armenian Cultural Foundation and recognizing Alan in the Arlington MA community. He has coordinated many of Alan's local concerts and has done so much for the community. He is always available and willing to provide support for any Hovhaness projects.

Jack Johnston – Jack grew up in Alan's neighborhood and was very close to Alan's father; he is still one of Alan's greatest supporters. An all-around great guy, an outstanding person in the community, likes to drink Moxie, and I'm waiting for his joke book to be published.

Michael Armanious – He helped to investigate Alan's personal life and interviewed many of Alan's old acquaintances. The information he uncovered and his interest in Alan helped inspire the completion of this book.

Marvin Rosen – I had heard Marvin's name several times when I was younger while Alan and my mother were alive, but after going through some of my mother's documents, his name reappeared, so I decided to contact him. He is a very dedicated follower of Alan and his music, and he motivated me to research further into details of this book.

Gene Caprioglio – I met Gene on a trip my mother and I made to New York. He has since retired as Vice President for New Music and Rights at Edition Peters Group.

A sincere appreciation for the publishing and marketing/public relations groups that carried me along the way to publishing this book. All the experience and knowledge they provided absolutely made all the difference in motivating this project into a major success.

Peanut Butter Publishing

Elliott Wolf – He has become one of Alan's great admirers and has provided ideas and information well beyond the scope of this book. We are forever thankful for his dedication to the Hovhaness projects.

Danielle Harvey – She was a major contributor for contract negotiations, book design, editing, and layout of this book. Her knowledge of the process very much made the book publishing experience straightforward.

Ruthie Little – She coordinated all the publisher meetings, contracts, and legal aspects for this book.

Amy Vaughn – She performed the book layout and cover. Any edit or design modifications were performed promptly and professionally.

Black Chateau Enterprises (BCE)

Desiree Duffy – She is the Executive Director of PR, branding, and business development for BCE. Desiree has exposed all the techniques for branding, coaching, and promoting a book.

Dave Duffy – He is the head of operations, social media, advertisement, and website development for BCE. I can't stress how much Dave has helped with his all-around knowledge for promoting the book and how to capture that knowledge into the website.

Special thanks to Michael York for taking time in his busy schedule to read this book and provide me with some of his memories. His reading will forever be associated with Alan's composition of the "Rubaiyat." Michael was very willing to provide support for this book, and he was an absolute pleasure to work with.

Foreword

In David Ewen's seminal book from 1982 about American composers, he begins his entry about Alan Hovhaness:

"One of the most prolific composers of the 20th century, with some three hundred compositions in all media and most in large structures to his credit. Hovhaness has arrived at an individuality of style by synthesizing the music of the Western world with that of the East."

In reading Hinako Hovhaness's wonderful book about her husband and their life together, I am reminded of Hovhaness the man, husband, and philosophical thinker. Each of those personas were reflected in his music. He was always true to his art and created a very large body of work that, no matter how they are influenced from Japan to India and Armenia, has a clear and poetic compositional voice.

He started writing music in the 1930s but was more broadly noticed as a student at Tanglewood in 1942. From all reports, it was not a good time for Hovhaness, but he established himself as an independently thinking composer even then. He certainly embraced particularly trendy forms such as aleatory, but as he wrote: "To me, atonality is against nature. There is a center to everything that exists. The planets have a sun, the moon the earth. The reason I like oriental music is that everything has a firm center. All music with a center is tonal. Music, without a center is fine for a minute or two, but it soon sounds all the same. Things which are very complicated tend to disappear and get lost. Simplicity is difficult, not easy. Beauty is simple. All unnecessary elements are remover-only essence remains."

I first played Hovhaness's music as a high school trumpet student performing his *Prayer of St. Gregory*. I was struck by playing a living composer who wrote music that was very beautiful and yet playable by students of every level. Interestingly, even today his music is better known by younger students than professionals.

In my article for *Gramophone* magazine in 2019 about important, lesser-known American composers, I wrote this about Hovhaness:

"I met Alan Hovhaness (1911–2000) when I was 16, recording his work for trumpet and band, *Return and Rebuild the Desolate Places*. His music is played often, but usually by student groups. It is very melodic, usually not too difficult to perform, and each piece selectively is evocative of the music of Armenia, India, Hawaii, Japan, Korea or America. Alan was always a very spiritual person, drawing on nature for inspiration. He also prided himself on his use of counterpoint and was disappointed his works were not studied in counterpoint classes."

He was highly prolific, having written approximately seventy symphonies. Like Haydn, the ones with titles are the ones most often programmed. His second symphony, *Mysterious Mountain,* is an evocative work, combining traditional white note (on the piano) melodies and harmonies with an underlying accompaniment often sounding not only harmonically unrelated but gesturing apart from the main material. The work has numerous solos for woodwinds and brass. It also contains an extraordinary double fugue in the second movement, and it ends with an exquisite full-bodied chorale for the entire orchestra. It was premiered by Stokowski during his opening concert as music director of the Houston Symphony in 1955. Reiner recorded it with Chicago in 1958, which helped make Hovhaness's reputation. In the last fifteen years, while it has had many performances, I could only find a handful by professional orchestras, other than my own. In fact, when I recorded it for PBS television with the All-Star Orchestra in 2016, many members of the orchestra, loving the work, asked why they had never heard the piece before. These were players from America's most important orchestras. Most composers of his time did not accept Hovhaness into their circle because of his simpler style. There were exceptions such as Howard Hanson and Lou Harrison. I remember David Diamond always speaking highly of him, especially during our time together in Seattle.

There have been several important conductors who have supported Hovhaness, including Stokowski, Kostelanetz, and Reiner. Both Dennis Russel Davies and I have continued to perform his works, and others such as Ozawa, Ehrling, and Rostropovich have performed his music.

On the 23rd of April 2001, a Hovhaness memorial concert was held in Seattle's Benaroya Hall and subsequently repeated in New York. For the first time the concert hall waived its rental fee. I read out a letter from composer Lou Harrison that declared Hovhaness "one of the great melodists of the 20th century" and "a master to us all." I paid the following tribute when speaking to the *Seattle Times*: "He was trying to add beauty and sensitivity to the world. He cared deeply about goodness and about nature, and he has had a tremendous impact. I've known Alan since 1963, throughout it all, even in the times when his music wasn't so fashionable, he stuck to his thinking and to his distinctive style, which had a passion and a great reserve. He stood out. Alan was amazing, he was one of the great composers of our time."

In 2011, I lead a weeklong celebration of the 100th anniversary of Alan's birth with the Seattle Symphony. I've recorded eight CDs of his music and continue to preform works each season and with great public success. His music has lived on and will continue to because of its beauty and passion.

– *Gerard Schwarz, Music Director: All-Star Orchestra; Frost Symphony Orchestra; Palm Beach Symphony; Eastern Music Festival; Conductor Laureate: Seattle Symphony; Conductor Emeritus: Mostly Mozart Festival Distinguished Professor of Conducting at the Frost School of Music at the University of Miami*

Table of Contents

Introduction

Written by Hinako Hovhaness
July 30, 2014

Alan Hovhaness: Unveiling One of the Great Composers of the 20th Century is based on the true events surrounding my husband, Alan Hovhaness, and the stories he told me.

In the year 2000, after his death, I started writing poems, which was the only way I could cope with my great loss. They were written with my limited English, yet they were spontaneous and poignant, straight from my heart.

After I had written hundreds of poems, it was not enough. I started writing stories from my memories about Alan, events I had experienced with him.

Then I realized, to write these stories, I needed help with my English. My daughter Joni, who was living in New York at the time, offered to help me. I faxed my writings to her daily and she corrected them over the telephone—hours at a time; she typed them and faxed them back to me. But by the end of the year, she confessed she could no longer do this anymore.

I looked for someone to help me edit my stories. I needed a person who was knowledgeable about English and literature; so I called Daniel Shelhamer, our long-time friend who Alan and I had met in the early 1970s when he was studying at the University of Washington graduate school. He was an all-around musician (conductor, bass singer, pianist, actor, and composer), so I thought he could help me find somebody with those skills. His wife answered my call, and I told her my need, then she said instantaneously, without pause, "My husband is the right one!"

That was it! Dan became my editor and English teacher. He has an excellent knowledge of English and corrected my bad English; but he was always careful not to change the personality and originality of my writing (including my made-up English words). So here we are, continuing to work together into 2014.

My book is not about Alan's music, but about him as a composer and a man. Often people asked Alan about his music—he said, "My music speaks for itself!" So why would I write about it? I would rather entertain people with his delightful stories.

Alan was a good educator and entertainer. When he was not composing, he taught me about the composers of the past he most admired: Handel, Mozart, Beethoven, Schubert, and Sibelius. Through their music as well as their true-life stories and love affairs (including musicians' gossip, which should interest everybody).

Alan often spoke of Francis Bacon, his master and mentor, whom he believed was the real Shakespeare, the true writer of Shakespeare's works. According to Alan, Bacon's secret messages and stories are hidden in code (cipher) in these works. Very few people can decipher these messages.

Alan was a master of counterpoint and an intellectual, yet he had many different sides to his personality, from being a polite, distinguished gentleman to a wild savage, idealistic, and old-fashioned man to sexy womanizer. He understood human nature and emotion, and I think that is why his music touches people's hearts and is loved by them, even though his music is built on an intellectual foundation.

Obviously, my stories are memories of the unforgettable events I experienced with him, which I wrote as they came into my mind; but I hope my stories give you a deeper understanding and interest in his music as well as Hovhaness, the man.

My book is not a long, continuous story, even though the titles are in chronological order, but each of them has its own story and title, so you don't have to read from the beginning to the end; you can choose any one of them to read by itself.

Finally, my stories are my tribute to my genius husband, Alan Hovhaness, the "giant" composer.

Alan and Hinako Hovhaness at Mt. Si

Stories of Alan's Growing Up

♪

Alan told me many stories of his childhood, and I know they were very important to him. Since Alan's death in 2000, I have written many stories about him based on what he told me and our experiences together, many of them being his childhood stories. Today, I have an urge to put them together in one chapter, not as my creative writing, but rather my biographical portrayal of his early life.

Alan Hovhaness at age twenty-three

Alan's Earliest Memories

Alan Vaness Chakmakjian was born on March 8, 1911, in Somerville, Massachusetts. He recalled when he was very young, barely walking, looking at the hills of Somerville and thinking he was in Florence, Italy. According to Alan, he believed Florence was where he lived in his last incarnation at a very young age; memories of his past life were still present.

He also had memories of the first place he lived; it was attic-like with a dump nearby. That was before his family moved to Arlington, Massachusetts, when he was five years old.

Alan's Father

Alan's father, Haroutioun Hovanes Chakmakjian, was an Armenian from Adana, Turkey, where there was a large Armenian settlement. At the time of the massacre of Turkish Armenians by the Turkish government in the late 1800s, Alan's father was teaching French in Beirut, Lebanon. His family escaped to Cyprus, but he headed to France in a boat called the "Poseidon." On board, the captain of the ship gave the steering wheel to a young child. Within minutes, the ship was grounded on a rock and shipwrecked. It happened right across the bay from a Turkish city, and Turks came to rescue the shipwrecked people. To avoid being captured, Alan's father pretended he was a Frenchman. By using his ability to speak French, he was able to finagle his way onto a boat to France. From there he came to America and settled in Boston. He taught chemistry at Tufts University; he was called the "professor."

Later he met Alan's mother, Madeleine Scott, at an Armenian charity newspaper where they were both volunteering.

Alan's Grandfather Walter Scott

Madeleine was born in Ossining, New York, to Walter Scott, a Baptist minister. He was often mistaken for the famous Scottish writer, Sir Walter Scott; he did not mind but was rather proud of it. Alan remembers him as being very talkative. One day he was giving one of his usual long, sermon-like speeches to his informal dinner guests—finally, his wife cut in and said to him, "Eat your dinner or else you won't get it," to shut him up. She was his second wife and much younger than him; she was the only one who could control his talk.

(I always thought Alan's talkative nature was from his Armenian side, but I realize it must have come from his grandfather's Scottish side.)

Alan's Grandmothers Sarah Pugsley and Kohar Chakmakjian

Alan's grandmother, Sarah Pugsley, was his grandfather Walter Scott's first wife. She was a descendant from a Scottish family who had settled in New England. They were stubborn troublemakers; one time they challenged the American government, and Sarah was part of the clan. She was living with her son's family in her old age. At bedtime, if any of her grandchildren came to her bedroom, she would say, "Shut up!" as if she knew what they would say beforehand.

Alan never met his Armenian grandmother Kohar, but he wrote a piece for string orchestra with her name and dedicated it to her.

Alan's Mother and His Home – Off Limits to Laughter

Alan remembers his home as being gloomy, as if laughter was off limits. His parents were stern and strict. Alan was their only child and had all their attention and expectations focused on him. He thought in his young mind that having a brother would soften the focus on him, but his mother never gave him one.

On Alan's birthday, there were many boys gathered at his home, and Alan was so happy he could not stop laughing. "Alan, stop it!" his mother said as if laughter was indecent. Alan's mother and grandfather were both very Christian, and she taught Sunday school. In class she would often cry from her overwhelming religious inspiration. Alan was very ashamed of her uncontrollable tears, but he inherited her tears, and he could not stop them when he was inspired or emotionally moved.

Alan's childhood home in Arlington, Massachusetts

At church services, Alan watched old ladies singing hymns; their shaking voices interested him, and he rather liked them. Alan did not object to voices with vibrato, and many of his songs were written with repeated wide trills or tremolo-like notes.

Alan would go wild after many hours of confinement at church. His father, who would stay home, would say to Alan's mother, "Madeleine, you brought a devil from the church!"

Alan loved trees and planted young evergreen trees (which grew up to be giant trees) in a small space in his yard that was not suitable to become woods. They were all taken away by his mother.

She was a nervous person, and she did not like children because they bothered her. There was a fruit tree at the side of their house; and children came to pick the fruit, which bothered her, and her only solution was to cut down the tree.

Alan's Cousin Winthrop

Since Alan could not have a brother, his closest experience to brotherhood was his cousin Winthrop. Whenever the two families got together, Alan would play with Winthrop. Their favorite game was what they called the "civilization game." They would build buildings with blocks, and once completed, they would destroy it and start building all over again. (They already had the instinct of the human species—we have been doing this, building and destroying, ever since we started.)

Uncle Frank

Winthrop's father, Frank, was a delightful person. He played piano and sang with his nice voice, and Alan often went nature painting with him. Those were such fun times for Alan; they climbed the hills, looked for spots with mountain views, and then they took their position to paint. Even though those were nice, clear days, Alan's childhood paintings turned out to be something awesome with wild mountain storms. His explanation was that peaceful mountain scenes were not interesting, so he put drama into his paintings.

One of Alan's childhood paintings

Alan was fascinated by mountain storms all his life, and he talked about the famous storm music from "William Tell Overture" by Rossini, and Sibelius's "The Tempest." In 1931, he wrote "Storm on Mount Wildcat," and in 1980, he composed his New Hampshire mountain storm in his symphony "To the Green Mountains." And in 1982, he wrote his most famous dramatic mountain music: "Mt. Saint Helens Symphony."

Uncle Frank was as happy as he seemed, and he kept his unhappy marriage to himself. Alan's parents told Alan not to ask his uncle about his wife (Winthrop's mother). From the little he knew, he thought she was struggling with mental illness. Later she died and Uncle Frank remarried, and Alan heard he was very happy.

Alan's Uncle's Farm

Alan's other uncle had a farm in New Hampshire, one of Alan's happiest memories was visiting his farm. In his uncle's newly built dining room, the two families spent many happy evenings together. From the back of his uncle's house, Alan could see the farm all the way to the foot of Catamount Mountain, which was shaped like a sleeping cat. *Alan often stood there, looking at the mountain.

Alan loved to climb hills and mountains, which he did better than other boys, even though he was not good in sports. In the summertime, the hills were filled with blueberries and Alan often went berry-picking with his parents. He picked the berries with them for a while but soon snuck off and climbed the hills. At the top of the hills, above the tree line, a magnificent view opened in front of him, and he found himself surrounded by mountains. Soon his parents became worried and started looking for him. They told him they would never take him blueberry-picking again, and they did not believe what Alan had seen on the top of the hill. The only person who supported Alan's story was his uncle Frank. He said he had gone there himself and saw the wonderful view.

*Alan's quote: "Catamount is near Pittsfield, New Hampshire. An old farmer and sage lived near the top of Catamount and used to look through his field glasses at the magnificent view of the distant White Mountains. I used to climb Catamount many times in my childhood."

Alan's Neighbors in Arlington

Alan remembered a young boy in his neighborhood that seemed to look up to him. He called him "Al," and every time he saw Alan, he would say, "How are you?" [sic].

There was another poor family in his neighborhood with many children. In the cold winter, they could not buy firewood, so their father took down pieces of his house, one by one, to put in the fireplace to warm his family. Alan noticed their house getting smaller and smaller.

Alan thought another neighbor was nice, but she periodically had a fit and ran out of her house, screaming and crying and leaving her husband. Alan was very young and did not know what was wrong with her, but he was very concerned. After each episode, a priest brought her home.

Alan often took a shortcut to school; the pathway was covered with wild bushes. One day he was passing through the pathway and his pants got caught on the bushes and tore. At the end of the pathway, he unexpectedly bumped into a neighbor lady; he greeted her politely, in his embarrassment covering his torn pants.

At this time in America, men were taught to be respectful and protective to women, often saying, "Ladies first." Alan always had that attitude towards women. Although that tradition has been lost, in old Japan, we Japanese thought of American men as "gentlemen," polite to ladies.

Speaking of ladies…

There was a very respectable old Christian lady who lived in the neighborhood. Every time Alan paid a visit to her, her parrot, sitting in the entrance hall, greeted him, saying, "Go to hell! Go to hell!"

Those were the only words the parrot had picked up from the old lady. It seemed to Alan that her parrot was exposing her bad habits behind closed doors.

Mr. Angelo was an Italian man who had a small farm. Alan often watched his old, beat-up truck going up the hill, and he wondered whether it would make it or not. When Alan was walking home from school, Mr. Angelo often gave him a ride in his truck. Alan was a little hesitant because his mother might not approve of him getting a ride from an Italian farmer.

Mr. Angelo was one of Alan's early audiences. He was appreciative of music, and every time Alan played one of his new compositions on the piano for him, he cried out, "I will die this time, I am sure I will die!" This was his expression of overwhelming appreciation, but young Alan took it seriously and was afraid he really would die. All his life he was afraid of anybody saying, "I will kill myself."

Alan's Family Dog Frolic

Frolic was a small, husky bull terrier with black fur and a white design on the center of his face and chest.

Alan used to do chores for his mother. There was a small country grocery store nearby, and he went there in a wagon pulled by Frolic. One day at the grocery store, Alan saw a dog peeing on a vegetable, so he reported it to the owner of the grocery store. She said, "That's okay," in her sing-song manner. Alan was surprised and worried that he might have eaten her polluted vegetables.

Frolic was gentle to his family but, according to Alan, he was a killer. Any time he saw chickens, he became wild and chased and killed them. Alan was the one to face Mrs. Angelo, the owner of the chickens. Each time a chicken was killed, he brought the dead chicken, money to pay for it, and an apology. Then she would say, "Tell your father to be sure to keep the dog on a leash!" But his father believed, "A dog needs freedom."

Frolic was wild in nature and chased anything that moved. But one time he chased a porcupine and got quills all over himself. He suffered from the leftover quills in his body for some period. He came to Alan in such a way that Alan knew what he wanted, for Alan to pull out the quills showing up on the surface of his skin.

At night, when everybody was in bed, Frolic would come upstairs to crawl into Alan's bed. However, Frolic was not supposed to be there since it was restricted by the mistress of the house. Frolic felt guilty every time he would miss the steps at the top of the stairs and wake up Alan's mother, who would yell at him, "Frolic, come down!"

The last time Alan saw Frolic was when he was visiting his father. By that time Frolic was old and blind, sitting at this father's feet (every dog needs somebody to belong to). He was Alan's father's dog—Alan's father understood him and gave him his freedom.

Alan's First Girl – His Choice

Alan disliked sports, so while the other boys were playing baseball, he would hide in an ashcan and the teacher had to pull him out to put him in the game. But neither team wanted him.

Alan was different from other boys his age because he was intellectually developed and was not interested in their childish activities. The girls of his age were usually attracted by the boys who were fitted for sports, so they did not understand Alan.

The one girl his mother approved of and thought good for Alan was a church girl, the "good girl," but Alan found her "not interesting." He liked the prettiest girl in the school, and she obviously knew Alan liked her. She told everybody that Alan had a crush on the homeliest girl in the school, which were her sadistic kicks to torture Alan. She was the "bad girl."

Alan at Jr. High School

Alan's memories of junior high were not pleasant ones. After school he was often beat up by Irish bullies, if not every day. Around that time, many Irish families lived in the suburbs of Boston. They were Catholic and outnumbered the Armenian Protestants, so Armenian boys were targets. (As usual in the religious sector, even kids were at war against other religions.)

Alan being very tall (Alan remembered he was the tallest of anybody), short and husky Irish boys had an advantage over him. They punched his middle first so he could not do anything but just pound their backs from above. Then he was knocked down on the ground and they all ended up on top of him, beating him. After that, he would go to a stream to wash the blood from his wounds, and then he went home as if nothing had happened. While all this was going on, his parents did not know.

Alan said to me that he did not have any troubles at his first junior high, but his parents changed schools because he had to cross a train track to get to school.

One of the boys at that school, Ottoson Jr. High, who sang the leading part in one of Alan's operas, coached Alan how to fight. Finally, Alan got up the courage to fight back against the bullies and face, who else but the leader of the Irish gang, face to face. They were surrounded by spectators who had come to see this spectacle. Alan was motivating himself by saying over and over, "I will knock out your teeth." Naturally, the bully did not believe him, but Alan did knock out one of his teeth! The bully was very surprised, more than anything else, and said, "He knocked out my tooth!" After that, he and his gang did not bother Alan anymore.

(Alan used to wear dentures. I never asked him how he lost his teeth, but I am wondering, did he lose his teeth from battles with the Irish? If so, how many teeth did he lose before he knocked out the tooth from the Irish bully?)

At this time, I would like to go back to Alan's early composing...

Alan, the Born Composer

Alan had been hearing melodies in his head for as long as he could remember, and he thought everybody else did as well.

His first attempt to compose was when he was four years old. He composed on an eleven-line staff (treble and bass clef plus one line) that he invented. His mother, who had a small harmonium organ, said she could not play his music on her instrument, so he gave up composing and went on to study astronomy until he was seven years old.

When Alan was in early elementary school, Schubert's music was being introduced to the class. Alan liked it and thought, "Mr. Schubert wrote down that music, but I am hearing my music in my head, so I should write it down." So he did, and that was how he started composing. Schubert's music continued to inspire him all the rest of his life.

During the Elementary School Years

Alan did not do well in school because he was bored in class and was always looking out the window, thinking of his music. His grades were bad, but in some special subjects, like astronomy, he knew more than his teacher. He even built a treehouse for his observatory to see the stars in the sky. (He said the last time he was there, his observatory was still standing.) But because of his bad grades, his parents thought he was lacking motivation, so his father showed him the picture of the muscle arm and hammer on the baking soda box to motivate him.

Obviously, his parents did not understand Alan writing music and thought he should study instead. Alan had to compose in secret from them, sometimes hiding his music from them under the bathtub.

He often woke up before his parents did and composed outdoors in the dark, using his cipher, which he had invented for that purpose; later he would decipher it in the daylight. One time, he made a mistake, he went out thinking dawn would come soon, but it was still night, and he was locked out of his house and had to stay out all night.

Alan's first music education was the piano. When he was eight years old, his mother sent him out to Mrs. Kay, a piano teacher who lived next door. She taught him a waltz, but that was the only thing she could teach him, so he had to move on.

His next piano teacher was Adelaide Proctor. Prior to Alan studying with her, she had had dreams about a woman and her young son and wondered about this occurrence. When Alan and his mother came to see her, she knew that young boy in her dream was Alan, so she took him as her student, by all means! Alan later studied with Henrich Gebhard; both encouraged him greatly.

Alan wrote operas, even in his childhood. His first opera was "Bluebeard," based on the story of the king who had six wives. Alan had difficulty writing the libretto for Bluebeard's love scene with his sixth wife, so he asked his mother to help him, but she dismissed him. She was very puritanical and could not speak of such a thing to her son. So, Alan had to improvise, and his libretto turned out like this:

> Bluebeard: The moon is flowing.
> Wife: His blue beard is not so blue after all. (She is beginning to like him.)

He also composed "Daniel," the biblical story when he was in junior high.

By the time he was in high school, he was known among the students as a pianist and composer. He and Edgar Hague (Alan called him "my librettist") established an opera workshop called "Atelier" to study and perform operas. Alan composed the opera "Lotus Blossom" from Edgar's libretto for the workshop. By the end of the school year, they all went to an ice cream parlor and ate ice cream, using up all the money they saved for Atelier and dissolved the workshop.

Alan's First Composition Teacher

Alan's first composition teacher was Leo Rich Lewis at Tufts College. He was a very obstinate Germanic teacher. His teaching started with him saying, "You are a Goddamn fool, nothing but a Goddamn fool," to intimidate Alan and make him obedient. His teaching was just as rigid as his manner. He would say, "I will knock out all your originality." Alan was obedient and mastered all Lewis's classical composing techniques. He composed pieces Lewis would like and presented them to him, and Lewis was pleased. Then Alan's mother said, "Why don't you show him the other one you have been writing?"

Alan thought that he had earned his trade by being obedient to his teacher; he thought he should show him his own composition he had been writing on the side. He presented them to his teacher, who then said, "You are a Goddamn fool, nothing but a Goddamn fool! You are too young to know anything."

When Alan got to study with Frederick Converse at the New England Conservatory, Lewis told Alan not to mention he had ever studied with him, but Alan always mentioned him as one of his teachers in his biographies. (I hope by now Mr. Lewis does not mind it.)

Alan's Mother's Death

Alan lost his mother when he was only nineteen years old. She had tongue cancer, which she had developed from a bad habit of biting her tongue.

During that time, Alan's father taught at school, commuting to a distant place every day, and young Alan thought his father might have had somebody he liked there. Alan's mother's unhappiness might have been due to his father's interest in another woman.

Her condition worsened, she was biting her tongue in her sleep, and it developed into cancer. By that time her dentist had pulled all her teeth out so she could not bite, but it did not help the cancer. She was in severe pain; Alan could not stand to watch her agony and wished her to die. Finally, she did die, and her suffering was over. Alan was relieved, but that was short lived because he missed her terribly and tried to find her by any means. I think that was how his interest in spiritualism started. He could not face the fact that she was gone. To believe she was still living as a spirit was the only way he could cope with his great loss.

Life with His Father

After her death, Alan's life was with his father, but their relationship was a strained one. At one time his father was upset with Alan and knocked him down on the ground. Alan picked up some object from the ground and pointed it at his father, to defend himself. But his father was very upset about Alan's action and said to him, "You assaulted your own father!"

Alan was not fond of Armenian food. He especially hated *madzoon*, Armenian yogurt. According to Alan, it was spoiled goat's milk, but his father said, "It is healthy," and tried to make Alan drink it. He would take Alan on long walks into the countryside, dropping in on various Armenian farmers he knew. Then he asked them to give *madzoon* to his son and, even though Alan was thirsty, he could not drink it.

Altogether, his father was disappointed in Alan and did not understand him writing music. The only thing he could understand was academic professions. Whenever he was displeased with Alan, he hit his own head and said, "Madeleine, what shall I do with your son!"

When Alan got older, he got his first music-related job, which was very difficult to get during the Depression, but his father went to the business and told them things to disqualify Alan's credentials, to stop Alan from getting the job.

It seemed Alan could not get his father's approval or make him happy. But finally, in 1958, Alan got his first honorary doctorate's degree in music. Alan's father was so proud of his son and cried with joy. He did not know a music writer could get a doctorate's degree.

For the first time, he realized what a treasure he had.

Eyes of Eternity

I will write and write your stories you have told me.
Pity—I cannot write them beside you in our old age,
But if you were here with me, how could I write?
Instead, we would be busy, fondling each other.

Let me take off my reading glasses and put on my brand-new distance glasses to see the whole picture,
I realize—It is meant to be, to be alone to write,
Write about you and your profound stories.
My road seems long and lonely,
But from the eyes of eternity, our long separation is just as short as
The blink of an eye.

Consuelo Cloos

Alan met many people in his lifetime and told me many stories about them. He was a storyteller, telling stories all the time, when he was not composing. He said that Armenians were very talkative people, and he was no exception! But now, I realize his storytelling was not just "talking to be talking," but subconsciously he was passing those stories on to me so they would not be lost. Many of these people were like storybook characters and made strong impressions on him. Consuelo Cloos was one of them. She was a singer and a poet and was one of the most unconventional characters Alan had ever met.

Alan's first meeting with Consuelo was in the 1940s in Boston. At that time Alan was a struggling composer teaching piano and playing organ in an Armenian church, as well as trying to produce concerts for his own music. One night, he was in his backstage dressing room and a woman and old man, who was shaking, came in; her makeup was drooping down her face like a ghost. She said she had come to Alan's concert because she had seen an announcement about it in the newspaper. One of the pieces, "Lament," the title, interested her, also the thirteen letters of the composer's name.

Consuelo had been living with this rich old man with Parkinson's disease; his family had gotten worried about his estate. He was getting old and still living with Consuelo; his family had to do something to control the situation, so they kidnapped him against his will. He must have been brokenhearted. Consuelo never heard from him again, and he apparently died.

Consuelo was not legally married to him but had lived with him for a long time, so she decided to get her share of his estate. Alan and Serafina, his wife at that time, tried to help Consuelo by taking her to California, where the old man's family lived. So, they hopped in a car and off they went to California. Alan drove the car across the U.S. with two backseat drivers in his car. You can imagine, it was quite a difficult trip for him.

At one time they stopped at an eating place by the road. After eating, Serafina took out all her money from a packet and put it on the table and started counting. Alan was nervous; somebody might mug them since Serafina was displaying the money for everybody to see. Alan was supposedly the protector of the two wild women, but he looked very thin and fragile. (He was especially undernourished at that time of his life.)

Finally, they arrived in California and went straight to his friend William Saroyan, the well-known Armenian writer. He found a good lawyer for Consuelo, and she was awarded one of the rich old man's houses. On the way back home in the car, Alan and Serafina constantly fought. (In New York, Serafina usually went to the theater while Alan was teaching. In the evening, he composed in the bedroom while Serafina was having a chat over coffee with her friends, so this trip was the first time they were exposed to each other all day.) Serafina, being hot-tempered, like an Italian peasant, and Alan being very sensitive, they fought like cats and dogs. They decided to divorce as soon as they got to New York; it was forgotten for a while once they went back to their usual New York routine. (They divorced later.)

Shortly after that time, Consuelo lived with her new boyfriend, a Russian bass singer. The two singers fought often, and he pleaded with her, "Wilt please to be normal." Every time, after their short separation, he brought her a bouquet of flowers and they made up.

Alan was hired by them as a piano accompanist for their singing. For his payment, they fed him. Alan remembered he was eating yams at their dinners, always lots of yams.

Finally, the concert day came. Alan was at the piano and the Russian bass came on the stage. But he did not sing, just stood there saying, "Very good, very good," as if he were admiring the hall. So, Alan played the introduction of the song, over and over, to help him come in. Finally, he played the singer's melody and the bass started to sing. (This happens often to many singers who have a large, impressive voice but do not have good musicianship.) When Consuelo and her boyfriend sang together, their voices were so loud that they would drown out Alan's piano accompaniment.

Eventually, I met her in the late 1970s in California. She was a painter then, painting ghostly faces and figures. We saw her in a restaurant parking lot. She came toward Alan and exclaimed, "Maestro!" and curtsied, bending all the way to the ground. She was very old then, but she looked distinctly original, thin and long faced.

Consuelo and Alan's friendship continued by letters. Her last letter ended with "…to my dearest Alan." After that, we never heard from her, so she must have died. But she lives vividly in my mind—one scene in particular.

Once, Consuelo visited Cape Cod, where Alan used to live with his first wife. Every night, Consuelo went out to the waterfront and rang a gong under the moon.

Recently, I saw her in a vision in my mind and wondered at her presence. So, I looked at her story that I had written in 2003 and realized I had to revise it. I hope this one is to her liking. I will conclude her story with one of her poems that Alan set to music.

Pagan Saint

The saint has died
The pagan rides this night
Once more…
Wild horses through the sea
The sky in all its mystery
Wildly she rides attended by
All the gods of love desire
Passionate pagan, fierce and free…
Sing your song of ecstasy
Sing your song, triumphant cry…
The saint has died…
The pagan rides.

Grace Deeran, Alan's Amateur Orchestra Violinist (Rajah Hoydn and the Kreutzer Sonata)

Grace Deeran* came to me in my dream so vividly this morning, but I was woken up by the noise of a garbage truck. Then I fell asleep and dreamed again. I was in an Armenian's house and the telephone rang; it was Alan calling. I could not remember what he said, but I was overwhelmed to hear his voice. Then I tried to say something, but he was not there anymore. Then I realized he didn't know who he was talking to. He must have been looking for me because he might have thought that since he died, I moved away from our house. Why didn't I interrupt him? I could have told him how I missed him and was glad to hear him. But what an amazing thing it was that I heard his voice. My dream brought it back to me. But why did Grace and Alan both come to me so clearly this morning?

Grace was an Armenian violinist who lived in Boston. She was about the same age as Alan and never married. After Alan had left Boston and lived in New York, Switzerland, and finally Seattle, she had been sending letters to Alan faithfully to report about Boston and the activities of their old friends. Her cards were always sentimental, childish cards. Alan said she was a good violinist but with no taste for the arts.

Alan and his painter friend Hyman Bloom were tickled about her being so obedient, writing letters to her old friends, as if she were the communication center of their old community. One time, she was so frustrated by Alan not answering her letters that she put white writing paper with her letter. The paper was supposed to be Alan's reply to her letter, and it already had written on it (by her) "Dear Grace...." That was her desperate attempt.

April of 1993 was the first and only time I met Grace. She had come to our performance at Harvard University in Cambridge, MA. I sang Alan's songs, and he accompanied me. I knew she was about Alan's age, but she did not look as I expected. She had a good-looking, strong face, and I noticed her strong hands when she shook my hands. (I thought her years of playing the violin had made her hands strong.)

One evening while we were there, another of Alan's old friends, Dr. Elizabeth Gregory came to the Sheraton Commander Hotel where we stayed, and we had dinner together in the hotel dining room downstairs. After dinner, the three of us thought we should see Grace. Dr. Gregory called her for us, but her answer was that she could not see us because she had something else to do. We were surprised because she had been writing to Alan all these years since he had left Boston, so Alan tried to see her despite his demanding schedule. Couldn't she make some effort to see him and talk to him in person?

In the year 2000, after Alan had died, I received many sympathy cards from people, but, as time went by, the letters stopped and their sympathy faded away, but Grace's letters continued. One day I called her and cried. She said, "You must miss him very much," as if she understood my grief. She must have known Alan like I did; he was a loveable man.

I would like to write Alan's favorite story that he told me many times...

When Alan was a starving composer in Boston, he was known as a "composer of no performance," so he organized his own amateur orchestra and performed his own music. He was the conductor and pianist. He conducted from his piano for his piano concertos.

Grace was Alan's faithful and valuable violinist. Often, she came to his apartment in the evenings to practice with him. One evening, they were practicing Beethoven's "Kreutzer Sonata" for violin and piano. Suddenly, Alan's black cat Rajah Hoydn jumped up on the piano bench and played wildly with his paw and looked at them with his serious eyes, as if he was affected by the serious passage of the sonata.

This experience was never forgotten by Alan and Grace, and this morning they reminded me of the story through my dreams, wishing me to write it so their story could not be forgotten.

* Grace died on December 25, 2002. I found out by letter from an Armenian lady who took care of her things after Grace passed.

One Holiday at French Village – Roy Stoughton

Roy Stoughton was Alan's composer friend who died in the early 1950s. Alan was eternally guilty about what had happened to Roy's music.

In the 1960s, Alan lived in apartments and moved around to different places: Switzerland, New York, Japan, etc., so he did not have much space. Elizabeth, his wife at that time, got rid of all of Roy's music, which Alan had kept for him, intending to help publish and promote them. She did this without Alan knowing about it, just to make room for Alan's gigantic amount of music. But she went to the extreme; she cut pages of books, even art books, to make them less bulky. By the time Alan realized what she had done, it was too late, and Roy's music had all disappeared. I would like to write about their delightful story, which Alan shared with me many times.

One fine holiday in the late 1930s, Roy and Alan were in Manchester, New Hampshire, watching an electric streetcar. It was beautifully decorated with stained-glass windows, and they were fascinated. Roy got an idea to ride in the car to a French village (mainly populated by French immigrants) to see the girls. Roy went for the blond French girls, but Alan was for the black-haired Japanese girls; however, he went along with Roy. They got off at their destination and fooled around the town, looking at the girls passing by. Suddenly, a whistle blew, and they were arrested by the police.

Around that time in America, labor unions were illegal but were still forming to help the workers, who had no voice, against the companies. There was a mill in the village, and the police thought Alan was a labor agitator. He looked wild, with his hairy near-Eastern look, and they thought Roy was a bookie because he was small and wore eyeglasses; obviously, he was not the physical type.

Alan and Roy were dragged into the police station and interrogated. They searched Alan's suspicious heavy briefcase, only to find music, his sketchbook, and a manuscript of his Symphony No. 1 "Exile." They realized they had made a mistake and apologized, but the policeman who had Roy was not about to let him go, because he was convinced that he had got the "real thing," a criminal. The policeman did not want to let him go but eventually had to.

In the 1950s, Alan had a brief marriage to a woman called Phylis. The part Alan never told me was that she was Roy's old girlfriend, and Alan married her after Roy's death. I found this out much later.

Alan spoke of her as a cheater who had tricked him into marriage and tried to get a lifetime of alimony; he truly disliked her. According to Alan, she asked him to marry her because she needed protection from her former husband, and if Alan married her, she would give him a divorce the next day. (This did not make any sense to anybody.) Alan married her and, naturally, she did not give him a divorce the next day. Alan had known her in high school, and she must have made an impression on him, but by the time he married her, she was a very messy painter. Their apartment smelled, with garbage piling up, even his composition students complained of it. The most awful thing was she left things in the toilet bowl for Alan to see. (Alan thought this was intentional.)

He could not stand her anymore and ran away, but his piano became her hostage, and she sued him for something like $100,000 at that time. Alan was in hiding and took almost two and a half years to divorce her. She did not get the $100,000, only $12 a week, even though it was a hardship for him at that time. Alan continued to send her a check every month until 1994.

In 1997, Alan showed initial signs of dementia, and his mind was drifting. One morning at breakfast, he looked at me and said, "You are so beautiful, you must be Phylis." I was shocked and upset. Why did he think of me as Phylis, the person he hated so much?

But now I know his memory must have gone back to his high school years, losing accurate sequencing. As I write, my tears fall from my deep sympathy for Alan.

Because of his dementia, I found out his secret. His guilt towards Roy was much deeper than I originally thought, not only losing his music, but also taking his girlfriend.

Letters from William Saroyan

I never met William Saroyan, but I feel as if I knew him because Alan often talked about him.

I had a hilarious experience in 2002, after Alan's death. For some reason, I felt Saroyan wanted me to look into his letters written to Alan, which I had kept somewhere in my house; so, I was looking for them, turning the house upside down, but I could not find them. The next morning, I found them on the top of the pile I had started from, as if they were laughing at me; then I knew it was Saroyan's trick; he wanted to give me a strong impression of him, and he did.

Alan was a very talkative person. He told me many stories of his life, but strangely enough, he did not tell me about the important event written about in Saroyan's letters. When I read them, I was shocked; Saroyan was the one responsible for the biggest breakthrough in Alan's career. I wrote in 2002, "I started reading his original letters to Alan and realized I do not have to add anything because his genuinely pure and beautiful letters speak for themselves." That was then, but today is 2007; I have an urge to construct his letters of 1941–1951 into a story. I know this is one of my most important subjects, and I have an obligation to let Saroyan's letters be known to the people.

Alan and Saroyan's correlative relationship started in the early 1940s. Alan composed music for Saroyan's plays and lyrics. Saroyan was a well-known and a popular Armenian-American writer at that time. One of his dramas, *The Human Comedy*, was made into a movie with Mickey Rooney, and several years later, *The Time of Your Life* was made, starring James Cagney. Also, when I was still in Japan, I heard one of the hit songs from the U.S.: "Come On-a My House." Later I learned the lyrics of the song were written by Saroyan. During this time, Alan met Saroyan while he was an organist in the Watertown Armenian Church in Boston, but he was desperately trying to make it as a composer. He organized an amateur orchestra and financed the performance of his own compositions. He was the conductor, and when his piano concerto was performed, he was the soloist and conducted from the piano.

August 19, 1941

Saroyan's first letter to Alan and his willingness to get to know him, a young unknown composer, and his music:

Dear Mr. Hovhaness,

Thank you very much for your good letter. I need not tell you that I have been hearing good things of you for some time, or that I have hoped to work with you on something. Unfortunately, the Armenian show must be postponed for the present. I am at work on another job, which may take two or three or even four or five months. I shall be thinking about the show, however, and if and when the time comes to return to it with full time and full energy, I shall do so. I have written two sketches for the idea, but actually nothing has started. I am eager that it will be very good; or not at all.

Your letter (as I read it again) is fine... and let's work together someday... an opera perhaps. I'm sorry it can't be just now, but I'm delighted that there is a good possibility for it in the future, if you are still interested.

Will you kindly let me know if any of your works have been recorded, so that I may obtain them, I look forward to listening to your music, I am particularly interested in your work in the Armenian Folk idiom, If [*sic*] this material, or some of it, is recorded, I should want to have it very much, If [*sic*] not, then anything else.

In 1932, I wrote in English a little Armenian song...the words are Armenian, but they are written in English. Perhaps you would like to see this very simple little song...and perhaps write music for it, in the Armenian Folk style. If you do so, we might have it published, and do other songs... while we are getting ready for a longer work. Doing smaller things would give us a chance to get acquainted. Consequently, I am typing out the song on another sheet of paper. I will type a sort of literal translation in English also, to clarify my writing of Armenian words, in the English alphabet.

Please let me hear from you again soon. With kindest regards,

Yours truly,

October 5, 1941

Alan's first opportunity to compose for Saroyan's play, *JIM DANDY*:

Dear Hovhaness:

I hope a copy of the play *JIM DANDY* will have reached you before this letter, so that you will have had a chance to read it for guidance in the making of the *JIM DANDY* Rhapsody.

I have been thinking about the use of the human voice in the composition, and if it doesn't work out effectively I feel this element of the composition can be eliminated, The [*sic*] important thing, however, as I see it, is for you to proceed as you feel you must, even if the whole work cannot be used technically in the presentations of the play.

But the whole work will stand by itself, and the ideal result will naturally be a work which is musically whole and separate. Any new variations, and new themes, any special emphasis or any isolation or use of ideas in the play are desirable, and whatever length the whole work takes will be just right. That is to say, do not let the fact that the play is involved limit you in any way in the making of the Rhapsody.

October 28, 1941

Dear Hovhaness;

Thanks a lot for your wonderful work for *JIM DANDY*, and please forgive me for not attending to the cost of the recordings sooner. I hope my telegraphed money order reached you O.K. Monday morning.

I hope it all works out well, and that you benefit from this work. As I telegraphed, if more money is needed, please be sure to wire me collect, and I will send it. I am a little off the beat financially myself at the moment, but all will be O.K. soon enough. This is no letter… I am rushing but let me only thank you and send you my very best…until I can write more leisurely.

Between the two letters October 5 and October 28, Alan completed the three movements, thirty-one-page score for *Jim Dandy* Rhapsody. That was an example of how Alan composed—he devoured the commissions like a hungry giant.

November 13, 1941

Dear Alan;

Here is a copy of the new play *AFTON WATER*. Don't let it intrude. If you find time to read it, read it, but don't go to work on anything. There is a chance that The Theatre Guild will be doing it, but nothing's set. When everything is set, then I'll be writing to you fully…if you are interested in doing the music. With the Guild of course, there will be a definite arrangement with you, and I will try my best to see that it is a good one. Now, there's no telling about these things. I've just finished writing the play, and I have only a hunch that it's O.K. There's always a chance that nothing will come of the whole thing. With warmest regards,

Yours truly,

I always knew Alan composed music for *AFTON WATER*. Just recently, I saw the score and found Alan's writing in the beginning of the score: "Adapted from William Saroyan's play *Afton Water*." Alan began composing it on April 14, 1951, and completed it on April 28, 1951.

January 2, 1942
Big Holidays Come Roaring Home

Dear Alan;

Please forgive me for not writing to you long ago, and many times, but I have been caught up in a good many new activities, all calling for tremendous work, and on top of that the two big holidays came roaring home keeping me busy being happy with my folks. Now, let me thank you for sending me the full score of the *JIM DANDY* RHAPSODY."

Without Being Too Much of an Impresario

While in Hollywood, a violinist...I forget his name at the moment... ran into me in the street and immediately spoke of you. Then he telephoned and suggested that I meet a conductor to talk about your work, which of courts [*sic*] I wanted very much to do, but as the fellow turned out to be out of town, I missed him, and the whole thing went flooey. I think your work will become very widely known. I do not want to intrude, as one always feels embarrassed about such a thing, but at the same time I would like to do anything I can, without being too much of a discoverer or impresario. I know at least three thousand people who have discovered me, and while I try to make them all happy by letting them continue to imagine that they are my discoverers, after a while the whole thing gets to be a nuisance. I look forward to the time when we shall meet and talk things over. I do not believe any good talent should go unnoticed, and I am all for erring on the side of pushing rather than erring on the side of being indifferent. I am eager to hear more of your work, too.

Expecting Royalty from *JIM DANDY*

I have no financial reports as [*sic*] yet from *JIM DANDY*, but you shall be getting them, along with a check, in the near future, I hope. At that time, I will send you a check. In the meantime, please do not feel embarrassed about writing or telegraphing me when you need money. This is always awkward stuff, but please just wire or write, and if there is any on hand, I'll send some along. There usually is, but today there isn't much...owing to the time of year it is, and to not having any theatrical income coming in, except *JIM DANDY*.

January 6, 1942

Dear Alan,

At last, a report and a check has come from the National Theatre Conference on *JIM DANDY*, and I quote from the letter:

"At the request of Mr. Norvelle, we are sending you our check for the sum of $747.00 in full payment of royalties for *JIM DANDY* received up to this date (30 December 1941). Gross royalty received amounted to $830.00. From this, we have deducted ten per cent commission for services and expenses." This is from Frederic McConnell, Treasurer.

I feel that out of this sum your share is $100.00, consequently I am sending you herewith my personal check, and sincerely hope you approve. If and when more money is received from *JIM DANDY*, I will report to you and send along your share.

Nothing new, otherwise. I hope all is well and send you kindest regards.

Finally, Saroyan's efforts paid off. Alan told me Saroyan earned considerable income from his writings, but it was unexpected to him, and he was rather apologetic about it. He was generous to people around him. From his letters I find how considerate he was to Alan—he always paid him. He understood the difficulties of creative people making a living.

August 29, 1942
Saroyan's Little Amateur Detective Work

Dear Alan,

After a little amateur detective work, I uncovered Stokowski's address and have sent him the music you sent me with the attached letter, which I trust will meet with your approval.

The man from whom I obtained the address...Meyerberger...urged me to send the material along to Stokowski because he said Stokowski was very eager always to read music and to uncover new talent. Otherwise, I would have been tempted to show the music to someone closer. But actually, it is no matter, because wherever the music is discovered it will be the same; that is to say, a good thing.

I wish my own affairs were not quite so unsettled and unfavorable at the moment so that I might be a little bit more direct and immediately helpful to you, which I assure you I would like to be.

Here's the best of luck and keep up with your good work.

Sincerely,

August 29, 1942:
Saroyan's Recommendation Letter to Stokowski
I Have a Hunch He Is

Dear Mr. Stokowski;

Mr. Michael Meyerberger was recommended to me by the Music Department of the *New York Times* as one who might know where you could be reached at the present time., [*sic*] I have just spoken to Mr. Meyerberger by telephone, and he was good enough to give me your address.

Under separate cover I am taking the liberty of sending you a number of the works of a young composer named Alan Hovhaness, who lives at 240 Huntington Avenue, Boston, Massachusetts. These works consist of two symphonies, and something entitles [*sic*] "Prayer." As I am not at all familiar with music in print, I can only hope that each symphony is complete so that it will be possible for you, if there is time, to judge this young composer's work.

I feel a great responsibility to any unknown talent that I hear about, and I have been interest [*sic*] in this man's work for several years and have been waiting patiently for him to become recognized as an important composer...which I have a hunch he is.

I know what a burden manuscripts can be to a man whose time is always taken up as yours must surely be. Therefore, I hope that sending you this manuscript will turn out to be an event of some pleasure for you and perhaps of some importance to the world of music.

If you find the music worthy, it would [sic] make me very happy to hear from you, and I am sure it would be perhaps the happiest event in the life of this young composer to hear from you.

With sincere thanks and warm regards, even though I have never had the honor of meeting you.

Yours truly,

Who could write a letter like this? It is a masterpiece. Who could not be moved by it? This letter was the cause of the biggest break of Alan's career.

August 31, 1942
Good News from Stokowski

I know a symphony of Hovhaness [*sic*] and think him to be a composer of exceptional talent. I hope to play some of his music this coming season.

I am arriving in New York about October 15th. Will you be there then? There is something I would like to talk over with you.

With friendly greetings

(Signed) L. Stokowski

September 4, 1942
Saroyan's Letter to Alan

I have received today a letter from Stokowski, a copy of which is attached. Most likely you will be getting a note from him, too.

I hope, as he says, he will do some of your music this coming season.

All the best,

The next year, on January 21, 1943, Stokowski performed Alan's Symphony No. 1 "Exile" with the Los Angeles Philharmonic Orchestra as a guest conductor. Since then, he performed many of Alan's pieces and became his champion.

Alan's masterpiece, Symphony No. 2 "Mysterious Mountain" was commissioned by Stokowski in 1955 and was dedicated to him. In the same year, on October 31, Stokowski premiered it for his debut concert with the Houston Symphony Orchestra. The symphony has become one of the standard repertoires for symphonic concerts.

October 25, 1950
Saroyan's Letter to Alan

"Lalezar"

"Lalezar" is one of the most beautiful things I have ever heard. It has enormous natural and irresistible power. By this, I mean it is sorrowful without that strange spuriousness of so much noisy music, as if the composer (and the listeners) were thrilled to be so sad. My cousin Archie (whom you met at New Joe's at lunch that day) came downstairs while I had the phonograph going with your playing the piece and he literally went berserk from being so deeply moved by the music. This is an Armenian thing which I am sure you know about. Of all the people I know only the Armenians (even those born in America) seem to be driven into paroxysms of appreciation, of joy. He literally fell to the floor and kicked his feet with thankfulness to you, saying, "Oh, man, Oh, man." It was much the same with me every time I heard the piece being played in Hollywood. Which brings me to the poor news. I went to Hollywood on schedule and went to work, to see about casting the play, about directing it, about making something of it. The people arrived. Florence Yacoubian, Hratch's sister, came and sat at the piano and played "Lalezar," then again, then again, then again and again and again, and each time it went deeper and deeper. Everybody who heard it was hushed. The stage of the theatre adjoins the bar and the restaurant, and people kept coming out of the bar and the restaurant to find out what the music was. Florence played it straight at first, and then asked if she might try putting left-hand stuff to it, and I told her to try it. I hope you will forgive my having taken that liberty. Well, something happened that I liked. I felt that nothing was lost, either.

Saroyan was not any different from his cousin Archie. When he heard Sibelius's "Finlandia," he was so moved he had to go to Finland to meet the composer and express his appreciation of his music in person. He met Sibelius in his home; the composer was smoking a cigar and a maid brought whiskey to the table. Saroyan was overwhelmed by the joy of meeting him; he practically fell to the floor to thank him. Then Sibelius said to him, "Drink, young man." Then Saroyan tried to ask him the question that he had wanted to ask ever since he had first heard "Finlandia," the important reason for his coming to Finland. But facing the powerful Sibelius, all his preparation became useless, and the only words that came out of his mouth were, "What made you write 'Finlandia'?" Then Sibelius said to him, "Drink, young man."

Alan was like Sibelius in this regard; when he was asked about the music he had already written, he said, "Music speaks for itself." Composers are not musicologists; they don't talk about music—they create it.

October 25, 1950, continued:
Written By a Desperate and Depressed Man

I kept working hopefully, and then suddenly I had to recognize a very cold and real fact: I either had no play at all that I could make come alive on the stage, or I did not have the players to make it possible for me to make the play come alive. Getting a play on the boards is exhausting work, and I did not want to come up with a fizzle, especially since it is an all-Armenian play. I insisted on withdrawing it, and it has been put aside. The stuff just would not breathe on the stage, that's all. I think it must be a bad play, although I intend to look it over again sometime. It was written by a desperate and depressed man...solely to keep a promise...so you can imagine how difficult it was for me to withdraw it. I know I did right, though, under the circumstances, I have been more dead than alive in my heart since I lost my family, which is all I have ever lived for and all I have ever wanted. I am in a perpetual daze, as if I didn't know what hit me. I am unconsciously inconsiderate of others, forgetful, more than half-irresponsible, and generally shot.

Saroyan was divorced from his wife, but it was not clean-cut, she called on him for help whenever she was removed from wherever she was staying, and her belongings were thrown out on the street. Saroyan rescued her every time.

In later years, he said his failure of life was because of his bad marriages, but his tragedy was not only his bad marriages. He was a gambler, he liked the feeling of being "on the beam," so he gambled, and finally his gambling caught up with him. He lost money and owed lots of money to the IRS for his income taxes and became a fugitive.

October 25, 1950, concluded
I Wrote the Only Kind I Know How

I have taken another liberty which I earnestly hope does not distress you. I felt obliged to do so, as I now feel obliged to make known to you precisely what I have done and how I have done it. This will all reveal itself when you have had a glance at the attached letters. I hope you will not mind my manner of recommending you for a Music Grant at the National Institute of Arts and Letters. I do not know how to write a formal letter, and so I wrote the only kind I know how. Let's you and I feel almost definitely that the Grant...one of them in Music...will not be made to you. I don't know why I must feel this, but I think we must. Still, I felt that I owed it to my own conscience to at least make known to Virgil Thomson and to the outfit itself my feelings about your music. In Hollywood, Photostats were made of the composition, and I sent a copy of the photo stated manuscript to Mr. Thomson. Nothing will come of this most likely, as I say, but let's know what's happened and then forget all about it. If we hear good news, fine, if we don't, God love them. Your work is irresistible. It will not be resisted, that's all. I don't know when or how it will be truly recognized and appreciated, but I don't know how it can fail in these things.

Saroyan is talking about a recommendation he wrote for Alan to the National Institute of Arts and Letters, in reply to the following letter:

To the Members of the Institute:

You have already been asked for suggestions for "Arts and Letters Grants" of $1,000 each in Art, to be given in 1951 to younger men and women of demonstrated ability who are not members of the Institute.

We are now writing to ask if you have any candidates to recommend to the Committee on Grants for Literature and Music. If so, please forward his or her name promptly, together with informative data, to the above address. Examples of the work should be supplied or mentioned by name.

In response to this letter from the Institute, Saroyan sent this letter of recommendation for Alan to Virgil Thomson, who was chairman of the Institute's Music Committee:

October 8, 1950

Here with "Lalezar," piano piece.

I believe you know his work. I am fond of it, I admire it, and it satisfies me deeply, I am grateful that he is composing. I believe he is under forty. I believe he teaches for a meager living. I most earnestly hope you find that he deserves a break.

"Lalezar" was written for a play that I have withdrawn. I have heard it in varying degrees of skill in the playing perhaps a dozen and a half times. When the skill is almost nearly what it ought to be the piece is irresistible. When the skill is ordinary the piece is still extraordinary. The composer's identification of the piece…"Piano Solo Imitating the Kanoon"… is only unimportantly accurate, if not in fact a mistake. The Kanoon is a plucked-string instrument of some sort. "Lalezar" imitates nothing; it just is. I would call attention also to his "Mihr," two-piano piece. I would call attention to everything he has composed.

He is in no group but let us not overlook him on that account. That is sometimes a good and necessary thing. The ones who are in groups help one another and that is also a good and necessary thing; but who is to help the group less one? God help him no doubt, but here before me is the invitation dated September 20th to recommend a candidate: Alan Hovhaness.

Saroyan genuinely believed in Alan's God-given talent. He saw it through his own extraordinary insight. Despite his own difficulties, his love and sympathy for Alan, an unknown composer, were vividly expressed in his letter. The letter was written in 1950, yet it has never lost its power. I cry (not just little tears) every time I read it. I salute the power of the writing; Saroyan lives in his words.

October 18, 1950
Letter to Saroyan from the National Institute of Arts and Letter

Dear Mr Saroyan:

The Committee on Grants for Music will of course consider Alan Hovhaness as a possible candidate, and at the proper time I will secure his music and records (without letting him know that he is being considered.) [*sic*]

As a result of Saroyan's recommendation, Alan was awarded a $1,000 grant from the Institute in 1951 and became a member of the Institute in 1977, the year of our marriage.

I would like to conclude Saroyan's story with his rather naïve poem that was sent to Alan to write music for it:

MEMORIES OF HEAVEN
A Song
Music by Alan Hovhaness
Words by William Saroyan

Verse:
A humble father spoke these words
To his motherless daughter.
Heaven itself heard the words
And put its own music to them.

First Chorus:
Angels in heaven
Play when you play.
Beautiful angels
Say what you say.

Pieces of heaven
Are now your toys.
Heavenly music
Comes from their noise.

Angels in heaven
Move when you move.
Beautiful angels
Love all you love.

You are my angel child.
You are my only life.
You gave to me all joy.
You gave to me heaven's own truth.
You gave to me all of life's worth.

Oh, I could never live, never live without you.
Oh, I could never live, never live without you.

Second Chorus:
Angels in heaven
Smile when you smile.
Beautiful angels
Sigh when you sigh.

Memories of heaven
Sleep when you sleep.
All hearts in heaven
Weep when you weep.

Beautiful angels
Go where you go.
Heavenly creatures
Know what you know.

Why does this little song make me cry? Maybe because the childlike, innocent spirit behind Saroyan's words touches my senses.

Does it make you cry, too?

My Dream of a Swiss Mountain (Alan's Bad Marriages)

I woke up at nine AM that morning. I was not sleepy anymore. I could have gotten up then, but I turned myself to the right and went to sleep again. My dreams usually come just before I wake up. Sure enough, I had a nightmare!

I was in England. Alan was there, but he was confused and didn't remember me. He was under the care of a tall, middle-aged English psychiatrist, but he had disappeared. The psychiatrist knew Alan had gone to Switzerland because he had been speaking of Switzerland. Alan's memory was back there, where he lived before he knew me.

The doctor and I took a long time to get to Switzerland. There was a cheap apartment beside a beautiful Swiss mountain range. The doctor found Alan in one of the rooms. Alan didn't look like the Alan I knew; he was a young, blondish man, not tall like Alan, but I knew that was him. I talked to him, but he didn't remember anything about me. But I was trying very hard, as if he were Alan. He said, "I don't remember you, but I like you." Then Alan's former wife (his fifth) Elizabeth, my rival who used to live in Switzerland with him, showed up, but she was rather nice to me.

Why was I at a Swiss mountain and losing him again? What does this dream mean? I always come back to this nightmare. Before I married him, he left me many times, and during his last sickness, he was confused and not remembering me. That was my waking nightmare. When I was sleeping, my unconscious mind reminded me of that bad experience, but what was the meaning of my nightmare this morning?

Then, suddenly, I realized I had to write it down—maybe Alan wanted me to do so. Alan used to tell me, "Write down your dreams; dreams have a meaning." I decided to write it down, regardless, whatever came to my mind.

In the early 1960s, Alan and Elizabeth were in Switzerland after the trip to India and Japan. The magnificent Swiss mountains impressed Alan very much, but his personal life was a very lonely one.

One day on the mountains, without any warning, Elizabeth ran to a precipice to throw herself off. Alan stopped her with all his might. He was afraid that if she would have killed herself falling from the precipice (it was so steep, almost straight down to the bottom), he would have been accused as a murderer, especially since he was in a foreign country and there were no witnesses. After that incident, he lost his sexual feeling for her completely, but his marriage continued for sixteen years.

Alan's Former Marriage to a Young Italian Girl: Serafina

In the 1940s, Alan married Serafina, his third wife, to avoid legal trouble because she was underaged while he was living with her. On the other hand, this was her wish because she knew Alan's potential of becoming a successful composer. This naive, immature girl thought that by being married to him, she could go to New York with him and study acting and dancing without paying rent or other expenses by herself. She studied in a Martha Graham dancing group and even swept floors in order to stay in the group, but Graham said that Serafina was "too fat to be a dancer." She also joined "Living Theatre," an amateur acting group, and got a part and performed. While she was seeking her own career, Alan was not being taken care of, not getting anything from the marriage.

In the meantime, Alan was getting up early to go to school to teach, and all he got from her was lots of coffee. In the evening she brought friends to their apartment to chat all night; while all that was going on, Alan composed in the bedroom. Finally, Alan got serious stomach trouble from not eating proper food, since she did not cook for him. To get proper food by himself, he had to get baby food from the grocery store. Every time he went to the store, he cleaned out the baby-food shelf. Eventually, one day, he fainted on the street and was carried away to a hospital. That's how Alan's lifetime of stomach trouble started.

Alan's Next Wife, Phylis

Sometime after his divorce from Serafina, a woman called Phylis showed up in his life. Alan had known her when he was in high school, and he had found her rather attractive, but later Phylis became a girlfriend of Roy Stoughton, a dear composer friend of Alan's, who had died by the time she came into Alan's life. He became involved with her because she said to him, "I will cook for you"—that was what Alan needed.

She persuaded Alan to marry her because she needed him to protect her from her former husband (I don't think Alan understood this, and neither did I), and she said she would give Alan a divorce on the next day.

Alan married this woman, thinking it would be just for one day to help her out and, instead, wound up paying her for a lifetime. I heard Alan's dislike of her and complaints for all these years; every month when he wrote a check, it reminded him of her—and his own stupidity.

Now, Back to Elizabeth

During the time of his hiding from Phylis, he met a pianist called Elizabeth. She had come to study piano with him, but he felt sympathetic to her because she was wearing an old coat and looked poor, so he bought her a new coat. She was a good pianist and smart, so he thought it might be good to marry a smart woman (for a change); most of all, she was a musician. "Musicians are honest." (That was what he thought.) But before the marriage, he heard a voice of warning not to marry her. "If you marry her, you will not see the spring." He was depressed.

At that time, he was divorcing Phylis, and she was suing Alan for something like $100,000, so he had to hide his money (whatever he had) into a new account with Elizabeth's name. He trusted her (because she was a musician), but she wrote checks without asking him (a total of $1,050) to pay off her old boyfriend in order to get freedom. Alan kept all the canceled checks she had written in an envelope and showed them to me. On the envelope, written in Alan's handwriting, was "Secrets against A. H."

After his divorce from Phylis, Alan and Elizabeth were married; then, that former Italian wife, Serafina, came into the picture. At one point, Elizabeth and Serafina had a confrontation. Serafina still behaved like she owned him and was telling people, "Alan and I are 'kind of' separated." She was wild and naive and even nasty; on the other hand, Elizabeth was quiet and smart and even shrewd. Plus, both of them were about the same age.

Elizabeth was no match for Serafina's fiery Italian temper, so the only way she could get even with her was to stop Alan from giving her alimony. (According to Serafina, "When I gave him his freedom, he promised to pay me fifteen dollars a week.") Elizabeth insisted that Alan stop giving the money and make Serafina behave because Elizabeth was insulted by Serafina, but Alan didn't take her side and continued to give Serafina the promised money, even though it was not legal alimony.

I am sure that is the reason for Elizabeth's suicide attempt. I am not especially on her side, but I understand her pain. It was only her first marriage and, knowing Alan had been married more than once, she needed to have the proof of his exclusive love and devotion to her, so she challenged him to prove his love for her by cutting off any money to Serafina. The tragedy of this was that she misinterpreted the money Alan was giving to Serafina as his affection for her, and this cost her the marriage.

While Alan was composing his music, his life was led by the women around him. At some point, he tried to correct things, but went through another cycle of wrong marriage, until he met me. With me, he tried to be a good husband as well as a good composer. He had always written his music in spite of others' opinions or criticisms, but now, simply because he was proud to be the man whom he had idealized when he was a young man, he composed with even greater conviction.

Florence Mesler
(One Summer Night Changed My Destiny)

♪

One day I was looking at the entertainment page of the *Seattle Times*. I saw an article spotlighting a singer whose name was Florence Mesler, a voice teacher at the University of Washington who was singing in oratorios and had been giving vocal recitals in recent years.

I thought I needed a teacher like her to help my voice. I had studied with a number of voice teachers, but none of them seemed to know what to do with my voice. I had an unusually big high voice and small low voice, with a break in between. One of the choir singers said to me, "Your voice starts where my voice stops!"

I don't remember how I got Mrs. Mesler, but I became her private student. She squeezed my voice lesson in between two other lessons. She was younger than I was unlike my former voice teachers. My previous voice teachers were retired from their singing careers, and they always seemed preoccupied and in a hurry. Her main objective was to be a successful singer herself, so her singing engagements came first. On top of that, she had to take care of her three children plus driving her husband to his work before she got to the university to teach.

Her lessons were unlike any I'd had in the past. It was the technical aspect of music and vocal production without the enjoyment of singing. I thought it must be "advanced college teaching" and I would have to go through this in order to become a professional singer.

At that time, in the early 1970s, I was married to Peter, and we were raising three children and my dog Koko. My singing had been interrupted by having children, but I wanted to sing again, and I started to sing in a church choir so I could have occasional solos.

One night, we invited Mrs. Mesler and her family to my house for dinner. They came late, and her husband, David, was very upset. He had lost his job and was at home, taking care of the children and helping with his wife's career. He had studied oriental literature and language at the university, and he could speak Japanese and Korean fluently. But what he told us was that he had been cheated by his Korean professor at the university. His professor had promised to publish David's book in the Korean language, but he never did and never did anything else that was promised, so all of David's studies came to nothing. He could not get a job using his knowledge of oriental languages, but he had too much pride to get an ordinary job. I recommended for him to work in the university library because they had an opening, but he said he could not work for such low pay.

Earlier that day he had been working at a booth, promoting Mrs. Mesler's record. He had been demonstrating her record by playing it, but the demonstrators in the other booths complained to him that they could not stand to hear such a shrill voice all day long. That night with us, he let out his frustration openly in front of Mrs. Mesler and the children and my family. Peter, who was very conservative and quiet, did not like David and could not stand his arrogance.

Mrs. Mesler was literate and intellectual, maybe because of the husband's influence. She taught me songs by composers I was not yet acquainted with, such as Bruckner, Dvorak, Schubert, Vaughn-Williams, and the literature of William Blake. She also introduced me to new songs by contemporary composers.

Just before Christmas, she had showed me two new Christmas songs. I liked one of them, which was "Watchman, Tell Us of the Night," by a composer called Alan Hovhaness. I studied and sang it for a church service on the first Sunday in December. People complimented me, saying, "That song sounded Japanese." I was encouraged and sang another Hovhaness song, "Out of the Depths."

Shortly after that I saw his name in the newspaper; he was going to be at Cornish School of Arts giving a lecture concert on July 12, 1973. I mentioned this to my teacher, and she said, "Hinako, his concert would be instrumental." She said this knowing I liked opera and vocal music.

But I said, "I don't care—I like his music," and I went to his concert.

There, I saw him: a tall, slender, and aged composer. I was fascinated by his music all the way through and was surprised to find that such a good contemporary composer existed. He understood the concept and spirit of oriental music. Halfway through the concert, his wife played "Komachi." She was a good, conservative pianist, but I liked his piano playing better—it was spontaneous and free. The first thing that came to my mind when I saw her onstage was, "Alan Hovhaness should have a more glamorous wife." Later I found out he liked "flashiness"; he enjoyed and appreciated *my* flashiness especially.

She wore a short, sleeveless black dress, and her hair was tied in a ponytail. It looked like she had jumped up on the stage with street clothes. At that time, in 1973, we were more formal, and we dressed up for concerts. At the end of the concert, Alan played a record of Symphony No. 21 "Etchmiadzin" on a phonograph player on the stage. He sat beside the phonograph and listened seriously. The audience all joined him, listening. It was a very unusual symphony, and I had never heard such sounds before. I liked it very much. In the last movement, bells came in every certain measure and finally climaxed with a clashing sound and decrescendo and disappeared. I saw in my mind many white birds being released into the sky, a symbol of peace. But after Alan died, in my mind, this movement became his heroic funeral procession.

After the concert, they announced that everybody was invited to a reception. I decided to go. My policy was that if I was impressed with the performance, I would go backstage to express my compliments to the performer. On the way to the reception, I saw the composer John Sundsten and his wife. I had never met her before, but she came up to me and asked,

"Are you Mrs. Hovhaness?" It was such a coincidence, of course, and I said, "No, I am not," but she must have felt a vibration from me mutual to Alan, or she had foreseen our future.

At the reception room, we guests were having refreshments and chatting, then Hovhaness stepped in through the center door to the reception room. At that instant, he saw me; there was a moment of astonishment, and I saw his eyes utterly somersault. His expressive dark brown eyes could not hide his emotion. I knew then that I had given him a strong impression. After that, he never looked at me straight; he was looking at the floor all night long, even though he stayed near me all the time. I had brought two of his songs, and told him, "I sang your songs and liked them very much," and asked for his autograph on the music. He said, "Certainly," but his autograph was so distorted, like the signature of a man who recovered from a stroke. Maybe that was because his wife was near him, and he was afraid she might discover what he was thinking about this Japanese girl. When his wife saw me, her eyes went from my head to my toes, as if she were examining me, but she was nice and gave me information about Hovhaness's music.

I was very happy that night. Before I had gone to the concert, I had only known two songs of his and came back knowing more of his wonderful music. Plus, I had gotten tremendous attention from the composer, an actual living composer. I slept happily that night. I didn't think anything more would come of it. But at the next lesson my teacher was smiling and told me that Mr. Hovhaness had been asking about me.

Two weeks later, on July 26, my voice teacher Florence Mesler was going to give her vocal recital in the North Seattle Community College Concert Hall. As her student I was supposed to attend her concert, as I always had done. But that day I was not eager to go, because her recital was dedicated to northwest contemporary composers' music, which I was not fond of. I called her and said, "I am not up to going to your concert tonight." But she insisted I be there, and she said, "Hinako—you should come," so I did. I drove for forty-five minutes and went into the concert hall. I spotted my usual location (I liked to sit in the center of the hall because I could hear the voice far enough to hear the acoustic sound yet close enough to see the singer's mouth.) Then I looked to my right side. There was the composer Alan Hovhaness sitting next to me. He was in a dark grayish-blue suit with his hair looking like it had not been groomed by anybody, and with a worn briefcase beside him. What an excitement it was! We had met each other just fourteen days before at his concert at Cornish School.

Hovhaness was so happy, he completely took me over, leaning over, whispering in my ear to give me information about the music all night. I heard his stomach making noises all the time; I interpreted that it was because he was over-excited. After my teacher's recital, he took me to another room to a harp concert; the harpist was performing one of his harp pieces. We sat there together. After the concert somebody was calling all the composers to come up to the stage to take pictures, so he was called up. I didn't know at that time, but I found out later, they were having a festival of northwest composers on the college campus that week.

He had recently moved to Seattle from New York, but already was included as a northwest composer. After he joined the other composers on the stage, I thought, "I have been with him long enough—I should not linger on any longer." So, I left.

Later, Alan told me he was so disappointed when he came back to find I was not there anymore, and years later, he confessed that he wanted to "take me to the woods" that night.

Alan and Hinako playing piano and singing together

Shortly after that, I introduced him to my family, and he wanted to help my singing by accompanying me on the piano. We practiced together whenever he was in town composing; I often picked him up at Roy Street, at the bottom of Queen Anne Hill. He walked down the hill to meet me because his house was on the top of the hill, and he did not want his wife to discover his activity, meeting with a singer.

One day after our practice, I took him to Mercer Street near the Opera House; he was going to walk home from there. He said he was leaving for Europe and wouldn't see me for a month. Then, suddenly, he kissed me on my mouth. I was in shock, and then I saw Mrs. Mesler outside of my car window walking with her children, pushing a baby carriage. I said hello to her, but I was so ashamed that I was with the composer, sitting in a car, and had just been kissed by him.

During that summer while Hovhaness was away, Mrs. Mesler gave a recital at the Seattle Center Playhouse. She sang songs by Greg Short, a young Seattle composer who was accompanying her. I did not enjoy the songs because they were so-called contemporary style of writing, which was an unnatural and shocking quality and not supposed to be beautiful and romantic. It needed endurance for me to sit through.

After the concert, we went out of the hall. It was a beautiful summer night with stars in the sky; then a renaissance procession started. The male dancers were in black tights dancing by. I had waited to see Mrs. Mesler with her other students. She showed up with Greg Short, and they looked like two lovers talking away ahead of us. He was young and tall and had lots of hair then; but later, he shaved his hair, and he lost his good looks with it.

While I was watching them pass by, a sudden loneliness came over me, and I thought of my composer, Hovhaness, who was away and was passionately in love with me. He was the composer who wrote music I liked, and I believed he was a great composer. I could have put all those other composers in one bunch, but they could not equal my composer, and here I was about to write to him, "I won't see you anymore." But I never wrote to him; it was the magical summer night that changed my destiny.

Mrs. Mesler used her spinto soprano voice to sing the songs of Greg Short, John Sundsten, Peter Hallock, and Michael Young. These were northwest composers whom she honored at her recitals. She promoted their songs, and by doing so, she put herself in the spotlight. All this time her husband, David, was a very strong supporter and impresario for her.

Just before the time I met Alan at Cornish, David had given him a libretto, hoping Alan would write an opera for his wife. It would have been a great advance for her if Alan wrote one, but his libretto did not inspire Alan. It was too sophisticated and dry for him. The libretto was based on a reincarnation staged in old Korea about a husband and wife. In the end of the opera, she dies, but the twist of the story was his wife was reincarnated and said to him, "Thank you very much for your devotion to me, and now I am reincarnated as a boy."

One night, I went to my teacher's home to get her advice about my relationship with Alan. By that time, we were having an affair, and Alan was saying that if he lost me, he would die. I was torn between Peter, my husband, and Alan. I was in love with Alan, but I was still married and had two children to take care of. They were teenagers, and it seemed they did not need me anymore. That night, Mrs. Mesler really took time to talk to me, and she told me about herself. She too had affection for someone else, but they decided to keep their relationship platonic. She was strongly against divorce and encouraged me to keep my love for Alan platonic and only to be involved through music.

In 1974, she was denied tenure from the university, and she fought them legally, but she lost. It was a very difficult time for her. I think her problem was that she had put too much effort into her own singing career, so her teaching became secondary. Sometimes I drove forty-five minutes to my lesson only to find a message on the front door stating that she could not teach. After she left the University of Washington, I went to her home for lessons. I never knew whether I would have a lesson or not until that morning. After her fourth child was born, she taught me with a baby in her arms. I put up with all of this for a while, but finally I decided to quit studying with her. My real reason to quit was that her method of forcing the middle voice did not work for me.

By 1992, Alan and I had been married for fifteen years, and my mother, who had lived in New York for three decades, came to live next door to us. On Sunday, October 11, the three of us went to Mrs. Mesler's home for composer Sundsten's birthday. By that time, Mrs. Mesler had divorced her husband and was struggling to make ends meet. She was still taking care of three children. She was also directing a church choir and taking care of Mr. Sundsten, who was practically bedridden. He was a local composer who had emigrated from Finland. I could tell by the way he was looking at her that he was an admirer of Mrs. Mesler. His wife was also a singer but had died in recent years.

Alan enjoyed listening to Sundsten talking about Sibelius. Alan admired Sibelius, and he himself had gone to Finland to meet him when Alan was in his twenties. At the party Sundsten was not in bed but was dressed in a suit and was very clear about everything even though he died within a few days later that week.

About Mrs. Mesler's Husband, David

Around that time, my mother had written a story about herself. She was born in old Korea and had gone to Japan and fell in love with a Japanese man and married him. Her story was written in Japanese, and she had tried to publish her book in Japan, but she found out it was not the right place because of their long-standing prejudice against Korea. She came back empty-handed, so I thought my mother's story could be translated into the Korean language and published in Korea. I thought that David Mesler was the right person to do this, since he had not done anything with his knowledge of Korean study. It was a good opportunity for him to do this, and I was excited, so I called him on the phone and told him of my wish to translate my mother's writing from Japanese; but what he said was, "I am no longer interested—I have become a carpenter and at least I can sleep at night." Shortly after my conversation with him, Greg Short told me that David fell off a roof while he was on the job and his new wife divorced him. Her reason was "I don't want to be married to a handicapped man."

I met Mrs. Mesler in October of 2000, the year Alan died, at the Highline High School auditorium. The Northwest Symphony was performing her son David's composition. He was a good composer, and she was a proud mother that night. She had dedicated her life to music and all her children were in music. She told me she had been studying Christian ministry and she was about to become a minister.

It was such an extreme change that it was hard to believe that she could go from singer to minister. Come to think of it, her father was a minister, and she had always had that religious quality. It seems to me her life was a suffering one. If she had been in different circumstances, she could have been a successful singer. She had a mixture of two personality types, professional as well as motherly. She had four children, and her last child came when she was in her forties.

To succeed in the fields of music, art, or literature is difficult. You must be extremely talented; also, you need financial support because you are following your dream, doing what you want to do and not working for a living like others.

Alan was one who made it among them. He had extreme financial difficulty early in his career. He survived by drinking coffee and eating mashed potatoes, but he kept composing before anything else like eating, clothing, housing, and marriage. Because of that he had a very unhappy life, but he became well-known and married me when he was sixty-six years old. He was one of the lucky ones; he got his fame *and* happiness in his lifetime.

Mrs. Mesler introduced to me the music of Hovhaness, who later married me and gave me his name. When I look back, I realize she played a very important part in our relationship.

In the 1960s, Alan had composed many short operas in contemporary style that was influenced by the music movement of that period and reflected his own personal life and his marriage.

"The Burning House"	Op. 186	1962
"Pilate"	Op. 196	1963
"Spirit of the Avalanche"	Op. 197	1962
"The Travelers"	Op. 215	1965

Just before we met in 1973, he had already started composing romantic music. "Pericles," Op. 283 was completed in 1975. It has lots of melodies and was written in the traditional "grand opera" style. When David asked Alan to compose music using his contemporary-style, sophisticated and dry libretto, Alan was no longer interested in composing in his old 1960's style.

"I Will Shake My Spear at Ignorance" Alan's Mentor – Francis Bacon

♪

During a telephone conversation with my daughter Joni from New York, she asked me if I had seen Alan's very old Shakespeare books, which she remembered seeing when Alan was here. I remembered seeing them in the basement. They were very large books with grayish-green covers and black and gold writing. She had asked me about them once before, but I completely forgot about them.

After the telephone conversation, I went into the garage where bookcases full of books were dumped. I could not find them; then I went into Alan's music storage room, and I found one book at the bottom of a shelf and another two books on the opposite side of the bookshelf, which was a total of three books: tragedies, comedies, and histories. The books were just as I remembered, large, heavy books, eleven inches wide, sixteen inches tall, and two and a half inches thick. I could carry only one book at a time. I could not find the date of the printing, but it said "A facsimile of the cert of the first folio of 1623" in the front piece. I realized these books were nearly the complete Shakespeare writings, and God knows what the value of them would be.

Alan left his music and books in the basement. He must have felt secure because his treasures are in my care. The woman he loved and whom he knew understood his wishes more than anybody else, even more than he, himself. Who would take care of them according to his wishes and for his welfare?

I went to bed late and did not wake up until 9:30 AM. My mind was blank at first; then suddenly, the memory of Alan's passion surrounding Shakespeare came to my mind, and I could not let it go. I really do not want to be inspired by anything now because I still have leftover Christmas things to do for people. I just need two days or so to finish them up, but I do not have a choice. My inspiration cannot wait for me, so I plunge into writing the memory of Alan's craziness over Shakespeare. No, it was Francis Bacon, because Alan believed Francis Bacon was Shakespeare, who was the real author of his plays and many other writings.

Whenever Alan spoke about Francis Bacon (Shakespeare), he got high, his speech accelerated, and nobody could stop him from talking. As if he were controlled by some power and had gone back into Elizabethan times. One evening my friend Leona and her husband, Walter, visited us. As soon as they came into our apartment, Alan started talking about Bacon and did not stop until the time they had to leave. They left without saying anything.

Alan had been a member of the Francis Bacon Society long before I knew him. The Society was based on the belief that Francis Bacon was the true Shakespeare, who Bacon used as a disguise. His name was spelled like Shakespeare, without an "e" in the middle, and was actually an unlettered man from Stratford. The members of the Society believed that Shakespeare could not have had the education or the background of experience to write his plays, while Bacon's great intellectual faculties were equal to the task. Therefore, Francis Bacon was the author of Shakespeare's works. In that time, freedom of speech was inhibited, and many books were burned. Bacon wrote behind this fake pen name to avoid persecution.

Alan's favorite Shakespeare books

Alan's Letter of April 13, 1974

In 1974, Alan visited the Bacon Society in England. At the time, he was still married to his former wife Elizabeth. While there, he wrote to me about a message from Bacon to him through a medium:

The Bacon Society came to the concert. They said the spirit of Bacon was there with them, and I felt this. The next morning a medium named Helen Greaves and Commander Martin Pares, who was the president of the Bacon Society, were gathered along with other members of the society. Martin Pares gave a long message from Bacon. His voice was very serious. He said, "The note has been struck in the music—it is still only a bud, but it sounds like the new age. It must deepen—I must not expect quick success. I may fail, but failure is better than success. They will not spare me suffering—they did not spare him. The truth in my music will anger critics and some musicians—later others will build on my music. These things are as they must be and should be. I will be given strength to finish my work. Fear not." Alan Hovhaness stated, "He compared my music to the 'Sower and the Seed.' Martin said, channeling Bacon, "'The Seed' falls on barren and fertile ground, is many times lost, but sometimes takes root and blossoms." Alan Hovhaness said, "He quotes from the parable of Christ in the Bible." And Bacon, through Martin, said, "Later I will show you the whole message."

In 1976, he visited there again. At that time, we were living together, and he had disappeared. Elizabeth had taken him on a long European trip, her desperate attempt to separate us by cutting off our communication completely. At the end of the trip, they stopped in England to visit the Bacon Society. Alan told me later what had happened there.

The psychic had been brought in, and they played Alan's trumpet piece "Prayer of St. Gregory." That was the obvious intention of the group, to help Elizabeth invoke Alan's spiritual consciousness so that he would realize the higher calling of his work and give up his personal needs like his love for me, but their intention backfired on them. Alan broke down in tears because he missed me, and the much-expected profound message from Bacon did not come through. Elizabeth became frustrated and asked the psychic why her husband Alan had not been touching her. In fact, Alan had not touched her for most of their fifteen years of marriage. The psychic's answer was that Alan had been confused, and she added that if he ever would marry me, he would be tortured by me, which was said to scare him. Anyway, the psychic reading went to a very low level and ended up in a fiasco.

The Story Alan Told Me about Francis Bacon

Bacon was the illegitimate son of Queen Elizabeth I and the Earl of Leicester (Robert Dudley). Essex was Bacon's younger brother, not Elizabeth's lover, as we have been told. She met Leicester and they fell in love during her imprisonment in Bell Tower. He was also confined in the Beauchamp Tower under the shadow of execution. After her sister Mary (Bloody Mary), Queen of England, daughter of Henry VIII and his first wife Catherine of Aragon failed to rule, England was brought into chaos. Her disastrous five-year reign came to a close and Elizabeth became Queen of England; but Elizabeth's legitimacy as the true heir to the throne was doubted by many in the opposition because her mother Anne Boleyn's marriage to Henry was not recognized by the Catholic Church.

She kept her personal life (private marriage to Leicester) secret and declared herself "The Virgin Queen" to protect herself and England. If her marriage to Leicester had become public, the queen herself would have broken the law because he was a married man, even though he did not love his wife, and such a truth could be the target of criticism. Moreover, the country could be divided by the public's split opinion. Also, she did not want to give Leicester power because she knew she was the only one who could rule England.

In the meantime, Francis Bacon was born and was adopted by the queen's friend Lady Ann Bacon, the wife of Sir Nicholas Bacon. They raised him and gave him the highest education in England and abroad. The queen's secret was well-kept by the Bacons, who were her faithful friends.

Bacon grew up to be a philosopher and ethical teacher; he even obtained a high position in Elizabeth's court. He was his mother's personal lawyer and counselor. However, in this dark time, it was dangerous for anyone to express their opinions freely, or more particularly, one who had great knowledge and spiritual values. Your voice could be interpreted as treason by government officials. You could be put in prison or executed at the drop of a hat. Even churches were tools of government. So, Bacon put his knowledge, criticism, and frustration toward his mother into plays and ciphers or codes within the plays and concealed his authorship.

At the young age of sixteen or seventeen, he fell in love with Marguerite of Valois, who was married to Henry IV of France. Their marriage had been a convenience, and they were about to divorce. Bacon used to visit her on her balcony in secret, and so the story of "Romeo and Juliet" was his own experience, his love affair with Marguerite. This affair was the beginning of his resentment towards his mother the queen. She did not acknowledge him as her son, her heir to the crown prince. Young Bacon wanted to be the king, only to impress Marguerite and win her love.

Alan told me many stories surrounding Bacon like "The Tragic Death of My Brother Essex," Bacon's disgrace by a conspiracy of the opposition, and on and on. Those subjects were annoying to me then, because every time he talked about them, he was in a trance and his mind left his body and I lost him. Besides, why were things that happened such a long time ago so important?

But today, after Alan has gone, my concept of the past has changed; everything becomes the past after all. Each one of us has a connection with the past, whether yesterday, 100 or 1,000 years ago. It does not make any difference. We Christians celebrate Christ's birthday every year and mourn His death, even though it happened nearly 2,000 years ago.

I know how important Francis Bacon was to Alan. He felt Bacon's frustration deep down in his heart. Bacon's life, the shadow of his mother Queen Elizabeth's refusal to recognize him as her heir, his monumental writings without recognition, etc. Alan, who had also believed in education, knowledge, expression (creativity/originality), realized Bacon's genius and sincerely wanted to unveil his secret and credit him as the true author of Shakespeare's works.

The origin of Bacon's Motto, "Shake a Lance at Ignorance" was taken from the Greek goddess Pallas Athene, who stood for "shaking her spear at ignorance." This was Bacon's cipher (code), which proves his true identity. "I Will Shake My Spear at Ignorance." The door to the mystery can be unlocked only by the power of intelligence to find the true meaning of Shakespeare's writings, written with hidden ciphers.

Alan's Compositions inspired by Francis Bacon

Op 31	Two Shakespeare Sonnets (Voice and Piano)	1939
Op 283	Pericles (Grand Opera)	1975
Op 402	Symphony No. 62 "Oh Let Man Not Forget These Words" (Text by Francis Bacon – Bi-lateral Cipher Contained in Henry VII 1622, Deciphered by Mrs. E Gallup in 1899)	
Op 417	"Why Is My Verse So Barren of New Pride?" (Text from Shakespeare Sonnet 68) (Baritone & Piano)	1988

DEAR BOKEY: Seattle, Wash. 98188
U.S.A.

THANK YOU VERY MUCH FOR THE CIPHER PLAY "TRAGEDY OF ANNE BOLEYN" AND THANK YOU FOR YOUR GOOD LETTER. ENCLOSED IS CIPHER MATERIAL WHICH MR HESILL GAVE ME 12 YEARS AGO. I WANTED YOU TO HAVE IT – I SET IT TO MUSIC IN MY SYMPHONY No 62. I INTERUPTED IT FOR SYMPHONY No. 63 – "LOON LAKE" COMMISSIONED BY NEW HAMPSHIRE MUSIC FESTIVAL, WHERE IT WAS PERFORMED IN 3 PLACES VERY BEAUTIFULLY. NOW I HOPE TO RETURN TO THE FRANCIS BACON SYMPHONY No. 62. (MY SYMPHONY No. I "EXILE" PERFORMED BY BBC IN 1939 WAS ALSO DEDICATED TO BACON.

COMPOSER ORLANDO GIBBONS SHOULD BE INVESTIGATED. THE WORDS OF HIS MADRIGAL "THE SILVER SWAN" MUST BE BACON'S. GIBBON'S GRAVE IS A CIPHER WITH 33 TALL Ts. WORDS OF MUSIC BY GIBBONS AND JOHN DOWLAND ARE "ANONOMOUS"

Alan's communication with Bokey, the head of the Bacon Society

I WAS HAPPY TO READ ABOUT ALEXANDER POPE'S SECRET VERSION OF THE TEMPEST POEM ON THE SHAKESPEARE MASONIC MONUMENT IN WESTMINSTER ABBEY – I OFTEN VISITED IT ALONG WITH HANDEL'S MONUMENT. PERHAPS HANDEL, MOZART, HAYDN AND BEETHOVEN KNEW SOMETHING OF THE 33RD DEGREE OF MASONS:– "THE DEGREE OF THE KING'S SECRETS." BEETHOVEN IS SAID TO HAVE TOLD PEOPLE TO "READ THE TEMPEST". BEFORE PERFORMING HIS D MINOR SONATA WHICH BEGINS WITH MASONIC CHORD

ALSO SAID EVERYONE SHOULD KNEEL BARE HEADED BEFORE HANDEL'S GRAVE – FORGIVE MY RAMBLING,

WITH ALL BEST WISHES,

Alan

Alan's communication with Bokey, the head of the Bacon Society

Vilem Sokol
(Who Brought Alan to Seattle)

♪

I got a call from Eileen Swanson, a violist. She is the wife of Al Swanson, the recording engineer who recorded Alan's music.

She had a message from Mr. Savage, the conductor of St. James Church in downtown Seattle. He performed Alan's oratorio "Magnificat" for the ninetieth birthday of Vilem Sokol, the former conductor of the Seattle Youth Symphony. He thought he could borrow the parts from me, but my answer was simply "No, I cannot," because it is published by Alan's New York publisher, C.F. Peters. People don't realize that once a music composition has been published, the composer does not have any rights except to receive a royalty; so I gave her the information on how to get the parts from the publisher.

After the conversation with her, I called Gene Caprioglio at C.F. Peters and found out the "Magnificat" is twenty-eight minutes long and they charge $400 for the rental fee. When I reported this to Eileen, she said they were not performing the whole oratorio but only one part for the Sunday Mass. Mr. Sokol came to Mass every Sunday, so they would be giving a birthday concert for him then. I was surprised that they would perform only one part from such a magnificent oratorio.

I thought about it for a while, and I understood why they came to me. They did not want to pay the entire rental fee for just one part. I decided to talk to Gene to reduce the rental fee to $100, and I would pay it by myself as a contribution to the church. By the time I talked to Eileen, the conductor had called Gene himself and had gotten the same special arrangement. So, I called Gene and told him I would pay the fee and make it as a birthday present to Sokol from Alan. After all, he had played a very important role in Alan's life. If he had not invited Alan to come to Seattle, he never would have lived here, and I never would have met him.

In the 1960s, Vilem Sokol approached Alan and asked him to conduct his well-known symphony "Mysterious Mountain" for a Seattle Youth Symphony concert. Alan was living in New York then and told Sokol he did not want to come just to conduct "Mysterious Mountain" unless he could conduct some of his new music. Alan thought, "Everybody is playing 'Mysterious Mountain,' but I am writing new music all the time. I want to introduce my new music."

Mr. Sokol agreed, and on the February 14, 1966, concert Alan got the last half all to himself, conducting "Mysterious Mountain," "Symphony No. 5," and "Variation and Fugue." As a result of this concert, Seattle Symphony Conductor Milton Katims invited Alan to be the composer in residence for the Seattle symphony for the next year.

Alan told me that while he was here for the Youth Symphony concert, Sokol woke him up early every morning and took him to radio stations for interviews. Alan had been a night owl all his life, so it was very difficult for him. Plus, he had to praise the Youth Symphony during the interview, which was over the radio as requested by Sokol.

During that next year with the Seattle Symphony, he stayed at the Georgian Hotel, a cheap hotel in the downtown International District. As far as the Seattle Symphony was concerned, it was disgraceful that their composer in residence was staying at such a cheap hotel. But Alan didn't mind it; in fact, he rather liked the place because an old Japanese maid who worked there helped make him comfortable.

From there he participated with the Seattle Symphony musicians in many performances all around Washington.

During that year while Alan was in Seattle, he left his wife Elizabeth in New York, and he was more or less independent from her. He was thinking that this separation could help him break up with her. He had an unhappy marriage with her for many years but could not break it off. So much of the time he was away from home with concert engagements, tours, etc. It became his lifestyle.

In 1972, he decided to separate from her, leave New York, and find a new place on the West Coast. But she ignored his wishes and came along with him instead. I never understood this, but according to him, his attempts to break away from her backfired on him many times during that marriage.

First, they stopped in Portland and met the conductor there, but they decided not to settle there and came up north to Seattle. That was the place to which Alan really wanted to come. He loved the mountains, and they gave him inspiration. That is why he loved Switzerland, a beautiful mountain country. But he discovered Seattle, a city sandwiched in between two mountain ranges, the Cascades on the east and the Olympics on the west over the Puget Sound. And his beloved Japan was just on the other side of the Pacific Ocean, so he resided here.

Sokol had conducted Alan's "Fra Angelico" in 1969, "Mysterious Mountain" again in 1971, and finally Symphony No. 22 "City of Light" on May 20, 1974. Alan gave me many tickets for that performance. In 1974, Alan was helping me with my singing. We met regularly to practice, and he accompanied me on the piano. Eventually, this led to our secret love affair.

I took my family to the concert and also invited my singer friends, the alto soloist from the church where I sang and my friend Leona. Our seats were on the front edge of the second balcony. We singers were so excited, like schoolgirls. Every time the climactic build-up returned at the end of the symphony, like the tide on the shore, we cried out for the music not to end.

After his symphony during the intermission, Alan came up to the balcony to meet us and jotted down some music notes in his sketchbook. Then he tore out the page and gave the music to me. It was two lines of melody and an accompaniment figure with his words over it, "Since I cannot live through Copland, please drown me in *sake*." I was all red inside of me from the embarrassment, and he was giving me a secret message. I was hoping nobody else recognized it.

After the intermission, Copland's music was performed. Alan hated Copland because he had discriminated against Alan's music in the past. But that night, Copland's "Appalachian Spring" was a "flat tire." All our excitement was exhausted over Hovhaness.

After the concert, the Youth Symphony made a record of Alan's "City of Light." But Sokol cut the beautiful third movement *allegretto grazioso*. Alan had taken it from his childhood piano piece "Dance Ghazal." He was complaining about that movement having been cut, and he said to me, "That movement is too sexy for Sokol." Alan was right; every time I heard that movement, I danced. In 1992, Alan recorded the whole symphony without cuts with the Seattle Symphony. And in Alan's 2001 Memorial Concert, I put that sexy movement in the program.

During 1975–76, Alan had been living with me, but he returned to his wife twice because of her desperate attempts to get him back. Finally, on the third time, she decided to get him back for good and took him to Europe. He disappeared from me, and I didn't know where he was for some time. Before he left for Europe, she took him to Vancouver, BC, to attend Yehudi Menuhin's violin concert. There he met Sokol and his wife! They offered to drive Alan and Elizabeth back home. All four of them were together on that long ride back to Seattle.

During that whole trip, Alan felt very uncomfortable and ashamed, as if he had been caught with the wrong girl. Sokol did not know what was going on; they all thought he was Elizabeth's husband. The fact was that he had been living with me, but at that particular time, he had abandoned me and was with Elizabeth against his own wishes like a borrowed cat. But he could not tell the truth in front of everybody, so he tried to behave normally. That was bad for Alan, because he came back to me and married me a year later. The Sokols must have felt that they had been deceived and thought Alan was immoral and scandalous. That event cost him greatly, personally and professionally, and Sokol never performed Alan's music again.

After Alan and I were married, we met Sokol a few times at the university, after my singing lesson. When he saw Alan, he came up to him and greeted him passionately. I said to Alan, "He really likes you. Maybe what you are thinking is wrong."

Alan had been saying to me, "Sokol is punishing me because he had seen me with Elizabeth in Vancouver. Then, I turned around and married you. Maybe his Catholic wife is influencing him to not play my music. Also, he does not play Wagner because he was a scandal, too. So, he performs Mahler because he was a 'good boy' and he had only one wife."

Despite what I thought, what Alan said was right, and it was confirmed by what we heard from a conductor who was married to a young violinist, a former student of Sokol's. That conductor had been divorced before and then married the violinist. He became the "black sheep" of Mrs. Sokol's clan. According to the conductor, half of her children went into convents, and the other half rebelled from her strict Catholic upbringing and married divorcees, etc.

In 1999, Alan was very ill. I took him to the hospital often for blood transfusions. One morning, he was sitting up in the hospital bed when a violinist came into the room carrying a violin. She introduced herself by saying she was Sokol's youngest daughter, Jennifer. In 1966, the first time Alan was in Seattle, he was at Sokol's house. She was just a little girl then, but she remembered Alan very well, and they were even in a picture together. There in the hospital room that morning, she played "Humoresque" for Alan. After that, I got to know her. She was a nun, but her mother became ill, and she left the convent to take care of her until her death. She was the angel of the family.

During Alan's last year of sickness, I thought it would be nice for Alan to see Sokol once more, possibly for the last time. But my attempts were never fulfilled. I don't know why Sokol did not make an effort to see Alan. Could it be that he never accepted our marriage, even after his wife's death?

On May 21, 1989, the year after Sokol's retirement, Ruben Gurevich, the new conductor of the Seattle Youth Symphony performed Alan's well-known piece "And God Created Great Whales." In 1991, he commissioned some new music from Alan. In the agreement he wrote:

I was absolutely delighted that you have agreed to write a piece for us. As we discussed, we would like a work of about ten minutes in length in a joyous, celebratory style.... One more personal note. Let me tell you that, as a longtime admirer of your music, I am particularly happy that your work will be the one that will be performed at the final concert of our 50th anniversary season.

Alan composed, not ten minutes, but a nineteen-minute-long symphony (Symphony No. 66 "Hymn To Glacier Peak") containing three movements. The symphony was completed on March 29, 1992, and premiered on May 10, 1992, on Mother's Day and conducted by Gurevich. Finally, Alan and the Youth Symphony had resumed their association.

SEATTLE YOUTH SYMPHONY ORCHESTRA

VILEM SOKOL, CONDUCTOR AND MUSICAL DIRECTOR

Seattle Center Opera House — 8:00 p.m., Monday, May 20, 1974

PROGRAM

DIVERTIMENTO FOR STRINGS VERRALL

Allegro moderato
Andante tranquillo
Allegro fantastico
Molto moderato

SYMPHONY NO. 22 "CITY OF LIGHT" HOVHANESS

Allegro moderato
Largo (Angel of Light)
Allegretto grazioso
Finale

APPALACHIAN SPRING (Ballet for Martha) COPLAND

INTERMISSION

CONCERTO FOR VIOLIN AND ORCHESTRA BARTOK

Allegro non troppo
Andante tranquillo
Allegro molto

Denes Zsigmondy — soloist

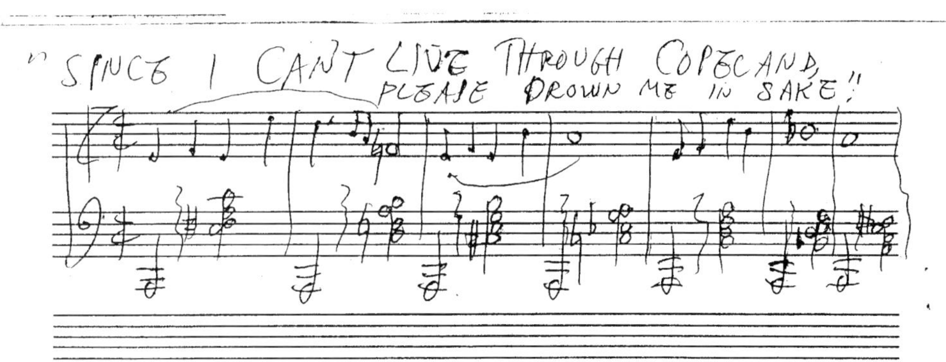

Top: Alan's program with the Seattle Youth Symphony Orchestra, bottom: Alan's writing to Hinako at the Symphony No. 22 concert "City Of Light" on May 20, 1974

Editor's Difficulty
(Letter to the Editor)

♪

Dear Gary,

May I tell you my story again, correctly—the story I was telling you on the telephone the other day, one of Alan's funny stories.

One day Alan got a call from a C.F. Peters Music Publisher's editor, a very conventional, conservative gentleman, who was editing Alan's music, but he was puzzled about Alan's "Dedication to Rajah." He said to Alan, "Mr. Hovhaness, you already wrote a dedication to Mr. Rajah in the beginning (of the piece). Do you really need a second one?"

Rajah was Alan's beloved black cat Rajah Hoydn. In a certain section of the composition, it describes a cat's movement, so Alan wrote it "especially to Rajah."

It seemed strange to the editor, but Alan could not tell him that Rajah was a cat.

Being an editor, you must have edited all different kinds, sometimes even animals.

P.S. Rajah's original name was spelled "Haydn." Alan named him after the composer Joseph Haydn, but he started to call him "Hoydn," which sounded more like Rajah's personality—a very special little black cat.

Rajah Hoydn (Magic Ruler)

Rajah was Alan's beloved black cat who lived with him during his early Boston era.

At that time, in the 1930s, Alan was the organist at Watertown Church. People recalled him as the "composer living with a cat."

Their inseparable relationship started early. One day, Alan had gone to a nearby river to swim and took young Rajah with him. Alan went into the water up to his neck. Suddenly, Rajah jumped into the water to get to him! He was worried that Alan was drowning and tried to save him. Obviously, Alan was the one who rescued him from the current of the river. Because of this event, Alan realized Rajah was not an ordinary cat, and he loved him so much.

In the morning, Rajah woke up early. Alan had been a night owl, and he was still sleeping, so Rajah threatened him by putting his paw against Alan's ink bottle to push it to the edge of the table, about to drop on the floor. So, Alan had to get up.

Alan took Rajah everywhere, even to his orchestra rehearsals. While he was driving, Rajah sat on his shoulder. Anybody who saw him was surprised and said, "What is that?"

Even though Alan was a church organist, his goal was to make it as a composer. He organized an amateur orchestra and created a concert in order to perform his compositions. Whenever contributions came to him, he used them to hire the musicians for his concert; he never spent them on himself. (I heard this from people who knew him in the past.)

During that period, Grace Deeran, Alan's faithful violinist friend from his amateur orchestra, came to Alan's apartment to practice music. One evening they were practicing Beethoven's "Kreutzer Sonata" for violin and piano. Suddenly, Rajah jumped up on the piano bench and played the piano wildly with his paw, looking at them with the most serious eyes, as if he was moved by the serious passage of the sonata. So, they played the same passage again, to see if he would do it again. Sure enough, Rajah jumped up and played the piano; he did this every time they played the "Kreutzer Sonata." (I know this, music is not only for people, but also for animals, and they have their favorites.)

At one time, Alan could not keep Rajah and left him with a farmer he knew, but he would visit him often. The farmer reported to Alan that, after his visits, Rajah was brokenhearted and did not eat for many days.

Finally, Alan got Rajah back, but their togetherness did not last long. Suddenly, Rajah got very sick; Alan took him to the vet, but he died. Alan watches his life going away from him, from his feet to his head. At that time Alan had had a brief marriage to a strange woman who hated Rajah. Alan believed she had poisoned him.

After Rajah's death, Alan desperately tried to communicate with him. He went to a psychic, even used a Ouija board. Rajah came through often to Alan by those means.

Often, Alan saw Rajah's black fur in the air, out of the corners of his eyes. Alan never forgot Rajah on Memorial Day; he put milk in a saucer and placed it on the table for Rajah's spirit.

Alan said to me, "Now Rajah is helping the dead animals, including dogs, enter into the spirit world." (He added the "dogs," knowing I am a dog person. He also used to say, "Rajah was like a dog," to make me like him.)

After Rajah, Alan had a number of cats. Bach was a fierce black cat who guarded Alan like a watchdog, scaring the people who would try to come into the apartment. One time Alan saw two repairmen come in; the next thing he knew, there was Bach, paws up in the air, his mouth wide open, as if to attack them, and the two big men, hands up in the air, backed up and pinned against the front door where they came in. Ramasa was a female cat; at one time she sat on the windowsill and Alan, without knowing she was there, closed the window and she fell from the second-floor window, but she was not hurt. *Sasa-no-yuki* (snow on bamboo), was a stray cat he found on Queen Anne hill.

But Rajah dwelled in Alan's heart and sat on a throne above all other cats.

After Alan's death, I found his writing on the front cover of his sketchbook "Rajah Hoydn—Magic Ruler" and a drawing of a black cat beside it.

Alan and Creston

I have been thinking, I should not keep Alan's important manuscripts and documents in my house forever. Where is the best archive for them?

I have had a request from the Yerevan Library in Armenia, but it is too far away and not a convenient location for people to get to. I thought of New York City, but there are so many other composers there, and Alan's music may be overlooked and buried among them. I thought of the University of Washington Library; it is a very convenient location for me. After all, Alan was a Seattle composer; they would be proud to have his music and would take good care of it for Alan.

Then I learned Paul Creston's music was in their archives; he was also a Washington composer. I sang one of his compositions "The 23rd Psalm—The Lord Is My Shepherd," and I liked it. That thought brought me back to an event that took place in the summer of 1974.

In the summer of 1974, Alan took me to New York to audition to sing in his just-finished oratorio "The Way of Jesus." In it he had composed two soprano arias for my voice and had written the arias so high that no other soprano (but me) could sing them, hoping I would get to perform them.

One day during our stay in New York, Alan was invited to dinner by Mr. Singer, the former conductor of the Portland Symphony. That afternoon, I went to a corner flower shop and bought a bouquet of flowers to bring to dinner. Before we left for dinner, we started talking about music, and I told Alan I had sung Paul Creston's "23rd Psalm" at a church service and liked it. Then, suddenly, his facial expression became wild, and he lay me down on the bed and got on top of me, as if he were raping me. He was not at all like the Alan I knew. Even though it was unexpected and drastic, I did not mind it because I was madly in love with him, but it was different, one of a kind; it was his red-hot fire of jealousy.

Sometime later, Alan told me this story. At one time, Alan and Creston were staying in the same building during the time their music was being performed on the same program. Their rooms were next to each other; I don't remember where it was. Could it have been a school guest house? For some reason Alan became very nasty to Creston and intentionally played the piano located near their bedroom loudly to irritate him.

These two stories coincide. I don't know why Alan behaved this way towards Creston; he usually was respectful and supportive of other composers. Alan introduced me to music by many different composers: Handel and Mozart (he especially liked Mozart and insisted that I like his music). He introduced Mozart's coloratura arias and accompanied me on the piano; we had a wonderful time studying the music together. Finally, I appreciated and loved Mozart's music.

He also admired Beethoven, Schubert, Tchaikovsky, and Wagner. Wagner's music excited him, starting from when he was a young man. Every time he took me to a Wagner opera, he was filled with passion, whispering in my ear, passing all his knowledge of Wagner's music to me.

Then Sibelius, who was living at the time Alan was in his early twenties. Alan's passion led him to Finland to meet Sibelius. Alan had corresponded with him for many years. (Unfortunately, his letters disappeared; Alan thinks one of his previous wives took them.)

Alan even introduced me to Mahler and Bartok, and he got along with many contemporary composers; he praised Randall Thompson's music. (They corresponded towards the end of Thompson's life—I have Thompson's letters.)

After all I have said, Alan's behavior remains a mystery. Maybe it was their personality differences or something about Creston's music that aroused Alan's competitive spirit, but as far as I was concerned, Alan did not have to compete with him.

I saw one of the photos in a book called *Stokowski: A Counterpoint of View by Oliver Daniel*; Alan and Creston were standing side by side next to Stokowski, who was sitting at the piano. Alan was tall, twice the height of Creston, and was smiling handsomely. I almost saw his powerful vitality overpowering Creston.

Nevertheless, what happened in that New York hotel room must have been his sheer jealousy. He didn't mind that I liked "dead" composers' music but did mind "living" composers; he wanted me to be in love with his music, exclusively.

Anyway, if I decide Alan's library should be at the University of Washington, where Creston's music is, it will be a conflict again. Alan would try to take over all the popularity to himself with his powerful force and charm.

Erick Hawkins
"Plains Daybreak"

♪

In March of 1976, shortly after Alan left me, Erick Hawkins, a New York dancer, called me to talk to Alan about commissioning Alan to compose for his contemporary dance group. I told him I would give the message to Alan as soon as he returned, but the truth was I didn't know where he was.

Alan was still married to Elizabeth, but he had been living with me. On March 15, he visited Elizabeth, but he never returned. During his disappearance, he was taken to Europe by Elizabeth, like a prisoner. She tried to get Alan to forget me by cutting off our communication completely. I didn't know where he was, and in the meantime, Alan had been worrying about what I would do. He thought he might lose me since he had left me without saying anything. Finally, he called me on June 9 from New York. When I answered the telephone, he was extremely happy to find I was still there in the same apartment, waiting for him. Then I told him about the commission from Erick Hawkins and gave him all the information to communicate with him. On the night of June 20, Alan came back to me for good.

Alan completed Erick's commission on December 20, 1977; it was scored for flute, bass clarinet, trumpet in C, trombone, percussion, violin, and contra bass, the instruments for Erick's regular chamber group. Alan had to follow Erick's long-winded scenario, precise timings, plus pages and pages of his analysis. Alan named the piece "Spirit Animals," but Erick changed the title to "Plains Daybreak." Alan let Erick help himself to his own title, but he said to me, sarcastically, "He likes the flatland like the Midwest—Iowa, Kansas, Oklahoma, but I like the mountains."

The first time I met Erick was December of 1975 in San Francisco. Alan had been invited for the performance of his piece "Meditation of Orpheus." Seiji Ozawa was conducting the San Francisco Symphony. Erick Hawkins and his dance group were to dance to Alan's piece. We stayed at the King George Hotel in the heart of downtown San Francisco. At the dress rehearsal, Erick made a big gesture and embraced Alan passionately in front of the musicians, I knew then how much he adored Alan.

December 3, the opening of the concert, was a somewhat distracting day. After we had been seated in the concert hall, we had to leave the hall because of a bomb scare, and later we came back to the concert. Just before Alan's piece, a nude man came out from the wing of the stage and crossed the stage, carrying something (I was not sure what) like a banner. I thought maybe it was a "streaker," and I looked around, but no one was making a fuss, so I told myself to be quiet about it. That was the prelude for Alan's piece, and then the music started. The dancers were dressed in see-through costumes over their nude bodies, in the style of ancient Greece. Erick danced also, but I never could tell about the style of his costume or his movement. He more or less stayed at one position and moved his arms and legs. According to Alan, his movements were original and philosophical.

I never saw a "porno" performance like his in a concert hall before; I was ashamed of Alan's music being used this way. Then, suddenly, some man came from behind Alan and said something. Alan yelled at him and stood up and chased him and went out from the concert hall behind him. He did not come back until the intermission and said the man blamed him for the dance, but Alan had nothing to do with it. Once the music had been published from the publishers, the composer has nothing to say and anybody can use the music any way they please, as long as they pay.

A note had been given to Alan after the concert; some man wanted to meet Alan in a certain place. I guess Alan's piece excited a gay man. When we went to Erick's backstage dressing room, Alan mentioned that note to Erick, but he did not have much to say. "Don't pay attention to such a thing," as if he were used to this kind of reaction from his choreography.

While we were backstage, we went to see the conductor Ozawa. He came from Japan and became well known in America. Earlier in the evening, at the performance, we saw him for the first-time onstage conducting. He moved his body and swung his long hair like a dancer, showing off his body movement; he looked like a young boy. He was well known for his conducting style.

But when Alan and I went into his room, I saw a heavy-set man in a gown, sitting on a chair that was Ozawa. He did not look at all like the conductor I had seen on the stage. Alan thought so, too, and said to me, "He looks like a Japanese *Yakuza* [gangster]." He shook hands with us but did not have very much to say, even though I was expecting him to show his interest in Alan's music because he was Japanese and Alan's music was very oriental. But I guess many Japanese were interested in European music, far different from their own. I saw his wife outside the room, tall and with her hair dyed light brown. I could not tell whether she was Japanese or not.

In 1982, the San Jose Symphony approached Alan, asking him if he could conduct his "Meditation of Orpheus" for their subscription concert, with Erick Hawkins' group dancing. We were shocked, that incident in San Francisco had never been forgotten by us. So, our answer was "No!" Alan had been blamed for Erick's nude dance; moreover, if he would conduct, the dance certainly would look like it had been approved by the composer. We said "no" to the young orchestra manager David (he was the son of Alan's violinist friend Gary Beswick who used to teach at Billings, Montana, and invited Alan to his school concerts), but just out of curiosity, I asked him how much the orchestra usually paid for the visiting conductors. Then he said, "As much as six thousand dollars." That amount in 1982 was quite a bit of money. We could not resist; finally, Alan decided to conduct his music with Erick's dance.

Whatever we felt about Erick's creation, the nude dance, Erick was sincere. His choreographies were from his pure concept of art and intellect. To the artist, the human nude body is the pure beauty of God's creation; nevertheless, we felt taking this job was like prostitution.

At the concert, Alan did conduct the orchestra with his back to the audience, but I felt his uncomfortableness. As before, a nude man came out with a banner and crossed the stage, the nymphs danced with their see-through coverings, etc. At the end of the performance, Erick and his dancers lined up on the stage and bowed. But, to my horror, Erick stepped back to get Alan, to put him in the center of the line. Hand-in-hand, skipping toward the front of the stage. Alan was not just embarrassed but tried to catch up with Erick's skipping feet with his confused, off-beat steps. Alan was more or less hiding behind the dancers, but Erick pulled him out and exposed him to the audience.

Alan told me Erick was a very idealistic dancer who had believed in using live music for the performances, not recorded music, like most dance groups used. He commissioned compositions from many composers, and he was especially fond of Alan's music and used it for his performances. Later, he commissioned Alan to write specifically for his group, not once, but three times, and he paid every bit of it himself. He was an idealistic dancer but, as was usual with music and performing-arts people, money was very hard to come by. Erick paid Alan his commission fee in installments, a small amount each time; and one time, Erick applied to the American Music Center for a grant, and Alan received $300 from them for copying and printing of parts.

His last commission "God the Reveler" took him four years to pay. I found the envelopes sent by Erick and Alan's writing—"Not Deposit able Check." It had Erick's letter and a $1,000 check for Alan dated March 25, 1978, and never cashed. His story was:

78 Fifth Avenue
March 28

Dear Alan,

I am enclosing one check for $1000. However, if you don't need to cash it at once, please hold off. We are doing a performance here at the Roundabout Theatre at the end of April, and are tight for money since one never knows what the expenses will be. If you see you need to cash it before May 1, let me know, otherwise hold it and then when you are about to cash it write to me.

I will not let you down! It is wonderful that you are having the work done and that you are going.

I will have the third $1000 during the month of June, that is by the latter half without any question, so you can count on that.

I am hoping now to premiere "Plains Daybreak" in San Antonio May 27th at the 4th International Congress of Art, Religion, etc. Had too many troubles here to premiere it in April here. Had to fire a manager etc. Can't find people to do the work.

Let me hear your plans. With my best,

Erick (Signature)

When I knew Erick, he was older and didn't look special; but, according to Alan, when he was young, he was a tall and handsome dancer. He was married to the famous modern dancer Martha Graham, and they danced together in the U.S. and Europe. She also commissioned music from Alan and danced to much of Alan's music, with her ballet troupe.** According to a story Alan told me, at a performance in Paris, during their duet, Erick dropped her onstage, by accident. She was very angry and never forgave Erick for that; after that accident, they divorced.

In the late 1980s, we drove to see him near Olympia, where he had a performance and wanted to meet with Alan. He took us to a restaurant by the water and we talked. He wanted to commission new music from Alan for the third time, and that composition eventually became "God the Reveler," titled by Erick.

That night, Alan and I were together, as usual, and Erick missed his girlfriend Lucy (Lucia Dlugoszewski), a New York composer. He had been living with her for a long time, and Martha was ancient history at that time. Back in New York, Lucy had gone back to her mother's house to take care of her dying mother. Erick must have loved her so much; he spoke her name many times that night.

After his death in 1994, Lucy did so much for his memorial; she published a book and video to keep him and his original concept and method of dance alive. I never met her, but now I understand why Erick adored her so much. I learned she died in April 2000.

*Music Commissioned by Erick Hawkins:
"Plains Daybreak" op. 295, composed in 1977
"Killer's Enemies" op. 383, composed in 1983
"God the Reveler" op. 408, composed in 1987

**Music commissioned and/or performed by Martha Graham:
"Ardent Song" op. 190, composed in 1945
"Circe" for ballet, op. 204, composed in 1963
"Dream of Myth" op. 260, composed in 1973

With My Voice Teacher Leon Lishner (Our Regular Routine – Good Music and Good Company)

I was dreaming about Leon Lishner all night long, the voice teacher I had studied with for six years. My dream was just the atmosphere of being in a party, surrounded by a crowd of people, like a party Lishner used to give often. I am not sure if Alan was with me or not, but he must have been because we always went to his parties together.

When I woke up, I realized my dream reminded me of Lishner; otherwise, I had forgotten about him. Our relationship with him was long and nothing significant happened. Alan and I just saw him once a week and enjoyed making music together.

For two days I dismissed the idea of writing about him—then, last night, I saw a movie called *The Sixth Sense*, which was about a young boy who had an unusual sense. He could see ghosts, dead people, and he had to do things for them, even though he was bothered by it. I realized I don't see ghosts (like him), but since Alan's death, many people I knew who have died appear in my dreams and in my thoughts, influencing me to write about them. Sometimes I am not up to it, but they persuade me, and this dream is the same case. But how can I make Lishner's story interesting? It is flat. But I cannot get rid of his ghost, and it seems to me even Alan is supporting him.

December 1975 – Alan took me to a Northwest Chamber Orchestra performance. The chamber orchestra was founded by Louis Richmond, a talented young conductor from Seattle. Alan had been very much involved with him when he was organizing the orchestra. They performed five program series each season, and Alan's music was played at almost every program.

That night they performed Alan's "Avak the Healer," a cantata for soprano, trumpet, and strings. Alan composed this cantata, inspired by a story in the newspaper about a healer. I was impressed with the soprano soloist Valerie Yockey. She had a very controlled, mellow voice. At that time, I was looking for a new teacher, so Alan and I went to her backstage and complimented her singing and asked her who her voice teacher was.

Her voice teacher was Leon Lishner. I had heard of him before; he was a well-known voice teacher at the University of Washington. He had produced many successful singers, and he himself was a fine bass from New York. I had seen him in several opera performances at the university in the past.

Alan asked him to teach me, and Lishner took me as his student. He could not say "no" to Hovhaness, the well-known composer. At that time, Alan and I were living together in an apartment in the south end of Seattle. Every week Alan came along with me to my voice lessons to accompany me on the piano.

Soon after I started studying with Lishner, Alan went to New York, persuaded by his wife. I showed up alone at my lesson in a disastrous mentality. My teacher noticed my condition and asked me what had happened. I said, "Alan left me. He cares about his career more than me." Then he came towards me and embraced me, I was surprised and thought he must be being sympathetic to me, but he was taking advantage of the situation. So, I said to him, "You must be a very emotional person," which was the only thing I could think of to discourage him without saying harsh words. He understood what I meant, and he stopped.

I thought of this event very seriously. I never had to worry about this kind of situation before because all of my former teachers were women. I thought I could have quit going to him, but why should I have to lose a good teacher because of that? I don't blame him; I understand a man's nature. God made men that way; they are attracted to women, but I don't want my voice lesson to become a "rat race." Finally, I decided to continue to study with him, but I would make myself clear to him, keep the student-and-teacher relationship. We never spoke of that event and behaved like that had never happened. Our relationship as a student and teacher lasted for six years, from January 3, 1976 – June of 1981, until he retired from teaching.

Finally, in July of 1976, Alan came back to me for good and our separation ended. Alan came with me to my voice lessons every time, to accompany me. Lishner was unlike the usual voice teacher who was only interested in and knew vocal music; he was an all-around musician and understood instrumental music as well. Alan enjoyed his company.

Lishner, being a bass, had a low voice, extremely different from my high coloratura voice. He was fascinated by my voice but could not help very much. A voice like mine, which is extremely high and long ranged, has a "break" where the low chest voice and the high head (falsetto) voice meet, so he had to strengthen the transition to make the voice even from top to bottom, it is one of the hardest things to do for a classical singer. He taught me to bring the voice down from the top in order to lighten the low voice to match the high voice, instead of bringing the chest voice up, so his method did not strengthen my voice but produced a beautiful-sounding voice. Alan naturally loved my voice; he had been attracted by my voice to start with. He and my teacher worked together with the same goal, to make my voice beautiful and perfect.

Since my voice was extremely high (I could sing to high F above high C, about three octaves), Alan and Lishner, together, selected very unusual songs for me and with a challenging piano part for Alan. Among them were Mozart's Concert Arias for Soprano. Many of these arias were composed for Aloysia Weber, the dramatic coloratura soprano. Mozart was in love with her, but she rejected him, and he later married her sister Constanze.

These arias were very demanding and very seldom performed. Alan was excited and delighted for me to study Mozart's songs because, all this time, he had been persuading and insisting on me liking Mozart's music. And he succeeded, I finally appreciated Mozart and loved his arias. My wish was to record Mozart's complete concert arias for soprano, but my dream was never fulfilled because Alan became sick.

Handel was Alan's favorite composer; he also wanted me to sing the arias from Handel's opera "Solomon." In order for me to sing the arias, Alan transposed the songs to a higher key. One of the arias he really loved was called "Blessed the Day." The queen sings to King Solomon on their wedding day:

"Blessed the day when first my eyes saw the wisest of the wise-
When I was led to ascend the nuptial bed.
But completely bless'd the day on my bosom as he lay,
When he called my charms divine, vowing to be only mine."

Then my teacher introduced the aria of Zerbinetta from Strauss's *Ariadne auf Naxos*. She is not the main character, and she sings only one aria in the whole opera, but her aria is twenty pages long, and all the skills and tricks of the coloratura are in this aria.

The three of us enjoyed studying this aria so much. Alan had not liked Strauss in the past, maybe because his favorite composers were Handel, Mozart, Beethoven, Schubert, Wagner, and Sibelius—composers he could relate to with melody and emotion. When he heard Strauss's music for the first time, maybe he did not get inspiration, and he had not heard much of Strauss's music since. I think that might be the case about him not liking Strauss's music. After he was introduced to Zerbinetta's aria by Lishner, he came to appreciate and understand Strauss's greatness.

Alan also composed numerous songs for us to perform together. *

When I started studying with Lishner, he taught me at his studio at the U.W., but after his retirement from the school, we went to his home for the voice lessons. His house was a large, three-story house near the university. I think he was interested in art; I saw good drawings displayed, even over the toilet. We met his wife; she was not young but had been a modern dancer from New York and was teaching at that time.

Shortly after that time, he sold his house. The house he had lived in for a long time, and moved to the other side of the U.W. His new house was also a three-story house, but it was unlike his old house, contemporary style, smaller, and conveniently designed like a studio apartment. Each floor was independent from the others and had a separate entrance, so the students could come and go without disturbing the rest of the house. Because of his years of teaching at school, his lifestyle was set, and he wanted to keep his independence, so he bought a house suitable for their needs. But in spite of their efforts, that house did not help the adjustment of their marriage, due to his retirement.

He thought his wife was weird; we noticed she was strange and other people did, too. We were at his voice recital and his wife was in the audience dressed like a hippie and making yoga-like solitary movements during the performance. Alan said sympathetically, "When he was young, he must have been attracted by her originality, but when he got older, his taste changed, and he became attracted to younger, more feminine girls."

Soon after that, Lishner was seen with a young, good-looking violinist. He had left his wife and bought a new house for himself, after he had spent so much money to remodel that new house to his liking, then he sold it and moved into another one.

He did this several times and finally he settled down in his last house. It was a nice newer house in wooded surroundings. We were invited to one of his parties. His girlfriend Beverly was there, helping with the party. I assume she had been living with him all this time, but she said that she was not. He could not stand living with his wife and had separated from her, but he did not divorce her. Although he loved Beverly, he did not live with her. He needed independence and his house had to be exactly the way he wanted.

Alan was oh, so different from him. Alan had to compose, that he could not compromise, but where all other things were concerned; he left them to me to be the way I wanted. And he did not need independence; he wanted my presence at all times, even while he was composing. Otherwise, he was lonely.

One time, Lishner and Beverly dropped by our house for some reason, and I did not have any refreshments for them, so I put what I had in my refrigerator (cold cuts, tomato, and lettuce, etc.) out on the table to make sandwiches. To my delight, they were so hungry; the four of us ate together with such intimacy. I assume by that time he had lost much of his money buying many houses.

In 1990, Seattle Opera was going to give the opera *War and Peace* by Sergei Prokofiev. It was the first complete presentation of this opera in America. Alan was looking forward to hearing this opera, but on July 31, he fell and broke his hip and was hospitalized. Our tickets for the opera were for August 2, so Alan could not make it. I called people to give away the tickets but, unbelievably, nobody had enough interest to go to the opera on such short notice, even my teacher Mrs. Berger.

Finally, on the day of the performance, I called my former teacher Leon Lishner, thinking that he must already have tickets for this opera. To my happy surprise, he was delighted to go. Immediately, he and Beverly drove from the north end of Seattle to see me in the hospital waiting room while Alan's operation was going on.

The last time we heard from him was just before the Fourth of July in 1995.

He had invited us to his birthday party on the fourth, but Alan did not want to go out on that day because he did not like the noise of fireworks, and he also wanted to stay home to protect our house from sparks of fireworks. Shortly after that, Lishner died. We learned about his death from the *Seattle Times* newspaper article written by Melinda Bargreen.

I started out writing this story "low key," but I became interested. I realized it was very important, the routine of our life, good music, and good company. Alan was younger then, and once a week we went to my lesson with Lishner and afterward dropped into the University District. I shopped and Alan sat in a coffee shop, composing, with coffee and desserts on the table. We were so fortunate to live life, doing what we wanted to do, composing, and studying voice and singing.

Once, Alan told me, "What we do for our development here, other than just survival of life, we are preparing for the next life, which is not material life. In that place, there is an order of rank. Persons who have developed intellectually and spiritually do not come back, but ones who are not developed [still in an animal state] must come back to life many times until they will be wholly developed."

I remember Lishner was a strong-minded and self-confident man, and he did not believe in God or spirits (unlike Alan, who was spiritual and believed in life after death), but when his old dog died, he needed to talk to us about Alan's belief of life after death.

I hope now he is there with Alan and is happily surprised he was wrong.

This is the music Alan composed for me:

Voice and Piano

op. 265 Two Biblical Songs for high soprano and piano
"How Long Wilt Thou Forget Me?" (1973)
"Let Not Your Heart Be Troubled" (1974)

op. 274 Three Sasa Songs for soprano and piano (1973)
"Where's My Cat?"
"Melancholy Cat"
"Sasa's Tarantella"

op. 304 "A Presentiment" for coloratura soprano and piano (1977)

op. 315 Three Songs for soprano and piano (1978)
"Genri"
"Strange Little Cat"
"Mysterious Harp"

op. 350 No. 1 "Star Songs Bell Song" for coloratura soprano and Javanese gamelan (1981) op. 365 "Shigure" for soprano and piano (1982)

op. 370 "Love's Philosophy" for soprano and piano

Cantatas

op. 292 "Glory Sings the Setting Sun" for coloratura soprano, clarinet and piano (1977) text by the composer

op. 298 "How I Love Thy Law" for soprano, clarinet, and piano (1977)

op. 305 Celestial Canticle for coloratura soprano and piano (1977)
Orchestral version available
"Prelude"
"The Lord Reigneth"
"Under the Shadow"
"Alleluia"

Oratorios

op. 279 The Way of Jesus, for soprano, tenor, bass, SATB chorus, and orchestra (1975)

op. 343 Revelation of St. Paul for soprano, tenor, baritone, SATB chorus, and orchestra (1980)

Operas

op. 283 "Pericles" Grand opera for two sopranos, tenor, bass, SATB chorus, and orchestra (1975) Libretto by composer.

op. 323 "Tale of Sun Goddess Going Into the Stone House" for coloratura soprano, soprano, tenor, bass, SATB chorus, and orchestra (1978) Libretto by Hinako Fujihara Hovhaness.

Unpaid String Quartet

I have just finished printing Alan's String Quartets No. 1–4. It took four days because I had to adjust his old manuscripts in order to print them. His music was written on all different sizes of papers, as if he had picked up the papers from the floor. Alan was that way when his inspiration came, and he was in a hurry. He used any paper he could find to write on, like the back of somebody's letters, even the back of shopping lists. These quartets were especially irregular and untidy, so I had to reduce, cut, paste, and bind them. Finally, I looked at my finished product and was pleased.

In 1988, we were at the New Hampshire Festival for the premiere of Alan's Symphony No. 63 "Loon Lake," which had been commissioned by the festival. two days before the premiere Alan's String Quartet No. 1 was performed. We did not know about it, but it was a happy surprise for Alan. Alan told me that his string quartets were seldom performed because string quartet players were "sophisticated" musicians, and they thought Alan's music was too emotional and "popular."

That string quartet had been written when he was twenty-five years old, yet it was never performed. Alan orchestrated it and called it "Prelude and Quadruple Fugue." It is my favorite, and I consider it one of his masterpieces.

Later, in 1994, Alan's four string quartets were recorded by the Shanghai Quartet for the Delos label. It was as if they had come out of the closet and were seeing the light. Finally, Alan's string quartets had become part of the repertoire of sophisticated string quartets.

On February 11, 1977, just before we were married, we were at St. Martin's Abbey in Tacoma for the premiere of Alan's String Quartet No. 5. It was performed by the Kronos String Quartet who had commissioned the work. Another piece on the program was by Penderecki; we heard his music often around that time and, he was considered "avant-garde."

The piece I heard that night had no melody, just "schocky" noise. Afterwards, I glanced at his score, and it had been written with no music notation, just drawings. But that was the thing to do then.

Alan said to me, "They [the Kronos Quartet] are ashamed of my music because I write melodies—that is why they are only performing at a monastery." What he said turned out to be true. That was the only performance that we know of, and on top of that, they never paid him! This commission came about before my time, so he composed it without a contract. After I married Alan, I protected him from having this kind of misery again. I got a contract for him every time—before he started to compose.

Alan was very sore about that string quartet being performed only once; and they never even bothered to pay him. On the day of the premiere after the concert, a mother of one of the quartet players asked Alan to write another piece. Alan was very insulted, and because of his anger, he orchestrated this quartet and called it "Symphony No. 31." It is a delightful chamber symphony, and in 1977, it was premiered by the Northwest Chamber Orchestra and recorded and then recorded again in 1994 with the Northwest Sinfonia for Crystal Records.

A few years after that premiere, we were at the Seattle Symphony and bumped into a young man on the stairway. Suddenly, Alan cornered him and attacked him verbally, saying something like, "Son of a bitch—you did not pay me for my composition!" I did not know what was going on at the time, but that young man was Walter Gray, the talented cellist who had been one of the Kronos Quartet and later joined the Seattle Symphony. Alan attacked him, but I don't know for sure if Walter was the one responsible for not paying Alan's commission fee.

Time passed, and Alan forgot that Walter was the musician from the Kronos Quartet. Walter was always respectful to Alan and was never offended by Alan's verbal attack at the symphony stairway. He participated in Alan's small eightieth birthday concert at a local church even though he had another engagement that day; also, he helped us in a recording session.

We never talked with Walter about what happened to the unpaid commission fee for the String Quartet No. 5.

So, it remains a mystery.

Curse of Divorced Wife

Premieres of Symphony No. 29
"Baritone Horn Concerto" and "Rubaiyat"

We left Seattle in May of 1977 for Minneapolis for the premiere of Alan's Symphony No. 29 "Baritone Horn Concerto." This concerto was commissioned by Henry Charles Smith, Associate Conductor of the Minnesota Symphony Orchestra, to perform on his instrument, the baritone horn. The premiere and the two following concerts were a great success.

Charles Smith was very popular among Minnesota concertgoers, and Alan had written a very challenging solo for him to show himself off. Since Alan had been writing solos for my very high coloratura voice, he composed with that capacity of range for the baritone horn. For the performance, Henry Charles Smith had to use all his strength to perform this demanding concerto. We all appreciated his vigorous effort and gave him a standing ovation for all the three performances. The concerto was performed at the end of the first half of the concert, and during the intermission, I went to the lady's room—there was excitement in the room. The ladies were complimenting the performance of Alan's concerto, and I was delighted to know the piece was an absolute success.

After the performances, we went to New York and stayed at our usual Hotel Wellington. We were there for the premiere of "Rubaiyat," an accordion solo and speaker and full orchestra, commissioned by the accordionist Carmen Carrozza, and to be premiered by Andre Kostelanetz with the New York Philharmonic Orchestra.

The day before the concert, while we were in the hotel room, Alan's former wife Serafina stormed in over the phone. We were surprised, for how could she have known where we were? (But now that I think of it, it was not difficult for her to figure out—it was the day before Alan's big premiere in Lincoln Center and more than likely he would stay at his usual hotel, the Wellington.) But we were very much surprised. Actually, we had been living together for a year but were not married legally yet and were waiting for his divorce proceedings; but Alan had bought me a wedding ring so people would think we were married.

Alan was on the telephone for a short time, and after that he told me about the conversation. Serafina had found out Alan was married again, and his new wife had been married before and had children. Even though Alan had divorced Serafina twenty-three years ago, she was telling people, "We were kind of separated," and she was upset about his new marriage and cursed us. "She makes me sick, leaving her children. This marriage won't last."

We were not married yet, but we had gotten a wedding greeting from her in advance. My comment was, "She thinks I left babies in the crib, but my children were all grown up, and the oldest one was married."

After that, I tried to call her on the telephone to explain that my children were not babies anymore and Alan still cared about her, but not as his wife; she hung up on me, saying, "I don't want to talk to you!"

I didn't understand her behavior, and somehow Alan and I started to argue, and we argued all night, as if we were affected by her anger—Alan told me she had a psychic power, but she could not help herself with it and her anger created negative power. I think his disastrous previous marriage with Elizabeth had been cursed by Serafina, too. I did not sleep all night, and my face was all puffed up from crying.

During our stay in New York, I wondered why Alan was not visiting his own publisher. C.F. Peters was the most important publisher of Alan's music. Originally, Walter Hinrichsen was the president and founder of the company. He was a believer in Alan's music and had promised to publish all of it, but unfortunately, he had died, and his wife became president of the company, and other composers had become favored by the company, so his promise was forgotten. Before I knew Alan, he had a deep resentment toward Peters, and he even had a lawsuit to get his unpublished music back, which was just sitting around on Peters' shelf.

After Alan told me the story of his relationship with C.F. Peters, I persuaded him to call Mrs. Hinrichsen, and he did. She was eager to see us both. The next day, the day of the concert, she invited us to dinner at a French restaurant across the street from Lincoln Center. I didn't think I could make it, with my swollen face, but in the evening, I did not look so bad, and we were picked up by Mrs. Hinrichsen at the front of the hotel in her car.

For dinner, she brought Stephen Fisher with her, and we all had a lovely evening together. Mrs. Hinrichsen liked me very much, and it seemed all the ice between Alan and her had melted and we were a family again and I had become a very important bridge between them.

After dinner, we crossed the street and walked toward the entrance of Avery Fisher Hall. Suddenly, Mrs. Hinrichsen fell on the pavement; Mr. Fisher, who was accompanying her, quickly lifted her up, but she had broken her wrist, and her face was perspiring from her severe pain. Then Alan and I realized—the curse of Serafina, intended for us, had gone to Mrs. Hinrichsen because she was with us. She was rushed to the hospital, and we went into the concert hall without her.

Alan and I sat with Alan's artist friend Hyman Bloom. The New York Philharmonic Promenade concert opened exuberantly; at tables near the stage, people were sitting and drinking wine during the concert. Amazingly, Alan wrote very good music for the accordion. It did not sound like usual accordion music but made me think of a near-Eastern instrument. John V. Lindsay, the mayor of New York at that time, recited the Persian poems with his manly voice.

For the curtain call, Carmen Carrozza, John V. Lindsay, Andre Kostelanetz, and Alan went up on the stage to acknowledge the applause, just the way Kostelanetz choreographed it.

After the concert, Alan and I, Larry Sobol, the clarinetist, and his wife and Martin Berkofsky, the pianist, and his wife, we all went to the Opera Café across the street from Lincoln Center. We had coffee and a snack; I remember Alan and I had a spinach omelet. While Alan was talking to Larry, I talked to Larry's good-looking, newly married wife; Larry completely took over Alan. Poor Martin, who was sensitive and inward, never had a chance. I could tell he very much wanted to talk to Alan, so I suggested to him to come to our hotel with us so he could talk to Alan exclusively.

We walked back to the hotel together, his Icelandic wife beside me, and Martin on the other side of Alan. But I sensed something was wrong, it seemed they were separating themselves in between Alan and me. At the hotel, she told me about why she had gone back to her home in Iceland without Martin—"to make him independent." I didn't understand what she meant.

By the end of the evening, we found out their real problem. Their 1966 Cadillac was parked on the pier, but apparently it was not a legal parking place, so the car had been taken away by the New York police. They had to pay a fine to get it back and, on top of that, it was damaged; we realized Serafina's curse had struck again.

We could not tell anybody about this curse because people would avoid us, and we could not tell anybody when we were leaving New York, because if Serafina were to find out, our airplane might crash.

Shortly after that, Berkofsky divorced from his wife, and we thought what had happened to them that night had something to do with their divorce.

After we got home, a letter from Serafina waited for us. Her message to Alan was: "If your marriage won't work out, I am here, waiting for you."

In old Japan, a woman's negative power is deadly. A woman's revenge play in the *Kabuki* theatre ends with a man expressing his fear in a stylized way—hiding his head between his fluttering kimono sleeves and saying, "Osolosiya—osolosiya [scary—scary]" accompanied by *samisen*.

Our Wedding Day

Our wedding day was June 17, 1977. It was the hottest day since the beginning of the year. I wore an off-white, long medieval-style dress, with a V-neck open almost to the waist and with bell-shaped sleeves trimmed in lace. It was so hot, my face perspired, and it seemed the makeup on my face all melted away. Alan was dressed in a white shirt and navy-colored suit and his favorite tie, wide and navy-colored, brocaded with a white and blue Japanese landscape. He always dressed in a white shirt and jacket, even while composing at home, so he seemed not to be bothered by the heat.

Alan and I had waited for this day for a long time, one whole year, and Alan's divorce proceedings took almost a week—it was not an easy divorce. He wanted to be fair to Elizabeth, so he got a lawyer just as a formality. His lawyer was Catherine Morrow, who had just graduated from law school. She had been introduced to Alan by Ivan, my singer friend who was studying at the University of Washington at that time.

On the contrary, Elizabeth was dead serious to get as much settlement as she could from Alan; she shopped around among the topnotch lawyers in town and found not one but two lawyers. So, from the beginning, Alan did not have any chance. The first day in court, the judge suggested that they settle out of court, but she and her lawyers never compromised, so they went back to the court to fight it out.

But Alan was not concerned about the outcome in court; somehow, he wanted to get it over with quickly and marry me legally. It seemed to me that was the only thing on his mind. We started our marriage license application during his divorce, and it was final on June 16, 1977—just one day before our marriage.

We both were divorced to get married, so, in my concern for others, I wanted our wedding to be low-key; even though it was very important to both of us, we had gone through so much to accomplish this. So, I told Alan's lawyer that we would marry at the marriage license window, but she persuaded us to come to her house for our wedding ceremony.

On the way to her house on Capitol Hill, we dropped into my former husband Peter's house to pick up my three children to come to the wedding, but Bill, my seventeen-year-old son, did not want to come, so I took the two girls with me. He did not say anything, but I understood his feelings, being loyal to his father, it must have been a difficult thing to accept.

When we got into the lawyer's house, Judge Horton Smith waited to marry us. He was a very well-known judge in Seattle at that time. Catherine, the lawyer, thought we should have a proper wedding and quietly arranged it for us. Right after we got there, we were busy signing legal papers. Then our wedding ceremony started.

Alan and I stood side by side and the judge stood next to the east window. I remember, at the time, Alan was supposed to put the ring on my finger, but he had a struggle. He could not put the ring all the way on, so I had to help him. The judge's concerned eyes were looking at Alan, as if he were thinking, "Can he make it, a man in his late sixties, marrying a woman in her forties?" This was caught on camera in a sequence of photos Joni took that day.

The photos were taken in a small, ordinary living room with two windows, and a child's potty chair on the floor behind Alan. But something happened; the light from the window gently surrounded us, most tenderly and compassionately, as if a blessing from heaven.

I know now, more than ever, it was our destiny to unite on that day.

Alan and Hinako's wedding

I WILL NEVER CHANGE —

IF HINAKO KILLS ME I DON'T MIND IT AND I AGREE TO IT. I WILL BE A FAITHFUL HUSBAND TO HINAKO ALL MY LIFE.

IF I FAIL I AGREE TO BE KILLED,

Alan Hovhaness

JAN. 22, 1983

Alan's writing to Hinako

On University Way –
Youthful Days in the University District

♪

Alan and I met there often; it had started before we were married. He took a bus from Queen Anne hill, where he used to live, and got off at the street where his printer was. I was studying voice with a university voice teacher as a private student, so the University District was a very convenient place for us to meet. After we were married, we went there every week for my singing lesson and Alan came along with me to accompany my singing during the lesson.

University Way was one block west from the University campus, running north to south. The street was filled with little shops, including the European restaurant toward the south end and a little up north was the Allegro Coffee Shop. To get to the Allegro, we had to go into a shabby alleyway, like a dark tunnel, filled with other small hippie shops. There Alan used to compose a cappuccino at the table, after going to the printer. The printer and post office were on the same street, practically next to each other, so it was a very convenient and necessary place for Alan to come to. Across the street there was a clothing shop that sold hippie-like clothes imported from India, colorful hand-dyed cotton clothes. While Alan was composing his cappuccino, I shopped there. Sometimes I didn't know which clothes to choose, because of the difference in colors, so I took Alan to the shop and asked his opinion. He usually wanted me to buy both because he liked to see me in different colored dresses. The shop next to the clothes shop was owned by the husband of the clothing shop owner. He was free-spirited and liked girls (I think?), and his wife was very nervous and jealous, but she was the one who had a younger boyfriend. But they still stayed married to each other and had shops side by side. His shop was called "Dr. Feelgood" and sold used art books and porno magazines (even "pot" pipes, I think). That was the first time I was introduced to porno magazines; it was a period of sexual freedom, before AIDS came. We caught on with that spirit, too—we were very expressive with sex then, but only to each other.

Next door to "Dr. Feelgood" was a health-food store. We went to the store often because Alan was a believer in health food and vitamins then. He took 1,000 mg of vitamin C and other vitamins every day. His sleep was disrupted by the large amount of vitamins; later, I reduced his vitamins and gave him good, balanced, healthy food instead. After that, he slept very well.

On November 24, 1981, when Alan's Symphony No. 47 "Walla Walla" (Land of Many Waters) was performed with the Walla Walla Symphony (I was singing in the one movement that Alan composed for me); we were in Walla Walla for the performance. One day during our stay there, we were to go up to Spokane to do a TV interview with the symphony conductor, but Alan's face and body had become completely red, like a tomato. The conductor came to the hotel to see Alan in person, but he was not sympathetic; instead, he was very upset about canceling the TV interview, more than anything else. Obviously, Alan did not want to cancel it either, but what could we do? He could not have been on TV with a red-hot face. So, I had to cancel the appointment.

Alan seemed okay, but not knowing what was wrong with him, he had to be careful (at my request). Suddenly, something hit me, I looked at the bottle with the vitamins he had taken that morning. It was a new bottle, just bought from the University District. Sure enough, it was not vitamin C, but niacin! The name on the bottle was printed in flowery characters, not in print, and I had picked it up from the vitamin C shelf. It must have been misplaced there and I had gotten it by mistake. Alan's red face went away after I stopped giving him the pills. Alan was perfectly healthy, but that conductor became our enemy forever. (He didn't have anything to do with us anymore.)

Next to the health-food store was a store called "Gibson Girls," which sold used antique-like clothes and jewelry. It was a narrow store, only as wide as an entrance door, but very deep, like a train. The owner of the store was a very large and heavy middle-aged woman; at first, I was afraid of her, but after I got to know her, she was actually a very nice woman. I used to see her sitting under a mysterious old Tiffany lamp, like a gypsy. Her name was Maria, and she came from Hungary.

Farther north, to the west of University Way on NE 43rd St, there was a "Copy Mart." They just made copies for their customers. We went there often. One workman there was Roupen Shakarian, an Armenian whom we had met a short time before in London. He was studying music at the U.W. and was trying to become a conductor.

In July of 1978, Alan and I went to London for a week-long music festival of Armenian music and musicians, organized by the Institute of Armenian Music. On our way to England, on the airplane, Alan bitterly complained to me about Loris Tjeknavorian, one of the organizers of the festival and an Armenian composer and choral conductor. Alan was upset because Tjeknavorian was getting attention from Armenians by making music, organizing amateur orchestras, etc., which Alan had done in Boston during the Depression, but he didn't get the attention that Tjeknavorian was getting now. There in England, we met him; he was short, and his hair was very curly, like a poodle. He looked like a young kid, very emotional and friendly. Anyway, when we met him, Alan forgot all about his complaints and liked him.

Later, Tjeknavorian was in Los Angeles, teaching. He called us about his project, to have a music workshop in a university. He was so excited to include Alan and his music in the workshop and also wanted Aram Gharabekian (who was also an Armenian conductor and composer studying in Vienna at that time) to participate in his project. So, in the middle of the night, he called Vienna, Austria, and woke Gharabekian up. We three were on the telephone, back and forth, talking about who else should be involved in this project. Alan thought the boy who worked at the Copy Mart (Shakarian) would be a good candidate.

The next day, we were excited, and went off to the Copy Mart and told Roupen we might be able to use him as one of the instructors of the workshop. Then, there was an unexpected reaction from him; he was cool as a cucumber and said, "I don't think anything will come of it, they [Armenians] behave emotionally, but nothing is in it." We were suddenly cooled off by him, and we hated him for not reacting to our excitement, but he was right, he knew more about over-emotional Armenians (including Alan and me) than we did. Sure enough, nothing came from that excitement, and it all died down.

We were young then, Alan was seventy-one years old, and I was fifty. We were young and free, hanging out on University Way like students—we were all there.

Dan Shelhamer worked at The Varsity Theatre on the same street while studying and conducting opera at the University.

Also, we often bumped into Yujin, a young girl from Korea who was studying ethnomusicology. She always talked enthusiastically while spitting from her mouth, with garlic aroma in the air.

One day we saw the composer David Lamb (at first, we didn't recognize him) putting his arm around a kind of homely girl, walking down the street like a teenager. We both thought, "Who is that kid walking with him?" It happened to be that girl became his wife and much later, in 1999—we found out she was a scientist!

It was our good old days. Our life has changed since, but it really happened, we all had walked on that University Way.

Alan Standing under a cherry blossom tree at University of Washington

Origin of Purple Poverty

A dream I had this morning reminded me…

Alan used to call himself "Purple Poverty"—this name was a sarcastic description of himself. Purple was his favorite color. He believed everybody had their own color, reflected by their aura, and his was purple. Poverty was the condition of his early composing years; he was determined to succeed as a composer, but he couldn't earn money from composing and was nearly starving. His diet was mashed potatoes and coffee, and late in the evening he got a banana from a nearby coffee shop.

He had to be a church organist, a ghost writer for jazz musicians, such as Artie Shaw, and a teacher. He taught composing at schools and for the WPA, a government program during the depression that was open to anybody who was interested (including the bums who came into the class to warm themselves up). When Eisenhower came into office, the program was eliminated.

By the time he was in his seventies, he was a very successful composer, yet he still thought of himself as that starving composer. He stated to me, "I will never become rich."

In the 1960s, when Alan was living in Switzerland with Elizabeth, his wife at that time, he was still giving alimony to Serafina, his previous wife, because he had verbally promised to give her alimony. But as far as Elizabeth was concerned, it was not legal; therefore, Alan should not give her any money. So, Alan had to give the money to Serafina secretly, and he did so for many years. Also, he got a P.O. Box in Switzerland to communicate with her and others, using the name "Purple Poverty." He got his kicks, getting away by using this phony name in a foreign country.

In the late 1970s, Alexander Broude, Alan's new publisher in New York at that time, asked Alan to write some piano pieces for their publication of a children's piano book. They wanted the pieces to be written in a progressively difficult fashion, but Alan composed delightful pieces, wherever his inspiration led him. The book was published in 1980, was called Hovhaness's "Sketch Book of Mr. Purple Poverty," and my daughter Joni did the illustrations for the book.

In the introduction of the book, Alan wrote, "Mr. Purple Poverty is an idiotic clownish poet who dreams himself in love with 'Lady Purple,' a great and beautiful poetess who lived around a thousand years ago in Japan."

Lady Purple was Murasaki Shikibu, who lived during the middle Hean Period of Japanese history (900–1087 AD). She was the author of *Genji Monolatry* (Story of Genji), and the heroine of the stories. They were stories of Genji's love affairs and remain some of the most famous classics of Japan. Genji was a very handsome man, who could have any woman he desired, even his emperor's wife bore Genji's child. His relationship to many women included his intellectual love affair, and his three wives, his jealous, nagging wife, a very sensual, emotional young wife, and Murasaki (purple). She was his ideal wife; she had the quality of all women in one body.

Alan always thought of that perfect woman, "Lady Purple," all his life. He said to me that every time he married, he thought, "Maybe this is the promised one," but he soon realized that she wasn't.

When he was a young man in Boston, during a psychic reading, a Japanese guide appeared. His name was "Morano" (I think his name was pronounced Murano, meaning "village of field"). He told Alan, "Your future wife-to-be is in the south of Tokyo; she is still a child and smiling now." He always wanted a Japanese wife; maybe that prophesy affected his subconscious mind. In the 1984 KCTS TV documentary called *Hovhaness*, he expressed, "I always find myself not married to a Japanese woman, until now."

My dream this morning brought back this memory, Alan's strange connection and attraction for "Lady Purple," the ancient Japanese poetess. Am I the reincarnation of Lady Purple? If so, I am glad Purple Poverty found her in his lifetime.

(In my research for Murasaki Shikibu, I found that she was a member of the Fujiwara family. Coincidence?)

My Memories Surrounding Andre Kostelanetz

I met Alan in July of 1973. At that time, I was a church soloist with an unusually high coloratura voice. Church solos did not require a high voice like mine, but that was the only place I could sing.

My real passion was to sing in the opera like Lily Pons, who was my idol, the prima donna of the opera. I was studying voice, singing opera arias, which were the only songs fit for my voice. Alan liked my voice and extended his help by playing piano accompaniment for my singing. We practiced together whenever he was in town, as often as once a week.

He was a mysterious figure, the famous composer who came into my life from nowhere and who chose to practice with me. But it was obvious he was in love with me, and practicing with me was his pleasure and also his excuse to be with me. Since then he got to know my family, Peter and my three children. He liked my family, so he settled for just practicing with me and not taking a chance of losing me completely.

The Day Alan Told Me about Kostelanetz

One day in the late summer, I drove up to the Olympic Hotel entrance. That was the place I usually picked Alan up to go practice. He came into my car, and it was an unusually hot day. I smelled his body odor. I am very sensitive to smell and did not like that certain smell. But it was strange, and I was slightly intoxicated with his odor. I looked at his profile, as if I were seeing him for the first time, and thought, "He is not bad looking—in fact, quite handsome. And he is not as old as I thought." He said he wouldn't be able to come to the opera with me that week. I had bought opera season tickets for the two of us, and we had been going to the opera together since the conductor Andre Kostelanetz was going to perform Alan's music in San Diego and he wanted Alan to be at that concert.

Kostelanetz always wanted Alan to be at his concerts when he was conducting one of Alan's pieces. He acknowledged Alan the composer at the end of his piece. It was his theatrical staging that entertained his audience, and he got added applause! This was the first time Alan told me about Kostelanetz. He said, "I have to be there—he is my boss!"

The First Time I Saw Kostelanetz

In 1974, I saw Kostelanetz for the first time in Hollywood. Alan wanted to take me there. Kostelanetz was performing Alan's "Fantasy on Japanese Wood Prints." This piece had been commissioned by Japanese xylophone player Hiraoka for his comeback and was composed for Kostelanetz to conduct with the New York Philharmonic.

At the Hollywood concert after the performance of the piece, Alan was called onto the stage to bow to the audience. He stood beside Kostelanetz and the soloist Hiraoka, who were two short people, and he looked like a giant! I could not believe my eyes. He did not look like a distinguished composer with the way he dressed. He was wearing a dark Sears and Roebuck grayish-blue suit. I could not even tell for sure the exact color. He also had worn-out pants popping out at the knees. But I could not do anything about that then. At that time, he was not my husband, he was my secret lover. But after I married him, I changed all that. He had a very elegant figure, and what he needed was somebody to help bring it out, so that's what I did.

After the concert, we were at the reception. Alan and I were quiet about being together, so he introduced me as a singer to Kostelanetz. A young dancer came in the room and took over Alan, and he looked at me as if to say, "Who are you?" But I had to take that quietly.

The "Rubaiyat" Premiere

The second time I met Kostelanetz was in May of 1977. He premiered Alan's "Rubaiyat" at Avery Fisher Hall in Lincoln Center with the New York Philharmonic Orchestra.

This piece was commissioned in 1975 by the accordionist Carmen Carrozza. As usual, this commission was in collaboration with Kostelanetz. He requested Alan to put an American president's speech with the accordion solo and orchestra, and he was hoping to get another successful piece, like Copland's "Lincoln Portrait."

Alan chose Thomas Jefferson's speeches, which was the only American president he liked. But when Kostelanetz saw Alan's manuscript, he exclaimed, "Alan, this is not president's speech—it is love music!" He immediately came up with the idea to put the love poems of the Persian poet Omar Khayyam with the music instead.

During that time, Alan and I were living together in a small apartment near Sea-Tac airport. On many evenings, Alan and I read the poems and selected them together; we copied, cut out, and inserted them between the music. Before the completion of the piece, Alan left me and went back to his wife.

Two years had passed, and Alan had come back to me for good and had been living with me for a year waiting for his divorce to be final. We were to go to New York to attend the premiere of his "Rubaiyat" together.

Before the trip, Alan had bought me a wedding ring to wear so we could pretend we were married for the trip. He wanted to tell the people I was his wife.

On May 20, 1977, the New York Philharmonic Promenade Concert opened luxuriously. Alan's painter friend Hyman Bloom came for the concert, and we three sat together in the center of Avery Fisher Hall. The stage full of orchestra waited and Kostelanetz entered; then came

Carrozza, the accordionist, and finally the narrator of the poems, John V. Lindsey, who was the very popular New York mayor at that time. He recited the poems with his macho voice. We were surprised about the choice of the narrator, but Kostelanetz had a plan all along to use this piece to draw in the crowd wherever he went and by having an influential person in that region recite the poems.

It was a happy surprise for me to hear the accordion solo. I never actually liked the accordion and neither did Alan. I was not sure how he could compose for the instrument, but he did well. It did not sound like accordion music I had heard in the past. He wrote complicated rhythms for the accordion, perhaps Arabic style. It was the most popular writing of Alan's music I had ever heard.

Immediately after the music ended, Hyman stood up and shouted, "It is great music!" Then Alan was called onto the stage, which was already crowded by the conductor, the soloist, and the narrator. The four men were bumping into each other, acknowledging the hearty applause of the audience.

After the concert, Hyman came with us backstage. We were surprised since we thought he was anti-social, but he was so impressed with Alan's accordion melodies he wanted to shake hands with the conductor. When we got to Kostelanetz's room, he was surrounded by old ladies who were his admirers. Alan introduced Hyman, but obviously Kostelanetz was distracted by his admirers and did not pay attention to Hyman. We were disappointed but understood his behavior. Why do you give concert, if you do not get attention from the girls?

Since Alan died, I have felt so personal about the "Rubaiyat." How vividly Alan captured our love in the music, and the poems were as if he himself were speaking of us. No wonder Kostelanetz said, "This is love music!" when he first saw the manuscript.

Three Poems of Omar Khayyam:
Here, with a loaf of bread beneath the bough,
A Jug of wine, a book of verse – and thou,
Beside me, singing in the wilderness –
Oh, wilderness were paradise enow!

Ah, love! Could you and I with fate conspire
To grasp this sorry scheme of things entire,
Would we not shatter it to bits – and then
Re-mould it nearer to the heart's desire!

* * * * *

Alas, that Spring should vanish with the rose,
That youth's sweet-scented manuscript should close!
The nightingale that in the branches sang,
Ah! Whence and whither flown again, who know?

Come, fill the cup, and in the fire of Spring
The Winter garment of repentance fling.
The bird of time has but a little way
To fly—and lo! The bird is on the wing.

* * * * *

But see! The rising moon of heav'n again
Looks for us, sweetheart, through the quivering plane:
How oft hereafter rising will she look
Among those leaves—for one of us in vain!

Ah, moon of my delight, that knows no wane,
The moon of heav'n is rising once again—
How oft hereafter rising shall she look
Through this same garden after me—in vain.

At Kostelanetz's House

In October of 1977, we went to Minneapolis for a lecture concert of Alan's. Alan had accepted this job mainly because he wanted me to have the chance to sing with him. He accompanied me on the piano and then we went to New York from there. During our stay in New York, I noticed Alan had not called Kostelanetz to pay his respects, so I asked him, "Why aren't you calling him to let him know you are in New York?"

Then he said, "I will wait until the last day to call him so he cannot ask me to change my score."

We went to Kostelanetz's penthouse and the security officer at the door let us in and we went up to the top floor of the penthouse. His spacious apartment windows opened to a view of the city overlooking the Hudson River. Kostelanetz played the just-arrived test pressing of the "Rubaiyat" on his phonograph player and was saying "The 'Rubaiyat' is a great success," repeatedly! We weren't that sure about it, but *he* believed it to be a big success.

He had been married once to Lily Pons, the Metropolitan Opera coloratura soprano who had the most beautiful voice in the world. She had been my idol since I was in high school. I asked Kostelanetz what she was like, and then he started to talk about her passionately.

He must have loved her very much. She was a beautiful, petite lady with a very high metallic voice. I heard people say he and Lily Pons gave many concerts together, and he arranged songs for her to sing. I never could forget "Estrellita" (Little Star), the Spanish song she sang most beautifully.

He told us she was very lazy and did not practice and was also very nervous before each performance. How could the temperamental soprano and conductor live together even though they must have been in love with each other? Later they divorced and she was married to somebody else and he remarried again, but it ended up in divorce also.

He told me about their last performance together, and it was long after they had separated and Pons had been retired from the Metropolitan Opera. She told him of her wish to sing again. She wanted to sing the most difficult coloratura arias, like the "Bell Song" from *Lakme* and the "Mad Scene" from *Lucia di Lammermoor,* etc. He thought she had not been singing for a long time and she might not be able to sing those demanding arias as well as she used to. He could not say so because he knew her temper and so he told her diplomatically, "Recently, Joan Sutherland made her fame at the Met by singing *The Daughter of the Regiment*," a French opera. The arias were supposed to be sung by a young, petite coloratura. Joan Sutherland was large and had a rich voice, not the so-called "traditional" lyric coloratura, but she was able to sing high. Because of people getting larger, the pure coloratura voice is becoming scarce and is being replaced by the larger, richer voices like Sutherlands.

Sure enough, Pons got excited and wanted to sing those arias. Kostelanetz knew she would think she could do better than Sutherland because she was French and petite and fit the part better than Sutherland. She was a success at Kostelanetz's Promenade Concert. That was their last performance together, and then she died sometime after. Though they had divorced, I could tell Pons was the love and joy of his life.

While I am writing their story, I cannot help but to think about Alan and me. Unlike Kostelanetz's love, Alan's love came toward the end. I was much younger than Alan, and he had already established himself and could afford to have me then. We had wonderful times together without any regret. He took me all over the world and we performed together; but he had to die before me, and I have to spend the rest of my time without him. However, I knew it and I chose it.

In January of 1979, we went to Washington, D.C., for the premiere of Alan's Symphony No. 36, for flute and orchestra. The famous French flautist Jean-Pierre Rampal was the soloist and Rostropovich conducted the National Symphony Orchestra. After the concert, we went to New York, and during our stay there Kostelanetz invited us to a French restaurant.

At the French Restaurant

We were to meet him in the French restaurant after his own concert in upper New York State, but on his trip back from the concert, he got very tired and told us he could not go.

He wanted us to be there as his guests, so Alan and I went. Soon, we went into the luxurious French restaurant, and we announced ourselves as Kostelanetz's guests. Then the owner of the restaurant was a beautifully dressed, middle-aged French woman who greeted us and led us to a table. Then she asked, "What wine would you like to have?"

Then I thought, "I don't know anything about wine—why do we have to waste Kostelanetz's money?" So I said, "We don't drink wine." Then I saw her face fill with horror, and then she left and we were completely abandoned for the whole evening.

We realized what had happened, and I guess us barbarians who didn't even know wine went to the most sophisticated, snobby French restaurant in New York. I thought about it for a while, but Alan and I didn't like wine, in fact, we didn't understand why people drank wine; but fruit juice was delicious! Alan and I were oh, so different in our appearances, like a greyhound and a Pekingese. But we were so much alike; we enjoyed the same food and everything else without wine. There were so many things to enjoy, we never had the need for going in that direction. Couldn't I be honest about not drinking? Actually, I never was ashamed of that fact.

We were lost for a while, but then we thought, "Kostelanetz paid for this dinner, why not make the best of it?" We ate exactly what we wanted to eat. We were practically all alone in the large dining room with the entire buffet full of delicious French pastry. We had my favorite, caramel flan. It was heavenly!

In Vancouver with Kostelanetz

In March of 1979, Kostelanetz planned to drop in to see us at our home on the way to his concert in Vancouver, Canada, but his schedule changed, and we drove to Vancouver to see him instead. He rented a room for us in the Bayshore Inn, overlooking the water. In the evening, we attended his concert.

I understood him that night; he was creating his own original kind of classical music performance. He would modify the performance to the right proportion, to not bore the audience, but to entertain them. His concert was a sheer delight, and he had a large following in Canada. I realized what he stood for in the world of music. He popularized classical music for a wider audience to enjoy.

One night, Kostelanetz took us to an Indonesian restaurant, Rumah Bali. His interest was "islands," whether Southeast Asia, Caribbean, etc. At the restaurant we ordered something familiar to us, like Chinese dishes, but we noticed Kostelanetz ordered authentic Indonesian food. There were many small bowls of individual entrees, about fifteen of them, with white rice. We ended up eating his food. It was delicious.

On the morning we were to leave, we decided to order food in our room. We had a luxurious breakfast, looking out over the water of the Pacific Ocean.

That Awful Day – January 14, 1980

We arrived in New York that day and went to our usual Hotel Wellington. Then we went into the hotel room and turned on the TV. The news came on and we heard that Kostelanetz had died. He had died on January 13 in Port-au-Prince, Haiti. He was supposed to have sat with Alan in Alice Tully Hall the day of the premiere of Alan's Symphony No. 34 for bass trombone and strings. Also, he was going to be in a Hovhaness documentary movie, which was being produced by KCTS channel 9.

A couple of days later, we had a call from a woman called Mary, who was supposedly with Kostelanetz on his last trip. We had met her with Anna a few years ago when Alan had a performance of "The Way of Jesus" in San Francisco. Alan had known Anna in the past because the San Diego Youth Symphony was interested in premiering Alan's opera "Pericles." The original premiere of this work some time before had been planned but had not materialized because the rich commissioner of the opera had died unexpectedly. Anna had been actively involved in producing the opera with the Youth Symphony, but she hadn't succeeded.

After the "Way of Jesus" concert, she invited Alan and me to a Polynesian restaurant and brought Mary with her. According to Anna, Mary had recently gone through a bitter divorce and had hired an expensive lawyer to get more money from her husband. But she lost money instead, which caused her to become mentally unstable. It seemed to me that even though Anna was married, they were hanging out together for some reason.

Anna told Alan about a "porno" movie they had just seen in San Francisco. The movie was about a man and a woman having sadistic sex, and it got to the point that she cut off his—you know. Mary said that the movie put her in some kind of ecstasy, and she persuaded Alan to go see it. I was shocked and said, "That is a very dangerous direction—we should not encourage such a movie. Sex should be a healthy thing."

Then she said, "Hinako, you are square." It was obvious to me the two women were together looking for excitement.

The dinner was excellent, and we had Polynesian curry. After the dinner, Mary asked Alan his birthdate and other personal information. I was unhappy about it, but she said she needed the information to find out his horoscope for him. Then she wanted my information, which I refused because I felt an unhappy aura surrounding her, and I did not want to be connected with her in any way.

When Kostelanetz was in San Diego for a performance, they drove him around and spent much time together. One night we got a call from him, and he was with them in San Diego. Alan was worried about him being with them.

What Happened in Haiti, According to Mary

Mary told us what had happened to Kostelanetz in Haiti. They had been having an affair, and one day he wanted to go to a far-off place with her so he could have freedom from gossip, and so he chose the island of Haiti. When they got to Port-au-Prince, he wished to stay in a different hotel that was across town from her hotel. Alan was wondering if he might have needed distance from her by that time.

Soon after Kostelanetz got there, he contracted a digestive disease and was sick in bed with a fever. He wanted to go back to the USA, but the airplane did not leave until a certain time, and he had to wait. While he was lying in bed, he was tortured by the sound of voodoo drums coming from up above his room. His condition worsened, and not much had been done for him in that primitive island. He died without proper care.

Alan was horrified by this story and blamed Mary for his death. He thought they must have told Kostelanetz they were Alan's friends, which was not true, and he'd trusted them. By the time he realized he was with a neurotic woman, it was too late, and he died in an island of hell. Alan lost his champion in such unnecessary circumstances.

On January 17, 1980, the day of Alan's premiere of Symphony No. 34, we saw a tall woman wearing a magnificent mink coat at the front of the ticket office line. It was Mary, and she was arguing with the ticket office woman and trying to help herself by saying she was Hovhaness's friend in order to get free tickets. We were astounded by what she was doing. Then she saw us and came close to us to take a picture of Alan. Later, when Alan saw the picture, he was "spooked up" because the upper part of his head was cut off in all the pictures she took.

After Kostelantez's death, his brother who was a lawyer took care of his affairs. A Kostelanetz Memorial Concert was performed by the New York Philharmonic Orchestra, conducted by Leonard Bernstein. Alan was not included in any way.

One night, I saw Kostelantez in my dream. He was eating green spinach. I told Alan about my dream, and he said, "He must be in the green plain." Spiritualists believe there are different colored plains and after death we go to one of them according to the level of our spiritual achievement on this earth.

I remember Kostelanetz used to call Alan for no apparent reason, just to talk to him. I persuaded Alan to call him, too. One time I sent our very personal wedding photo to him as my expression of affection to him.

I have concluded some of his personal letters to us:

My dear friends:
This is for you—
I miss you
And hope to
see you soon.
With much
affection Andre—

Note from Andre

Andre Kostelanetz
10 Gracie Square
New York, N.Y. 10028

May
15
1979

Mr. and Mrs. Alan Hovhaness
1040 South 320th #14
Federal Way, Washington
98003

Dear Alan and Hinako:

I have just played your SYMPHONY No. 38, and it is simply beautiful. It was a great surprise and pleasure to hear Hinako sing. This is the first time I have heard her. She has a beautiful voice, and the high notes and intonation are perfect. She certainly has a most unusual coloratura soprano, and I am sure she will make a fine career.

I want to thank you for the two photographs which just arrived and for your kind inscription on them. I will have one framed as soon as possible.

We will always remember with pleasure our meeting in Vancouver. Please let me know when you are coming this way. We must keep in touch.

With love to you both,

As ever
Andre -

Letter from Andre

30 GRACIE SQUARE
NEW YORK
NEW YORK 10028

December 28, 1979

Dear Alan and Hinako,

Thank you for your Christmas greeting.

I am looking forward to hearing your new work and hope I can attend the performance on January 17th. Please let me know when you are here in New York.

Happy New Year and much happiness!

In friendship,

Andre

Letter from Andre

P.S., I happened to find this letter when I was cleaning out a drawer of Alan's manuscripts, program notes, etc. It shows further insight into the background of his composing of "And God Created Whales."

Alan and Ohan Dourian

They Performed Together in 1978 and 1987
toward the End of 1977…

Every morning Alan woke up and sat on the edge of the bed, burying his head in his hands. He was depressed because of what had happened to him. He had been commissioned to compose for an Armenian Concert in Los Angeles, which was a commemorative concert dedicated to the memory of the Turkish massacre of Armenians on April 24, 1915. Originally, there were two main sponsors for the concert, and one of them was for Ohan Dourian, who was from Vienna, Austria, and the other was for Alan. Both of them had been commissioned to write music for the concert as well as to conduct it in the concert.

Alan composed Symphony No. 27 with tremendous inspiration, starting after only one phone call. He could not stop, and so he wrote another symphony, No. 28, in Armenian style to please the Armenians. But Alan's sponsor disappeared. So what could he do but to be stuck with two symphonies and without payment and no premiere? After that bad experience, I had to get him the contracts for the commissions first and did not let him compose until the contract was signed.

His depression continued until one day, we heard from the other sponsor of the concert. A rich Armenian grocer from Beverly Hills, California, named Archie Dickranian was the sponsor of Dourian. He decided to fill the financial gap that the other man left to pay Alan's commission fee and all the concert expenses. Finally, Alan's depression ended, and the concert date was set for April 23, 1978, at Dorothy Chandler Pavilion in Los Angeles.

In April, 1978, when we got to Los Angeles we were picked up by a car and chauffeur who told us that the Dourian's were to come to meet us at the airport. However, his wife Alice was sick and they could not come. When we got to the hotel, we went to his room to see how Alice was doing.

Alice was an Armenian dramatic soprano from Marseille, France, living with Ohan in Vienna. He had a wife and son in Russia, but he was in love with Alice, and they were performing together. There is a story that one day at a performance where he was conducting the orchestra, he was supposed to accompany Alice. When he came on stage, he saw a big Russian soprano waiting for him instead of Alice. She was sponsored by the Russian government, and they had replaced Alice without Dourian's knowledge. He was so upset, he walked out from the stage. After that incident, he defected from Russia and had been living with Alice in Vienna. In 1976, When Alan was in Europe, he visited Ohan's house in Vienna. Ohan showed his English brochure that had been translated from German. It said, "Dourian stopped the breath of the audience for fifteen minutes with his magnificent conducting." Alan was laughing and said to me, "His audience was all dead, not breathing for fifteen minutes." Alan made a new brochure for him with the right translation.

Alice was tall and serene, with coal-black hair with a white complexion. She told me she had been sick since she had gotten there. I knew it then because of my experience, and her trouble was the air conditioning. I told her to turn it off, especially during the night while she was sleeping, so she did. She was okay in a matter of a day and became normal.

Alan and I were there for five days just for the rehearsal, followed by the performance. Dourian went there months before the performance to prepare his composition. It seemed to me that he was not concerned about his expenses since he behaved as if he was Wagner, the "King of Opera" and people ought to pay for his luxury. They even brought their parakeet in a cage, plus room service for their meals. For dinner they treated themselves to wine, making the most of their privileges. On the contrary, Alan and I were very careful and ate modestly, breakfast and dinner only; we did not drink wine, just coffee for Alan. We knew Dickranian was paying our expenses, and we did not want to abuse his generosity.

One evening, we ordered fillets of sole, but it tasted bad. After the dinner, we went back to our hotel room, and I went into the bathroom. While I was sitting on the toilet, Alan banged on the door. I was surprised and said, "You cannot come in!" But he barged into the bathroom and vomited in the basin. After that, we learned not to eat fish while traveling because fish is not always as fresh as we were used to in Seattle.

On the day of the radio interview, I went with Alan and Ohan. Alan was wondering about Ohan's composition called "Universalism," which was supposed to be Ohan's original invention, and he was making a big thing about it. During the interview, Ohan explained about his universalism. Every section of instruments of the orchestra played a different melodic motif repeated at the same time to create a very original sound. Alan was very upset because that was his invention called "spirit murmur." Ohan had taken it and called it *his* invention.

The rehearsal day came, and the rehearsal time was to be shared between them and Ohan was to rehearse first, after the break Alan was to rehearse his two symphonies. But Ohan had forgotten to bring his set of parts from his hotel room. By the time his parts arrived, he had lost half of his rehearsal time. But he extended his rehearsal time into Alan's portion and Alan's rehearsal time was cut short. But Dickranian could not pay the overtime for Alan's lost rehearsal time. Alan was the one who lost because of Ohan's carelessness. To lose so much rehearsal time was unheard of in this country because orchestra time was paid by union rate, and a big orchestra of seventy musicians would cost thousands of dollars.

Dickranian was so upset; he sat on a seat at the back of the concert hall and buried his head. Being a grocer, he never would have realized that one concert would cost so much money. He had to pay for the hall, the musician's performance, rehearsal, the conductors, broadcasting, the publicity of the concert, and not to mention the hotel and food, especially for Dourian's luxurious lifestyle.

The day of the concert, Alan appeared on the stage with a not-so-confident look. He had been overpowered by Ohan, even though Ohan was half his size. But Ohan had that commanding personality that many conductors have. On the other hand, Alan was sweet, kind, and never bragged, and the musicians loved him.

He conducted the three movements of his Symphony No. 27 that was just about as much as the Armenian audience who were not symphony goers could take. Then Alan's other symphony, No. 28, came directly after, without a break, as if the two pieces were one symphony with six movements. Being a composer, he was thinking only of the music, and he did not think how to present the music in the best, most effective way. If I had my way, I would have separated the two symphonies, a tone at the beginning of the concert and the other at the end. But I am sure it could not have been done that way because Ohan had taken the end of the concert for his glory. And that is exactly what he did. He came out with tremendous self-confidence, swung his hair, and cued the orchestra to stand up at the beginning of his performance by taking over the stage and the audience. His "Universalism" was just like himself, very boastful with big orchestration. Alice was the dramatic soprano who screamed over the orchestra, symbolizing the cry of the Armenian people, which Alan hated. He said that was so much like many over-emotional Armenians he was familiar with. So the concert was completely taken over by Ohan, and Alan's music was buried by Ohan's noise.

After the performance, Alan wanted to stop in San Francisco, where we had a good time in the past. We had stayed at the Mark Twain Hotel and ate at Omar Khayyam's Armenian restaurant. This time we stayed at the King George Hotel. The next day, Alan took me to a Japanese tea house, and he *had* to be there to sit with me. We sat in the tea house, overlooking a Japanese garden.

That evening, we went to the Omar Khayyam restaurant. We expected a house full of people, but the restaurant was practically empty. George Mardikian, who was the owner of the restaurant, had died shortly after his wife's death. His son had taken over the restaurant and apparently was not making it a success. A middle-aged Armenian waiter came to our table and started talking to us about Ohan, who had stayed at his home for a long period of time and had taken advantage of him.

Alan Met Ohan Again in 1987...

Alan got a call from the Diocese of Armenian Church in New York. They were planning to have a commemoration concert in Avery Fisher Hall at Lincoln Center, in memory of Khrimian Hairig; His Holiness Vasken I, Catholicos of the Armenian church. He was coming from Armenia for this occasion.

They wanted Alan to conduct some of his compositions for the concert. Alan suggested his trumpet piece "Khrimian Hairig," which was inspired by the heroic Armenian priest who was the subject of this concert. It has a beautiful trumpet melody and obbligato over strings and equally as beautiful as his famous trumpet piece "Prayer of St. Gregory." Alan also suggested "Talin," the name of a ruined 7th century Christian Armenian cathedral, for viola and strings. He was trying to help them by not using a whole orchestra, just solo instruments and string orchestra in order to save their concert expenses.

But it was a futile effort, because later we found out that Alan was to share the concert with another conductor, and it was none other than Ohan Dourian. By that time, Ohan had separated from Alice, and I assume she had gone back to Russia. He brought his wife for this concert. He must have been selected as conductor for this important occasion. So you can see, he did not care about the expenses since he used the largest orchestra he could possibly get.

Many New York Armenian performers were participants in this concert. It was just like a talent show, and among them were Metropolitan soprano Lucine Amara and baritone Ara Berberian. They all hated Ohan's personality since they openly expressed this, and they adored Alan.

At this concert, Alan was on the first part of the concert, and history repeated itself because his performance did not go well. His string pieces did not have enough sound for the big Avery Fisher hall and the soloists were not with the orchestra and were either ahead of them or behind. It sounded like many contemporary compositions were intentionally dissonant and awkward.

Dourian took the stage after the intermission. His piece was called "Gomidasiana," and it was an arrangement of a composition by an Armenian archimandrite and composer Komitas Vartabed, who Alan very much admired. It used a full orchestra, and again Dourian took over the concert triumphantly. When I first heard that he was coming, I knew this would happen to Alan.

Alan said this to me about Dourian's composition; if he were to arrange Komitas's music it would be very different. Komitas's music was never boastful or bombastic but was very spiritual. Alan would have orchestrated his music following Komitas's inspiration and being sympathetic to his music by not changing his simplicity of beauty to something else like Dourian did.

Answer to Mr. Shelley's Letter

♪

I have been thinking about a letter from Mr. Shelley...

He is the conductor of the Air Force Command Band of Australia who bought Alan's Wind Symphony "Star Dawn" score and parts from me. He wishes to perform the symphony throughout Australia and to make it known to their people.

In his letter, he wrote that he is also a composer and recently had the premiere of his new symphony. He asked me, "It made me wonder whether composers with a large output such as your husband ever became immune to the joy of hearing a work premiered, or whether every premiere was a joyous occasion." His question led me to my recollection of some of Alan's premieres, and I would like to write about them.

In the 1940s in Boston, he was the organist at St. James Armenian Church in Watertown. Alan played for Sunday services like weddings and funerals to support himself. But the performance of his music did not come easily. In fact, at that time he was known as the "composer of no performance." So he organized an amateur orchestra and conducted his own music. Much of his Armenian period music was premiered at Jordan Hall concerts in Boston like the "Psalm and Fugue," "Avak the Healer," "Vahakn Symphony," etc., in 1947.

His New York Town Hall debut was in 1945. Lou Harrison was the composer and critic for the *New York Herald Tribune*, and he came to the concert and brought John Cage with him, and wrote a rave review for Alan. Their friendship lasted for the rest of their lives.

In 1939, Leslie Heward, who was the director of music for the BBC radio, discovered Alan's music and performed Alan's First Symphony "Exile." Unfortunately, he died shortly after that. As a result, Leopold Stokowski heard the symphony and conducted it for an American audience in 1942. Since then, he has performed many of Alan's works. Alan's masterpiece, Symphony No. 2 "Mysterious Mountain," was commissioned by Stokowski and premiered by him with the Houston Symphony for his inaugural concert in 1955.

Later, Andre Kostelanetz became Alan's champion, and he commissioned and performed numerous works from Alan. One of them was "And God Created Great Whales," which premiered in 1970 in the New York Philharmonic Promenade Concert. Despite the big splashy premiere of "Whales," the newspaper reviews were bad. There was a big headline in the *New York Times*, "Hovhaness Was Harpooned." But this piece did not die, but instead it became one of Alan's most popular pieces. So a bad review is not necessarily bad. As my mother said,

"A bad review is better than no review at all. They write because they are giving attention to it and know their negative headline will arouse the people to read their reviews." She was right!

Speaking of criticism, Alan did not take it very well. In that respect, he was like Tchaikovsky, who was very sensitive to bad critics. At one time in Alan's early career, he was so upset about a bad review he stormed into the newspaper and confronted the critic.

In 1978, Alan was asked to write a symphony and conduct it for a commemorative Armenian concert in Los Angeles. He was sharing the concert with Ohan Dourian, an Armenian conductor and composer who lived in Vienna. Alan composed not one, but two symphonies for the concert, Symphonies No. 26 and 27. However, one of the sponsors of the concert who was particularly committed to Alan disappeared, and the concert was up in the air for some time. But what could Alan do? Two symphonies and no performance!

Alan was depressed. Every morning he sat on the edge of his bed and buried his head in his hands. Later, the rich Armenian grocer Archie Dickranian, who was supporting Dourian, came to the rescue. He paid all the expenses for the concert. It was an exorbitantly expensive concert, especially because of Ohan Dourian's unreasonably high expenses. Dickranian was overwhelmed, and he, too, buried his head in his hands.

Alan had many colorful premieres in his life, but in between times he was composing away from people and in a very different world. After the completion of a work, he was busy preparing for the premiere by copying the parts and printing them, etc. At the premiere, for the first time, he heard the music in the midst of the audience and not just in his head. Suddenly, he was surrounded by the people and was hearing their comments, gratitude, enthusiasm, and criticism.

Often people asked him, "You have written so much music, but which one of them is your favorite?" He could not answer because his music was like his children, he loved them all, and each premiere was like the birth of a newborn.

Did I answer Mr. Shelley's question? "Did your husband ever become immune to the joy of hearing a work premiered?" No! His every premiere was a joyous occasion because he lived for that moment! In fact, he was very unhappy about some of his works never having been premiered. Every time a new commission came, his word to the commissioner was, "Don't let it sit—be sure to perform it!"

Family Concert – February 25, 1978

Meeting with Alan's First Wife, Martha (Patt) Brand-Erichsen

On February 25, 1978, Alan and I performed a concert in Berkeley, California, with his daughter Jean Nandi, who was a harpsichordist. She enthusiastically arranged the concert, and it was important for her to perform with her famous composer father. It was just a church performance, but a newspaper picked up the event and wrote a big announcement.

Jean was Alan's only child, who was separated from him when he divorced her mother Patt over forty years ago. She was later adopted by Patt's new husband, Brandt-Erichsen. Alan's visitation rights were taken away and they had just recently communicated with each other. Jean was married to an Indian scientist, and Jean herself was a scientist also. But she changed her course to become a harpsichordist. She had an unknown genetic disorder, but she was okay then. Her husband was very protective of her, and they were conscientious about eating healthy food.

During the performance, we stayed at their house. They lived in a strongly built old house and we stayed upstairs, separated from the rest of the house. In the mornings, I came down to the kitchen to prepare breakfast for Alan. One morning, I was looking for a non-stick pan for the scrambled eggs and could not find it, but I found a new pan and used it. Her husband, Ranu, found out and scolded me, as if I were just Alan's Japanese maid.

The *San Francisco Chronicle* concert review was large and critical:

> "The concert was a real family affair, for it included not only Hovhaness as pianist, but his daughter, the Berkeley harpsichordist Jean Nandi, and Hovhaness's wife, soprano Hinako Fujihara…"
>
> "The Harpsichord Sonata written for Nandi was meditative and liturgical, in the style of a hymn. 'Ananda' Sonata, performed by the composer, created a dynamic tension that was driving and relentless and Fujihara, a high soprano of modest talent…" This was about "Presentiment," which had been composed for me.
>
> "It was apparently a life-long ambition of Hovhaness to set the Bryant poem to music; this he did last summer in his individual style. But the ghost of Schubert-Goethe lingers, as if to say, 'Why?'"

Alan's intention to help Jean in her small town of Berkely backfired on us because of the big newspaper criticism. Ordinarily, a local concert like this would attract little attention, but because of Alan's name and reputation, the newspaper got into it.

After the concert, Jean wanted Alan to visit her mother, who lived in a small California town called Solvang, which was mainly populated by Danes. There was no transportation to get there except by driving. Patt had lost her husband many years ago, and she was getting old and very much wanted to see Alan. On February 27, we flew from San Francisco to Santa Barbara and rented a car and drove to her place. It was a good three hours' drive.

* * * * *

Patt's birth name was Martha, but she was called Patt. The first time Alan met Patt, he was in his late teens, not even twenty yet. Alan had lost his mother just before that, and Patt was a Baptist minister's daughter and was very religious. She took Alan to church every Sunday, and she taught Sunday school. In his teens, he was not allowed to go to young people's gatherings, and even movies were considered evil. Her "approved" girls were, in Alan's own words, "not interesting," and Alan did not have experience with girls and never even learned to dance.

In the meantime, Patt was trying to correct her lesbianism. She was in therapy with a psychiatrist named Dr. Adler. He thought that having grown up among lesbian sisters that she had been influenced by them, but this might not have been her true nature. He also thought that if she married a man, she could be corrected. I think that is why Alan was chosen. Alan was much younger than her and did not know about girls, so he wouldn't object to her sexual habits—unlike a boy who had already experienced sex with girls.

Alan married the first girl he was involved with. He did not do well with his love-making. He did not know about sex, but yet he was very uncomfortable with her sexual requirements, and he hated it. He could not satisfy her, and she complained, saying, "You have to do better." Because of this, he developed an inferiority complex, and he consciously learned about sex by reading the *Kama Sutra*.

Soon after they were married, she became pregnant. Again, this was Dr. Adler's idea for correcting her sexuality, and she went along with him. Alan, who had barely reached twenty, was composing, and his creativity was uncontrollably blossoming. He had to make something of himself, but here came a child, a strange existence, who seemed to be taking away Patt's attention from him. In his heart, he was still a young boy, and what he needed was a mother, not a wife.

On top of that, he could not get a job. It was the Depression in America and difficult to get a job, especially for Alan, who was married to a rich wife. They lived in one of her father's houses in Cape Cod. Patt's father was a very rich and powerful man. At one time, he tried to be president of the United States. Alan resented the situation, and this was one of the big reasons for divorcing her. Alan believed he should be the one supporting his wife, and because of that experience, he was never interested in rich women.

At one time, their friend Edovard Duburon and his wife stayed at their house. His wife was much older than him, almost like his mother. One day, according to Patt, she was in her kitchen and Edovard came in. They looked at each other and suddenly a flash of sparks hit them, and the next thing was they were on the floor and were on top of each other. Then his wife walked in and saw them and left. Edovard was shocked and ran after her to find her. Alan ran out to look for her also, but she was not to be found. Later, she divorced him.

Actually, this incident did not bother Alan because he was not in love with Patt. But he used this incident to divorce her. In fact, he asked her to divorce him in order to save her pride. Later, he told me that he was very guilty about what he had done to her, but he thought that was the only way he could get out from that relationship without saying, "I don't love you."

Alan got visitation rights to see his daughter and gradually developed affection for her. He composed much piano music for her to play instead of giving her toys. "Slumber Song" was dedicated to Jean Brand-Erichsen.

Later, Patt remarried their old friend, a Danish artist Brandt-Erichsen, who had been married to a sick wife that had killed herself by jumping from a second-story window. Patt had been hoping for Alan to come back to her, but after she had married Brand-Erichsen, she got him to be on her side by punishing Alan for leaving her and her child.

Her new husband wanted to adopt Jean and asked for Alan's signature for the adoption papers. Alan signed the papers reluctantly because of their persuasion, not knowing his visitation rights were being taken away, and they stopped him from communicating with Jean completely.

Obviously, Alan was not a real father, and just sending piano music to a child does not make a father; nevertheless, he suffered. I think that is why he went for younger women, maybe to fill the place of his lost daughter. I am twenty-one years younger than Alan, and I know I was his daughter, yet I was his mother also, the mother he lost too soon.

* * * * *

We arrived at Patt's house in Solvang. It was a large, studio-like single floor house built by her husband, and his art object sat in the front of the house. She was in her seventies and was nice and kind, and she welcomed us.

She put us in a bedroom, which was dark and small. While I was in the room refreshing myself, Alan went into her living room and played the piano. I knew he was entertaining her. Then she said, "Alan used to be a very good pianist." Alan and I understood it was not a compliment, but it was an insult. She meant that Alan had been a very good pianist but not anymore. Then Alan remembered the way she was. That she never hesitated to say anything.

She prepared dinner for us with a young woman's help. She cooked a Danish dish for us with sausage and sweet potatoes. She was a good cook even though I didn't like sausage, but I ate hers. In the evening, I put on the dress I wore for the concert and sang Alan's songs with his accompaniment. She liked my singing and said, "You have a strong voice." After that, we talked, well actually, they talked and I listened. She was worried about her daughter, Jean, and had her own theory that her condition was mental. She said that Jean was okay for now, but she had lost coordination in her body, like muscular dystrophy. She had been a scientist working with her husband, who was also a scientist. But she realized she could not ever surpass her husband, and as an excuse, her body gave up. So she could not continue as a scientist. Then she became a musician like her father. But again, she realized her limitations that she could never be like her father. She could not admit her failure to herself, so her body gave up. According to Alan, Patt's interpretation was always influenced by Dr. Adler. Psychology was everything to her, which took the place of religion.

Then Patt started telling us about her recollection of when Alan was the father. After Patt had delivered the baby, he came to the hospital. Alan was so absentminded, he got lost and a nurse had to look for him instead of taking care of the baby. According to Patt, he did not care for the baby. So one day she left the baby with him in order to get him acquainted with the baby, but when she came home, he was still composing and the baby had been left alone.

One time, the baby was crying and Alan made a gesture to throw her from the window, but Alan denied that. "I just scared her to stop her crying." I realized Patt was punishing him in front of an audience and in front of me, who was his new wife. Alan knew it too, but he took it like he was a boy being scolded by his mother.

She said one day his friend saw Alan on the street and said hello to him, but Alan was thinking of his music. His mind was far off, and he didn't know who he was, so Patt said, "Alan was a moron." That hurt him very much. He said to me, "That was not true. I was not a moron. I was very talented, and in high school I composed an opera, and they performed it. Patt is trying to cut me down." Then she made a statement. "I cannot live without Beethoven and Mozart and Schubert, but I can live without Hovhaness." It was so obvious to us what she was doing to Alan, letting out her resentment.

But her most important question was, "Why did you leave me?" He knew that she wanted to hear that he loved her, but he had left her because he was jealous of that incident on the kitchen floor with Edovard. But Alan could not answer that, and he was afraid to tell her the truth because it would hurt her. She said she loved Alan and never knew why he left her and her daughter.

After that long evening, we took a bath. The bathroom was a little way from our bedroom. Alan came along with me, and we took our bath together. Her bathroom was very dry, and there was no trace of anybody ever taking a bath. Her paintings were hanging over the bathtub. We had to be careful not to splash water. After the bath, I quickly went back to our bedroom. Alan was behind me and bumped into Patt in the hallway. According to Alan, she intentionally waited there to see him. The next morning, she complained about the bathroom being wet and said, "Alan was naked." He was embarrassed.

In spite of her sweet revenge, Alan was grateful to her and talked about her respectfully. She is the one who took him to Finland to meet with Sibelius to make his dream come true, and she took care of him when he developed lumps on his chest from some form of tuberculosis.

Several years later, she had an operation for her cancer and lost both her legs, but she continued to paint. Jean praised her, saying, "She is a fighter." At last, when Patt was dying, Jean told Alan her mother wanted him to see her for the last time. Alan could not go because he was afraid she might ask him that question, "Why did you leave me, because of that incident in the kitchen?" Alan could not provide her the answer and the salvation she needed to hear.

She wrote a letter to us after our visit to her home in 1978. Most of her letter was concerning her daughter, and it concluded:

> I really felt very good about your visit here with Hinako. She is a lovely little lady and understands you and accepts you as you are. After a life on a rather stormy sea, you must feel that at last you have reached a safe harbor.
>
> My love to both of you,
>
> Patt

I think she is one of the angels sending good thoughts towards me.

"Parting Friends"

While I was cleaning a pile of papers, a paper marker fell from a book. I picked it up to see what it was; it was Alan's handwriting on an old envelope. I looked at it and thought, "Is it worth anything?" and threw it in the waste basket. But then I picked it up and put it back in the book where it had been. The book was called "Social Harp," a song collection of old southern shape-notes. Alan got it from Mrs. Joan Applegate in Pennsylvania, where she taught piano. She introduced the book to Alan during his visit to her school, hoping he would be interested. He became fascinated by the songs.

I saw the page where the marker was, "Parting Friends." That was the melody Alan used for the third movement of his Symphony No. 60 "To the Appalachian Mountains." The words go:

"Farewell my friends, I'm bound to Canaan
I'm traveling through the wilderness.
Your company has been delightful,
You, who doth leave my mind distressed.
I go away, behind to leave you,
Perhaps never to meet again.
But if we never have the pleasure,
I hope we'll meet on Canaan's land."

I understand that these words are speaking of life and death. My tears fall, as if Alan is speaking these words to me. Our destiny is in God's hands, but I sincerely hope to meet him in the land of Canaan.

His notes for "To the Appalachian Mountains":

"I got into the mood of Appalachian history of study shaped notes and mountain music and folk poetry, and the third movement is a variation of 'Parting Friends,' anonymous song from before 1820. All other melodies are original."

Today I am not just missing him but mourning for the loss of such intellect. As I am looking at his pen marking notations on the pages of the book he had been studying, I realize I did not know the depth of his intellect wholly.

The book *Social Harp* is by John G. McCurry. It is one of the rarest of Southern shape-note songsters, a collection of his melodies and the old folk melodies that were passed on to him. He had learned the tune “Parting Friends” from Mrs. Catherine Penn when he was only eight years old. Those melodies were original, developed independently from sophisticated European music.

My mind has been circling around the year 1979, even in my sleep I was back there, especially the time Alan and I went to Pennsylvania.

In July of 1978, Alan received a letter from Dr. Cowdrey of Shippenburg State College in Pennsylvania. He wrote:

> We are planning a music festival similar to a festival I presented in 1975, featuring the music of Aaron Copland. Mr. Copland was present and participated in a seminar and conducted our concert choir and college/community orchestra. He was very pleased with the programming and performance. Your personal involvement in the music festival is flexible; however, we are interested in having you conduct a program of your own music and participate in a seminar on contemporary music…

Alan’s letter to him:

> This is to confirm agreement that I will come, hold workshops, conduct, April 4th to 8th, 1979, coming earlier in the week April 1st—to 8th as is convenient for you, receiving $1,000 and $500 expenses, total $1,500.
>
> In addition to the religious anthems, motets, brass pieces, my wife will sing arias from my new opera “Pericles”—I conducting the overture and the arias—possibly if I can prepare chorus parts the chorus SSA and SATB might also join for ending scene of opera.
>
> Sincerely,
> Alan Hovhaness
>
> P.S. There will be no charges for my wife as she always travels with me.

Just before leaving for Pennsylvania, the Three Mile Island nuclear disaster occurred, so we had to change the air tickets at the last minute to avoid going near there. Originally, we were to land in Harrisburg, PA, and to go to Shippensburg from there, but we changed arrangements to travel to Washington, D.C., instead. So Dr. Cowdrey, who was the planner of the festival and the conductor, came to get us in Washington, D.C., and drove us back to Shippensburg. It took many hours of driving, but we passed through many battlegrounds that I had heard of from American history.

The day we arrived, we were invited to Mrs. Applegate’s house for dinner, along with dozens of other people who came to meet Alan. She was the professor of piano at the college and was what I think of as a true American lady, gracious and kind. (They are becoming fewer and fewer.) Later, on Friday, April 6, she was the pianist for Alan's "Khaldis" piano concerto performance.

We arrived in Shippensburg on April 3, and the festival continued until the eighth, a total of seven concerts, with numerous pieces of Alan's being performed (vocal solos, cantatas, anthems, wind, and orchestra music). On the last day of the concert, Alan conducted, and I sang three of his arias from his opera "Pericles." During the festival, Arthur Hamilton, who we had met at the Interlochen Music Camp earlier, came to see Alan from Michigan. He had been studying there and had been interested in Alan's new opera and wanted to find somebody to produce the opera. He arrived at the festival with a knapsack on his back. I felt sorry for him and took him to a restaurant to feed him.

One evening, Dr. Cowdrey and his wife invited us to a restaurant for dinner, but I had to take Arthur with us. Dr. Cowdrey was not happy, maybe because he knew Arthur was the kind of student who helped himself by latching on to influential people. Alan and I were not experienced with this. Maybe he was right. Alan spent substantial money to make an opera score, and he gave it to Arthur, but the performance never materialized, and the opera score was never returned.

In Alan's own words, his gloomy childhood was maybe the reason why he had been so fascinated by the music of other places. But regardless of whatever his interest was, he always looked for the origin of the music. Finally, after he had traveled to far-away places, he came back to his own roots, the early American heritage he had grown up with. It was my wish for him to write his American music, he should because he was an American, from the country I so admire.

Mrs. Applegate gave Alan the book *Social Harp* containing the rudiments of shape-notes. Alan kept this book close to him, always. (I appreciate Mrs. Applegate for giving the book to Alan.)

2911 SOUTH 200TH
APT. 2.
SEATTLE, WASH. 98188
AUGUST 29, 1978

SHIPPENBURG STATE COLLEGE

DEAR DR COWDREY:

THIS IS TO CONFIRM
AGREEMENT THAT I WILL
COME, HOLD WORKSHOPS, CONDUCT,
APRIL 4TH TO 8TH, 1979, COMING
EARLIER IN THE WEEK
APRIL 1ST — TO 8TH AS
IS CONVENIENT FOR YOU
RECEIVING $1,000., AND
$500. EXPENSES. TOTAL $1,500.
IN ADDITION TO THE RELIGIOUS
ANTHEMS. MOTETS. BRASS
PIECES, MY WIFE WILL
SING ARIAS FROM MY
NEW OPERA "PERICLES"
I CONDUCTING THE OVERTURE
AND THE ARIAS — POSSIBLY
IF I CAN PREPARE CHORUS
PARTS THE CHORUS SSA
AND SATB MIGHT ALSO
JOIN FOR ENDING SCENE
OF OPERA —

SINCERELY
Alan Hovhaness
(ALAN HOVHANESS)

P.S.
THERE WILL BE NO CHARGE FOR
MY WIFE AS SHE ALWAYS TRAVELS
WITH ME —

Writing from Alan

Ruffles Motel

Port Angeles, what a wonderful and nostalgic place! Located between the north end of the Olympic peninsula and the south end of Vancouver Island, on the inland water of the Strait of Juan de Fuca, it is a three-hour drive from my house in south Seattle, crossing the Hood Canal Bridge. There are many attractions of nature, but the most spectacular showing is Hurricane Ridge, which is located to the south of Port Angeles, parallel to the main road of the town, which runs east to west. From this road, drive up a steep hill for fifteen minutes, then suddenly, a wide-open panorama view of overlapping Olympic mountains appears in front of you. This was Alan's favorite place to come.

In 1976, Alan and I went to Port Angeles, right after Alan came back from our separation. Before our marriage, we were so much in love; we were like just-married teenagers. We stayed at the Ruffles Motel, located below Hurricane Ridge, on the main road of Port Angeles. The next morning in the motel, a maid came into the room for cleaning; we were still on top of each other. We didn't realize their check-out time was eleven AM; cheap motels kicked you out early in the morning.

A year after we were married, June 13–16 of 1978, Alan and I went back to Port Angeles with my teenage children June, Joni, and Bill, and we went to the same Ruffles Motel. I had brought cooking equipment to cook breakfast for everybody secretly in the motel room (I had been cooking breakfast for Alan in hotel rooms in every place, even in foreign countries, because Alan being a night owl had difficulty getting up in time for the hotel breakfast). After our day's activities outdoors, we got together in the room. I decided to cook something for everybody, so I took out a small electric stove from my hiding place and started to cook. I think Joni was drying her hair at the same time, then "poof!" the lights went out! We looked around, and the lights were out, not just in our room, but in all the motel rooms. We were so afraid; we all went to bed. We knew from the beginning that the motel manager was very tight, but we never imagined this extreme. He fixed each room to have just enough electricity, so if we used any extra, the electricity would shut off. What a cheap guy!

The next morning, we had a family conference about what to do. We already told him we would stay there for three nights, but we could not stay because we could not cook. On top of that, he must have known we did something illegal last night. Everybody was scared, and then I had an idea. If I had acted guilty, he would have had an advantage over me, so I should be one step ahead of him: I should complain to him instead.

That is what I did. I never gave him a chance to complain. I told him we used a hair dryer, and then the electricity went out! I could not stay in such a motel, so I paid for one night and safely drove away. We found another motel (the Chinook) farther west on the main street in Port Angeles. It was a much nicer arrangement; there were big rooms and a bedroom and kitchen. I no longer had to perform illegal cooking.

Later, a telephone call came, and my daughter answered. That was a call from the manager of the Ruffles Motel. (How did he find out where we were?) He was very naggingly regretful, and he told my daughter he had a big family unit with a kitchen on the basement level and wished we would have asked. But the way he looked us up and called us in another motel was a very scary moment.

Many years later (by that time my daughter June was married and lived near Port Angeles), Alan, my mother, and I traveled to Port Angeles. It happened to be it was a very crowded day in Port Angeles, and my daughter could not find any other motel vacancies, so she had to make reservations at the same motel, the Ruffles. The day we left, we had all kinds of delays at the ferry boat. At one point, in our frustration, Alan yelled at another car, "I will kill you!" That expression made my mother feel very much at home. In her old country, Korea, their over-emotional expression was, "I will kill you!"

We got to the motel late, and that stingy manager had already given our room to somebody else, so as not to lose any money. Alan was so upset, he yelled at him, then suddenly he got pale and sank into the car seat. I was afraid he had had a heart attack, but he recovered.

After that, we looked for another place to stay and found a hotel (not a motel) at the edge of the water, the Red Lion Hotel (Bayshore Inn). They found rooms and treated us nicely. We ate breakfast in the hotel restaurant overlooking the water. Only the amount of money made a difference. After that, we went back to this hotel every time, and we never went back to the Ruffles Motel.

Lucerne, Switzerland – Alan Took Me There

♪

I dreamed about Alan this morning; we were at a hotel in Lucerne. Somehow, we were moving from our room to a different room upstairs. There were only two suites, and the hotel personnel were talking to us for a long time, checking our identifications. Alan seemed not strong, and I felt his frustration. Then he started talking to them in a European accent. After I woke up, I thought, that was so much like Alan used to be. Sometimes, when he could not get through to people, suddenly he started to talk in German. I asked, "Why?" He said that German was a very command-sounding language and you could get through to people better.

Alan and I were in Switzerland from August 14-20 of 1978. During a visit to London for a week-long music festival of Armenian music and musicians (organized by the Institute of Armenian Music), suddenly Alan wanted to take me to Switzerland. Because we were already in London, from there it would be easy to get to Switzerland by Swiss Air. He said Swiss pilots were the best in the world.

When we were transferred to Swiss Air, they treated us with their chocolates—they were delicious! (I think their sense of taste is different from the English.) Soon we were greeted by the beautiful Swiss Alps under our windows; no wonder Alan loved this country and lived there. It was not just the mountains, but it was the cleanest place I had ever seen, as if everything was touched and cleaned by hand. (But he did say Swiss girls were too "white" for him.)

Alan wanted to take me to an expensive hotel at the edge of the lake, but it was too expensive ($70 a night), so we looked for another hotel. Alan knew of the Hotel Balance, where he used to stay, but he avoided going there because he had been there with his former wife Elizabeth. He was afraid that if we would go there, they would recognize him and notice a different girl with him; according to Alan, the Swiss were puritanical and, by now, Elizabeth's Swiss friends would be against him because he had divorced her. He even dreamed of being stoned by them.

Anyway, we didn't have a choice; the Hotel Balances was reasonably priced and also was overlooking the lake, so we checked into that hotel. When we got in our room, a box of chocolate and bottle of champagne were waiting for us, and the manager of the hotel came to talk to us. I am sure he was scornful of Alan because he was with a different girl, but he didn't stone him.

That night, Alan was very excited, like a kid, showing off to me, taking me to places he knew. Then he took me to a very expensive restaurant, the Old Swiss House, and treated me to a luxurious dinner and a *krup Denmark* for dessert. He often talked about *krup Denmark*, flaming hot chocolate over cake, and the richest dessert you could imagine. But, I was so tired from the trip, after the airplane flight and the hours of train ride from Zurich to Lucerne, I could not eat very much.

The next day, August 15, he was still excited with tremendous energy, and took me to Mount Pilatus. We went up a long railroad tram to the top. There we saw many lightning rods. He said so much lightning hit the top of Pilatus that that was why they needed so many lightning rods, for protection. And he told me his opera "Pilate" was inspired by the legend of Pilatus. This is the place Pontius Pilate supposedly threw himself to his death. Pilate knew Jesus Christ was not an ordinary man, yet he ordered his crucifixion, demanded by the mob. His guilt led him to suicide.

In the evening, we walked around the lake, under the moon. There were a dozen birds on the driftwood over the water, lined up, sleeping, but always distracted by somebody invading their position. We were laughing about their uncomfortable sleep.

In the morning, I left Alan in the hotel room, composing, while I went to a store. I left a large box of chocolates (it had whiskey in each section) for Alan, but when I returned the box was empty, so I asked, "What happened to the chocolate?"

Then he answered, "It went down nicely!" From that time on I called him "Chocoholic."

One day he took me to Richard Wagner's museum, across the lake to Tribschen in a small boat. It was a simple, square, three-storied house. This is the house Wagner lived in with his wife Cosima and their three children. I saw Alan's oriental instruments on the first floor of the house; he had donated those years ago, when he lived in Lucerne. In Wagner's living room, I saw Wagner's piano and his white death mask on it.

Alan's Wagner fever started when he was a young man; and even on that day in Switzerland, he was telling me about Wagner's stories with tremendous excitement. Wagner was such an extravagant man, and he was always in debt. King Ludwig II of Bavaria believed in his music and supported him, not just with his opera performances, but financially in general. He needed to do this without government approval, so he gave the money to Wagner by coins in huge sacks, carried into his house secretly. Wagner bought expensive gifts for his friends, but they knew he could not afford his generosity, so they returned his gifts to the store without telling him. He was a man of exceptional extravagance and impracticality. I think that is why he could write such a huge opera cycle like "The Ring." This is one of the stories Alan told me surrounding Wagner's inspiration for "Das Rheingold."

One day Wagner went out on the lake in a boat in the sunset and threw coins into the lake. Every time the coin flickered in the sunset, he said, "Rhine gold." This story was just like him, who else could have thought of such imaginative things beyond our common practicality? The libretto of his enormous opera "The Ring of the Nibelungen" was written by the composer himself. Many nights he would gather his friends to recite the wordy libretto all evening long.

After we left Wagner's house, we went to Bruneian. There, we stood at the lakeshore, overlooking the Swiss mountains, where Wagner's vision for the performance of "The Ring" came from. His idea was to build a stage on the exact spot where we stood, at the edge of the lake, using the surrounding snow-topped mountains for the background scenery.

After we left that location, we went to a nearby Italian restaurant and ate steak and French fries; it was the only edible thing on the menu. Why did we choose to eat American food in an Italian restaurant in Switzerland? It was the worst meal we had during the whole trip.

Alan took me to the small church where Wagner and Cosima were married. Cosima's father, Franz Liszt, was against their marriage, even though he strongly believed in Wagner's music, and he was the promoter and conductor of his operas. Previously, Cosima was married to Wagner's friend, the conductor Hans von Bulow; she claimed her children, not just one but both of them, were Wagner's, and later she divorced von Bulow and married Wagner. It was the scandal of the century, but what can you do after you know Wagner? I did the same thing; I married Hovhaness and abandoned my family. Something about a composer is irresistibly fascinating, especially to a singer. Every morning we ate in a simple, clean breakfast place, even the hot tea was in a clear glass cup. Unlike in America, I had to order orange juice, eggs, toast, etc., separately, and the coffee came with only two squares of sugar. I had to ask to get extra.

A few times we ate breakfast at the hotel. The hotel came with a complimentary continental breakfast, but we had to special order ours because we needed a very extravagant breakfast, eggs and fruit and everything. We saw many young Japanese tourists in the dining room. They were having coffee and croissants, the continental breakfast. Switzerland is almost the farthest country from Japan. They had come far to see Switzerland, a very different country that fascinated them, and so they had to eat a very "white" breakfast. We looked at them with sympathy.

During our short stay in Lucerne, I noticed we foreigners were confined to the tourist section. We needed more orange juice because we had gotten a very small glass of it in the restaurant, but I could not find any grocery stores, so I asked the cashier in a store, "Where is a grocery store?" The answer was, "Tourists eat at the restaurant."

In the past, when Alan lived in Lucerne, he ate every meal in the restaurant and Elizabeth never looked for a grocery store. But I wanted to solve the mystery of my suspicions. "Are we confined in a section just designed for foreigners? Where do the ordinary Swiss get their food?"

I went out from the tourist section and saw a woman with a baby carriage and asked for a grocery store. I was right, the grocery store was hidden from the tourist section and there was an abundance of fresh fruit and juice, even from Italy and France, and at a price they could afford.

One day, we were sitting at an outdoor table, looking at the beautiful mountain and lake, Alan pointed out one peak and told me his unfortunate story.

When Alan and Elizabeth were in Lucerne, shortly after their marriage, on the way back from their India and Japan trip, they had gone up into the mountains often. But one day, suddenly Elizabeth ran to the edge of a cliff to throw herself off, and Alan grabbed her with all of his might. That precipice was very steep, straight down to the bottom. If Alan had not caught her, she would never have had a chance. That incident affected Alan very deeply. He thought that if she killed herself, he could not defend himself in a foreign country. Without witnesses, he would have become the murderer. That was his early experience of that tragic marriage. The marriage lasted for sixteen years, but he never regained his intimacy with her.

Despite Alan's effort to experience a new and happier Switzerland with me, I was not quite ready, because his tragic relationship, the ghost of his past was still there. As he said, he was very lonely in that beautiful Swiss landscape. I felt I was in somebody else's territory.

Years later, I wanted to go back to Switzerland with Alan. By that time, our marriage was all established and his past was not painful anymore, we could have had our own Switzerland to enjoy, but we never made that trip.

Alan, as I write, I miss you so much. You took me to places of wonder where I never could have gone without you. Nobody could have loved me like you did, you gave me a wonder of life I fervently treasure.

Symphony No. 36, "Flute Concerto"

Alan's commission for Symphony No. 36, "Flute Concerto," came in the spring of 1978. It was commissioned by Bob Bialek, owner of the Discount Record Shops in the Washington, D.C., area. This was his fifth such commission and was specifically for Jean-Pierre Rampal to be performed with the National Symphony Orchestra.

Alan had just completed Symphony No. 34 for bass trombone and strings, and other commissions were still waiting for Alan to compose, among them a commission from the Criterion Foundation for the piano, Symphony No. 35 from the Seoul, Korea Cultural Arts Festival, etc. Alan seemed overwhelmed with too many commissions then. The commission from Seoul, Korea, was for a full orchestra plus Korean *ah-ahk* orchestra, together in one symphony. He could not find music paper large enough for the score for the symphony, so he had to paste two music papers together. His composing did not come easily, and he struggled with it. He said to me, "It would be much easier when I will compose the flute concerto." But it did not happen that way, because he had as much difficulty as he had had with Symphony No. 35.

While he was composing the concerto/symphony for Jean-Pierre Rampal, the internationally famous French flautist came to Seattle for a performance. He was supposedly the soloist for Alan's Symphony No. 36. I expected Alan to meet Rampal at his concert, but Alan never mentioned seeing him, so I asked him "Why?" His answer was that, if he would see him, then he would be influenced by him, and he wanted to have freedom to compose. But this concerto was too demanding for him, and his difficulty was because it was to be performed by a prestigious national symphony orchestra and conducted by the world-renowned conductor Rostropovich, who had defected from Russia and without saying, flute solo by Rampal.

In the beginning of 1979, the premiere of Symphony No. 36 was set for a January 16 and 18 concert. However, we had no word from the symphony orchestra. I thought I had to do something, so I called them and asked, "Aren't you going to invite the composer, my husband, for the premiere?" Then to my surprise, they were so ashamed and apologetic for their lack of courtesy to the composer and immediately made our hotel arrangements for us. What a difference one telephone call made!

They put us up in the luxurious Watergate Hotel, where the Watergate scandal had taken place just the year before. We had a spacious suite surrounded by large windows and a kitchen unit behind closed doors. It was a very cold day when we arrived there, and the fountain water outside was frozen, and we felt cold air coming from the windows.

On the sixteenth, my daughter Joni arrived from New York to join us. We were surprised when we saw her, and I saw her face was red and swollen up from crying. Her beautiful face was completely ruined. Her reason was that her jealous Italian boyfriend had made trouble for her because he did not want her to go. But she recovered quickly and joined all our activities.

Joni and I found our hotel bathroom very elegant. One side of the bathroom wall was all mirrors, and the makeup tables were against them. I had brought rice and a rice cooker with me, and I cooked beef stroganoff and rice for Joni and Alan in our hotel-room kitchen. It was delicious and Joni commented that, “It was the best food I ever had.” I agreed. I think their gas stove had something to do with it.

During our stay in D.C., an old couple, Mr. and Mr. Hustings, called and introduced themselves as somebody who had met Alan at some party in the past. According to them, Alan should have known them, but he did not remember them. But he took their word to be polite. They didn’t seem to care whether Alan remembered them or not. They helped themselves to being with us and joined our activities. We went to the National Art Gallery, where an exhibition of French arts was going on. I remember seeing the original painting of *Scream* by the artist Munch, which I had seen in my mother’s art book before. Then they took us to an exclusive club for dinner, where there was a table full of buffet food that had all kinds of meats, even pheasant. But I could not eat them because they were hardly cooked and made me think of hunters and men’s club food, cooked by men.

The day before the concert, we were invited to Mrs. Klee’s apartment next door to our hotel for a dinner party. She must have been an important person for the orchestra. Mrs. Klee greeted us at the door. I noticed she had a collection of original paintings from famous painters. One of the paintings that caught my eyes was Paul Klee’s original. This just happened to be the same as her name. Then we met the conductor Rostropovich, who was seated in the center of the party like a rooster. He greeted us and especially noticed my daughter Joni’s beauty. Joni and I were dressed to kill that night; she wore a striking beige-colored kimono-style raglan sleeved dress with a distinctive design going through one end of a sleeve to the other. The whole evening the conductor kept his attention on Joni and said to us that his favorite people were Armenian and Japanese. He had quite a personality and was a diplomat. For the dinner, a caterer had prepared the food. It was a simple chicken dish and rice and vegetable, but it was exquisitely done.

Alan admired Rostropovich, and he told me, “He did not waste the rehearsal time.” Alan used to correct the mistakes of his parts at the rehearsal, especially for his new compositions. He called it “getting the bugs out.” He could detect any misprints or mistakes by just hearing them. He was very precise about what he wanted, and there was no compromise. At that rehearsal, Rostropovich corrected the mistakes, even before Alan could say anything to him.

The night of Alan’s premiere, Rampal had his music on the stand in front of him, like a rehearsal. I thought it was unusual to see a soloist using the music for the performance, so maybe he could not memorize it because Alan had composed it super-difficult to impress Rampal and the orchestra. But he overdid it.

The last piece of the concert was Gunther Schuller's Concerto for Bassoon. The bassoon is not usually a solo instrument, and I thought it sounded bad because, unlike Alan's melodic style, Schuller did not hesitate to emphasize the repulsive part of the sound of the instrument. At that time composers were writing "ugly music," but it was considered the thing to do.

Sure enough, Alan's concerto review was bad. It said something like "Hovhaness concerto was like a child lost in the garden." That is all I remember; I must have thrown away the review. But later, the *Washington Star* newspaper review came out, dated Friday 19, 1979, and written by Theodore W. Libbey, Jr. It was based on his pre-concert interview with Alan and Rampal and Schuller, but it had no mention of Schuller. There was a large, two-page article with a photo of Alan and Rampal. Mr. Libbey wrote so observantly and sympathetically of Alan, starting with a big headline "Hovhaness: He Is the First Composer in 200 Years to Complete 36 Symphonies" and "Alan Hovhaness at 36 Symphonies." His article was all about Alan.

Here are some clips from it:

> Sipping black coffee at a kitchen table hastily converted to a work-desk, his slender hands trembling slightly as they pour over the pages of his new score, Alan Hovhaness seems bemused, but not bothered, by the notion that he is the first composer in nearly 200 years who has had to worry about the reception of his 36th symphony.
>
> Not since Mozart wrote his "Linz" Symphony in 1783 has a composer reached that dizzying plateau of three-times-a-dozen symphonies. While Mozart had no idea that history would record the "Linz" as his 36th, Hovhaness' score, written out in his own hand, carries not only the number "36" but the official designation "Op. 312" as well.
>
> Hovhaness does not pretend to be unaware of the added context which such numbers lend to his works. "I'm working on my 40th right now. When I began it things went along smoothly enough, and then I thought of Mozart's 40th, and I realized that I'd have to make mine better—oh no, not better than Mozart—just better than it was."
>
> When asked if he thinks there is any truth to the claim of some composers that the symphony as a form is dead, his own efforts notwithstanding, he replied quite sincerely, "I hope not."

Alan continued to talk about his concerto:

> "I've adapted the symphony to the long melodic line," he says, summing up his enormous output. "My symphonies are really half concertos and half symphonies; even the ones which are for solo instruments."
>
> The flute solo in the present work, according to the soft-spoken composer, "should have an improvisatory quality. It should sound somewhat mysterious. I use the flute as a voice—so while

> it is mysterious it also has a very *singing* part, a long melismatic line. At several points I treat it like a coloratura part, with an extended high range – but I am not so interested," he adds, with a somewhat gruff gesture, "in terribly piercing high notes."
>
> For fear that his last remark will be misunderstood, he allows as how, "in the cadenza, the flute *does* go up to a high C and D-flat—because I thought Mr. Rampal should have something worthy of his attention.

During that time he composed many songs for *my* coloratura voice; he was thinking of my voice when he was composing, especially for some instruments.

Rampal continued, talking about the concerto:

> Rampal himself characterizes the work as "a big song for flute and orchestra."
>
> "It is a very conservative piece," Rampal explains, "very melodic except for a few moments, and very well written for the flute. The solo encompasses all registers, from very low to very high, but there are passages where it stays a long time in the upper middle range, which can be very tense because your lips get tired after a while."
>
> Rampal, when asked for his opinion of the work, says characteristically: "When I play a work, I always believe that it is the best work. It is like love…you cannot make love to one person and think about another while you are doing it."
>
> While the Gallically good-humored Rampal is all flair and passion as he speaks, Hovhaness seems more contemplative. Aside from his lively brown eyes, he radiates gentleness and spirituality with an almost monastic meekness.

He beautifully described Alan. I remember him that way, and he was a darling man, but he had that volcanic passion inside of him. I passionately adore him.

National Symphony: Hovhaness and Schuller premieres

For Alan Hovhaness, the appellation "symphony" has been known to cover a broad range of musical phenomena. In the case of his Symphony No. 36 for Solo Flute and Orchestra, premiered by the National Symphony on its subscription concerts of January 16-18, both the three-movement form and the solo-accompaniment format are as much like those of a concerto as a symphony. Flutist Jean-Pierre Rampal was featured soloist in the new work, his presence alone enough to guarantee a standing-room crowd each night. Rostropovich conducted.

Composer meets composer: Alan Hovhaness and Gunther Schuller together at the Kennedy Center after double premiere; Jean-Pierre Rampal looks on

Hovhaness achieves with the symphony a subtle play of texture in the juxtaposition of the flute with various orchestral and instrumental groupings. When he calls upon the full orchestra to play, it invariably makes a beautiful sound, the hallmark of one who has written for this medium extensively. One might criticize the work for a certain long-windedness, yet in its relaxed flow of melody there is also a sense of serenity and at times even a feeling of majesty. The sweetness and regularity of the writing remain, however, just one step away from platitude. Rampal played the mellifluous solo part with liquid softness and a radiant purity of tone. The second movement cadenza, with its pulsing internal rhythm and fluidity, was brilliantly characterized.

HIGH FIDELITY / musical america June 1979

Newspaper Article of Alan

Alan's Record Ventures

Poseidon Adventure

In 1978, Alan and I started a record venture. We recorded Alan's new music symphonies and songs that he composed for me. I sang and he conducted. We made a total of five records.

Alan's record venture was not anything new. In the late 1950s he had produced acetate records of himself playing his piano music, using a small tape recorder.

In the 1960s, after he married Elizabeth, she took over his projects herself. She thought his record-making was clumsy and unprofessional; they named the company "Poseidon"—God of the Sea. Also, it was the name of the boat Alan's father was aboard when he was escaping from the Turkish massacre. They recorded many of his orchestral pieces in England. At that time, to record orchestral music in England was not as expensive as in the U.S., but it was still substantial. They lived in an apartment because most of his money went into the recordings instead of a house and cars.

There was no doubt the Poseidon project helped Alan's career greatly. He was not just the composer of the music, but also conducted it to show to people how his music should sound. But his personal life was a lonely one. It seemed Poseidon was the big reason they were together. Alan began to have affairs, and this led him to a deceitful double life. But Elizabeth had power over Alan because of Poseidon; she knew his career was in her hands. In fact, she developed the belief that sacrificing her personal happiness for Alan was her divine duty.

When he met me in 1973, he genuinely fell in love with me, but he could not break from Elizabeth, not until after she took him to Europe in order to break us up for good. That separation between us made him realize what his life would be like without me. He had to decide between love and his career, and he chose love. He came back to me.

He immediately filed for divorce, but Elizabeth was not about to exit quietly. He had to fight with her in court and three lawyers between them. As a result, he had to pay a large amount of alimony to her for the rest of her life. Alan called it alimony, but she thought of it differently. She said she was not just his wife but also his business partner and that the money from him was her share from their investment. She also took Poseidon from Alan and for her advantage to use as a hostage.

After their divorce, Alan had received from her the Poseidon expenses, which were just numbers written by her handwriting on scrap paper that she expected him to pay to her. Finally, Alan thought, "Enough is enough" and quit dealing with her.

But her revenge did not stop there. We got a proposition from her lawyer, saying that since Alan refused to pay for the Poseidon expenses, she could no longer continue the company. So she decided to sell Poseidon to Alan for something like $100,000 at that time. We did not have that kind of money; then she turned around and asked for $10,000 to sell it to anybody except Alan.

She did not want to give him back Poseidon, which was lawfully his with his records, his own compositions, conducted by him. And every bit of it had been paid for from his compositions. Finally, Crystal Records bought Poseidon for less than $10,000, which I heard from some source. It was the end of Alan's Poseidon adventure. Since then, Crystal Records has been converting Alan's records to CDs and marketing them to record shops. It is on a small scale, but at least his music is still available.

Pandora's Box

In 1978, the Northwest Chamber Orchestra asked Alan to be their guest conductor for their October concert. He got the second half of the concert to himself. So Alan thought this would be a good opportunity for him to put me on the program. He composed a long symphony (No. 38) and wrote the third and fourth movements for my voice and strings. After the concert we recorded the symphony for the purpose of making a record.

Glenn White was the recording engineer. He was a professor at the University of Washington and the best engineer for classical music in Seattle at that time. After the concert, he introduced Al Goldstein, a local record maker, to us. His company was called Pandora Records. It was our record venture together, and it started with him. Goldstein started the record business in order to record his wife Martha's harpsichord playing, and he must have thought including Alan's music would help his venture.

Goldstein was a fairly young man in his late fifties, dark and stocky, with the looks of some typical Jewish men. On the other hand, his wife, Martha, was tall and thin, a very white Norwegian. She looked much older than him, maybe because of her washed-out look, which was the opposite from her husband's. Even though Alan and I are also very different from each other in looks and age, we were still amazed at their contrast and wondered how they had ever gotten together.

Martha told us many things about them. They married when they were very young and had a baby girl. But they divorced and Martha never married again and raised the girl all by herself. On the contrary, Goldstein had married again and had produced a large family. Many years later, they bumped into each other on the street and decided to marry again. I assume by that time his children were grown up and he was free to remarry Martha, and so they did.

They lived in a large old house on Capitol Hill. It was once a very good neighborhood and many rich people lived there, but they had left and the place had become rundown. Martha was afraid to go down in the basement because rats lived there.

I remember Martha was a very sweet and innocent old lady. She was completely under his power even though she had raised her girl by herself. She often said, "That is too expensive." Those were his words and he had trained her to be thrifty. She could not go clothes shopping alone, for he came along with her to make sure she would not buy expensive stuff. But they were generous to us and often they treated us to refreshments and sometimes dinner after our sessions. Alan and I hated their food, and we could not eat it.

One night I went into their kitchen while Martha was preparing the dinner. She was sitting in front of a big boiling pot, stirring spinach. She looked like a Halloween witch stirring a pot of brew. Her spinach was all mixed together, not like the Japanese would do. Japanese prepare spinach this way; after washing spinach, we put them together in a bunch and boil them; then we take them out, cut them the same length, squeeze the water out, place them neatly on the plate facing upward with the cut edge on the top and bottom, then sprinkle sesame seeds and pour soy sauce over them.

Then one day Goldstein invited us to a restaurant. We were relieved and thought at least we could eat something. They took us to a Chinese restaurant called Tai Tung's in the International District near downtown Seattle. We were shocked that we could not eat at all. It was the most crudely-prepared food we had ever eaten. I think bad Chinese food is the worst. On top of that, Goldstein said to us that any time we would go out to eat, we would only come to Tai Tung's because they were very cheap.

Goldstein was so cheap, by the time we were to make Alan's next record, he was thinking of pressing the records himself to save money instead of pressing them at a California company. Our next record was Alan's Symphony No. 31; it had been recorded at the same time with Symphony No. 38 with the Northwest Chamber Orchestra conducted by Louis Richmond. On the other side, we were to put my singing that was accompanied by Alan's piano. Then Goldstein suggested using Martha's piano in his living room. He would record it himself to save money. I thought her piano sounded dry, and we were not happy about that setup, but we recorded it anyway.

Goldstein did not understand nor appreciate my extremely high coloratura voice and did not know how to record it. He sent us the test pressing between our concert tours, but we must have overlooked it; when we heard the finished product, we were shocked. Then we realized the record was so unprofessional, we had to stop it before the records were released. It happened because of our carelessness, so we offered to put up our money to do it again, but Goldstein was not about to do that. He had already distributed the records, and he did not understand how bad the record sounded—like his taste in food.

Our battle began.

Goldstein Case

Alan and I sought help from Michael Cohen, the lawyer who had incorporated our company, Fujihara Music Co., Inc. He was a young Jewish man who thought he could settle the matter with Goldstein by just one casual meeting. Alan's request to Goldstein was for him to give us the record rights for Symphony No. 38 and Symphony No. 31 so we would be able to repress the record and make a new recording of my songs on side two.

Alan's letter to Cohen – June 4, 1980

> Goldstein himself also said he does not want the partnership. He said he wants to negotiate and argue. We only want to speed this process. We waited weeks for his estimate paper. We will pay as we already have, but we want to know exactly how much. Goldstein told us he would give use of the records of his expenditure... The letter we sent was to explain how much we paid already and to give you an idea of what we had paid and to help with negotiations.

But what Cohen thought would be easy negotiations did not happen that way. One of Goldstein's letters to Cohen – July 26, 1980

> ....Since my last letter, I have called you three times. You are virtually inaccessible. The next time I try, I'll say, when your secretary asks who it is, "Your mother" instead of Mr. Goldstein.

Cohen could not stand Goldstein and gave this nasty job to his associate David Leshner. He was a CPA as well as attorney and had a different temperament from Cohen.

Goldstein requested $6,000 to give us the rights for two records. This amount was based on future sale of 8,000 empty record jackets. He stated $2.50 as the adjusted gross income for each record and the expense of making the record would be $1, so the profit per record would be $1.50. He multiplied 8,000 by that to get $12,000, then divided by two and $6,000 would be his portion.

Mr. Leshner calculated from Goldstein's obscure record of expenditures and what we had already paid to Goldstein for our portion of expenses. We had paid from his handwritten numbers without a printed statement or receipts and not counting what we had paid to the Northwest Chamber Orchestra for the recording of Symphonies No. 31 and 38. Leshner's argument was:

1. For all 8,000 jackets to sell would take many years and, judging from Hovhaness records, Alan had received one check for $35 from Goldstein as royalty for the first record.

2. To get money now or receive it later would make a difference in the money value.

3. In the years to come, the expense of making records could go up and the amount of profit would change.

He took all of this into account and his brilliant calculation came to $2,000. Goldstein made a counteroffer to our offer. To receive $2,000 directly to him and we would drop any other claims, offset against the expenditures he owed us, etc. Leshner urged us to take his offer because if we did not, we would argue back and forth and take a longer time and eventually wind up paying more to the attorney's fees.

His suggestion was a good one. Goldstein agreed to accept $2,000 and gave us the rights for the two records, Symphonies No. 31 and 38. We established Fujihara Record Company and our new record venture kicked off.

"Okay" Guy

We again asked Glenn White for someone to produce our record. He suggested Al Swanson. Then I asked him what Swanson was like. He said, "He is an okay guy." We did not understand what he meant, but we got the impression of a low-key person.

Al Swanson was not a stranger to us, as we had first thought. He was a professional recording engineer, and his recording company was called Location Recording. His wife was a violist we had known. She had been playing in the Northwest Chamber Orchestra from the beginning of its establishment. I remember her very well; in 1977, the Orchestra premiered Alan's Symphony No. 31 and she played viola; during the fifth movement (Allegro Vivace), she swung her head right to left so lively. Since then she had married Swanson and they had two children, a girl and a boy. I thought he and his wife looked so much alike since they both had very light complexions, and my impression of them was that they were like school sweethearts.

I understood why Glenn White had said, "He is an okay guy." Swanson did not talk much and was not expressive either. But one day Alan said to me, "For the first time, he showed his passion towards his son." One night we were editing our recorded music tape in his basement studio. His young son was just a toddler then and came downstairs to get father's attention. Swanson talked to him so lovingly; then we glimpsed the tender emotion inside of him and found out who he really was.

Fujihara Record Co. produced a total of five records, two of them recorded by Swanson; but times had changed and CDs had come in and our record-making became a thing of the past. Since then, we have let major CD companies produce our recorded music.

Al Swanson became the Seattle Symphony recording engineer. In the year 2000 when Alan died, he was one of the few people who came to Alan's very private last viewing. And Leshner continues to be my personal and corporation lawyer.

Love Song Vanishing Into the Sound of Crickets

"Love Song Vanishing Into the Sound of Crickets," one of Alan's piano pieces, was composed for my Valentine's gift in 1979.

Wayne Johnson, who had recorded the piece in his piano album for Crystal Records, was interested in Alan's piano music. Johnson was Professor of Piano at Pacific Lutheran University. Alan met him often in his studio on campus and they would talk about his piano pieces while I was taking a voice lesson upstairs.

Johnson wrote in his CD liner notes:

> ...piece was written by Hovhaness in 1979 as a valentine for his wife, coloratura soprano, Hinako Fujihara. It begins with a tender expression of great beauty and simplicity... Perhaps Hovhaness had Hinako's voice in mind. During the middle section, the exquisitely contoured melody soars effortlessly above a background of gentle triplets, eventually fading out completely as the sound of crickets slowly becomes a part of the listener's consciousness.

But the real story is that during the time Alan was composing this piece, he was hearing a noise in his head that sounded like crickets. We tried to do something about it, but the doctors didn't know what it was. August 1, 1995, was finally the first time he didn't know who I was for a short time. Then we knew what was happening to him for sure. This music is a premonition of a tragic love song. His love for me was slowly fading away and taken over by the sound of crickets that was surely not his choice.

And I remain alone, remembering for both of us, his great love for me.

Alan's Lost Manuscripts

♪

It happened in 1980 after our concert tour. We went to New York and stayed at our usual hotel, the Wellington. It was located in the center of New York City and was a very convenient location for Alan because his publishers and BMI were within walking distance from there. But the hotel was old, and every time we stayed there something broke down. So that we would not have any more inconveniences, we decided to stay in an expensive room on the top floor, thinking that they must be different from the cheap rooms downstairs that we used to stay at. There were only a few rooms there and they were spacious. As soon as we got in the room I tried to figure out how to use the double lock to the door, but it was so outdated that it did not have any system and worked only by chance. I was trying, but finally Alan said to me, "I beg of you, please don't try anymore, and don't use the double lock." He was impatient because that night we had an engagement to go out to dinner with my mother and daughter Joni, who were living at that time in New York.

The four of us left the room in a hurry, without double-locking the door, and went out to a Korean restaurant called *Arirang*, near Patelson's Music Store. The restaurant was very small and narrow but very high class. Usually Korean food is very hot and primitive; using lots of red pepper and garlic, but the food in this place was modified to fit our taste. We all enjoyed their exquisite food.

When Alan and I returned to our hotel room, we immediately noticed Alan's briefcase was missing. It had Alan's symphony that he had just finished composing, and I was going to bring it to the publisher the next day. Also, my box of earrings and camera and other things were stolen, but I did not know that until later.

I don't know how this news got to them, but the next day a TV news crew came to our hotel room and interviewed us while the camera was rolling. Later I saw myself on the television, desperately telling what had happened with terrible broken English.

Alan thought that his flashy new briefcase I bought him before the trip had attracted a thief. He may not have known the value of the manuscript and may have thrown it away in a trash can. Alan randomly opened the neighborhood garbage cans, searching for his symphony. According to one of his publishers, you can get any hotel room key on the black market in New York. So our disaster was unavoidable, but penthouses were the most attractive targets for thieves.

Alan never found his manuscript, but he composed another symphony (No. 40) and said, "My new symphony is even better than the one I lost." This was one of his disasters, and there was another big one to follow.

Alan had so many compositions that he wanted all of them to be published. Realistically, no single publisher could handle the volume of his music. Then we had an idea to make our own music publishing company so we could take care of all his unpublished music. He named the company "Mt. Tahoma Publishing Company, Inc." and he stated in their brochure, "*Mount Tahoma Music Publishers* is named after the original American Indian name for Mount Rainier. The Indian name means *The Mountain That Was God.* This is my publishing venture to offer the public some of my new music as well as some of my older unpublished music." He also said to me, "It is an insult to call this ancient mountain by some American politician's name."

In 1977, we found a publisher called Alexander Broude in New York to distribute music belonging to our company, including music copied from Alan's manuscripts as well as his published music books. Broude was a very new company and had handled little music at that time. Just before the contract was signed, we had a meeting at Broude. Robert Bregman was the young president of the company, and others were there. During the meeting, I questioned Bregman, and that upset him; then I knew he was not completely honest with us. But instead, Alan was upset with me because he thought I might jeopardize the project and told me not to come to the next meeting, so I had to promise I would shut my mouth.

When Alan wanted to do something for his music, he was in a hurry and never stopped to think of the consequences. He trusted people without asking questions or getting anything in writing. Earlier in our marriage, as soon as he heard of a possible commission over the telephone, his inspiration came ahead of him and he started to compose, even before the contract came. Some of them never came through and he had many painful episodes because of his "hyper-eagerness."

He kept his original manuscripts at Independent, which was a New York printer. When Alan took me there, I was surprised. His manuscripts were in one of their filing cabinets marked "Hovhaness," but anybody could have taken his music because it was not even locked.

One day, Sahan Arzruni, an Armenian pianist, called Alan from New York and said to him that some Armenian sponsor was interested in recording *all* Hovhaness music. I thought it was too good to be true, but Alan was excited and wanted to go to New York immediately; so we went, only to find they were supporting Arzruni to make records of *him* playing Hovhaness piano music and not Alan's orchestral pieces. Arzruni did not tell him the whole story, or Alan did not ask.

On June 9, 1977, Mt. Tahoma and Broude reached a distribution agreement and our business had started rolling. In 1980, we renamed the company Fujihara Music Co., Inc. Again, this was Alan's inspiration. He always loved Japan and wanted to be entwined with it. Fujihara was my maiden name, and he thought it was a beautiful name. Mt. Fuji is the most beautiful mountain in Japan, and my name means "Slope of Mt. Fuji" in Japanese.

Alan started sending his manuscripts to Broude, and his reason was that in order to make the copies, they needed the originals. Bill Sisson was the young man in charge of music and took care of Alan's music. He seemed knowledgeable about orchestral music and understood Alan's music language. From this relationship, our relationships with Broude blossomed. Bregman respected Alan, and he was proud to be Alan's agent. Many of Alan's commissions came linked from Broude.

One of the commissions was Symphony No. 34 for bass trombone and strings. In 1980, when it premiered at Lincoln Center in Alice Tully Hall, Bregman, his newly wedded wife, and all the Broude staff were present.

After the concert, Bregman took all of us to a restaurant. His wife encouraged me to order a whole lobster dinner, and then she helped me eat it!

Fujihara Music Co. published symphony scores and piano books, a total of twelve different books. Two of them were made through Broude, but all were paid for by Alan.

One day in 1986, without warning, we had a call from Verona Music. They said they could not acquire music from Broude, so they came to us to get help. After our frantic search, we discovered Broude had gone bankrupt and was no longer in business. Sources informed us that Bregman owned Broude jointly with another person named Lefferts, and Bregman sold his share to him around 1983. Bregman could not collect $100,000 from Lefferts; therefore Bregman, being a lawyer, sued him. According to Bregman, it was the biggest lawsuit in New York, and it seemed he was proud of it. As a result, Broude went bankrupt.

Our immediate concern was, "Where is Alan's music?"

We found Bill Sisson's telephone number and immediately called him. He was already working at Boosey and Hawkes, the well-known music publisher. He was indifferent to what had happened to Alan's music, and his excuse was that he and Dean Streit, another person working with him at Broude's, were fired and had to leave the building the same day. He should have called Alan to let him know, but he didn't.

On the other hand, Bregman rescued only the music owned and published by Broude and had already distributed that music to Kalmus Music in Florida. He was surprised that Alan had been sending his original manuscripts. Earlier that year, Alan had considered sending the manuscript of his new concerto. I begged him not to until a copy had been made, but Alan was in a hurry to send it, he could not wait for just one week.

We could not find anyone who knew or was responsible for Alan's manuscripts, so we hired David Guinn, a New York lawyer, to find Alan's music. After many documents back and forth and paying the fees, a result finally came.

David Guinn's letter of August 13, 1986:

> 575 Eighth Avenue. I spoke with the superintendent of the building (Manny). Unfortunately, I learned that when Broude closed shop they left practically everything behind. Manny told me that the landlord had to call in a rubbish man who spent an entire week cleaning out the offices. Filling

and dumping four large containers of rubbish. This included a "great deal of new sheet music." According to Manny, this material was disposed of as rubbish and cannot be reclaimed. I fear that this is what happened to your music.

As a result of his ordeal, Alan lost a large amount of hair from the top of his forehead. Every time I washed his hair, a handful of hair fell off and I could see his scalp through his thin hair.

Alan learned a lesson from this and realized he had to pay attention to my logic and intuitive opinion and, as he often said to me, "your Japanese smartness." This event came to pass, and we continued Fujihara Music Company—small but consistently.

After Alan's death in 2000, Dan Shelhamer suggested adding Hovhaness to the company name: Hovhaness-Fujihara Music Co., Inc. So, I did.

Alan's music lives on, as if they were his children. He left them with me for my care; our company has become my purpose of living.

As for Alan's lost music…

Broude kept thirty-six manuscripts; 2,610 music books were printed in New York. The 1,546 printed scores and piano books that we had printed in Seattle and sent to them all disappeared. I heard Bill Sisson was renting music from his home and Dean has a storage warehouse.

Now, the question is, who has Alan's manuscripts?

I think somebody is hiding his manuscripts underground, as an investment, waiting until the right time to bring them out.

Alan said that what had been done to his music was a criminal act. What do you think?

I think that this is a fault of the American legal system; anybody can get away from their financial responsibility in the name of "bankruptcy."

After all this…

In the year 2000, all of Alan's pieces that were owned by Bregman and distributed through Kalmus Music were destroyed by a big flood in Florida; fortunately, I have one copy of each of them that was lost.

Now, in 2011, over twenty years have passed, and Alan has been dead for eleven years. I unexpectedly heard from Mr. Bregman; he now has an important position with Morgan Stanley Smith Barney in New York City. He has generously returned the rights for all of Alan's music he owned, eight pieces including a piano book that had been published by Broude.

*The agent for composers and songwriters to collect fees from the performance and/or broadcast of their music.

**There is a difference between publishing and distribution. If a company has published music, it means they print it themselves and take over the rights to that music, and then they have an obligation to pay royalties from the sale of the music to the composer. If they only distribute the music, the ownership remains with the composer or publisher, and they sell the music for him/them.

Lou Harrison – Alan's Friend, Colleague, and Competitor

An all-Hovhaness concert took place in town hall in New York City on June 17, 1945. Lou Harrison talks about that concert in his interview on the CBC program "Alan Hovhaness Profile," broadcast in 1994:

> I think that he is himself, alone, actually. And one of the proofs of that was the occasion which I first heard his works was in the Town Hall in New York, many, many years ago, during the war.
>
> I was a reporter for the *New York Herald Tribune* then and one of my frequent guests was John Cage, and so we both went to that concert and it opened. We were quite startled by the beautiful opening cello line of the "Lousadzak" piano concerto and we thought any minute it would break, but it didn't and the whole piece went through, perfectly beautifully and then the second piece—we thought, well this had to be a dud, it can't be that good all the way through and, on the contrary, it was. The "Tzaikerk" violin concerto was equally beautiful as "Lousadzak," with string orchestra and some percussion.
>
> At the end of it, we went out for the intermission and the nearest thing I have ever been to one of those artistic riots was going on in the foyer. The Americanists, the French-Americanists, the Viennese twelve-tone people, you know, were there and they were all fighting because here comes someone from Boston nobody ever heard of doing completely neither, so it was really quite a surprising thing. John was very excited too and he went to the backstage to meet him after that premiere and he found a lady sitting on the stair saying, "I am going to marry him, I am going to marry him." She did, indeed—later.
>
> And then I went to the *Tribune* and wrote a rave review because it was a dazzling and a wonderful thing and I was delighted beyond words—well not actually beyond words because I did write the review.
>
> That was our introduction and I became better acquainted with him. John went to Boston to get better acquainted and then, when Alan came to New York I became better acquainted with him too. We had a community of music interest which was very pleasurable, indeed.

That was how Alan and Lou Harrison met and their friendship started.

Alan was a struggling composer in Boston, teaching composing and piano (some of them were beginners, so young that their mothers left them for a little while for Alan to babysit—that's what Alan felt.) as an organist in Watertown church in Boston. At the same time, he was performing with two Armenian sisters, Maro Ajemian (piano) and Anahid Ajemian (violin). Those young sisters were well-known musicians in that region. Alan was, as always, prolific; he composed much music for them, so they took his compositions for granted.

After that performance in town hall, Lou Harrison, the newspaper critic, became a composer. I assume he must have been a composer, but he was taking much of his time as a newspaper reporter to make a living. But after he heard Alan's music, he must have become inspired to compose and became an "orientalist" like Alan. According to Alan, he borrowed Alan's scores and studied them. Later, Lou got a commission from the Ajemian sisters and got paid a commission fee from them.

Alan had composed much music for the Ajemian sisters, yet he never got paid and they never thought of paying Alan. Unlike Lou, Alan was a born composer; he could not do anything else except music, and he was practically starving, yet Lou got paid. Alan was very much hurt. The Ajemian sisters thought that performing Alan's music was doing him a favor. Alan never forgot that event, and he complained to me about it even fifty years later. In spite of his resentment, Alan and Lou's friendship lasted the rest of their lives.

Both of them were "orientalists," even though they were so different. Alan loved and admired Mozart and Lou was for Bach. Lou had the look of the actor Orson Welles, at least when I knew him. According to Alan, when Lou was younger, he was the beauty of the gay circle. He was kind and spoke flowery, with distinguished English. On the other hand, Alan was tall and slender and shy and looked like the painter El Greco. In spite of his fragile appearance, he had a determination to compose, whether he would live or die.

In Lou's CBC interview, he talked about Alan's former Italian wife. "The lady sat on the stair saying, 'I am going to marry him, I am going to marry him.'" She did, indeed—later. The story became the gossip of the gay circle, a peasant-like Italian woman coming to Alan's concert and saying, "I am going to marry him." Everybody thought she was crazy, but Alan did marry her. He became their laughingstock; even forty years later that story has not been forgotten by them. (But Alan could not say anything about Lou, so he told me the stories. May I write them? I hope Lou doesn't mind.)

In New York in the 1940s, the artistic circle (art, music, theatre), everybody knew about any happenings. One of their favorite gossips was "Lou froze at the breakfast table." One woman (who was known to only go for men who rejected her) had a crush on Lou, knowing he was gay. She forced him to sleep with her, but the next morning, at the breakfast table in the restaurant, he froze (realizing who he had slept with—a girl!).

During one period of his life, he was trying to change himself to like girls and was undergoing psychotherapy. During that time, a girl from the country came to New York, intending to marry him, not knowing he was gay. Everybody in his circle was worried; they thought she should be notified that he was gay. Despite Lou's efforts to change himself, he could not be converted. He was disappointed, but John Cage comforted him, saying, "Lou! All forms of love are beautiful." (John was the guru and philosopher of the circle.)

Lou went to Japan, but Japan was not his style. They were a polite-speaking people, but not knowing what they were thinking inside of them, he thought Japan was like a theatre. But Alan loved that theatre, along with their ancient music and girls. But Lou loved Korea; they were emotional and even crude. He loved their temperament and felt very much at home (especially after Japan) and spent a romantic evening on the beach with a beautiful Korean boy (Lou's words).

In the early 1960s, Alan got a letter from Dr. Lee Hye-ku, the Korean music scholar. In his letter, he said, "Lou has married Bill. They are happily together, their shaving mugs side by side." Lou must have had many friends before, but this was his marriage, and they were together for over thirty-three years until Bill's death.

I met Lou and Bill when we were in California at Alan's concerts. They faithfully came to meet us every time we were there. Among the people who came to see Alan regularly in California were Scott MacClelland, Gary Beswick the violinist and his wife, Charles Amirkhanian the avant-garde composer, Vahe Aslanian the choral conductor, Charles Uomini and his wife Dr. Uomini, and Alan's daughter Jean Nandi.

For the Cabrillo Festival in Aptos, California, we were there between August 16–31, 1981. During the preview concert, Alan conducted his new symphony, No. 43, op. 334. It also featured the composition of a woman composer, Pauline Oliveros. She sat in the center of the stage in a mediating position and hummed one pitch and changed to other pitches. Then the crowd of people on the stage and in the audience joined in and moved around the stage and increased in number. She controlled the people by just sitting. The newspaper review made a big thing about her composition, and Alan's more traditional melodic music was treated as passé. Music at that time of the festival was going away from pure music towards "gimmicks." (A composer no longer has to write music.)

The festival performances were done in different churches and halls around Santa Cruz. Alan's Symphony No. 2 "Mysterious Mountain" was at Cabrillo college Theatre on August 21, and "Fra Angelico" was performed on August 28. My performance was at the Holy Cross Church in Santa Cruz. I sang Alan's compositions composed for me. One movement from Symphony No. 38 "Lullaby," op. 314, "O Joy at the Dawn of Spring" from his opera "Tale of the Sun Goddess Going Into the Stone House," op. 323, and Marina's "Song of Healing" from the opera "Pericles," op. 283.

During the festival, we stayed at Lou's new home, which was under construction. That was a generous offer by Lou to help us and the Cabrillo Festival, but Alan was unhappy staying there. A floor was not yet finished along with everything else. Alan complained about inconveniences every inch of the way. But his discomfort was not just that. He was uncomfortable being surrounded by "men's atmosphere." All the paintings on the wall were of men; he was used to "girlish" surroundings.

I did cook for him in the kitchen, but, it being an unfinished house, ants came in and made lines everywhere. I had to get an ant trap to control them. I didn't like them, especially the California ants—they were very aggressive.

Bill was finishing the house, one piece at a time by himself, getting the materials from (it looked like to me) a demolition site, very interesting old antique tiles, etc., to put in his new home. I thought I used to like chandeliers, but after I saw their chandeliers, I didn't like them anymore. No wonder, I realized theirs were old and made out of glass, not crystal, and some of them were even plastic.

During the time we were staying in Lou's house, we ate at a restaurant every night. Our favorite was a Japanese restaurant called Persimmon House (Kakino-uchi). One day, we invited Lou and Bill for dinner there. Strangely, Bill was very grouchy that night and complained the minute he got in and said their food was not even authentic Japanese. But, to the contrary, Lou was relaxed and enjoying the evening with the food and our company; it was as if they were intentionally annoying each other. Alan and I thought it was an excellent restaurant; that evening, the owner offered to give me anything from their sale case, in appreciation of Alan and me. I asked for small, navy-blue ceramic earrings.

I think Bill was getting old and grouchy, even before that day. One evening, at Vahe Aslanian's house, Lou and Bill came late for our gathering, and the minute they came in, Lou said to Bill, "You are always doing this," complaining bitterly in a loud voice. We all were smiling and noticing, they are just like us, a married couple, even though they look different. Later Alan said to me, "Lou complains, just like a big wife."

Previously, in July of 1980, Alan received a letter from Vincent McDermott, the composer and music professor of Lewis and Clark College in Portland, Oregon:

> Lou Harrison suggested I write you. He felt sure you'd enjoy doing a piece for a concert of his in Portland scheduled for February 18, 1981. Lou's visit devolves upon a central Javanese Gamelan newly arrived here and my insistence upon using it for traditional Javanese music as well as for whatever composers here would like to make of it…
>
> Lou's imagination and graciousness, though I hope not presumptuousness, in suggesting a piece of yours is a marvel. I hope you'll be able to accept though I fear there is no money, the grant and the budget were long ago fixed, but I can promise warmth, concern, travel and overnights, and hopefully even a touch of graciousness on our part.

Alan accepted his invitation without pay because of Alan's loyalty to his friend Lou. On February 15, 1981, we drove to Portland for the concert and, after three hours of driving, we finally got to the school, but the place was desolate, and it took a long time for anybody to come to help us. Eventually, somebody opened the school guest house, where we were supposed to stay; then we went in and found the kitchen and two bedrooms in the opposite sides of the house. I chose the nicer bedroom for us and settled in; later, the school orchestra manager took us to a nice restaurant near a stream.

The next day, Lou and Bill arrived, and they found out we had taken the better room for ourselves, and they seemed unhappy. (But why not—I am a girl. Don't I have the advantage over men, and shouldn't Alan get that advantage by having me?) I prepared food in that kitchen for Alan and me for the whole time we were there.

For the concert, he composed a song for me to sing, using his poem "Stars Sing Bell Songs," accompanied by the *gamelan* orchestra. He also composed "Pleaides" with the same instrumentation. (His notes: "It is to the beautiful constellation of suns or stars with that name.")

Alan's interest in the sky started when he was a child. At the age of four, he made his first attempt at composing, using his own creation, an eleven-line staff. His mother, who had a small harmonium organ, said she could not play it, so he gave up composing for astronomy until the age of seven. Later, while still in school, he built an observatory treehouse and watched the stars.

At the performance, I wore a silk dress made in India. The dress was light blue with pink flowers spotted all over the dress, and with an intricate design at the bottom of the sleeves and skirt.

Alan loved my clear but warm coloratura voice; he used it as the distant twinkling stars effect in my song. Then came "Pleaides," and this piece gives me the impression of traveling between the stars in the universe.

Then came McDermott's piece—it was his grand, major work. We realized his intention of inviting Alan to his concert (in order to use Alan's name to draw the audience) to show off his (McDermott's) major work against Alan's more modest composition, written in between his other commissions. Despite the difference in the scale of their works, the audience loved Alan's two pieces; they sparkled like jewels in the sky. (Precious things come in small boxes.)

At the back of the hall, the procession started. Lou and Bill proceeded into the hall and onto the stage under a colorful canopy, in Javanese style. It was lavishly staged by Bill to entertain the audience. The concert concluded with Lou's elaborate *gamelan* compositions.

Later, Alan arranged his two *gamelan* pieces for percussion instruments, glockenspiel, two vibraphones, timpani, and tam-tam. He did so because a *gamelan* orchestra is hard to come by but not the standard percussion orchestra, and he wanted to make it possible for anybody to perform the music.

One evening, the composers and school music staff gathered at our guest house. We had just bought pastries from a downtown Portland pastry shop, so I treated the guests with coffee and pastry. But Lou was burnt by the hot coffee I had made; I always felt guilty about that incident.

The last time we saw Lou and Bill was at the Cornish College of the Arts in Capitol Hill near downtown Seattle. We met them at a reception the day before a concert. The next day, January 25, 1992, we had dinner together at a Japanese restaurant near the school.

The concert program included two pieces of Lou's and two of John Cage's. My mother and I liked Lou's oriental piece, but Alan thought it was too much like his own music. The last piece of the program was John Cage's "Ryonanji" (a famous Japanese Buddhist temple "*Ryuanji*"). There was no melody, just occasional percussion and occasional voice, slowly screeching up. It reminded me of the most sophisticated ancient Japanese music. As soon as the piece was over, my mother stood up (a small, white-haired Japanese old woman) and shouted in a loud voice, "That is not a *Ryuanji*," with her protest. Alan and I had to quiet her down.

That was the last time we saw Lou and Bill together. Lou died February 2, 2003, following Bill's death on March 1, 2000. Bill (William Calvig) was a musician, instrument builder, engineer, and mountaineer. (Dr. Barbara Petersen of BMI gave me this information.)

Lou took marriage very seriously; he did not pay any attention to me before Alan and I were married, but he respected me when I became Alan's wife.

I would like to close this story with Lou Harrison's poem sent to Alan for his eightieth birthday concert at Carnegie Hall on October 6, 1991. It was read by Martin Bookspan at the opening of the concert, along with Dominick Argento's letter to Alan.

FOR THE HOVHANESSIAD: LINES OF 8 & 6
IN HONOR OF ALAN HOVHANESS

Alan's self is slim and rhythmic,
eyes lovely, large and dark.
He stands before us in golden
fields, Hinako with him,
sighting beyond us into still
& central quietude.
Mountains he loves, & mountainous
his art & his music
rise in memory around us.
He lifts us cups of tune
sung full fresh from fountains worldwide
of the human music.
Fecund; yet he went thought end-time—
ripped away old music
to hunt ancestral instruments,
hunt song & mode & time
to find a full-time house of heart
where melody has hearth.
All are tender, & thus we slash
in rage against ourselves.
He can endure the tenderness,
& sings in streaming tune,
in roving triads of chorale,
the arch-lyric beauty.

14. VIII.'86, Cheltenham

2/11/07

Alan's Oratorio "Revelations of St. Paul"

Last night, while I was sorting out the pile of papers on my kitchen table, one letter caught my eyes. It was from Vance Wolverton, the professor and choral director who had written about Alan's choral music in a choral journal in the past. Then I found another article about Alan written by a man called David W. Music.

Alan wrote much music for the voice oratorios and choral music. Then one particular piece of music came to my mind—"Revelation of St. Paul," his large oratorio for three soloists, chorus, and full orchestra, composed in 1980. It had been commissioned by Donald V. R. Thompson, a young businessman from New York. He was a board member of Musica Sacra, a well-known sacred choral group in New York. He wrote the libretto (words taken straight from a new translation of the bible, passages from Paul); he was specifically interested in this particular subject because no major choral work had been written on the text of Paul. He chose Alan to be the composer for the work from among other prominent composers of the century and expected Alan to write a grand work, like Verdi's "Requiem." It was to be performed by Musica Sacra and conducted by their own conductor, Richard Westenburg.

In a letter from Thompson dated February 8, 1980, he states:

> Dick Westenburg has asked if you could use the 4 soloist voices in your score. He also wished that the orchestra be as large as possible (or as you personally feel could be easily playable.) (26 violins?) For the strings.
>
> The libretto is composed of important passages in Paul's epistles from both the Modern English and the Revised Standard Editions. No words were changed or added in the entire text of the libretto.
>
> As per our brief phone call, my only request and Dick's also was a double chorus—Adult and Boys choir; moreover, I was hoping for perhaps even 3 timpani for a dramatic ending; one person at Musica Sacra was wondering if a harp and soloist could be one part, but I told them that you have your own ideas and don't want to diverge from your concept.

But Alan was not supposed to write a requiem because of my superstition surrounding them. If he would write one, it might become his last work (he might die), based on the story of Mozart's "Requiem" that Alan told me. Mozart had been asked by a mysterious commissioner to write a requiem to be performed at the man's wife's memorial. But his real reason has come under suspicion; he may have planned to use Mozart as a ghost writer and then credit himself as the composer of the requiem.

At that time, Mozart was very ill—actually, he was dying. He felt he had been writing his own requiem. In his own words, "My head is in turmoil. The vision of that unknown stranger is ever before my eyes. I see him entreating me, urging me and impatiently demanding the work." He had composed many monumental works of music in his lifetime, but he could not finish this last work; his pupil Sussmeyer completed it. So there is a controversy, how much is Mozart's work? It continues even to this day.

This story scared me, so I made Alan promise not to write a requiem. But how could he refuse such a superb opportunity (and also the considerable amount of the commission fee)? So, in order for Alan to write it, the title of the work had to be compromised, so it was changed to "Revelations of St. Paul." (My watchful thinking paid off, and Alan lived another twenty years after the completion of the oratorio.)

Thompson's libretto was long and wordy. Alan was familiar with the King James flowery translation and found the new one awkward. He said, "This is like an insurance man's sales pitch."

"If you give to charity, give with all your heart;
If you are a leader, exert yourself to lead;
If you are helping others in distress, do it cheerfully.
Love in all sincerity, loathing evil and clinging to the good.
Let love for our brotherhood breed warmth of mutual affection.
With unflagging energy, in ardor of spirit, serve the Lord.
Let hope keep you joyful..."

So I told him not to use all the words, but just write music for the passages that were usable. To my amazement, he devoured the whole libretto, set them to his melodies, and intentionally used awkward words to create very interesting rhythms. I think that in itself makes this oratorio a masterpiece.

The oratorio is made up of twenty-six choruses and arias plus a prelude. Alan composed two soprano arias for me:

No. 6 "If You Confess With Your Lips."
No. 10 "If We Live, We Live For the Lord"

His intention was for me to get to sing in the oratorio, but he could not tell anybody before the commission had been signed. If he would have demanded his wish, he could have jeopardized his commission. In the music business, the composer is supposed to be the most important person, but the actual power is with the conductor and the performing organization. Once the Finnish composer Sibelius said to Alan, "We are at the mercy of the conductor."

So what Alan did was to compose two arias so high that no other singer could sing them. In the first one he put eight high Cs, one high D, and an E above high C; in the other aria he put two high Cs and a D. I had a very high voice, not just an occasional high voice, but with a high tessitura (sustained high voice). So those songs were custom-made for my voice.

After the completion of the oratorio, Alan told the conductor of his wish for me to sing the soprano arias at the premiere performance, thinking the conductor could not find any other singer to sing them and he would then ask me to sing them. But the conductor turned down Alan's request.

Westenburg's letter:

> I hope it does not cause you concern that it is not possible for Hinako to sing the part which, as you told me, you thought would be very good for her. We do have a contractual obligation to Rita Shane, who is truly a wonderful coloratura, and one who will undoubtedly do a splendid job, and a job that will please you. She is with the Metropolitan Opera, and has performed important roles also with Covent Garden and the San Francisco Opera companies; and also, she has performed the other work on the program requiring a soprano, namely the Schubert Mass in G (which she did with Commission in Baltimore within the last season or two). I know you will understand the necessity of our honoring this commitment. Also, we had approached her because of her fine reputation in this city. For this season and the next, we were lucky enough to get a grant to enhance the quality of our soloists, and the donors were especially eager that we use soloists who were well established in New York. As I say, I know you will be pleased; she knows your music, of course, and is looking forward to learning and performing this newest of works.
>
> As for the title, I will review the libretto and decide from one of the ones you suggested; and it will certainly NOT be called a Requiem!

On January 28, 1981, Alan's oratorio was premiered with a lavish production at Avery Fisher Hall in Lincoln Center—Rita Shane, soprano, Vinson Cole, tenor, William Parker, baritone, full chorus and orchestra. It was the grandest oratorio performance of Alan's life. There was superb singing by Cole and Parker, but the poor soprano, her dramatic coloratura voice could not be kept high to sing like an angel's voice from heaven. Everybody noticed that her voice did not fit the songs and that she was in obvious trouble. After the concert, many people came to Alan and asked, "Was that soprano chosen by you?"

In spite of that, the performance was a great success and was broadcasted live. But as far as the soprano arias were concerned, even a Metropolitan Opera singer could not please Alan. He had composed those arias for me; while he was composing them, he was hearing my voice, a bird-like, petite voice. I was not given an opportunity to sing in that performance or another of Alan's grand works, "The Way of Jesus," or his never-performed opera "Pericles."

It was as if he had composed those songs for me in vain, but today I am finding greater meaning in this. Even though he died, his love lives on—on the pages of his music, as if the songs are his testimony of love to me.

There was a dispute over splitting the future royalties between Alan and Musica Sacra. They claimed Thompson had the copyright for his libretto, so they should have half of the royalties, on his behalf. But the conclusion was that any word taken from the bible or its translations could not be called a libretto, so Musica Sacra lost its argument. Since then, there has been no performance of this work by them. They claimed they had lost the orchestra parts, which they had copied and, as a courtesy, should have returned a copy of the parts back to the composer. So Alan did not even get any parts. Thompson, who had put so much money into this work, again paid for the copyist to make new orchestra parts for Alan for future performances.

My inspiration to write about this oratorio did not stop here; I would like to promote this oratorio. I hope I will live to see the performance of this work once more, on behalf of Alan, the composer.

Memory of Chandelier

A memory of a chandelier brings me back to the year 1981…

Alan received a commission to compose for trumpet and organ from St. James Armenian church in Watertown, Massachusetts. (Alan was organist there in his early days.) When they commissioned him, they may have thought that Alan would write another "Prayer of St. Gregory," written for trumpet and strings, his masterpiece.

We were in Watertown on May 13 for their fiftieth anniversary and premiere of that new composition "To the Divine Fountain," sonata for trumpet and organ, op. 349. We were at rehearsal, and I was fascinated by a ceiling full of chandeliers. Father Davidian caught my interest in their chandeliers; he proudly spoke to me, "We Armenians love chandeliers. Every time we get a large contribution, we decide to buy another chandelier." It was a magical experience, looking at chandeliers in the church.

(I also love chandeliers, even though I am Japanese. Then I thought, "If the church thinks it is okay to have such a luxury, I may have one for myself, too.")

Then my memory goes back further, to a time when we were in New York City…

Alan and I were invited by the Armenian bass Ara Berberian, Metropolitan opera singer. His wife, Ginney, and her uncle were with us. They took us to the famous Tavern On the Green restaurant. The bare winter trees outside were all decorated by small lights, like Christmas trees, and as we stepped into the restaurant, there were hanging chandeliers covering all the ceiling. I stood there in amazement. Ara said every year all those chandeliers were cleaned by hand. Can you imagine how many people it takes to do this?

We sat under the chandeliers; after a while, Ara's wife, Ginney, pointed in the direction of the doorway. We all looked at the table close to the entrance; there in the doorway, we saw a woman standing, medium-dark skin and large-built in the bust. She was kissing every man she saw who came in the door. It was a curiosity for a while, but as we feared, she reached our table and sat beside Ara.

She behaved like she owned him, and Ara was interested in making conversation with her. I knew Ginney was not happy; her uncle was making a remark to her, "See what happens while you are at home!" Ara was a very outgoing person, and being a Met singer, he was away from home often. Her uncle was worried that if Ara got too much freedom, he might get into trouble, so he was trying to persuade her to go with her husband everywhere he went. And still, nobody seemed to do anything. Then the woman became more intrusive; now she kept on looking at Alan with peculiar interest. He sat quietly in between people, as if he were trying to hide, his eyes downcast to avoid eye contact with her so as not to be targeted by her. Then suddenly, something came over me and I said to Ginney, "I'll beat her up if she tries to get Alan!" Ginney was very surprised to hear such a "macho" statement come from me, and besides, I am a small Japanese, half the size of that "kissing woman." I was thinking to myself, "If that woman touches Alan, I will beat her up by surprise. I am smart enough to win this duel, I know it. Then, tomorrow's *New York Times* headline would be:

Composer Alan Hovhaness's Wife Beats Up
Woman in the Tavern On the Green.

I was ready to participate in this action, but I didn't have to, for the story decrescendoed by itself.

Ever since my experience with the chandeliers, I have collected my own, one by one, and named them Fountain, Magic Lamp, Chinese Bird Cage, Weeping Flower, Gala, Contessa, and Lady Strauss. Our last chandelier I called "Crown." It sits on a king's head: Alan's.

Come With Me to the Place Alan Took Me – Symphony No. 46 "To the Green Mountains"

I have been thinking about the trip Alan and I took in 1981, from April 28 to May 21, from Vermont to New Hampshire, Boston to New York. As usual, before I started to write, I looked through my records—concert programs, airplane tickets, and hotel bills—every receipt of that trip. Then I remembered one of Alan's photos I took during that trip. He was standing in front of Mt. Washington, but when I found the photos, to my surprise, I discovered Alan's writing "Mt. Adams" with a pencil on the back of his photo. The mountain was Mt. Adams, not Mt. Washington. Then I opened the map of the New Hampshire Mountains and started to trace the route we took. My memory of the past began to open up, as if the past had always been there, just hidden under the lid, waiting to be opened. Now I realized that trip was the most important trip we had taken, and I had to record it as accurately as I could.

Call from the Conductor

In January of 1980, we were in New York for the premiere of Alan's Symphony No. 34 for bass trombone and strings at Alice Tully Hall in Lincoln Center. A telephone call came to our hotel room; it was from Alan's old acquaintance Guigui, the conductor of the Vermont Symphony. He wanted Alan to conduct his own music in Guigui's 1981 concerts, with a fee of $2,000 plus expenses—hotel, airplane, etc. Alan accepted the offer on the telephone, but when the contract came to be signed by Alan, the amount of the fee was only $1,000. I was surprised at the difference and told Alan to talk to the conductor before he would sign it, but the contract disappeared. After I questioned him repeatedly, Alan confessed he had signed it and sent it out without telling me.

He said he really wanted the job and did not want it jeopardized by arguing with the conductor. By the time I talked to the symphony, their attitude was, "You already signed it, too late now." (In the past, Alan had made many bad business judgments, composing commissions without contracts, with a result of no payments, etc. The worst time was when he trusted the wrong music distributor and lost many of his manuscripts as well as printed music. So I had to come into his business to protect him.)

But now I realize, regardless of the small pay, how important that concert was. Alan had all the second half of the concert to himself, and he could let me sing his music, which he had composed for me. Plus, he already had the inspiration to compose a new symphony (which

I did not know about at the time) for this concert. After all, Vermont was the region of his childhood and the place of his nostalgic memories.

We headed to Vermont on April 28, stopping at New York for one night and then to Vermont for the rehearsals on the thirtieth and concert on May second.

Symphony No. 46 "To the Green Mountains"

At the performance, I could not see Alan conducting his new symphony because my singing performance came right after his symphony; I was waiting backstage in the wings. He conducted his premiere of Symphony No. 46 "To the Green Mountains," then I sang four of his songs, one from his oratorio "The Way of Jesus" and three from the opera "Pericles." His part of the concert concluded with his "Mysterious Mountain."

Alan started composing Symphony No. 46 after he had heard from the conductor, he composed it without a commission. It was written by his sheer inspiration. During that period, he had been composing mostly for commissions, but he never paid any attention to the fees, for he just wanted to compose. And even that was not enough—he composed between commissions! He said to me, "I have to write the music I have always wanted to write!" That is the case for this symphony. He never forgot the time he visited his uncle's house in New Hampshire when he was a youngster, where he saw the White Mountains and also the Green Mountains in Vermont. He climbed many hills and mountains, so he had to write about them, his childhood memories of mountains.

The symphony was written in four movements:

I. Prelude
II. Hymn and Fugue – the "painting" of the mountains.
III. River and Forest Music – this beautiful melody came from his opera "Pericles," composed in 1975, written for a chorus of women's voices, sopranos and altos. Right after he finished composing this chorus, he showed it to me and we recorded it as a duet. I sang soprano and my friend Leona sang alto, and Alan accompanied on the piano. He used this melody in the symphony because the performance of the opera did not materialize. He arranged it for the oboes to take the place of the voices.
IV. Mountain Thunderstorm and Thanksgiving Hymn – he had always wanted to compose storm music, like composers in the past. He told me, "Rossini composed a storm in the William Tell Overture, Sibelius in 'The Tempest';" so Alan wanted to compose his storm, the storm over the New Hampshire mountains. The symphony ends with a hymn to the beauty of God-given nature.

He began by calling it "Vermont Symphony," even though he officially gave it the name "To the Green Mountains." In his mind he must have composed this symphony for Vermont—but are they worthy of it? I thought they would be honored and proud that Alan had composed a symphony for their state, but I never have heard anything from them since, or of any new performance of the symphony.

Meeting with Gloria Shaw

At the concert we met Aram Gharabekian, an Armenian composer/conductor from Boston, along with his friend. We also met Gloria Shaw—Alan had known her mother, a violinist. Once upon a summertime, when he was a young man, she invited him to her summer house in Vermont. They played music together and other musicians joined them. Alan accompanied them on the piano, and I could tell how he enjoyed that summer.

At Gloria's House

Gloria was between Alan's and my age; she was in her sixties then. She had met Alan once when she was very young.

After the concert, she took us to her home. Her large house had been built according to her own plan, with an enormous living room and entrance room to receive a large number of guests. There was a narrow spiral staircase to the upstairs bedrooms; it was the only way to get upstairs. Contrary to the large living room, the kitchen and dining room next to it were unusually small.

The day after we got there, Gloria gave a party for us, not in the large, spacious living room but in that kitchen/dining room area, the smallest rooms in the house. Many plain wood tables were placed there and five people sat around each of them. Alan and I were separated; Gloria sat with Alan, along with her other important guests. It was very unusual to be separated from Alan, but some people do that so a husband and wife can get acquainted with the others for a change, but Gloria's idea was definitely to have Alan all to herself. I sat with a retired conductor and others. I did the best I could, listening to the old conductor's lamentation on losing his wife.

After the party, we went into the room downstairs, on the other side of the study, the room we had not seen before. It had two twin beds on opposite sides of the room. Alan cried, then he dragged one bed and put them together, but he squeezed his body beside me and slept on my bed anyway, because he could not sleep on the crease between the two beds. He complained that he would much rather have stayed in a hotel.

The next day Gloria realized the bedroom was not working out for us and gave us the upstairs room. We went up there by the narrow spiral stairs. The room must have been occupied by a child before; it had a wooden rocking horse. Alan did not like that. Strangely, the bathroom across from the bedroom had just partial swinging doors in the middle, with the top and bottom open, and we did not like that either. On top of that, we did not have a car in the vast countryside of Vermont, and somehow we felt we had been confined by Gloria.

One evening, we invited her to the fish restaurant Ice House, a place we already knew about because the first day we had arrived in Vermont the manager of the Vermont Symphony took us there. The fish was very fresh, and, to my surprise, Gloria ate raw oysters. We enjoyed that restaurant very much. Alan and I felt our usual freedom there.

The last night of our stay, we sat in her dining room and talked. Gloria told us her story, which she really needed to tell. She was from a rich family, and she had married a young man and had children from him, but she had grown out of that marriage and lived with a famous playwright in New York. During a European trip, she met a rich businessman. He proposed to her, saying, "May I have your hand?" She married him, and he was the love of her life, but one day, without warning, he died from a heart attack. She was in despair, and at the end of that year after his death, she tried to kill herself, but she was saved by a psychologist. We realized that the man we saw in a picture with Gloria in her bedroom was the psychologist she had been speaking of. That was why she had put us in the room downstairs at first, but even though she had been sleeping with this psychologist, I thought she was still very much in love with her husband.

Finally the day came when we were free to leave her house. I don't know why we felt that way; we rented a car and off we went to our freedom.

During the concert in Vermont, we met the son of Vilem Sokol, the conductor of the Seattle Youth Symphony. The young man was playing violin in an orchestra and had been studying at Dartmouth College in Hanover. We talked about visiting him there, but Alan did not want to go out of our way to visit him. He wanted to go straight to New Hampshire, the real reason for his coming.

Mountain Behind Him – Mt. Adams

We left Middlebury, Vermont, on May 5 and drove across the state to St. Johnsbury and stayed there overnight. The next day we drove on Highway 2 and crossed over the state line to New Hampshire. From there we went into a mountain road between the White Mountains. Our first stop was at the side of the road where we could see a clear view of the snow-covered mountains. All the trees were still without leaves in May—spring comes late there. I took a picture of Alan in front of Mt. Washington. That's what I thought, but he corrected me, even after his death. It was Mt. Adams behind him—how important the names of mountains were to him.

How excited he was to come back to the place he loved! I feel his excitement, just looking at his photos.

Castle in the Woods

We continued to drive south, and I saw in the distance a big white building with a striking bright red roof, as if I were seeing an old European castle from the past. I was excited and wanted to see it. It was the "Mount Washington Hotel" in Bretton Woods. I was very attracted by it, so we got out of the car and Alan took a picture of me with the hotel behind. Alan had seen this building when he was a child. At the time, he and his parents were visiting his uncle in New Hampshire. They all went camping and Alan saw this red-roofed building in the distance with Mount Washington behind it. He was fascinated, so they camped at that spot. It was a magical place for both of us. Alan found the place once more, but this time we found it together.

North Conway

Then we proceeded to drive south between the mountains, following Highway 302 until we arrived at a town called North Conway on the edge of the mountains. Alan wanted to stay there for a while, to be near the mountains. We decided to stay at the Ledgewood Inn. There were twelve restaurants in one little town, and we could explore the White Mountain National Forest, driving north on Route 302. We ate at a different restaurant every night. Usually I don't remember the hotels we had stayed in, but I remember this one because there was a small, early American style wooden table in our room that I liked it very much. Alan and I sat at it and ate breakfast. I felt very cozy; it made me feel like we were a traditional couple, married for a long time. (During our early marriage, when people asked how long we had been married, we were so ashamed of not being married for a long time, so we added the number of years until we had passed ten years in our marriage.)

One morning we were sitting at the table and saw a small dog, so we went outside to pet him. Then a big collie dog across the courtyard looked at us and came toward us and chased the small dog away, forcing us to pet him. I was surprised about his obvious jealousy.

Mount Chocorua

One day we visited Lake Chocorua. There we saw Mount Chocorua across the lake, under the sky. This mountain had a characteristic shape with a hump at the top. Alan sat at the edge of the lake and composed while I drew the mountain, but soon we were attacked by an army of bugs occupying the surroundings of the lake. They chased us all the way to the car. Later, his music sketch became "Mt. Chocorua," sonata for piano. He completed it in March, 1982.

Program notes by Alan Hovhaness:

"Chocorua Mountain and lake are near the town of Chocorua, NH. It is a rocky peak of great majesty and beauty, towering above the mountain forest."

"Catamount" – View From Uncle's Farm

We left North Conway on May 9, drove around the north end of Lake Winnipesaukee, and got to Weir's Beach on the edge of the lake. We stayed there for another two nights and visited Pitts-Field, where his parents were buried. The village was empty, as if the place was abandoned by the people. Alan was astounded; it was not at all the way he had remembered. He thought what had happened was that all the young people had gone to the city and the old who were left there had died away. He did not take me to his parents' graves. I don't know what his reason was, but I assume, by the looks of the place, he did not want to feel sad and guilty, looking at his parents' graves not being taken care of.

Then we drove to his uncle's house, where he used to visit when he was a child. There we saw signs that somebody had been living there, but it was so rundown, not like the place it once was. To visit his uncle's house was one of the few happy times of his childhood. The beautiful dining room his uncle had added next to the house was all boarded up. Alan looked for the maple tree that had been destroyed by lightning, but he could not find the stump. The only thing left was a view of the Catamount to the south, overlooking from where his uncle's farm used to be.

His piano sonata "Catamount" is dedicated to me, but I didn't know it until recently; I was surprised to see my name "To Hinako" on the top of the title page. It is in six movements. The first is Mysterioso, the third is Grand View Farm (memory of his uncle's farm) and the fourth is Love Song.

Program notes by Alan Hovhaness:

"Catamount [shaped like a cat] is near Pittsfield, NH. An old farmer and sage lived near the top of Catamount and used to look through his field glasses at the magnificent view of the distant White Mountains. I used to climb Catamount many times in childhood."

To Boston – the Hotel Sheraton-Commander

On the eleventh, we drove straight south to Boston. There we met people from the Armenian church. They put us up in the Hotel Sheraton-Commander. We visited Boston many times over the years, and every time we went there, they put us up in the same hotel. The head of the hotel was Armenian, and he contributed his hotel room to the Armenian Societies for their guests, but we didn't know this until later, and we never had the honor of meeting him.

Watertown Church Where Alan Was Organist

Alan and I traveled to Watertown, Massachusetts, where Alan received a commission to write a trumpet and organ piece for St. James Armenian Apostolic Church, where Alan had been an organist when he was a young man. I think they were hoping to get another "Prayer of St. Gregory"(Alan's masterpiece for trumpet and strings, which he had composed in 1946 when he was thirty-five years old, inspired by the Armenian St. Gregory) for their fiftieth anniversary celebration, which had taken place on May 13, 1981. Alan named the composition "The Divine Fountain" and had completed it earlier that year.

We met Father Davidian, who had been communicating with us, and Zephyr Yazijian and her husband. She gave a party for us in her house. For Alan to come to Boston was a very important occasion for them. The time he was there in his youth he had just been an organist but, since then, he had become a well-known American composer and a hero to the Armenian people. At the party, a young woman came and expressed her appreciation of Alan. She was recalling that she had seen him at church when she was a child.

There were many Armenian foods. Alan had never gone for Armenian foods, especially a sweet baklava made of nuts and honey; Alan hated that. It was overly sweet to him, so we avoided it. (But in later years he changed his mind about baklava; he must have been prejudiced against it, having tried it only once.)

During the rehearsal at the church, I was fascinated by the many chandeliers covering the ceiling of the sanctuary. Father Davidian caught my interest in them and proudly said to me, "We Armenians love chandeliers; every time we get large contributions, we decide to buy another chandelier." It was a magical experience, looking at the chandeliers in the church. So after the trip I bought a chandelier. Now I have eight of them in my house, I have collected them one by one over a period of twenty years. I am sure Alan did not mind it because he was half Armenian.

At the Day of Celebration

The commemorative concert was given in the church sanctuary, and the program was dedicated to Alan's music. The anthems "*Getso Der*" and "*Djashou Sharagan*" were sung by the St. James Chorale. It was a surprise to Alan because he had forgotten the music had ever existed. When he was organist there, he had composed these anthems for the choir to use in the church services, using Armenian church texts. Next, his well-known clarinet piece "Lament" was played and then the premiere of "The Divine Fountain," with trumpet and organ. The second part of the concert opened with his "Partita" for organ, followed by the tenor solo "*Bahaban Amenaynee*," which means "Protector of All." They said this song had been sung in the church at every Lenten service and had become their church tradition.

I don't know how much music Alan had composed for the Armenian people in their language. In his early years, he composed so spontaneously (as always) and gave away his music. He could not make a living by his composing, so he took the job as the organist in the church.

He told me stories; during the worship service, he was thinking of his music in his head and composing between his organ playing. The Armenian services were very long (because Armenians were very talkative people; Alan himself was no exception), and they took all morning. Towards the end of the service, Alan could tell people were hungry and smelled the *shishkabob*, in their minds.

Alan also played organ for the wedding and funeral services for money. One day at a funeral service, he decided to do a musical experiment. He played some music in a certain mode (scale) to see how people would react; people became emotional and started to cry. Then he stopped and played again; sure enough, people started crying again. He learned by his experiment that some modes affect people's emotions in certain ways. I am sure he knew exactly which mode to put in his music to get an effect from us.

Alan talked about the Father of the church often: he was a tall, attractive man. Each morning he greeted Alan, saying, "*Abriss Hovhaness.*" (various meanings: "Long live Hovhaness," or "What a boy, Bravo," etc.). When Alan was directing the choir, the priest would stand behind him, imitating Alan's movements. He and Alan had a mutual fondness for each other. He was not like the other priest, he liked girls. Later Alan heard that he was married by a rich girl and gave up the priesthood.

Celebration and Reception

After the concert, we went into a large auditorium for their big fiftieth anniversary celebration, but it seemed as if it was centered on Alan, a celebration of his return. He and I were on the stage, and I was introduced to the people as Alan's wife. According to Alan's friend Dr. Gregory, people welcomed me with open arms and accepted me as Alan's wife (even though many people knew Alan had been married before).

Then Deran Dinjian, the former choirmaster and singer, came onstage. As soon as Alan saw him, he went to him and shook his hand passionately. After Deran's speech, he handed Alan the music "*Yar Nazani*," which Alan had composed in 1938 for bass-baritone. Alan spontaneously went to the piano and accompanied him, and Deran's rich voice filled the auditorium. It was the highest point of the great celebration and reunion.

After this impromptu performance, refreshments were brought in, people were vigorously helping themselves, and the large cake was getting smaller and smaller, yet Alan was still surrounded by a crowd of people, talking. I was afraid he would not get anything to eat after all that work, so I dished up a plate for Alan and held it for him. I didn't understand how they were so excited about Alan but never thought of his refreshment. Why didn't they give him the first piece of cake?

Memory of Deran Dinjian

Alan had spoken of Deran often; he was Alan's dear friend. His wife, Mariza, told me her recollection of Alan, a strange young composer who lived with a cat, and how they helped him by buying a new suit for Alan's debut concert in Jordan Hall (because Alan did not have the money for clothes nor did he care about his appearance). According to their daughter Sina (she had not been born yet but had heard the story from her parents), Alan needed money for his debut concert and people contributed money to him a little bit at a time. Every time he got a contribution, he said, "With this money, I can get one more musician for the concert." He never thought of spending the money for himself.

While we were there, Mariza assisted us by driving us places. That was a good opportunity for her to talk to Alan about her past and her lifetime of resentment.

Deran was a very handsome, likeable man with a good voice. Mariza was an opera singer, and Deran very much adored her because of this. She was on her way to the top professionally, but she had to choose between her career and becoming Deran's wife, she chose to become his wife. It was a long time ago, but it seemed to me, after all these years, she still was not sure if she had made the right decision or not.

At their wedding, Alan was the organist. Somehow, the bride-to-be did not show up in the ceremony for a long time. (She may have had second thoughts.) Alan had to pull out all kinds of music to play; after all, he had to entertain the church full of guests. But that marriage did last the longest time, and Alan complimented Deran for that.

Alan told me his painter friend Hyman liked Deran very much. After Deran had married, he came along with Mariza to see them. She had the physique of an opera singer, big and heavy. Alan and Hyman felt the air was thick and uneasy because of her presence.

I learned from Mariza that Deran had died in January of 2004.

Evening with Hyman Bloom, Alan's Best Friend

The next day, on the fourteenth, Alan called his artist friend Hyman Bloom and invited him to join us at a restaurant for dinner. We went to Ferdinand's Restaurant in downtown Cambridge.

Hyman was a well-known Boston painter and Alan's best friend. In the 1930s, when he was a "composer of no performance," Alan and Hyman met in the evenings and spent time together. One night, they met Herman di Giovanni in a Greek restaurant, where Giovanni was working as a waiter. He was a psychic, and he became Alan's spiritual teacher and guided him to finding a new direction of his composing. The three Bohemians supported each other, like the three musketeers, until Alan left for New York and Herman died on a Greek island.

Hyman came to the restaurant and was very excited to see Alan. He was short and black-haired, brown-eyed, and of Jewish descent. He was in his seventies, about the same age as Alan, but he made me think he was a young man. Like Alan, I think of them as "men without age." But he was very different from Alan, very independent. He could get along very well by himself, not like Alan, who could not even make coffee. Also, Hyman liked blond-haired girls and Alan only liked Japanese black hair. They talked and talked, ever so passionately. I wondered why he had never called or written to Alan.

After the dinner, we all went back to our hotel room and Hyman decided to call his wife, Stella. She was working at a Greek restaurant and was supposedly home by that time. We noticed Hyman was in trouble on the telephone, so we asked him what had happened. He was a changed man, and like a wet dog, he said, "I am in the dog house." What had happened was after Hyman left home, Stella called home to check up on him, for he was supposed to have been staying at home, painting. But he was not there, so Stella was frantically looking for him. When Alan called him, he got so excited, he forgot about being married and left home without telling his wife where he was going.

Hyman had married just recently, but he did not tell us. If Dr. Gregory had not told us, we would never have known about it. Hyman did not tell people about the marriage because, to him, marriage was personal—nobody else's business. When I called to congratulate him on his marriage, he did not say very much, so I asked him, "Is she blond?" Then he said, "No." Then I asked him what she was like. His answer was, "She is healthy."

Hyman was very nervous; he was not used to married life and behaved like he was a "free spirit." Stella was trying to make him a married man, so she put restrictions on him, but tonight it failed. Hyman was very miserable and could not help complaining, "Is it worth it?" (being married).

Then Stella came in the hotel room. She was a big Greek girl, much taller than Hyman, with a good-looking, articulated face like the Greek opera singer Maria Callas. Even though she was much younger than Hyman, it was very obvious she had control over him, but she was nice. She told Hyman she was worried about him; he should have just called her and told her where he was going.

We met them again the next day. This time they took us to another restaurant, and then we went to their studio apartment after dinner. Stella told me how their marriage came about. When she was working in a Greek restaurant, Hyman came to eat there often, so she had gotten to know him. One day, she dreamed that she was in his bed and knew the dream was a prophecy of her future. She visited him, and her dream came true.

E. Gregory and Hyman

The next day, we visited Alan's old friend, Dr. Elizabeth Gregory, an Armenian pediatrician. She was one of the circle of "girl friends" Alan and Hyman had in old Boston. Strangely, those girls had never married. She was ten years or so younger than Alan, not tall and with that heavy, box-like figure that most of the elderly women have. She talked bluntly, without hesitation. Even though she was a children's doctor, she never had her own and did not have the sweetness of a mother.

That day she told me she was very bitter about Hyman. They had nearly forty years of friendship. At that time, Hyman had divorced from his wife Nina and was living alone. One day, he wanted to talk to Dr. Gregory seriously, and she thought he might have been thinking of proposing to her or at least suggesting some sort of living arrangement with her. But at that time, she was about to leave for a trip, so she said to him she would talk to him as soon as she returned. But when she came back, there was no communication from him, and she learned he had married Stella, without any explanation to her.

At "Fish Restaurant" (Boston)

That evening, we were meeting with Hyman Bloom and Stella at the Fish Restaurant for dinner. Their old friend Jim Rubin was joining us; he was a specialist in Indian music, and he had brought many well-known musicians like Ravi Shankar to the U.S. to perform at Carnegie Hall. I asked Dr. Gregory to come along with us and meet her old friends; then she said she did not mind Stella, but she did not want to see Hyman. I insisted on her coming along with us and told her to sit with Jim.

At the restaurant, just before we got to our table, a towering woman stood in front of Alan and said to him, "Do you remember me?" as if he was supposed to know her. She was demanding for him to say who she was! Alan was absolutely overpowered by her; she was taller than Alan. How could he remember her, even if he had once known her, it was a long time ago, and he could not remember people anyway? Alan got into this kind of embarrassment often (not remembering girls' names), but this was the most dramatic incident; I can never forget it. Later, Alan remembered her name; it was Esther Peterson O'Brien; she was one of the girls he knew from his old Boston time.

I was right! Jim was so nice to Dr. Gregory. He kept her company the whole evening, even though he was much younger than her. It was a happy surprise for her; she was sitting down with her old friends Alan, Hyman, and Jim, just like it used to be. I was very happy for her, but Stella felt differently, even though Dr. Gregory was much older than her and not as good-looking as her. Stella told me Dr. Gregory was a dangerous woman.

She told me that her reason for disliking her was this: Stella was planning to have a surprise birthday party for Hyman, and she had sent invitation cards to people. It was meant to be a surprise because Hyman was antisocial. If he would have found out about the party, he would not have come to it. But Dr. Gregory sent a letter to Hyman, saying she could not come. Stella snatched the letter from Hyman before he could read it; otherwise, his party would have been ruined.

Performance of *"Lousadzak"* Piano Concerto in New York

On May 17, we left Boston and took a bus to New York. There we checked into the Hotel Esplanade, near Lincoln Center. The next day we attended the American Composer's Orchestra performance at Alice Tully Hall. My mother, who had been residing in New York, and my daughter Joni, studying at Cooper Union Art School, joined us. This special concert was dedicated to American contemporary composers' music, the music of Joan

Tower (young woman composer), William Schuman, and Ralph Shapey, along with Alan's "*Lousadzak*" piano concerto.

This piece had been composed in 1944, the name of the concerto "*Lousadzak*" is an Armenian word that means "Dawn of Light" or "Coming of Light" and was suggested by Herman di Giovanni, Alan's friend and spiritual teacher. After the incident at Tanglewood in 1942, when Alan's music was ridiculed by Copland and Bernstein, Alan destroyed most of his early compositions. It seemed he had lost his direction in composing, and Herman suggested that Alan find his own roots, so he went deeply into the research and study of ancient Armenian music, his ancestral heritage. And so he found his new path for composing.

The performance was conducted by Dennis Russell Davies, and the piano soloist was Keith Jarrett, the well-known jazz pianist. I heard that, at that time, he was trying to advance his career as a classical pianist, and so Alan's "*Lousadzak*" was chosen as his transition piece. That night, the concert hall was packed, probably because of Jarrett. We sat in a box, located on the first balcony. Joan Tower and her friends were sitting to our right side, toward the front; she was a rising composer at that time. We overheard her conversation.

We were amazed at what we heard. She had composed her first symphony not long before and was complaining that it had not yet been performed. Alan's first symphony "Exile" had been composed in 1936. The British conductor Leslie Heward discovered it and premiered it with the BBC Symphony in 1939, three years later. But many of Alan's thirty-seven symphonies (at that time) were waiting for performance; some of them had to wait ten years or longer, sometimes never.

Her performance started, but I never heard a melodic line or any melody I had been acquainted with. All I heard was just a cluster of noise and suddenly, unbalanced loud crashes. I put my hands on both my ears and screamed every time that happened, but nobody heard me because it was that loud! The next piece was by William Schuman, which was the same way. You could imagine, I was in agony. When Alan's music started, it was an oasis, even though that particular piece was not conventional classical music. But very original and with sounds I had never heard before. The repeated piano notes over the orchestra together created a wave-like melodic line, steadily rising to a climax.

After that performance, "*Lousadzak*" was recorded with the same performers, along with Alan's "Mysterious Mountain," and released as a CD by Music Master in 1989. To their surprise, it made record sales.

After the concert, the reception was given by BMI to honor Alan for his seventieth birthday. I saw the photo taken at his reception with the president of BMI, William Schuman, and Keith Jarrett. Alan was smiling sparklingly; it was a high moment of his career.

Our memorable trip ended there, but I am so glad I captured it all in these pages.

Symphony No. 48
"Vision of Andromeda"

♪

Symphony No. 48 "Vision of Andromeda" was commissioned by the New World Festival of the Arts in Miami, Florida. This ambitiously planned festival lasted a month with performances of plays, dances, operas, and symphonies and included many well-known performers. Alan's commission came in March, 1981; after he completed his symphony, he sent the score and parts to the Minnesota Orchestra, which was assigned to premiere Alan's symphony for the festival. Shortly before the concert, in April of 1982, while we were attending a series of Alan's concerts at the Interlocken Center for the Arts, a call came and Alan answered it. In the middle of the conversation, his voice became very violent, and he swore at the person at the other end on the telephone. After the conversation, he told me the call was from the manager of the Minnesota Orchestra; he criticized Alan's just-finished score, Symphony No. 48. After that incident, Alan was strangely affected by his criticism and seemed to be ill. (Alan was not alone in this; he told me that Tchaikovsky was supersensitive and was very much hurt by criticism of his music also.) This condition lasted long after the premiere of the symphony. His bleeding stomach started then and eventually he died from this condition in 2000.

This commission from the festival was his highest paid, other than his Symphony No. 60 "To the Appalachian Mountains," but when we got there, the situation was not what we expected. First of all, I could not find a picture of Alan in the large, thick brochure of this festival. Instead, there was a picture of a young composer whose work was being performed on the same program as Alan's. The day before the concert, we had dinner together with the director of the festival, the young composer, and also Conductor Leonard Slatkin, who was conducting the Minnesota Orchestra and was premiering Alan's new symphony. Alan sensed the conductor was "for" this young composer and that that was why Alan and his music were being ignored. (I think their intention was to promote this young composer, but they needed Alan's name for the concert.)

At that time, the Minnesota Orchestra was looking for a new conductor, and Leonard Slatkin was one of the candidates. The musicians of the symphony came to us before the concert and told us they were upset and were wondering why Slatkin had hardly rehearsed Hovhaness's music. Alan's symphony was premiered with just a run-through.

On the second day of the performance, an unexpected thing happened. Just before Alan's symphony, the conductor interrupted the concert by stepping up to the podium and, instead of conducting the orchestra, turned to the audience and started talking. He expressed his reflections on Alan's music, this enormous subject of Andromeda that no human could imagine or write about; he thought that this composition was rather a mental vision or insight of the composer Mr. Hovhaness. He must have had second thoughts after he had performed Alan's symphony the day before. It was a moment of consolation for Alan and me, and the second performance was done in a different spirit.

This Symphony No. 48 remains with me, and whether this symphony will have a future or not is "in the hands of God," as Alan said.

P.S., In 2013, I recorded this symphony with the Eastern Music Festival Orchestra in North Carolina; it was conducted by Maestro Schwarz and the new CD was released by Naxos.

Alan and Seattle Composers

♪

In 1966, Alan was invited by Vilem Sokol, the conductor of the Seattle Youth Symphony, to guest conduct his own music for their concerts. As a result of those concerts, Milton Katims, the conductor of the Seattle Symphony, invited Alan to be Composer in Residence for the Symphony the following year. Seattle is a most beautiful city, sandwiched in between two mountain ranges, the Cascades and the Olympics. He fell in love with them and had to come back, so in 1972, he left New York and settled in Seattle.

To reiterate, immediately, Alan was included in the Seattle composers' groups and was called a "Northwest composer." There were a number of composers in Seattle, but they were not as well-known nationwide as Alan, so his being included among them made the group more important. He became the idol of young Seattle composers; because of his independence, he was a loner and did not follow or belong to any school of contemporary music or movement. He created his own original style of music and made himself known on his own. But some of the older composers must have been jealous of him because he was a newcomer, yet he outshined them.

Vilem and Alan with Seattle Youth Symphony

William Bergsma

William Bergsma was a renowned American composer, and at that time he was a composition professor at the University of Washington. He was not as popular a composer as Alan, but he was well-known and respected in the academic field.

In the 1980s I used to go the University of Washington campus to get vocal lessons and Alan came along to accompany me. One day we saw an announcement of an upcoming university concert, and Alan's music was one of the pieces in the program. We were surprised at this because it was the first time Alan's music had been included in a U.W. concert. The piece was called "Mysterious Horse Before the Gate" for trombone and percussions, and it was being presented by Bergsma. I did not know this piece and thought, "What a funny name," and I also thought it was odd that this happened to be the one chosen from Alan's long list of music. In the past, I had heard that the university disrespected Romantic music, specifically Puccini, Tchaikovsky, and Hovhaness, and they were not to be played on the campus. I thought, "It just so happens that these composers were the most beloved of all, so to boycott them must be from their sheer jealousy." But Bergsma broke the barrier and introduced Alan's music to the students.

I remembered we had been involved with Bergsma in the past. In 1977, at the time Alan was divorcing Elizabeth, she got two lawyers, one of the lawyers was a top-notch lawyer from Seattle and the other was a vicious woman lawyer. She used a "nitty gritty" trick to get more settlement for Elizabeth. On the other hand, Alan felt guilty because he was divorcing her, so he got a lawyer who had just graduated from law school. She was introduced to us by Ivan, a singer friend from the U.W. graduate music school.

Elizabeth's lawyers were trying to get the maximum settlement for her and came up with the theory that Alan's music was an investment because compositions bring in royalties. So she claimed she was part owner of all his music and should get a share of the dividends since she helped promote them by putting most of Alan's income into the promotion; therefore, they did not have a lot of property, like most people had. The argument was whether a composition is one's personal creation or if it is a possession or property, like a stock or an investment.

So Alan called Bergsma to get his opinion since he was a composer like himself. Alan thought he would understand and have sympathy to what was happening to him. We three, Alan, me, and Peter, my former husband, who I had divorced by that time, went to Bergsma's house to get help. He had a very strong opinion against the interpretation of music composition as property, and he offered to come to the divorce court to help Alan.

The day of the hearing, Alan's lawyer did not allow me to be in the courtroom (his reason was that I was too honest!), but Alan told me later that Bergsma came to the court and made an idealistic speech: "musical composition is not property." After that, Alan sent him a check for his time and effort, but it was returned. Bergsma told Alan that he had done this not just for Alan, but for all composers, to set the status of composition and to protect them in the future.

In 1986, Alan received a letter from Bergsma unexpectedly and also six pages of his writing "Coming to Terms – Counterpoint in the Twentieth Century." Alan thought he must have been discouraged teaching counterpoint to his students whose attitude was "Who cares?" So Bergsma needed someone to talk to and share his knowledge with, so he chose Alan.

Alan's reply to Bergsma's letter was a nine page-long letter, which started out, "Thank you for your letter which opens up such vistas which have no beginnings and no endings." And his P.S. took three more pages and ended with, "Now I must stop to avoid page 13! That might bring bad luck counterpoint!"

It is a wonderful writing, filled with his personality; his knowledge of counterpoint surpassed its rules and strictness and made it enjoyable. He used to practice writing counterpoint in a coffee shop when he was on a break, between commissions. If he had been the counterpoint teacher, he could have made his students interested in counterpoint and they would have enjoyed writing it, as Alan did.

After that I expected their correspondence would continue, so I made a special file for it (Correspondence Between Alan and Bergsma, August 23, 1986), but, strangely enough, Bergsma never answered Alan's letter. I think he needed to talk to someone at the time, but Alan's letter was so energetic and full of life, like his music. Bergsma was overwhelmed by it and gave up.

Once, Alan told me a story… At one time his cat Rajah decided to be friendly to a big dog by putting his paw cautiously on the dog's forehead. Then the dog got happy, wagging his tail, panting his tongue to show his affection to Rajah and the cat gave up. He wanted to be friendly to the dog, but he did not expect that reaction! Alan and Bergsma were like two different animals, but in this case, Alan was the dog.

John Verrall

John Verrall was a renowned American composer and Professor of Music at the University of Washington for forty-five years. He was also an editor of G. Schirmer, the well-known New York publisher. He made a piano reduction for Mozart's "Concert Arias for Soprano," the music books from which I used to sing.

He looked much older than Alan, but we learned he was only three years older. We often met him at Joel Salsman's piano concerts. Salsman was a Seattle pianist giving free concerts around Seattle, in libraries and churches; he believed it was his duty to introduce new music to the people. Alan admired Salsman's dedication and productivity, so he composed many piano pieces for him and attended his concerts.

Verrall also composed many piano pieces for Salsman. Alan heard his music and liked it.

One day Alan said to him, "We should get together." Then Verrall replied, "Let's, and talk about anything except music." Alan and I did not understand that, two composers together, not talking about music?

A few years later, Verrall was no longer showing up at Salsman's concerts. Alan was worried; he thought he should see Verrall while he could. And since he did not want to talk about music, he could talk about Francis Bacon and the Bacon society, a subject Verrall was also interested in. (Francis Bacon was Alan's master. Alan believed he was the illegitimate son of Queen Elizabeth and the true author of Shakespeare's works.) So I called him to invite him and his wife to our home, and Verrall replied, "Your house is too far. I am not going anywhere." So I offered to meet them at a restaurant near his home; he said, "That is still too far," and added, "I don't understand Alan. I never understood him."

I don't understand why he said that; he must have disliked Alan. Poor Alan—he liked him.

In this world there are two kinds of people, ones who are fascinated by people like Alan and others who are jealous of them. But who cannot love him? He was the most loveable man I ever met—I adore him passionately.

Alan's Cousin Winthrop

Previously I have written about Winthrop, Alan's cousin, in "Stories of Alan's Growing Up, Told by Alan," but I realized I need to write more about him.

Alan was an only child, and his closest experience of brotherhood was his cousin Winthrop. Whenever the two families got together, Alan played with Winthrop. Their favorite game was to construct buildings with blocks and call it "civilization." After that, they broke the buildings down, destroyed it, and started building all over again.

Since then they had not seen each other for a long time, since the 1930s, when Alan played organ for Winthrop's wedding. Alan recalled Winthrop's bride, Elva, was a rather homely girl; unlike Alan, Winthrop married this girl for a lifetime. Alan admired him for that.

In the early 1980s, a few years after Alan and I were married, I learned that Winthrop and Elva had been living in nearby Burien, a fifteen-minute drive from us. I wondered why Alan was not seeing them; his explanation was that his former wife was not interested in associating with them and that is why he had not communicated with them for many years. By all means, I urged him to see them.

The day we invited Winthrop and Elva to come to our house, I glanced at them through the window, and I was shocked—I knew them! They had a used clothing store called "Exchange Store" in Burien. I used to go to that store after my daughter's dancing lessons on Saturdays. I remembered her as a very mean person who intimidated people who brought used clothes to the store for their inventory. The man with her was Winthrop; I never knew that couple would become my family. But it was okay since they didn't even remember me, and they were very nice to me.

As they were leaving, we went out with them, and my dog Koko came along with us. Winthrop bent down to Koko and said, "I am so glad to have met you," as if Koko was a person. I was very much touched by his words and thought of a poem written by Mary Baker Eddy*, which ends with "...Speaks kindly when we meet and part."

To me this short but profound line opens me up to the vista of our mystery of life and death. There must be a place we came from and return to, there we may meet again or meet in different circumstances. So after all, we are all connected in some way, expressing kindness to others, including dogs, is an expression of our love to the living and, moreover, respect to our supreme inventor.

Winthrop and Elva invited us to their home, when his sister Libby and her husband were visiting them. I found Elva snappy and blunt, but good-hearted! She called her husband

"Lord and Master" at some point in the conversation (could it have been sarcasm?). Also Winthrop spoke of her, "She puts up with me." I always remembered his kind words to Elva, but now something has dawned on me; I think that Winthrop's gratitude came from the fact that his mother had a mental illness and his father had endured an unhappy marriage until her death. Despite this knowledge, Elva married Winthrop, knowing that they should not have children because of the fear of his mother's mental illness being passed on to their own offspring. But they had a dog, a black poodle, and he was like their child, sitting on Winthrop's lap all through our family conversation.

One evening, Alan conducted his oratorio "Magnificat" in the Congregational Church in downtown Seattle. After the concert, we took Winthrop, Elva, and my son's family to a restaurant. Elva wanted to eat at their usual restaurant, but I thought her place was for elderly people and that we would need more lively food, especially for Alan after he had been conducting, so I took them to the buffet restaurant Sizzler, a place they were reluctant to go to. After we got in the restaurant, I left them seated while I went to order food for everybody; when I came back, they had moved and were sitting way back against a wall. I was surprised and immediately moved them to a table in a big open place. Winthrop grumbled all night, and later Alan told me he had been afraid from the beginning this would happen, knowing our differences, they liked enclosed, private places, and I like spacious, open places.

After that we did not hear very much from them. Apparently they sold their home, from which Winthrop had resisted moving for years, and went to an assisted living home in downtown Seattle. By the time we talked to Elva on the telephone, Winthrop had been dead for three years and she did not remember me anymore.

I called her sometime in 2000, but she was not there anymore; they said, "No such person lives here." I knew they had an adopted son, the only person I could ask about her, but we never knew his name or where he lived.

Later, after Alan's death, I got Elva's death certificate from a kind funeral home director, who took care of Alan when he died. She had died on December 9, 1998, and Winthrop died February 20, 1993.

Today I woke up with full of vigor to finish writing about Winthrop, since I am the only one who can tell the stories. After all, he was a very important person in Alan's life, his childhood buddy!

*Mary Baker Eddy was the founder of the Christian Scientist Church and many of her poems were set to music for their hymns; among them, the most beloved hymn of them all is Hymn No. 30 "Love." Its last stanza goes:

"Thou to whose power our hope we give,
Free us from human strife.
Fed by Thy love divine we live,
For Love alone is Life;
And life most sweet, as heart to heart
Speaks kindly when we meet and part."

"Mount St. Helens" Symphony and it's Surrounding Stories

♪

The "Mount St. Helens" Symphony was commissioned by C.F. Peters, Alan's main publisher. Henry Hinrichsen was the president of the company at that time. His father, Walter Hinrichsen, was the founder of the company, and he believed in Alan's music and had promised to publish every composition of his, including all of his future compositions. But he died unexpectedly in a hospital from complications during a routine physical test. It was a tremendous loss for Alan. After his death, his wife Evelyn took over the presidency.

According to Alan, Mrs. Hinrichsen was unlike her husband. Her taste in music was sophisticated, and she very much admired Arnold Schoenberg and favored John Cage and other *avant garde* composers. And so, Mr. Hinrichsen's promise to Alan was forgotten. During that period, Alan's music was not appreciated by the company, even though they were making good money from it.

Alan felt isolated and became insecure. According to Mrs. Hinrichsen's daughter Martha, who was working there at that time, "Alan showed up at the publisher's every day, nervously helping himself, looking through his file of music." That made Alan and the publisher's relationship uneasy. Finally, he sued them and got back all of his unpublished music that was "sitting on the publisher's shelf" (Alan's words). All of this happened before my time.

In 1977, we were in New York for the premiere of "Rubaiyat," and I was wondering about him not calling C.F. Peters; after all, they were his most important publisher. I insisted on him calling Mrs. Hinrichsen to say "hello," and he did. A few days later, she came to our hotel and took us to dinner at a French restaurant near Lincoln Center. I met her for the first time, and she also brought Stephen Fisher, her important assistant. She was very much a lady and liked me so much.

We had a lovely evening together, with elegant French food and wine. That night I became a bridge between Alan and Mrs. Hinrichsen, and their previously good relationship seemed restored.

In May of 1981, Alan took me to C.F. Peters after many years of absence. Everybody welcomed us, and our relationship blossomed like spring. Alan's music was displayed all over the office. I was surprised to see the amount they had published. I had been hearing Alan's complaints about them not publishing all his music, but I thought, all things considered, they were doing very well for him and his demand was impractical.

We met Henry Hinrichsen, the new president; by that time, Mrs. Hinrichsen had given her position to her son. The four of us walked to a nearby French restaurant on Park Avenue. We had a lovely lunch together and Mr. Hinrichsen made an announcement about commissioning Alan to write about Mount St. Helens, the mountain that had erupted on May 18, 1980.

Alan received a letter from Henry Hinrichsen, dated June 9, 1981.

> It was most pleasurable to see you and Hinako again a few weeks ago in our office. We especially value the continuation of our long personal and professional friendship.
>
> ...Although this amount is definitely smaller than other commissions you have accepted, I will tell you that this is the first commission fee ever paid to a composer during my ten-year association with Peters and represents a significant milestone and investment as far as we, as publishers are concerned.

The contract was signed on August 31, 1981 and Alan completed the "Mount St. Helens" Symphony No. 50 on January 24, 1982. In his premiere program notes, he stated:

> Ever since 1966 when I was invited to the Northwest by Vilem Sokol to conduct my music with his* wonderful Seattle Youth Symphony Orchestra, I have loved the Cascade and Olympic Mountains. Since 1972 I have made my home near these sublime peaks. Many years ago in my childhood I climbed many times the mountains of New Hampshire, and I loved those ancient worn-down mountains covered by forests, with rocky peaks rising above the trees. Now I live between the young volcanic Cascade Mountains and the oceanic Olympic Mountains with rain forests, and I find inspiration from the tremendous energy of these powerful, youthful, rugged mountains.
>
> When Mount St. Helens erupted on the morning of May 18, 1980, the sonic boom struck our south windows. Ashes did not come here at that time, but covered land to the east all across the state of Washington, into Montana. Ashes continued to travel all around the world, landing lightly on our house a week later, after its journey all around our planet.
>
> On August 7, 1980 we had to travel to Walla Walla to arrange details for one of my new symphonies. Before we began our journey I had a feeling that Mount St. Helens would erupt again, but as we drove across the Cascade Mountains the beautiful summer day made me forget my premonition; but after a while a strange darkness came over the landscape and the sun disappeared behind weird colors. Blackness covered the sky, stretching from behind the Cascade Mountains, extending from the western horizon, over our heads. People were taking pictures by the roadside of this new eruption coming from the direction of Mount St. Helens, beyond the western horizon.

In my Mount St. Helens Symphony I have tried to suggest a musical tribute to the sublime grandeur and beauty of Mount St. Helens and the surrounding majestic Cascade Mountains. I use the word "tribute" as the Northwest composer and mountain climber Michael Young says of his own music, "It is a tribute to the mountains."

Mount St. Helens Symphony is in three movements:

I. The first movement tries to sound the praise of mountain majesty before the destruction of May 18, 1980. The opening rising theme in horns is followed by lyrical extensions and elaborations in long melodic lines leading to a grand fugue in praise of the mountain before the eruption.

II. The second movement "Spirit Lake" is a lyrical tribute to the visionary beauty of Spirit Lake, before its violent destruction. Gently vibrating bells lead to expressive melodies for English horn and solo winds. A very lyrical duet for flutes dissolves into vibrating bells. This music pays homage to the memory of a paradise lake, a paradise lost forever.

III. "Volcano" is the third and last movement suggesting the morning of May 18, 1980. A brief dawn-like hymn is heard in horns over mysterious murmuring plucked basses. A rising solo flute passage is interrupted by a violent explosion in drums. Eruption music follows in brass, power of pressure of molten force rising from beneath the mountain, wild stormy strings, violent trombone glissandos, a strict blazing triple canon in twenty voices of winds, brass, and strings and percussion describe the monstrous volcanic eruption. The dawn hymn reappears and becomes an Alleluia-like fugue ending in the Dawn Hymn of Praise to the youthful powers and grandeur of the Cascade Mountains, the renewing vitality of our beautiful planet—the living earth and the life-giving force building mountains, piercing clouds of heaven.

Alan Hovhaness
January 6, 1984

This commission was unlike his others; usually commissions come from a symphonic organization or individual musicians for a specific premiere. But this one was from a publisher, so we had to find the right orchestra for the premiere.

In October of 1982, Alan was invited by the San Jose Symphony to guest conduct his "Meditation on Orpheus." George Cleve, the symphony conductor, had something to do with inviting Alan to his concert. He was a young and attractive man; Alan said he reminded him of Brahms.

After the concert at the party, we sat with him and started to talk about Alan's just-finished composition, the "Mount St. Helens" Symphony. Cleve was interested in conducting it for its premiere and also recording it. We liked his conducting, a very classical approach and thought he would be the right one to premiere it. We expected to talk more about it because, after all, it was a very important premiere and we needed to hear a more definite confirmation. But after the concert, he did not care about anything but drinking, so we, the sober, were left out in the cold.

Around that time, Alan had also been communicating with Rainier Miedel, the conductor of the Seattle Symphony about the premiere of this symphony. He had conducted Alan's "Floating World" in 1981 and was performing Alan's music at other locations when he was guest conducting. Also, he was going to perform "Fra Angelico" in the 1982–83 Seattle Symphony season.

His letter to Alan, dated October 25, 1982:

"As I expressed on the phone to your wife, I am in principle very interested in doing your new symphony, if the cost of rental material is indeed within the range she indicated. Peters quoted a completely different, and much higher amount. I would also inquire about the possibility of telecasting this performance as soon as I have a date clear. This should happen within the next month. The decision as to which orchestra does the world premiere of your piece is naturally yours."

Alan and I were absolutely frustrated. San Jose was offering a premiere plus a recording and now Seattle was offering a premiere and nation-wide telecasting. We could not make a decision; finally Alan said, "Let's flip a coin." And that was how San Jose got the premiere.

Alan wrote to Miedel on October 28, 1982:

Thank you very much for your letter of October 25th. I decided to write this most difficult letter, I will write honestly and hope you will understand. I gave permission to George Cleve, conductor of San Jose Symphony. After I wrote to you Sept. 27 I didn't receive any answer, and saw daily the news of Seattle Symphony's financial problem. We thought you must have great trouble—a much greater problem than my symphony. On October 11 we went to San Jose to guest conduct my "Meditation on Orpheus" for 3 performances. We were given such kindness and their excellent conductor Mr. Cleve was very interested in my music and wanted very much to do the premier performance of "Mt. St. Helens Symphony." I found myself more or less committed to him.

We found your letter dated Oct. 8 when we came back to Seattle on Oct. 18th. I phoned C.F. Peters and also called you but could not reach you right away, so I gave final permission to Mr. Cleve. You phoned 5 minutes later.

We understand now why we didn't receive a definite answer from you for so long. We only blame C.F. Peters for such a high fee ($8,000.00). I wish we had known this earlier. After all, we originally wanted you to conduct the premier performance of "Mt. St. Helens Symphony" and it

> would have been most meaningful to us. We again phoned C.F. Peters and they regret this also. Peters told us that if they do not receive a satisfactory contract within the next two weeks from San Jose Symphony they will certainly contact you in regard to the symphony premier.

In the meantime, Miedel had fallen ill. On the evening of January 10, 1983, after the performance of Alan's "Fra Angelico," we went backstage to meet him. He was in severe stomach pain and could hardly keep his usual composure. Later we learned he had pancreatic cancer and that the doctors could not operate on him; they just had to let it take its course. In other words, just let him die.

We could not do anything for him, but we talked to his wife Cordelia and offered to help communicate with a faith healer in England, George Chapman, to let him pray for her husband. But we never got permission to do so. I think, first of all, they did not believe in such a thing as faith healing; also, they were private people and wanted to keep his last desperate hours to themselves.

Symphony No. 50 "Mount St. Helens" was premiered on March 2 and 3, 1984, with the San Jose Symphony. At that time, Jean Walkingshaw, a moviemaker from Seattle KCTS Channel 9, was making Alan's documentary and wanted to put the "Mount St. Helens" premiere in it. During that time, a camera was following us all over the place, even to San Jose, but the musician's union did not allow them to videotape the performance, so they had to settle for a rehearsal. Later the scene was synchronized with the actual film clip of the eruption.

The next day after the rehearsal, my son Bill and his newlywed wife, Coleen, arrived at our hotel. We had invited them on this trip as their honeymoon gift from us. Before the premiere, we had dinner at a nearby restaurant, and Alan's daughter Jean and her doctor friend joined us.

Jean was Alan's daughter from his first marriage with Patt and she was born soon after their marriage, when Alan was barely twenty years old and not ready for a child. He had lost his mother at an early age and needed a mother more than anything else. Their marriage ended in divorce and Patt later remarried, and her new husband adopted Jean and Alan's visitation was denied. So Alan lost communication with Jean until just a few years before that time. She was a harpsichordist, but she had developed a mysterious condition similar to Parkinson's Disease and was in a wheelchair. But with the help of a new drug, she was walking then.

During the dinner, whatever I said to her with good intention was returned by her with short, hostile sentences, even though we were usually on good terms. I had met her before on a few occasions and we had even given a concert together, but this time it was different. My children were with us, and Alan seemed like their father. I understood what she felt and took her hostility quietly.

The symphony was a smash hit; all three performances got absolute standing ovations. I was happily surprised about the reactions of the Californians; they had been all excited over the eruption of the mountain, as if it were their own.

The day after the concerts, we took Bill and Coleen to Carmel, a town by the sea where Alan and I had had good times in the past. At the end of the day, we went into a French restaurant. Before the dinner, Coleen stood up to go to the restroom, Bill followed her, and they went in together, like a pair of young kids who had to be together in everything.

On the way back home in the airplane, Coleen cried; Bill was concerned and asked her, "Why?"

She said, "My honeymoon is about over." I understood what she felt; it was an unforgettable trip for me, too. Alan was a very special man, and whoever was exposed to his presence got a splash of his glorious moments.

After Miedel's death, Seattle Symphony concerts were conducted by visiting conductors, and at the same time, the symphony was looking for their permanent replacement among them.

In 1984, Gerard Schwarz became Principal Conductor of the Seattle Symphony. He was a young man in his mid-thirties. Alan had known him in New York as an excellent trumpet player, and he was the soloist in the recording of Alan's trumpet concerto "Return and Rebuild the Desolate Place."

I thought that, since Alan knew him, and, since it was about time for the Seattle Symphony to schedule Alan's music, Schwarz should perform "Mount St. Helens" Symphony. In the past, the Seattle Symphony had performed Alan's music often; in fact, their former conductor Milton Katims had invited Alan to Seattle in 1967 as Composer in Residence for the Symphony. As a result, in 1972, Alan came back to Seattle and lived here ever since.

I suggested that Alan should see Schwarz and introduce the "Mount St. Helens" Symphony, but he did not want to be like some composers who visit conductors backstage after a concert and promote their own music. But I insisted, and so we met the conductor and his wife in the Hilton hotel in downtown Seattle where they were staying.

We sat in a reception room and talked. His wife looked so young, like a teenager, and she was a beauty, a new kind of beauty. (I knew he had to marry her. Musicians are all alike, and Alan was no exception.) After our brief conversation, they left us for another meeting; we were left with a table full of refreshments; what else could we do but eat them, all by ourselves in the empty room?

Later, Alan received a letter from Schwarz, dated December 13, 1984. (Apparently, Alan must have written to him after that first meeting):

> "Thank you so much for your letter of December 10, 1984. Although we are working very hard on our programming for next season, we cannot yet commit a date for the Mt. St. Helens Symphony. The Symphony understands your predicament, and since we cannot commit to a time at this point, unfortunately, we will have to decline the honor of doing the Northwest premiere.
>
> I hope to do this piece sometime in the near future, and I thank you for giving the Seattle Symphony right of first refusal."

Alan was very upset by Schwarz's letter—his pride was hurt. First of all, seeing the conductor had not been his idea and, on top of that, he was now rejected.

By 1988, we noticed Schwarz's attitude toward Alan was changing. Whenever we saw him, he called "Alan" affectionately and came to greet him. Then one day we got a call from Edward Birdwell, the General Manager of the Seattle Symphony. He said a possible commission was coming to Alan from a person connected with the Seattle Art Museum. He wanted Alan to compose a tone poem surrounding a painting of Morris Graves, who was well known for his bird paintings and was living in Seattle at that time.

But Alan did not receive any contract for a long time. Finally, the telephone call came, and it was from Birdwell. He said to me apologetically, "The commissioner has disappeared." He was genuinely ashamed and asked me, "What piece would you like us to perform instead of it?" By that time, the Symphony had announced their new 1989–90 season, and Alan's premiere was scheduled for May, 1990. I answered without delay, "Mount St. Helens Symphony" and gave him my word—guaranteed standing ovations!

On May 20, 1990, Mount St. Helens erupted again in the Seattle Opera House. I was right; the symphony got absolute standing ovations for all three performances. I am sure it was a surprise to Schwarz, and he must have come to an understanding of Alan's greatness. Since then our friendship has grown, both professionally and personally.

Schwarz recorded the symphony twice, one for the Delos International label in 1993 and later for Telarc in 2003. In 2001, after Alan's death, I presented Alan's Memorial Concerts with the help of Schwarz, on April 23 in Benaroya Hall with the Seattle Symphony and on November 1 in Alice Tully Hall in Lincoln Center. The "Mount St. Helens" Symphony was featured in both concerts, conducted by Schwarz.

In the past, Alan had great conductors performing his music and some of their favorites became the Hovhaness trademark—Leopold Stokowski with "Mysterious Mountain," Andre Kostelanetz with "And God Created Great Whales," and now Gerard Schwarz with "Mount St. Helens." He carries out the music with conviction and respect to the composer, who breathes beneath the music like the mountain itself.

I would like to give credit to Don Gillespie of C.F. Peters for his original idea of a composition about Mount St. Helens composed by Alan Hovhaness.

*"Wonderful Seattle Youth Symphony"—that was the wording Sokol insisted on Alan saying at radio interviews when he was performing with them. Sokol woke Alan up early in the morning and drove him to the radio stations for the interviews.

Alan and Maestro Schwarz

Alan's Movie Connections

In 1945, after Alan's New York Town Hall debut, he went back to Boston and was going back and forth between Boston and New York for some time. Finally, in 1951, he settled down in New York City.

To support himself was not easy, but there were many opportunities there. He taught at Eastman School of Music, composing for dancers; he even did ghost writing for jazz musicians. Alan also worked for the Voice of America by making musical programs to broadcast to the Middle East. He taught composition under a government program that was free to anybody who could not pay the school tuition. So he was teaching homeless people, too, and they came to class to warm themselves up.

He did all of these jobs for his survival, but his formal education was as a classical contrapuntalist (a composer who specializes in counterpoint). It was like Bach, in order to be a traditional orchestral composer. But he was versatile and open minded. His knowledge of different systems and styles of other country's music enabled him to compose for different levels of musical taste. In that sense, he was like Mozart, who told his father, "I am writing music for everybody, including 'long ears,' too." Alan's music also had a popular quality, and it appealed to the young audiences.

Alan also composed for the movies, among them was *Nehru*, which was about the first prime minister of India. It has shown in many libraries all over the U.S.

At one time, Alan's publisher C.F. Peters reported to him that his music, specifically "The Holy City," had been used in a "porno" movie without their permission. They asked him to find out specifically how many measures of music had been taken, so he had to go to a "porno" movie theatre to investigate. He sat among the gay crowd watching the movie, with open score and pen in hand. Then C.F. Peters sued the moviemaker, but after all that effort, all the money that was collected from the lawsuit got gobbled up by a lawyer.

In 1972, he left New York and moved to Seattle, where he met many influential people. One of them was Wayne Johnson, the well-known *Seattle Times* music critic. He shot Alan's documentary movie by himself, and Alan composed an orchestral piece, "Ode to the Cascade Mountains," for it.

The movie was shown at schools around Seattle for their educational programs. The music was performed "live" by the Seattle Symphony, conducted by their assistant conductor Varoujian Kodjian, and synchronized with the picture. At each performance, Alan was on the stage watching the movie, holding a metronome in his hand and giving cues to the conductor whenever the music was supposed to come in.

While Johnson was shooting the movie, he wanted a certain effect of a mountain with just enough mist to make it look like a Japanese Sumi painting. But he had difficulty with it because you would never know what a mountain would look like on any given day. Mountains can be different every day, even moment to moment. Alan was puzzled by his attempt and said, "Why doesn't he like a clear mountain?" When a mountain shows up, it is a miracle. Alan much preferred the view of a clear mountain.

Around that time, Jean Walkinshaw, who was a moviemaker for KCTS Channel 9 Public Television, and cameraman Wayne Sourbeer wanted to make a movie surrounding Van Gogh's painting *Starry Night*. Alan composed a five-minute long piece for flute, xylophone, and harp called "Starry Night" for the movie, but the project failed.

Sometime after that, Walkinshaw produced the documentary *Three Northwest Artists* with Guy Anderson, Theodore Roethke, and George Tsutakawa, using Alan's music. It was unique with its own distinctive Northwest flavor. The movie was broadcast from Channel 9 and was well received. She became a noted moviemaker in Seattle because of that success, and soon after that, she made an attempt to make another documentary but this time only about Alan. However, it came out to be just a ten-minute-long film clip and was included as part of a longer film with others.

Finally, in 1984, Channel 9 got the funds from many institutions to make their documentary about Alan. He and I got a contract and were paid by the stations as the subjects of the movie. We became actor and actress as the camera followed us everywhere for some time.

The movie started with Alan's music storage room. At that time, we lived in Fairwood in Renton and our house was a small one-story home. We had just finished adding a whole upstairs to the house. Alan's storage room was on the east end upstairs. Alan was, as usual, looking for his music. Mumbling, "So much music—I try to find something, but I cannot." Then he looked down and all the pens in his jacket pocket fell all over the floor. He did this spontaneously. Walkinshaw had not given us any direction or scenario to go by. She expected us to say whatever came to our minds while on camera. It was difficult, but Alan was quite the "ham actor," playing throughout the movie.

In one scene, Alan sat at his new concert grand piano and started talking: "When I was four years old, for the first time I attempted to write music, but my mother said she could not play it, so I lost interest in music." He wrote his music on the eleven-line staff instead of the normal five lines, so his mother could not play it on her harmonium organ. "The first time I heard a good piece of music, a song of Schubert's, I thought 'Mr. Schubert wrote that music—perhaps I should write down the music I am hearing in my head,' since I was always hearing a melody in my head. That is why I wrote music from that time on."

The camera turned to a painting on the wall behind him, a psychic painting by Hermon di Giovanno, who Alan called his spiritual teacher. Alan said, "One's talent is the accumulation of many lives and many experiences. I had some kind of a life before, in the time of Leonardo da Vinci in Florence. My teacher taught me 'When you write, imagine yourself in infinite space. Our space is like a little speck, surrounded by the infinite cosmos.' This thought influenced my fourth symphony. The movie *Cosmos* used movements from my fourth symphony." Then Alan played a piano piece composed when he was eight or nine years old. It already sounded unique and original.

In another scene, at our kitchen, we were sitting at the table. This scene was also up to us to improvise while the camera was rolling. We had to talk about something, so Alan started to talk about his admired composer Sibelius and Stravinsky, who was Sibelius's opposite. Alan became emotional and started to criticize Stravinsky in order to defend Sibelius and put his music on a pedestal. I had to remind him not to because we were being filmed.

Then suddenly, we decided to go to the piano to practice a song called "Love's Philosophy" that he had composed for me to sing at my son Bill's wedding. Then the scene dissolved to Bill's wedding, and I was singing the song. Alan's voice was heard over the scene saying, "To me, Japanese women are the most beautiful. In an earlier time in my life, I found myself not married to a Japanese woman. Since I married Hinako, marriage is the most important thing in my life."

Later, that song was published by C.F. Peters, called a wedding song. On the top of the first page was a written acknowledgement, "For the wedding of Bill and Coleen Holst." Plus, I found my name on the top of the music with a dedication, "To Hinako."

They took us into the country where there was a view of a mountain with an old shed in the foreground. There, Alan was made to jump over a little stream and talk in the blowing cold wind. But the cameraman made Alan do this stunt over and over again. Later, we found out from Walkinshaw that the cameraman was new to the station. He had gotten his job by a false resume and that was the reason for our difficulties, and all through the movie the pictures were not consistent.

They filmed another scene at the coffee shop by the side of Highway 99, where Alan had composed his "Starry Night." We used to live near there in a small apartment after his costly divorce. Alan recreated a scene. He went into the coffee shop and sat at the counter between the truck drivers and composed as before. Then the scene changed, and we heard "Starry Night" over the painting of Van Gogh's picture *Starry Night*. Finally, Walkinshaw captured her vision of Starry Night in her film.

They followed us to many places and to San Jose for the premiere of Alan's "Mount St. Helens" with the San Jose Symphony, and then to Anchorage, Alaska, for "Mysterious Mountain" with the Anchorage Symphony.

In another scene, we were at the Japanese Garden at the University of Washington arboretum. We sat on a bench near the tea house. Alan's voice was dibbed over the scene, speaking of me affectionately, "Hinako is the joy of my life. She brings out the best in me… My music gets higher and higher." He loved my high voice and was very much affected by it; all through the movie we heard of his affectionate love for me. Then my singing was heard over the scene of rain on the pond, and the scene opened up to a rehearsal room. I was singing and Alan was beside me conducting the Seattle Youth Symphony. The movie ends with Alan conducting upbeat with his hands up in the air.

Walkinshaw's movie-making technique was not at all conventional. She set up scenes, but it was up to us to act and speak spontaneously. Then she used film clips and recorded interviews, selecting them and putting them together like a puzzle by following her inspiration. I think her technique was very much like John Cage, the contemporary composer; his philosophy was "chance—happening."

In 1985, PAL Productions was making a documentary called *Winds of Everest*, about an expedition to Mount Everest. This was being done by the well-known local mountain climber Lou Whittaker, along with a group of local climbers. They successfully reached the summit, but one of the women climbers, Marty Hoy, fell from the mountain to her death. It was the producer Laszlo Pal's inspiration to put Alan's music into this movie. He approached Crystal Records to get permission to use some of Alan's music from their record collections, which had been purchased from Alan's former wife. But Crystal asked an unreasonably high fee, so Pal came to Alan for help. Alan worked for him personally to put his recorded music, which did not belong to Crystal, into the movie.

Alan chose the most beautiful music from his Concerto No. 8 for the scene of Marty Hoy riding a horse over the meadow. I know why Alan's music had been chosen for the movie. It was because the expedition was successful, yet the loss of one of the members made this movie unique and melancholy. In 1986, the movie won an Emmy from the National Academy of Television Arts and Sciences. Alan got a trophy for his music.

In the year 2000, after Alan's death, David Ferre, the organizer of Contemporary Artist's Support Association, gave me a few videos of Alan that he had shot around the time of Alan's eightieth birthday. One of these was his birthday concert. That day, Alan was playing piano solo for one of his own piano concertos. Alan was supposedly conducting the concerto, and his composer friend Greg Short was the piano soloist, but Greg had a stroke prior to the concert and could not play the piano. So they switched positions at the last minute and Alan played the piano and Greg conducted. Alan did this in good spirits.

During the performance, Alan turned the page of the score too far and lost his place. The orchestra paused for him, and Greg went to the piano and found the right page for Alan and the concert resumed. It was a demonstration of their beautiful friendship.

In one of David's videos taken at our home, during Alan's interview, I saw myself, bubbling with vitality, bossing Alan around. He gave me that confidence, and I am envious of that girl who was called by Alan "Darling."

Olive's East Coffee Shop – "Chocolate Decadence" *

Olive's East Coffee shop! We used to go there almost every afternoon. Alan composed there with coffee and dessert. "I have to change my chair," he said. Since he was sitting and composing most of the day, he needed to move and change the scene.

His composing in a coffee shop started very early in his life in Boston. He lived in a small, one-room apartment and kept all his music underneath the piano, so he needed to leave his apartment every day.

Olive's East Coffee Shop was located in the Southcenter shopping mall; it was a long, narrow room with two rows of tables across the room. At the entrance, next to the cashier, was a tall glass display case that had luscious desserts displayed on a turntable to attract those with a sweet tooth.

His favorite was Chocolate Decadence. After he settled at his usual table with coffee and dessert, I left for my dress shopping. I had an addiction, and I called it "compulsive shopper," so it had worked out very well for both of us. I got to go shopping, and he got the freedom to compose.

Anna, the manager of the coffee shop, was a tall woman with a distinctive face. One day, she asked Alan, "Why don't you shop with your wife?"

Then he answered, "She can shop, and I can work here to pay for her shopping."

It seemed to me coffee had something to do with his inspiration and creative power. I often wondered how he could write in such noisy places with the noise of people talking and music playing. He said that life around him gave him a "vibration of energy." I did not know anybody like him. He had an amazing power of concentration. While he was composing, he blocked out outside noise and heard his music in his head.

In 1984, Channel 9 TV made a thirty-minute documentary movie about Alan. The producer of the movie was Jean Walkinshaw, the well-known successful documentary moviemaker who had been producing movies of northwest artists. She wanted to put Alan's everyday life in the film, so the camera followed us to the coffee shop. In one of the scenes, Alan was sitting at a table, a girl was bringing coffee to him, and Anna was talking about Alan on camera. She was such a good actress that she stole the scene.

Finally, the many years of Alan's movable studio came to an end, and Olive's East has closed. I heard that the owners of the shop, Mr. and Mrs. Harrington, had divorced, and the two coffee shops they had owned had been sold; Mrs. Harrington got a large divorce settlement, including Alan's original composition "Chocolate Decadence," which he had given to them in appreciation. It had been displayed in the show window in the front of their shop all these years. After Olive's East closed, we found a coffee shop upstairs at Nordstrom Best. Alan composed there for the rest of his life.

All this happened many years ago. Just the other day, I bumped into Anna, and we talked. She told me Mr. Harrington had died and Mrs. Harrington was bankrupted and had lost all her money. I asked Anna, "What happened to Alan's composition 'Chocolate Decadence'?" I wanted to have a copy because I could not find one. Alan must not have made copies when he gave it to her. It was a delightful composition about chocolate decadence using his words.

Anna promised to write to her so she could send me a copy. Three days later, I received a letter from Anna.

January 22, 2004

Dear Mrs. Hovhaness,

This is a copy of the note your husband sent me in Sept. 1982. We had discontinued his favorite dessert and he asked me to order it again, which we did. All the girls in the Olive's East tearoom were so fond of him, he was so kind and unassuming. It was such an honor for me to have known him. I wish you much success in writing the book.

Sincerely,
Anna M. Bernhard
P.S. My children have instructions to keep this note in our family.

Alan's note to Anna:

Sept. 1, 1982

Dear Anna:

I heard that you are discontinuing "Chocolate Decadence." I happen to like that very much. I always come here to eat that as it is the very best chocolate I have ever had. Is there any possibility that you might change your mind?

Sincerely,
Alan Hovhaness

SEPT. 1, 1982

DEAR ANNA:

I HEARD THAT YOU ARE DISCONTINUING "CHOCLATE — DECADENCE". I HAPPEN TO LIKE THAT VERY MUCH. I ALWAYS COME HERE TO EAT THAT AS IT IS THE VERY BEST CHOCLATE I HAVE EVER HAD. IS THERE ANY POSSIBILITY THAT YOU MIGHT CHANGE YOUR MIND?—

SINCERELY

Alan Hovhaness

Alan's letter to Anna about Chocolate Decadence

New York City, NY

New York City, NY, was the place of Alan's important publishers and where his main source of livelihood came from. We went there often and whenever he had major concerts and premieres of his new compositions.

In the early times of our marriage, as soon as we got to New York City, Alan changed. The sweet, fun-loving husband became a nervous man. This is the place to get work done. People are busy and they move like a tape recording or DVD in fast-forward. Every time we took a taxi it was such a rough ride, and we both almost had a heart attack. How can they drive in New York?

My first experience at a restaurant in New York was when the waitress came to our table to take our order, and I was not ready, and then she left and never came back that evening. After that, I was afraid to go to restaurants and realized I needed to decide what to eat before we got there. On one incident, the waiter decided for me what to have and I had to sip a soup I didn't like.

People in New York don't smile at each other like country folks do. When we stayed at the Empire Hotel near Lincoln Center, I went to a nearby grocery store. When I stepped into the store, a very ugly middle-aged woman who was sitting at the counter looked at me. The way she looked at me clearly said, "I don't like you!" But I had never seen her before; she didn't know me, so how could she hate me? I thought her expression might have come from her being ugly, or maybe this is the way New Yorkers treat outsiders.

But New York City is the city that never sleeps, like Alan and me.

There are many good restaurants, if you know where to go. One time, my daughter Joni came to our hotel, and we went out to eat dinner, but we didn't know where to go, so the three of us walked in the night streets, looking for someplace to eat; we went into some ordinary restaurant and sat down, but we left because I was afraid I might not like the food. I did that several times, and finally Joni and I decided to go to an expensive restaurant, so we wouldn't have to keep fooling around. Why didn't we do that in the first place? Because at that time, we had to watch our money situation? We decided to go to the Russian Tea Room, one of the most expensive restaurants (a "must-see" for tourists) so I would not complain. We went into the tearoom, and Alan and Joni ordered the main dinner, beef stroganoff, but I was worried about our money situation, so I ordered the cheapest thing they had on the menu (I think it was chicken salad). It was the most delicious salad I ever remember eating—the chicken was exquisite. I had been there many times before, but I don't remember the food being that good.

New Yorkers don't go to expensive tourist restaurants. They know very good restaurants where the food is well priced. The heads of the classical music department of BMI, Ralph Jackson and Dr. Barbara Peterson, took us to a wonderful small French restaurant during Alan's eightieth birthday concert in Carnegie Hall. The restaurant had many wines, and it seemed as if all the expense was in the wine. I was amazed, because Alan and I don't drink wine.

In 1980, on the way back from another tour, we dropped in to New York and stayed at our old hotel, the Wellington, but this time we decided to stay upstairs in the penthouse. In the past, we had stayed in the cheap rooms below and service was terrible, and the rooms were practically falling apart. Usually, something was not working or breaking down, so this time Alan and I decided to stay in the expensive top room, thinking this would change the situation.

Later that evening Alan and I went out to a Korean restaurant. When we returned to the hotel, we found that someone had broken into our room and had taken several of our belongings. One of which was Alan's brown briefcase, which contained his new symphony manuscript, along with many additional personal items.

The disappearance of his Symphony No. 40 was a shock to Alan, but he composed another Symphony No. 40. He said the new symphony was even better than the one that was stolen.

Once Alan said to me, people who live in New York choose to live there, the same as people who live in Hell. It is their choice; Heaven is too boring for them. New York, New York, whether good or bad, it is the center of the world, and we rotate around it. My memories carry me back to New York and the times we had there together, during those wonderfully productive years of Alan's career.

Spirit of Trees

I got an e-mail from Craig Yarbrough, the guitarist who lived in Flagstaff, Arizona. He bought Alan's "Spirit of Trees," sonata for harp and guitar, from me, and he sent me a CD of his guitar playing. It made me cry when I heard it. I felt his free and innocent spirit, very much in tune with nature.

"We are planning a performance in February, and we were wondering if you may have additional information about the work. We are curious to know if the individual movements may represent certain forests or regions. The imagery that is evoked by this music is full of elements of nature and beauty, and we would like to perform and interpret this sonata in a manner that most closely realizes your husband's intent. I am at my happiest when surrounded by natural beauty and wonder, and I believe this is why I feel such a strong attachment and attraction to this sonata. I can feel the wind rush through the forest canopy, smell the humus of the moist floor, and sense the energy and history of the trees' lives. Any insight you may be able to offer will help us to understand and communicate more effectively this wonderful music."

Alan composed "Spirit of Trees" in 1983; it was commissioned by the world-renowned Spanish harpist Nicanor Zabaleta. He performed it in 1984 in Carnegie Hall with the equally well-known guitarist Narciso Yepes. They performed this piece all over the world together, until Yepes' death. Later, in 1999, Yolanda Kondonassis, the beautiful Greek harpist, recorded the piece for the Telarc CD label with guitarist David Leisner, and it became a much-demanded piece. Other than that, I don't remember Alan saying anything about it, so, in order to give any information to Craig, I needed some research, but I kept my homework on the table, and one night I decided to resume my research and went into the basement to get the 1983 file, which had Alan's performance programs and reviews. But it had disappeared, along with the 1982 file. I looked all over the place, even in places where it was not likely to be found. I cried out and continued to look for it until the morning. The next day, I quit thinking about it and again put my homework on the table. A couple of days later, I looked into the 1984 file, and there it was! I found the concert program and program notes written by Alan.

In January, 1983, Alan received a letter from Nicanor Zabaleta:

> I hope you are in good health and being in that beautiful state is really wonderful, especially for you that love the trees so much.
>
> I will explain why I am writing you. My good friend the famous guitarist Narciso Yepes and myself have decided to give some concerts in DUO. We already have some important dates; April

> 8, 1984 in the Kennedy Center, Washington D.C. and April 9, 1984 in Carnegie Hall, N.Y. My question is: will you be willing to write for the DUO? It could be a SUITE lasting about ten minutes. I know that you could do a wonderful thing for that combination.
>
> In case you would be agreeable to write the work we would need it by the end of August, in order to prepare it.

In 1954, twenty-nine years before, Alan had composed "Sonata for Harp," op. 127, inspired by Zabaleta and dedicated to him, but it seemed he was still picturing Alan as that young composer, striving to make it. But in 1983, he was no longer that forty-three-year-old kid. He had been a well-known composer for quite some time; in other words, he had been making his living by composing. For a while, Alan hesitated to reply, but I encouraged him to be honest with Zabaleta, so he wrote to him, saying that he would compose a sonata for him for the modest fee of $1,000. Zabaleta understood and agreed. (But today I found only $500 from him in my records.)

Zabaleta wanted about a ten-minute piece, but Alan composed a twenty-seven-minute sonata with five movements. He completed the piece in less than two months, by March 15, 1983. In 1984, we heard that Zabaleta and Yepes would perform Alan's sonata "Spirit of Trees" at Carnegie Hall. Even though there was no invitation from them, I thought Alan should be at that concert, so we hopped onto an airplane and off we went to New York.

At the Carnegie Hall concert, my impression was rather gloomy. First of all, on the big stage, there were only two instruments; also, Carnegie Hall, at that time, was just a few years before its restoration, so it badly needed a facelift. Later, in 1991, at Alan's eightieth birthday concert, the restoration had been completed and made a world of difference.

After the concert, Zabaleta and Yepes invited us to a Spanish restaurant, along with their wives. They appreciated our being at their concert and, at the same time, must have been self-conscious about their lack of courtesy to the composer. Zabaleta and his wife were both tall and distinguished-looking, with formal mannerisms; on the contrary, Yepes was short and frisky, full of life. His wife was not young or good-looking, but she had a lovely personality and was very supportive of her husband. Yepes talked about his concert in Japan with excitement, for he loved the country and the people.

Alan and I didn't know Spanish food at all, so we ordered the same dish as everybody else. One rice dish, *paella*, had everything in it, fish and shellfish and vegetables. We had an intimate evening together, even though it was our first meeting (and it became our only meeting).

A month later, in May, we received a letter from Yepes' wife, Marysia, and another letter in October. She wrote of her husband's wish to have Alan compose a concerto for him. Later we learned he was almost blind and that she had been writing his letters for him. Her letters were delightful, full of life, and without hesitation; she wrote freely, in her broken English. Alan agreed to compose a concerto for him.

In her letter of October 29, 1984, she wrote in part:

"I also have to tell you that Nicanor and my husband played three concerts this summer and of course they included in the program your 'Spirit of Trees.' It is better and better every time they play it and they enjoy terribly playing. The audience is delighted with your composition and really now it sounds more fluent, more mysterious and even more beautiful than the time you hear it in New York."

Her letter of January, 1985, in part:

"Please write [concerto] as your heart inspires you. Be free in composing for my husband, because he is very clever and will be able to play all you write on his guitar."

Alan completed the guitar concerto in June, 1985, and sent the score to Yepes, but we did not hear from them until September, for he had been ill.

We found this out in a letter from his wife, dated September 29, 1985:

"Thank you for the score of the concerto. It arrived with a long, long delay. I suppose because of summer posts… Narciso was ill, he had troubles with his back and could [not] work, but now he is well. He says that he likes your concerto but he had no time enough to work it and to study it deeply.

Anyway I send you a cheque of 2.000 dol. As the second amount of the sponsoring of your composition. In October Narciso will have his tour in the States. I hope he will find time to call you and exchange some impresions [*sic*] about the concerto. Many good wishes and regards for Hinako and for you."

After that, we did not hear from her for a long time. Finally we heard from her about the tragic death of their son. He was deaf and could not hear an oncoming train and was run over by it, she explained. In Spain, things were primitive; they did not have gates at the railroad crossings to stop people from oncoming trains. Yepes took this very hard, and it seemed everything had stopped for him.

Finally, we heard from him in 1990. He was going to premiere Alan's concerto in the Granada Festival, but after the concert, we had received only one program. Alan was disappointed and persuaded him to pay the remainder of his commission fee. He finally paid it off on December 9, 1990, but we never received the orchestra parts Yepes had promised to give to Alan nor the publication of the concerto from Schott (well-known European publisher). Yepes died shortly after that.

Now, it is 2005. Alan has been gone for nearly five years, but today I found his program notes from December, 20, 1983:

> "The music is an expression of adoration to the trees of the world—ancient, majestic trees; gentle, mysterious trees; trees in mist and snow; hymns, dances and arias of thanksgiving to the trees for giving life to the world and making animal and human existence possible on this planet. All trees seem to communicate with each other all around in a mysterious oneness."

Many years ago, at the beginning of our marriage, we lived in a small apartment. One day, Alan pointed out a tree standing across the courtyard from our bedroom window and said to me, admiringly, "Look at that tree! She is dancing in the breeze with beautiful rhythm."

I know he thought of trees like individuals; they danced around him in all different rhythms, and he heard their songs.

John Cage said about Alan, "...A music tree who, as an orange or lemon tree produces fruit, produces music."

His Music Is Not for Snobs, but for All the People

♪

I called Don Gillespie at C.F. Peters, Alan's New York publisher with the largest collection of his music. I had three subjects to talk about, one of them regarding the *New York Times* article he sent me about a film director.

> "Bruce Beresford, on his recent trip to the New York Tower Records bought a CD by soprano Phyllis Curtin, one by Ms. Fleming, some Rossini cantatas, and four discs of music by one of his favorite composers, Alan Hovhaness. 'But don't make too much of that,' he said of Hovhaness, laughing, 'the classical music establishment doesn't think much of him.'"
>
> – *New York Times*, June 10, 2001

Don added, "Here is another example of the academic bias against Alan's music." Then I asked Don, "What does this article mean?" But instead of getting the answer, I expressed my opinion. Why does one of this world's most prominent film directors have to have an excuse to buy Alan's music? Isn't it important what you like? If he believed in himself, buying Alan's music could even change the opinion of others.

Alan used to say, "I like it, I don't care what other people say, only my opinion counts." All his life he insisted on writing what he believed from his heart and his instinct—he didn't compromise, in any large sense.

Previously in April, when Don was here in Seattle for Alan's Memorial Concert, I had a good conversation with him about Alan's biography he was writing. I told him, "If you feel uncomfortable about Alan's music not being accepted by the academics, you shouldn't write about Alan." Don denied that and said, "Why would I waste my time writing about a composer I don't believe in?" But after he said that, he told me a story that happened many years ago about somebody who bought a Hovhaness record but had to hide the record when she came out of the shop.

I am sure Don adored Alan and his music. It was his original idea for Alan to write music about the Mount St. Helens eruption, and on his own, he later recommended the piece "Mount St. Helens" Symphony for a Pulitzer Prize. Alan knew he would never get it and thought Don was wasting his time.

But for some reason, Don was overly sensitive about this particular issue of Alan's music not being accepted by academics and was making a big issue out of it.

Before my time with Alan, perhaps about thirty years ago, he sued C.F. Peters to get back all of his unpublished music that was sitting on the C.F. Peters shelf... I was very much surprised to hear what he had done to his own publisher.

Shortly after we were married, we visited the C.F. Peters office together; I was amazed at the amount of Alan's published music in C.F. Peters. I knew Alan was thinking all of his music should be published, but I thought that might be too extravagant in Alan's thinking. During that New York stay, we had dinner at a French restaurant with Evelyn Hinrichsen, the president of C.F. Peters, and Steven Fisher. We had a lovely evening together and Mrs. Hinrichsen and I got very close; we even sent flowers to each other in New York. We have had a very good relationship with C.F. Peters ever since.

But after Alan died, since Don brought up that Alan's music is not accepted by the "academic group," something dawned on me. I seemed to hear Alan's voice for the first time. Alan told me many times that C.F. Peters were not publishing all of his music, but I didn't pay very much attention, and I thought of Alan's complaints and the complaints of young, spoiled kids. Alan spoke of Walter Hinrichsen, who was the president of C.F. Peters at that time. He was very much a man of his word, and Alan admired him for that, and he believed in Alan's music. He promised he would publish all of Alan's music as well as all his future compositions. He was very regretful that "Mysterious Mountain," which was Alan's masterpiece dedicated to conductor Leopold Stokowski, went to G. Schirmer. Also, he was the one who told Alan to set his own words to music; otherwise, he would have to share royalties with the librettist.

It seemed Alan's career as composer was set and it would be a smooth ride to the top, but Walter Hinrichsen was sent to the hospital for a routine checkup and died. That was a terrible remorse for Alan.

After that, the situation was changed, and his wife Evelyn took her husband's position as president of the company, but she was advised by somebody new and went in for the sophisticated, avant-garde direction, and Schoenberg was the center of her admiration. So, Alan's music was overlooked by his main publisher. Instead, John Cage, Alan's composer friend who had been introduced by Alan to the company, became an important asset to them. According to Alan, Cage used to write beautiful melodic music, but after he went to France, he changed, and his music became atonal and non-melodic.

One time, on the radio, Alan's and John's music was broadcast together. First Alan's classical form of melodic music, and then Cage's music called "Silence." I didn't hear any music nor sound after the introduction.

Alan had to write; he could not theorize music; music was his knowledge, passion, and expression; therefore, melody was his voice. He couldn't think for one minute about not writing music.

Then John Cage was "in" and Alan Hovhaness was "out," so to speak. Alan thought C.F. Peters was thinking Alan's music was too popular and shameful because he wrote "melody."

He must have suffered that prejudice and alienation. I don't know why, but now I feel what Alan felt. That is why Alan took action to sue C.F. Peters, and they didn't do what Alan expected of them.

In 1975, in Peters' Contemporary Music Catalogue with composers' letters, Alan wrote:

> "Composer, publisher, and performer unite in beautiful cooperation for altruism of a better civilization. The composer, as in old China, joins heaven and earth with threads of sounds, the publisher promptly prints the music, the performer promptly plays the music and the world promptly receives the benediction."

As he aged, his music has been performed regularly by symphonies and, unlike in his past, the music reviews have become respectable and favorable to him, but there are still not so many major symphony orchestra performances, and I am still hearing this "...not accepted by the academic group."

I wonder why the academics cannot recognize that Alan's music was constructed on a highly intellectual foundation. After all, Alan was a contrapuntal symphonic composer who blended his highly developed European music technique with his mastery of a number of ancient Oriental music systems. But he also had a certain popular element in his music that came from his personality and manhood. The music of many master composers in the past like Mozart had those qualities. Mozart said to his father, "My music is for everybody, including long ears [animals], too."

Many of these so-called academically accepted avant-garde composers can't even write counterpoint! I wonder why Alan's music has never been accepted by them. I think, ironically, it is their lack of knowledge; therefore, they cannot recognize the depth of Alan's music. Or maybe it is just their sheer jealousy of Alan's popularity.

> "My purpose is to create music, not for snobs, but for all the people—music which is beautiful and healing, to attempt what Chinese painters called 'spirit resonance in melody and sound.'"
>
> – Alan Hovhaness

Drops of Water on Hot Sand – Symphony No. 59 "Crystal"

One afternoon, I got a call from the Netherlands; the voice on the other end was echoing, and we had great difficulty communicating. A man wanted to purchase a CD from my company, Hovhaness-Fujihara Music Co., Inc. I tried to explain that my company was for printed music; CDs were released from various labels, but it seemed he didn't understand the difference between the music company and the record company, so I told him I would get catalogs and information from the CD companies for him.

A few days later, I got a fax from the Netherlands, and by that time I had completely forgotten about the call from him. His name was Fred Van der Kley, and he wanted a recording of Alan's Symphony No. 59. I had forgotten all about that symphony, so I looked through Alan's catalog. It was composed in 1985, and I found the score and parts, which looked used, so I thought there must have been a performance. I remembered Symphony No. 59 was commissioned and premiered by the Bellevue Philharmonic Orchestra, conducted by R. Joseph Scott, a long-time admirer of Alan's music. He had performed many of Alan's works in the past, including the oratorio "Magnificat."

Alan and I attended rehearsals for the symphony, and also the concert preview; those nights we sat with Richard M. Farage, the young president of the Philharmonic. (He was a businessman in the swanky city of Bellevue.) His impression of Alan's symphony was "crystal," and he was kind of suggesting that Alan call it "Crystal Symphony." (He may have been a jeweler.)

The concert was at the Bellevue Westminster chapel and recorded on a built-in recording system on the chapel balcony. Conductor Scott and Alan strongly wanted to make a record of the symphony, even though the recording was not good enough for my standards, but Alan insisted, saying, "At least people can hear the music." So we pressed a record and made extra copies for the orchestra to sell at their concerts. I remember boxes and boxes of records were carried into our house. That was the fifth record by our company.

We started to make records by ourselves and called it Fujihara Record Company. This was Alan's idea to help me with my singing, composing songs for me, accompanying for my singing, and writing movements with soprano vocal lines in several of his orchestral works. We made recordings from those performances, but now the company no longer existed.

Now, back to the present…

I could not believe my discovery of Symphony No. 59, and even the recording. I listened to the symphony while looking at his score; I was in tears from all the memories of our early life together and how energetically he wrote. It is over forty minutes long; he called it "long, giant melody." He was right; he wanted to record this piece, and what an unexpectedly wonderful thing happened to him, even after his death. Recently, I thought, "How can I get rid of these records when nobody wants them?" But I didn't have the heart to get rid of them. Now, seventeen years later, a person in far-away Netherlands wanted to buy them.

It was late, but I took a chance to call Fred in the Netherlands to give him the good news. I was hoping the telephone would be clear this time. He answered; he was asleep, but he didn't mind. His time was later than I thought, one AM instead of eleven PM England time. I told him that I had the Symphony No. 59 and four other records. He wanted to have all of them and insisted on paying. I told him these records were complimentary from me, just pay for the shipping.

He didn't realize that because of him, I found Alan's symphony, which was resurrected from a long sleep, and I had an interesting story to tell. I said to him, "I am very sorry to interrupt your sleep—please go back to sleep." Then he said, "How can I sleep after this, I am so excited!"

Later, I found out from Marco in England, some copies of Alan's LP of the Symphony No. 59 were auctioned off on the internet by someone called Scott and sold for $50 each on eBay. By the time Fred approached, it was sold out, so he was frantically looking for the record.

After he received the records from me, he wrote:

> "By the way, it's no wonder you couldn't find us on the map. Musically speaking, we aren't. After Sweelink (16th Century) nothing happened here. The name "Hovhaness" is practically unknown here. How I nevertheless discovered your husband's music, I'm putting on paper. I'll send that to you as well next time. How one finds water in a cultural desert. All I can do is let others listen to it. Its drops of water on hot sand, but maybe somewhere a plant will flower."

Alan's Cap

I was in the front door closet, looking for something, and I saw something over a garment bag—it was Alan's cap. It must have been left there all this time, since he stopped wearing it because he became ill.

He used to wear it whenever he went out. It was made in Ireland, brown tweed, woven wool, with the name of the weaver and his message written inside of it: "Joy and health to you who wear this."

Every morning, Alan put on a white shirt, brown pants, and sport jacket. He looked good in brown; it softened his strong, distinct face and gave him a warm look. He wore a necktie every day, whether he was going out or not. That was his ritual.

I noticed two big holes in his cap, one large and a small one on the other side. I remember this very well. I used to go to my singing lesson every week, and Alan always came along with me to accompany my singing on the piano. One day at my lesson, Alan took off his cap and sat on the couch, waiting for me to finish my vocalizing. My teacher's cat Zizi got hold of Alan's cap. We did not know this until after the lesson. When Alan picked it up from the floor, it was all chewed up. My teacher was horrified and could not find any words to say, and then Alan said, "I am very honored that my cap was chewed up by the cat." And he put his cap on, a cap with violently torn holes on both sides. I meant to mend the holes, but I never did. (After a while, the holes from Zizi's attack were not so noticeable.)

This cap tells me many stories...

In 1986, we were in Tennessee for the premiere performance of Alan's Symphony No. 60 "To the Appalachian Mountains." This symphony was commissioned on August 6, 1985, by Martin-Marietta Energy Systems, Inc. (a big electric company in that region) for the occasion of the recognition of "Homecoming '86," a state-wide celebration of the cultural heritage of the state of Tennessee. They paid the biggest commission fee Alan had gotten up to that time. The next year, in 1986, it was performed by the Knoxville Symphony, conducted by Kirk Trevor.

At the rehearsal, the Brahms Violin Concerto came first. For some reason, Alan did not like Brahms, and especially that night*; they put so much importance on Brahms and didn't leave enough time for Hovhaness. Alan's symphony was just one quick run through.

Suddenly, from the edge of the balcony, Alan yelled at the conductor, "My music is not as simple as you think!" The empty hall was shaken and echoed with his voice. He was mad at the conductor, who had no respect for his music.

Later, Alan told me when he stood up and yelled it was as if he was losing his consciousness and he had a pain in the low abdomen. We didn't know what it was, but he had that sensation often when he was very upset. That day, at the rehearsal, he lost his cap, which he left on the seat. We never found it; I think somebody took it for a souvenir.

After the rehearsal, in the hotel room, he had an inspiration to write opening music to be added before the start of the symphony: a clarinet solo in old mountain music style, then flute 1, 2, 3, and harp joining in together. The next day, the music was delivered and performed. This kind of luxury very seldom happens to an orchestra.

Today, I found Alan's writing on the cover of the prelude to Symphony No. 60. Alan writes, "This prelude was composed to slow down the conductor who had no feeling for music and conducted like a machine at a rapid tempo, destroying melodic and contrapuntal beauty."

Before the first performance, the violin soloist Nadia Salerno-Sonnenberg strained her wrist and couldn't perform; some other piece was put in instead of Brahms. That was Alan's gain and Brahms' loss; the Hovhaness world premiere was the attraction of the night! But Alan's symphony was murdered by the conductor; even though Alan attempted to slow him down, he rushed through the piece. All the important Martin-Marietta officials were there for the premiere, and as a result, this symphony was not recorded by Martin-Marietta.

One evening, we had a dinner with a few people; the conductor and Sonnenberg were there. (She was introduced on the Johnny Carson show and was famous because during one of her performances, her violin string broke and she continued her performance.) At dinner, she ordered snails, and she was going to let me taste it, but I refused. (I thought that, by that time, she must have been eating many exotic foods and had exhausted her tastebuds, so she had to eat snails.)

Alan and I were there for a few days, and we drove to the Smoky Mountains every day; from Knoxville to Route 441, straight to the south to the Smoky Mountains. On the way back, we dropped into a tourist town, Gatlinberg; Alan liked this town very much. He sat in a coffee shop and composed coffee on the table. While he was composing, I visited the town and bought Alan's new cap; that cap is the one I found on the top of the garment bag in the closet today.

This cap was here all the time since Alan had put it here the last time.

I am happy to find Alan's 1986 Christmas message in it about Knoxville, Tennessee; I would like Alan's writing to conclude my story "Alan's Cap."

MY SYMPHONY NO. 60 "TO THE APPALACHIAN MOUNTAINS" COMMISSIONED BY MARTIN MARIETTA ENERGY SYSTEMS INC. IN RECOGNITION OF HOMECOMING "86," WAS PREMERIED BY THE KNOXVILLE SYMPHONY ORCHESTRA CONDUCTED BY KIRK TREVOR APRIL 24 AND 25.

I GOT INTO THE MOOD OF APPALACHIAN HISTORY BY STUDY OF SHAPED NOTES AND MOUNTAIN MUSIC AND FOLK POETRY AND THE THIRD MOVEMENT IS A VARIATION ON "PARTING FRIENDS" ANONYMOUS SONG FROM BEFORE 1820. ALL OTHER MELODIES ARE ORIGINAL. I LOST MY OLD CAP IN THE REHEARSAL BUT WE WENT INTO THE SMOKY MOUNTAINS AND STOPPED IN A NICE TOWN "GATLINBERG." HINAKO BOUGHT AN IRISH CAP FOR ME IN AN IRISH SHOP. WE DRANK DELICIOUS MOUNTAIN WATER IN A RESTAURANT. AS A RESULT I VISITED MY DOCTOR WHO SAID I MUST HAVE DRUNK BEAVER DROPPINGS.

Writing from Alan

PRELUDE TO SYMPHONY NO. 60

THIS PRELUDE WAS COMPOSED TO SLOW DOWN THE CONDUCTOR WHO HAD NO FEELING FOR MUSIC AND CONDUCTED LIKE A MACHINE AT A RAPID TEMPO DESTROYING MELODIC AND CONTRAPUNTAL BEAUTIFUL.

Writing from Alan

*I am not sure whether Alan's dislike of Brahms was because of his music or more personal. Alan admired Schumann, and he may have blamed Brahms for Schumann's insanity at the end of his life because Brahms was in love with Schumann's wife, Clara. Another story Alan told me was the gossip he heard from musicians, that Schumann became insane because he contracted syphilis from Clara, which she got from Brahms. Brahms visited prostitutes to avoid any romantic attachment with any other woman because he loved Clara.

Alan in his cap

At Alan's 75th Birthday Concerts

♪

On June 17, 1986, at our wedding anniversary, Alan conducted his own seventy-fifth birthday concert in Haik Kavookjian Hall in the Diocese of the Armenian Church of America in New York City, one of the largest Armenian churches in the U.S. Their archbishop Torkom Manoogian wanted to celebrate Alan's birthday at his church. Manoogian was naturally interested in music because an Armenian priest is like a cantor, and their services are carried out by not speaking but by improvisational singing or chanting. He fervently admired Komitas Vartabed, an Armenian priest and composer, and was his diligent scholar. So was Alan, and he found Komitas's music simple and pure without the influence of European music. In fact, Alan played and recorded Komitas's piano music on his own record label, Poseidon.

The concert was combined with the anniversary of the genocidal massacre of the Armenians by the Turks in 1915. The day before the concert, after the rehearsal, we had dinner with the archbishop and a few other people. Among them was Mrs. Kavookjian. Later we found out she was the donor of the concert.

In the early 1940s, when Alan was a starving composer ("composer of no performances") in Boston, he created an amateur orchestra in order to perform his own music. He was the promoter, conductor, and pianist. One time, before a concert, he gave all the tickets to an Armenian man whom he trusted; the man was supposed to sell the tickets for him, but he didn't; instead he kept them to himself in order to ruin the concert. The concert day came and there was no audience. Alan did not have any choice but to conduct the orchestra in an empty hall. What was the reason for the man not selling the tickets? What he said to Alan was, "You were very conceited, so I had to give you a lesson." But what was the reason for the revenge? The only possible reason Alan could think was that one day that Armenian tried to help Alan by carrying his briefcase. But Alan did not let him because it was Alan's most important possession. He carried it everywhere, and it had his manuscripts of music and his sketchbook full of his ideas.

On the contrary, at another of Alan's concerts with his amateur orchestra, a different Armenian man came to see him after the concert and handed him an envelope. After he had left, Alan opened it and inside was a $100 check! Alan was surprised, but he used that money to organize another concert. After that concert, the same Armenian appeared and handed him an envelope again and it was another $100 check! These episodes continued so that Alan could continue to have concerts with his amateur orchestra. He became Alan's most important supporter during his early career. His name was Haik Kavookjian, which was Mrs. Kavookjian's late husband. Alan's seventy-fifth birthday concert was benefited by her on behalf of her husband.

Dinner at the church was formal. The main course of the dinner was lamb, tastefully prepared by the women in the kitchen. They were working like servants, serving the archbishop and his guests. It seemed to me the Armenian Church was still keeping the old tradition of "women were not supposed to speak in church—should be in the kitchen."

The next day at the concert, Alan received honors from the Catholicos of all Armenians, Composers of Armenia, and from Broadcast Music, Inc., presented by Dr. Barbara Peterson. I sang two movements from Alan's Symphony No. 38; it had been composed for me to show off my coloratura skills and had many high E's and were a very tricky coloratura writing, like flying on a trapeze. In order to sing this, I had to be in top condition, but that day I was having throat trouble. While I was singing, Alan's conducting score fell from his podium. Since the score was accordion fold with all the pages folded in one long paper, it hung from the podium, all the way to the floor. It was an embarrassing moment for Alan, and I think he must have been worried about my condition.

Then Ara Berberian, the Metropolitan Opera bass, sang several of Alan's songs. Alan knew him from the 1950s. Ara had composed many songs for him, and they had made recordings together, with Alan playing the piano accompaniment for him. Ara did not have trouble like me; I was the finicky coloratura soprano. It seems the higher the voice, the more it has difficulties. I heard that Lily Pons, the famous Metropolitan Opera coloratura, had difficulties every time before a performance.

Then Alan conducted his Symphony No. 9 "Saint Vartan," a forty-four-minute long symphony written in twenty-four movements. My mother, who was seventy-nine years old at the time, was in the audience and made surprising comments. She said, "The more the music went on, Alan got more energetic. Why not let him conduct all night?" She was so impressed with him, and the audience was mesmerized by his spirit. After the concert, I told Alan what my mother had said about his conducting; then he replied, "I was enjoying it ecstatically."

Despite my imperfect performance, she praised me saying my singing was celestial compared to Ara's large, deep earthly voice, and she added, "If you think you could have done better, you are vain and unappreciative."

Later that year on July 27, we headed to New York for another of Alan's seventy-fifth birthday concerts. This time, Lawrence (Larry) Sobol, a clarinetist and conductor, organized a concert for Alan and was to conduct Alan's Symphony No. 50 "Mount St. Helens." He was Alan's long-time musician friend and admirer. In 1972, he had commissioned Alan's "Firdausi" op. 252 for clarinet, harp, and percussion. It was composed for him and his Long Island Chamber Ensemble of New York. They premiered the piece and recorded it on July 29.

Larry organized a press conference at BMI and invited the press, publishers, and important people in New York City. There Alan was honored and had a picture taken with Larry. Larry was also an active impresario, an organizer and promoter. His approach was formal and professional; as a result, the *New York Times* wrote a big review of the concert with a picture of Alan and Larry together.

On August 3, the day of the concert, a limousine was to pick us up from the hotel. John Duffy was riding with us, and he was the director of Meet the Composer, which was an organization giving out grants to the schools to help pay for inviting composers to the schools for workshops, concerts, etc. When Alan and I went down to the hotel lobby, there we saw a woman named Shoghere sitting on a couch and chatting with Duffy. She invited herself to ride with us. She was a tall Armenian woman with a good-looking face but bad complexion. Alan knew her from a long time ago, and at one time he had taught her piano. The first time I met her was near our Hotel Wellington when we bumped into each other on the street and Alan introduced her briefly to me and that was all. I knew he was avoiding her. Then she called our hotel room. Alan was not in the room at that time, so I answered. She introduced herself as Alan's old friend and said, "I knew Alan long before you knew him; therefore, Alan should talk to me." Alan avoided her because she was a friend of his former Italian wife, and not only that, but at one time in New York, the Turkish ambassador had been assassinated by Armenian extremists in revenge for the 1915 genocide massacre of Armenians by the Turks. Alan was horrified at the news, but Shoghere and her mother thought that action was justified. Because of their attitude, Alan developed a fear of them.

Since Duffy and Shoghere were well-acquainted, we did not need to introduce them. We all got in the limo and Shoghere and Duffy sat together like a pair. My mother, who was with us that day, thought they were a married couple until I corrected her. In the car, Shoghere took over the conversation by talking about the old times long before I knew Alan; she kept reminding Alan of the events that happened then. My mother and I were completely outcast, so we talked by ourselves in Japanese.

The concert was at Lakeside Theatre in the Eisenhower Park in Long Island. It opened with Alan's "Alleluia and Fugue," then "Avak the Healer" for soprano, trumpet, and strings. Barbara Martin was the soprano soloist. Then came the presentation of an award to Alan from Meet the Composer and BMI for his lifetime achievement and contribution to the art of music. The concert concluded with the "Mount St. Helens" Symphony, conducted by Larry Sobol.

At the concert, Archbishop Manoogian was with us. He could not help noticing and wondering about Alan's over-cautiousness to the women who came around him, including the soprano soloist. So he said to Alan, "You are so careful about women." I think the way Alan behaved was due to the many mistakes he had made in the past with women. Since he was well-known, many women came to him, and they were pushy and had their own agenda. This time, he wanted our marriage to be successful, so he was putting extra effort into letting them know his intention.

On the way back in the car, Shoghere wanted to give me a bracelet of her mother who had died recently; I did not take it and told her to keep it for herself. When the time came for Shoghere to get out of the car, we all were naturally expecting Duffy to go along with her. But he didn't, and instead he remained in the car. It was a surprise to everybody, especially to Shoghere. What had happened to his intimacy with her? Was it just polite courtesy to the lady guest?

At a later time when we were in New York, Shoghere invited Alan to her penthouse apartment for an interview and picture-taking and for her publicity as a pianist. Alan declined, and as a result, she wrote an article about Alan in the Armenian magazine and put a picture of him and his former Italian wife of some thirty years ago and wrote about her as a wonderful actress and psychic, completely ignoring my marriage to Alan. It was her obvious revenge, and then Alan's fear of her became justified.

"McMinnville"

February 28–30, 1987: Alan was invited to go to Linfield College for a performance of his music and also for him to conduct part of the concert. The college was located in McMinnville, Oregon, a small town south of Portland. We drove three hours to Portland, then another forty-five minutes to McMinnville. By the time we got to the motel, it was dark and it seemed we were all by ourselves. They told us to eat at the motel restaurant, so we went to the restaurant at the end of the motel. We found ourselves all alone in the dining room, but we felt rather comfortable and relaxed. Alan seemed happy having me all to himself. (He always wanted to take me out to restaurants so he could sit with me.) We thought this was a little different from any other trip; usually, as soon as we arrived, they kept us busy.

The next day we were at the rehearsal. In the audience we saw Joseph Rowe, Oregon Public Broadcasting music director, the young man who had been promoting Alan's music over the radio. After the rehearsal, the three of us drove a little way to Roger's Restaurant, a nice little restaurant some people had recommended, located in a wooded setting with a stream. It was constructed of beautiful natural wood, and all the lighting fixtures were clear glass. The waiter came out and announced, "Chinook salmon is in. This is seasonal and a limited-time treat." So, all three of us ordered the Chinook salmon.

That night, Alan and I had a fantastic love-making experience in bed. We were both surprised. The next day, we went to the same restaurant and had Chinook salmon. Again, another fantastic night! Then the next night again—this continued for three nights. We finally figured out that the salmon was responsible for this. He often said, "McMinnville," and this became our secret password.

In 1991, McMinnville College again invited Alan. This time they wanted to give him a doctorate degree. As soon as we heard this, our eyes lit up and we looked at each other. Alan said, "I already have four doctorates, I don't need any more. But I would like to go to 'McMinnville' again." So we did.

We went to the same motel and to the same restaurant, but no Chinook salmon this time, for it was not in season. The next day, May 26, we were at Linfield College in the office of the president, Dr. Charles Walker. We had a long conference, and there was an outdoor ceremony combined with the graduation of the students. It was a very cold, windy day. Alan had to sit on a high, stair-like stand for a long time with the other recipients. He was completely frozen and worn out. The second time at McMinnville was a complete flop. We blamed the Chinook salmon for this.

The trip was sponsored by Meet the Composer, a New York organization. At Linfield College we met the teachers and students. They were quiet and non-opinionated. (Or, if they had any opinions, they didn't say much.) It was so different. Suppose this meeting had taken place in a big city, you can imagine the tremendous discussion. But I thought that the way they were; unexpressive and conservative, was maybe because they had not been exposed to outside influences.

When we were there, we went to only one place other than the school, the thrift shop across the street from the motel. I bought old clothes I didn't even need, and Alan sat in a chair in the store, composing while I was shopping. We had kind of a good time.

Alan and Hinako influenced by salmon

Loon Lake Recording Session at Glasgow, Scotland, 2007

♪

I am in the hotel room, across the street from the Royal Glasgow Concert Hall. I am here for the recording of Alan's music with the Royal Scottish National Orchestra.

Early last year, I got an idea to record Alan's Symphony No. 63 "Loon Lake." Since the symphony had been commissioned and premiered by the New Hampshire Music Festival Orchestra, I thought they might perform it again and record it at the same time.

The commission came in 1987 from the festival in conjunction with the Loon Preservation Society; they specifically requested the sound of a loon cry to be in the symphony. A large portion of Alan's commission fee was donated by Mr. and Mrs. Huntington Damon.

Alan composed a twenty-five-minute symphony in two movements and put two bird cries, a mountain thrush, and a loon, in succession, played by the piccolo, in two different sections of the symphony. The mountain thrush lives in the New England countryside, and Alan had heard their songs when he was young. He said that they repeated the same phrase, but each time in a different key. That fascinated him; he never forgot them, and he took this opportunity to put them in his symphony. As usual, he tried to please others, and at the same time, he did something for himself, too.

In 1988, at the time of the premiere of the symphony, we were invited to attend the concert. They put us in their guest house; as usual, I carried pots and pans to cook breakfast for Alan.

One evening we were invited to a catered dinner party at the Damons', along with other important guests from the symphony and the Loon Society. Before dinner we were warned by the festival coordinator to be careful of Mrs. Damon, a former violinist, who was now in the early stages of Alzheimer's. But I did not have any difficulties with her; I found she was a little bit childish, but that was all. She seemed normal, but I could not help thinking of her uncertain future. After the dinner, we sat in a room with a view of the lake and talked; it must have been a memorable evening for the Damons, and it became my precious memory as well.

The day before Alan's concert, there was a string quartet concert that we did not know about. The program included Alan's String Quartet No. 4, and it was a happy surprise for him because his string quartets were seldom played up to that time. According to Alan, string quartet musicians were the most sophisticated, and his music was too "popular" for them. Before the concert, Thomas Nee, the conductor of the orchestra, spoke onstage; he then called Alan, who was sitting in the audience with me, to come up on stage and introduced him as the composer, and then Alan also spoke. All this was done spontaneously and added attraction to the concert. (Speaking of attraction, Alan looked like a giant beside Nee, who was a very small man.)

During our stay, Marvin Rosen, a pianist from Princeton, NJ, came to Alan's concert and brought his newlywed wife, Beata, with him. I could tell that they were very much in love. They took us to a restaurant for dinner, and although Beata also enjoyed Alan's music, I knew she was doing this for Marvin.

After dinner, they insisted on driving us to the concert, even though we had a ride already. The festival concerts were all at different locations, each of them miles apart, through winding country roads.

Before the performance of "Loon Lake," the conductor again asked Alan to come up on stage to talk to the audience about his symphony. He must have wanted to repeat the successful presentation they had the day before.

Alan started talking about his childhood memories of the country, which were the inspiration for the symphony, and it seemed he forgot there was a stage full of musicians sitting behind him. He talked about him and his parents visiting his uncle's farm in New Hampshire; it was one of his happiest childhood memories. In the summertime, the hills around there became blue with blueberries, and they went to pick them. Alan picked berries with them for a while, but soon snuck off and climbed the hills because his interest was to see the mountains. His parents were so worried because they thought he was lost, and they told him they would never take him blueberry picking again, and they did not believe what a wonderful mountain view Alan had seen at the top of the hill above the tree line. He also talked about the view of the "Catamount" (a mountain shaped like the back of a sleeping cat) from his uncle's newly added room. There, Alan had many happy family gatherings.

He also described his lamentation over a maple tree that had once stood at the edge of his uncle's farm and had been destroyed by lightning. Alan talked and talked, telling his nostalgic stories. We all realized he had been talking for a long time, interrupting the concert. Later, the festival coordinator reminded me not to let Alan talk so long.

By 2006, Alan had been gone for six years. I approached Mr. Graham, the president of the New Hampshire Music Festival and presented my idea: his festival orchestra performing Alan's "Loon Lake" again, recording it during and after the performance, then giving the master to Naxos to produce a CD. He liked the idea and wrote to me:

Dear Hinako:

How wonderful it was to hear from you yesterday.

I've contacted our recording industry specialist and he indicated "a tentative agreement has been reached with the American Federations of Musicians, and after it is ratified some time later this summer, will permit orchestras to make 'live' recordings on a MUCH lower cost basis than the Limited Pressing Agreement." He will send me a summary of the new deal as soon as it is available.

This sounds like good news for the recording industry and orchestras in the United States once it is ratified. So the rate is not available now, or for this season, but if all goes as expected, it will be available for our next summer season.

I forwarded his e-mail to Mr. Heymann, the president of Naxos. Because of his brilliant business mind, Naxos was practically the only CD company doing well with classical contemporary music. Surprisingly, his reply was simply, "Why bother?" He had been successfully recording music in European countries, especially England, where recordings were not as expensive as in the U.S. because their orchestras were supported by their governments and there were not as many union restrictions as in the U.S. He did not want to get into the unknown difficulties later with the U.S. musicians' union.

Besides, Mr. Calderon, the guitar soloist who was to play Alan's guitar concerto on the same CD, had gotten a grant specifically for this project and could not wait until the next summer for the New Hampshire Festival.

Mr. Heymann appointed Charles Padley in England as the coordinator for this project. He approached the Royal Scottish National Orchestra and got a recording session date on January 12 and 13 of 2007. Since I was paying for this project, I asked Charles to get Gerard Schwarz to conduct this recording, for he had conducted many of Alan's recordings and had just finished recording Alan's Symphony No. 60 with the Berlin Radio Orchestra in Berlin last summer. But Charles came back to me and said Mr. Schwarz could not conduct on that date and suggested asking other conductors who had been working regularly on Naxos recordings. But I got an inspiration to get Stewart Robertson.

Alan and I had met him in 1982 when he was a young English (his face looked "English" and reminded me of Prince Charles) conductor with the Monterey Youth Symphony. He had invited us for the performance of Alan's Wind Symphony No. 7 "Nanga Parvat," which he conducted. He also later invited us in 1985 to a Mid-Columbia Symphony concert in Richland, Washington; there I sang several of Alan's songs, accompanied by Alan. Robertson also played Alan's piano sonata "Ananda."

After the concert, we went to the Holiday Inn coffee shop and talked. Robertson had a taco salad (I distinctly remember this because I thought it was an unusual combination; an Englishman eating Mexican food). Then Alan had to have his usual sweet with his coffee; it was unthinkable to him not to have his favorite chocolate decadence after his concert. But by that time, the coffee shop was about to close and all they had left was mint cheesecake. I knew Alan hated mint, so I warned him, but he insisted on having it and then could not eat it.

Much later, in the 1990s, I saw the contemporary opera "Central Park" conducted by Robertson on Channel 9 and was very impressed. Since then, Robertson has become the director and principal conductor of Florida Grand Opera in Miami and also the Glimmerglass Opera in Cooperstown, New York. I got in communication with him, and he was delighted to conduct a recording of Alan's music. I found out he was not British, but Scottish like Alan, and he had a home in Scotland. It just so happened he would be there in January, so he would already be there for the recording sessions. This would work out well for both of us.

In the meantime, I called Mr. Schwarz because I thought I should talk to him in person to find out for sure if he would not be able to conduct the January recording sessions, before I got another conductor. Our conversation was disastrous, and he was very upset with me and called me "disloyal," even though he was my first choice and had been asked first. He said he was an "in demand" conductor and that we should have first asked him of his availability for a recording session. But it was not possible, under the circumstances, because in order to make a recording, there are so many other things involved: orchestra, soloist, recording site, etc.

It was a big shock to me; I did not know what I had done wrong. The only thing I could have done differently was to have talked with him directly in the beginning. I wrote a long, desperate letter to him; later, I called him with a new possible recording date and caught up with him in the Frankfurt airport between flights. By that time, he was not upset with me; but, again, that date did not work out for him either.

Here I am, having gone through all these difficulties to get here. Poor Alan, he has to rely on me, a small Japanese woman weighing less than ninety-five pounds, to do this gigantic task. But intelligence is not weighed by the size of the body. Alan used to say "Japanese smartness" to compliment me.

I am trying, wrapping my valuables around my waist, pulling my suitcases all over the airport, going wherever the recording session takes place.

Company Without You, Without Music

What a boring evening I had at Kay's house the other day. She meant well; she had invited me to a dinner party along with the conductor of the community orchestra that she plays in as a violinist, and two other couples. One of them was a retired conductor (that was what I thought).

When I went to her house, two of the couples were there, and they looked at me with surprise to find I was Alan's wife, but only for a moment; after the introduction, I was completely ignored. I was not even offered punch, which everybody else was having. While Kay and her husband were busy in the kitchen preparing the food, the young conductor arrived and came into the room. He was tall, not heavy but solidly built, and dressed in a perfect suit and tie, and every bit of his hair was neatly combed, just like coming out of a men's fashion page. I knew this conductor, since I had had correspondence with him, and just recently he had conducted for a new release of a CD containing three pieces of Alan's. I started to talk about that CD, but he didn't react or show interest. I was seated at the end (that was okay because I usually sit at the end of the table). Then the dinner started!

First, a little bowl of Japanese *miso* soup that was too salty (in the restaurant I usually put a little tea in it to dilute it) and with too much raw green onion; it seemed I was the only one who could not drink it. Then the salad; the mixed lettuce was so tough, I decided not to chew it anymore. Next, the main course. She had made many sauces from different vegetables, and we had to "quiz" to determine what it was. I don't know what the main dish was, some sort of meat, maybe roasted turkey? I chewed it like rubber. The elderly conductor's wife complimented them on what a treat the meal was; it seems I was the only one not appreciating it.

My mind was beginning to wander; maybe something was wrong with me. I always have been "finicky," but I am getting more so as time goes by, so I eat only the food delicious to me, and I eat almost the same thing every day. Alan was that way, too, when I met him. The only meal he liked was breakfast; after that, no other meal interested him. For dinner I cooked a variety of foods, including cooked vegetables, which he never had cared to eat before. So he came to enjoy eating, like Henry VIII. The last few years before he died, I cooked fresh food "from scratch" for a long time to make it soft so his body could take it in, and I joined him with the same food. Anyway, we liked soft, natural food, with just a little salt and pepper to let the natural taste come through.

Meanwhile, back at the party, I was the only one not eating. The conductor who sat beside me, his plate was completely cleaned up! In the meantime, the conversation was going on without break, with mostly one man, the white-haired conductor talking about locations (where he had been, etc.) but not about music, so I could not enjoy just sitting through hearing about locations (on TV, I can at least see the places).

And I could not help thinking that when Alan was here, company was so wonderful; wherever we were invited, everybody wanted to hear him talk; to them that was their once-in-a-lifetime experience! Everybody tuned in to Alan, and he talked and talked for a whole evening, with his knowledge and experience about Shakespeare, great composers, conductors, musicians, and their gossip.

In 1977, we were invited by the Minnesota Orchestra for the premiere of Alan's Symphony No. 29 for Baritone Horn and Orchestra, op. 289. It had been commissioned by their assistant conductor, Henry Charles Smith, for him to perform as soloist. He was very popular among the Minnesota concert-goers; he displayed a virtuoso performance and received standing ovations for all three performances.

After the opening performance, Alan and I were invited to a dinner with the important orchestra members (conductor, president of the orchestra, etc.). After the dinner, everybody listened to Alan talk; nobody else talked that night. Alan talked about when he lived in Switzerland, in the evening he heard the church bells, near and far, all simultaneously, all different pitches and durations. He described the sound in such a fascinating way, the way that composers hear it, and we all were mesmerized by the way Alan talked. What a wonderful evening it was; I am sure that people who were there that night felt the same as I felt.

Meantime, at Kay's dinner party, the dessert was brought in, all iced with cream and topped with multi-colored fruit. It looked luscious, but I was thinking to myself, "I have to be careful this time." So far, I had failed to eat anything, so I told Kay ahead of time to slice half of a piece of cake for me. I was wondering what was inside of the cream; at my first bite, the thing stuck to the roof of my mouth, and I could not get it off. It was like the texture of caramel. (Later, I found out from my editor Dan that he thought it could have been something called nougat.)

Whatever it was, I did not want to try it again; in the meantime, while I was struggling, the conversation kept on going. What was I to do? The conversation was not interesting, and I couldn't eat, so I decided to cut in and bring up an interesting subject and even shock them. I overplayed the story with over-action of hands and mannerisms, but that was it. Nobody caught on or developed it, and the result was the same—they went back to talking about locations.

Speaking of strange food… At one time, Alan and I were introduced to the Scandinavian delicacy called "lutefisk" at a college dinner party in St. Peter, Minnesota. It was like a clear jellyfish, and one of the dinner guests explained to us what it was, a fish that is caught and then buried under the frozen snow for a long time, until it becomes transparent.

It was in the year 1989, at the end of November just before Christmas, when a man from St. Peter, Minnesota, called and said that his name was Adrian Lo, the music professor at Gustavos Adolphus College. He was going to perform Alan's music "And God Created Great Whales" for a performance on December 1, 2, and 3, 1989, at a Christmas Mass. He wanted Alan to attend his performance. I didn't want to go on such short notice before Christmas because I had so much to do, but he kept trying to persuade us over and over. He even said that he would take us first class on the airplane and would pick us up at the airport by limousine to the hotel. Anyway, he talked us into going.

St. Peter was located in the south of Minneapolis and had a population of mostly very white Scandinavian people. It was funny to see Adrian, a small Chinese man, mixed in among them. When we got there, we gradually found out the situation. Adrian was not the head of the music department but was rather new. On his own, he had invited Alan in order to impress the people, but his scheme backfired, and he put Alan in an awkward position. Usually, Alan would be invited by the head of the music department of the school, but not in this case. We saw strong resentment among the music department heads, but we could not help taking Adrian's side because, after all, he was the one who had invited us; also, he and Alan both had a musician's temperament, which made Alan feel at home.

One of those days before the concert, while we were there, Adrian took us to the chaplain's office. The chaplain was a very handsome middle-aged man, not like a conventional priest, but very human. According to Adrian, he was always in trouble, and at the present time, he was in the midst of trouble because he had announced, "No mink coats for this concert because the theme of the Christmas Mass is for animals." So he offended the rich sponsors' wives who would have otherwise worn mink coats to the concert. They had already been saying there would be no support for next year's concert. It seems Adrian and the chaplain were the life of this community, always stirring it up. Without them, nothing would have happened, and the town would have had nothing to talk about.

After the rehearsal, all the music department staff and the chaplain and his wife were gathered and chatting. Alan was very relaxed and started talking about a red-haired priest in the Armenian Church in Boston where he had been organist in his younger days. The priest always greeted Alan with, "*Abriss Hovhaness*," which means in Armenian, "Long live Hovhaness." He was a tall man and often showed up during the choir practice while Alan was conducting the choir; he stood behind him, imitating Alan. He liked the girls, and the last Alan heard of him was that finally, a rich girl "got" him and then he quit the priesthood and married her.

Then suddenly, in the middle of Alan's story, the chaplain's wife stood up and left. Then the chaplain said, "Oh, oh, my wife left me." I knew it was trouble; later, Adrian explained that they were having difficulties because of the chaplain's interest in or interest from the girls. Alan's story of the red-haired priest must have reminded her of her husband. You can't imagine such a puritanical town. There the men have no peace. Anyway, Alan made a mistake, but it was fun.

We had another funny incident while we were there. Once, I needed to go to the drugstore so Adrian drove for us, but it happened that Alan wanted to stay in the car to compose, so Adrian came along with me into the store. The next day, the whole town was talking about Adrian and Mrs. Hovhaness together in the drugstore! What a town that everybody knew everybody else's business, and they enjoyed making up gossip about them.

The Christmas Mass was performed at their chapel at the college. Alan's piece "And God Created Great Whales" was performed as a processional, but not even the whole piece. It had something to do with their musician's capabilities. We wondered why Alan had been invited just for this!

On top of that, Adrian wanted to commission Alan to write a piece for twelve-part flute choir. Why twelve flutes? He must have had twelve flutes at that time and wanted to use them in some way. Also, the chaplain wanted Alan to write a piece for him. The subject of the composition was to be "Chaos." We were puzzled by such a subject from a priest, but we thought he must have been thinking of the chaos before the existence of the universe.

Alan never wrote for their unusual requests because it was beyond his creative inspiration.

On the way back to the airport, we did not get limousine service. Just because we took Adrian's side, the music department downgraded us!

During Kay's dinner party, we never talked about music. I thought they were conductors. Why didn't they talk about music? And come to think of it, they didn't even once mention Alan's name. Since Alan had died the previous June, I expected at least to hear their condolences. Maybe it was because they were not for Alan's music. Nobody can force one to like certain music. But why had the young conductor recorded Alan's music for a CD? Maybe he was using Alan's name in order to help the other unknown composers that were on the CD. Now I realized I was in the enemy's camp.

In 1978, we were at the house of Vahe Aslanian, a choral conductor in Salinas, California. We were in the company of Aslanian and his wife, the violinist Gary Beswick and his wife, and a man and woman from Seattle Opera. We were talking about a production of Wagner's "Ring Cycle." Then they started criticizing Wagner about his writing of "Jews in Music" and his character and sexuality. All six of them ganged up on Wagner the great composer, the great genius. Strangely enough, Alan was not saying anything.

Alan was the one who gave me an education about Wagner's operas; he talked with tremendous excitement about Wagner's music. He often entertained our friends and houseguests by playing Liszt's piano transcription of Wagner's "Love Death" from the opera "Tristan and Isolde." Every time he struck the "Romantic Chord," he was so absolutely "passion-stricken," he jumped up from the piano bench, almost as if he would hit the ceiling. Alan told me, “When Wagner introduced the Romantic Chord, it was revolutionary, and it changed the world of music forever.”

Wagner’s personal life was also sensational aside from his notorious love affairs; his marriage to Cosima, the daughter of Franz Liszt, was the scandal of the century. Before her marriage to Wagner, she was the wife of Hans von Bulow, the well-known conductor who premiered “Tristan and Isolde.” While she was still married to him, she bore a child and declared the child was Wagner’s.

What was I to do? Even though, according to them, Wagner was a scandal, I could not sit there not saying anything. After all, he was a composer, and somebody had to be on his side. I said, “He was a genius—to write music like he did, he must have had overwhelming and uncontrollable emotion, so we can all forgive him.” Then Gary the violinist said, whiningly, “I have emotion, too!” Then Aslanian’s wife said to her husband, “Watch out!”

Wagner was criticized even 100 years after his death. There are two kinds of people: one kind admires God-given talented or successful individuals, while the other kind is envious of them. So Wagner was the target of the latter’s criticism. This applies to Alan, too. Even though he was a prominent composer before he met me, his personal life was always in shambles, and he went from marriage to marriage. So while Aslanian and his guests were criticizing Wagner, they must have been thinking about Alan in the back of their minds too. No wonder Alan was quiet all that time. He took their criticism of Wagner personally. So after all, I was defending two of my beloved composers with my spontaneous impulse.

Finally, Kay’s dinner party had ended. Thank God. I realized the company was not the same as when Alan was here. He left a big empty space among us.

Alan, Alan, I miss you—you are my beloved composer. When I speak of you, I see you before me, standing ever so triumphantly!

*In 2011, I had an occasion to talk to Adrian on the telephone. Now he is teaching at Bethany Lutheran College and his colleagues are Chinese. Every morning on his way to the school, he drives by his old school, and he remembers the difficulties he had there and realizes now that he is in a better place.

As to the lutefisk, he explained; first catch the fish and soak it in lye. It is like soap and is poisonous, so before eating, you must soak it in a pot of boiling water for a long time to get rid of the poison.

The Day Alan Broke His Hip

♪

That awful day Alan broke his hip…

We were in our car in the basement garage, and I was about to start the car to go to my singing lesson. Then I realized I had forgotten something, so I went back upstairs with Alan following behind me on the stairway.

To get to my teacher's house took over forty-five minutes of driving, and I was in a hurry. Alan was sluggish that morning, so I yelled at him, "Hurry up!" from the top of the stairs. He was on the third step of the stairs at that time; then he became confused by my voice, lost his balance, and fell off the stairs. I rushed to him, where he was lying on the basement floor. Then he tried with all is might to stand up, but he had to fall back down on the floor. Later, he told me that when he stood up he heard something breaking inside of him.

I called an ambulance, and they took him to nearby Riverton hospital. I followed them in my car. When I got there, I found out they had to move him to a larger hospital in Burien in order to treat him. I was hoping the doctor could do something for him right away, but we had to wait until the next day. Alan's hip had broken, and the doctor had to put a pin in his hip to patch it up.

Before the operation, I asked Dr. Witham, the young surgeon, "Is there any chance that I may lose him from the operation?"

He answered bluntly and emotionlessly, "Yes, it is a major operation. That is a possibility." I guess nowadays doctors have to cover everything that could possibly happen so they will not get sued. To think positively and optimistically is the healing, but those thoughts are a thing of the past.

During Alan's operation, I was in the waiting room outside of the operating room. My former voice teacher Leon Lishner and his girlfriend came to get our opera tickets for "War and Peace" by Sergei Prokofiev. Alan had been looking forward to going to that opera, but the tickets happened to be for the day of his operation, so I had to give them away to someone who would appreciate it as much as Alan.

Finally my agonizing wait was over, and Alan came through the operation okay. The doctor told me he was resting in a recovery room but didn't expect him to recognize me for a while because he was still under the anesthesia. When he came to, he started shouting, "Handel!" and speaking about him in a loud voice ecstatically, all by himself, and he did not pay any attention to me. There I was, having waited for a long time thinking he might die, and I was so hurt I decided to leave him alone to talk about Handel.

I went home and worked in the garden to ease my hurt; then my son Bill called and asked about Alan's condition and was surprised I was not with him. Bill persuaded me to go back to the hospital with him. So everyone went together: me, Bill, his wife, their four children, and my mother. By the time we got there, Alan was normal and was happy to see me.

During the twelve days of his hospital stay, I was with him most of the time. But the hospital did not let me stay after midnight. Alan and I agonized over that separation. Up to that time, we had never been separated. We had always been together, and Alan composed anywhere I went.

According to his roommate, as soon as I left the room, Alan made a big fuss. Every night at midnight, the nurses changed shifts and a young Korean nurse came in. Alan was confused and thought that since she knew that he was a famous composer, she took advantage of him by touching him or doing something to him to make it look like he had something to do with her in order to make an advance for herself. Most of all, he was afraid this might jeopardize our relationship. His experiences were so real, I almost believed him. Another story he told me was that a male nurse tricked him and tied his fingers to do things to him, so Alan said to him, "Don't you pull a fast one on me!"

A man who was sharing the room with Alan and his bed was on the other side of the room, near the entrance. He also had had a hip operation and was confused like Alan. In the evening, after his family had left, he behaved weirdly. He picked up the phone without dialing and called his wife, saying, "Elaine, Elaine!"

He became frantic and told me she had left him, so I said, "I don't think so—I just saw her a little while ago with you." I tried to call his home for him, but he did not remember his home telephone number. Other patients with hip operations had similar conditions, so I think their confusion was due to the anesthesia given to them before the operation.

Alan's confusion continued. One night I was so worried I called the doctor and left a message, insisting he call me back. When he called, I asked him if Alan's confusion was temporary or not. Again, he could not give me a comforting answer, so he told me he "could not tell for sure."

One morning, I got to the hospital and all the staff were making a big fuss over was Alan. He had taken off his catheter and the other tubes connected to his body and had bled all over. He had decided to come home. The doctor was very unhappy and, according to the hospital staff, Alan was the wildest one. To take off a catheter would have hurt badly. It had a plug on the end, but Alan yanked it out.

So when it was time for Alan to leave the hospital, the doctor decided that Alan should come home with me instead of going to a rehabilitation center like other patients. He thought Alan's case was exceptional and that going to a rehab would not help him. So Alan came home, but for just one day. The next day, August 13, he had a complication so the ambulance took him to the hospital and he stayed there for another four days.

After the help of a physical therapist, he could walk again, but he used a cane to be extra careful. The breaking of Alan's hip was the beginning of his physical breakdown. His confusion went away, but that was a premonition of what would come.

For the rest of his life, we were in and out of the doctor's office and the hospital. I watched him and took care of him like a nurse. As the hospital staff said, "He is the most troublemaker." That he was! He was the "colorful" composer, and so was his sickness. He gave me plenty of troubles, but how colorful it was. He did not just "shut up and die." He came back from his battles with sickness and gave me my life back every time for nine years.

John Cage – All I Know

♪

This morning after I slept well, John Cage came to my mind. I have just written about him in a story about Lou Harrison, but now I realize I have to write about Cage in a separate story.

Alan met John on June 17, 1945, backstage at Town Hall in New York. That was Alan's New York debut concert, and it practically created riots among the composers in the audience. Lou Harrison said in an interview, "The Americanists, the French-Americanists, the Viennese twelve-tone people, you know, were there and they were all fighting because here comes someone from Boston nobody ever heard of doing completely neither..." John was very excited about Alan's music and came backstage to meet Alan and said to him, "Lou is writing a review for you." Lou was the music critic of the *New York Herald Tribune* then, and John was Lou's frequent guest, so they had come to Alan's concert.

I was married to Alan in 1977, but I did not meet John until 1991; I only knew of him from what Alan had told me. Alan said, "He used to write beautiful music, but after he went to France, he changed completely and is doing very *avant-garde* stuff." Alan must have thought he might not be able to communicate with him because John's direction of music had changed, and their musical thinking had become so far apart.

In 1960, while Alan was in Japan, John came to Japan for an *avant-garde* concert. Alan attended that concert, and it went like this… A composer came out on stage and suddenly cut another man's necktie with scissors. Was it musical "shock-effect"? Alan didn't like it at all, and he felt cutting one's necktie was like cutting off one's manhood. Next there was a man, all wrapped around with electrical wire, about to be turned on with a switch. Alan laughed from nervousness, in the dead-silent audience, and then the serious Japanese audience scornfully told him to be quiet.

Alan was farther and farther away from John's direction of music. Alan was a truly classical composer in his spirit and his knowledge. I think he was a very old soul who just landed in the 20th century by God's mistake. Or if it was intentional, Alan's purpose on the earth was to bring back music of the past. To him, music of the past meant not a few centuries, but all the way back to the source of music, adding the fresh air of a new age and originality to create unique contemporary music of the 20th century. Most of all, he wanted to write music, but he could not join the direction of *avant-garde* music because by and by, they were not writing music.

In 1980, Alan's and John's music was broadcasted over the radio. After Alan's melodic music, there was an announcement of John's composition called "Silence," but we never heard anything after that, just silence; and we never heard the end of it. John's "Silence" and many other works were published by C.F. Peters; I assume they did not spend very much money because there was not much music to print. But would anybody buy blank paper?

Alan told me he had introduced John to C.F. Peters. After the death of Walter Hinrichsen, who was the president of the company and a strong believer in Alan's music, his wife Mrs. Hinrichsen, became the president. Her taste in music was different from her husband's; she admired Schoenberg, a composer of sophisticated, atonal music, a different direction from Alan's music, which was melodic and more traditional. She favored other New York *avant-garde* composers, especially John Cage. Alan felt he was an outcast and he was very anxious and nervous about his own music; that made his relationships with C.F. Peters edgy.

In 1960, after his trip to India and Japan, he went to Switzerland and lived there for a number of years and finally came to live in Seattle to write music under the inspiration of mountains like Mount Rainier and the Cascade and Olympic Mountains.

After I met him in the early '70s, and with my encouragement, he composed in true classic form, that which was natural to him and which won the audiences' acceptance and approval. After many years of a cut-and-dried contemporary music period, the audience needed to hear the fresh spring air of Romanticism. Alan was the pioneer of neo-romantic music. He could not stop but followed his own instinct.

One day, Richard Kostelanetz, a nephew of the well-known conductor Andre Kostelanetz made an appointment to see Alan to interview him at our apartment; the appointment was at midnight. I don't remember for whose convenience it was. Before the appointment, we had gone to see Joan Sutherland, the Metropolitan soprano's recital at the Opera House. Her husband, Richard Bonnyng, was her piano accompanist. Alan was rather sarcastic about the recital, and he did not want me to tell Kostelanetz where we had gone. I was surprised that he was a changed man, but he had a reason why he behaved that way. Richard Kostelanetz was an *avant-garde* writer from New York and an admirer of John Cage. Alan was very sensitive because of his experiences; one example was in 1942 at Tanglewood. One of the reasons he had been ridiculed there was because he admired Jean Sibelius, one of the last great composers of the Romantic period. At that time, anything to do with classical music was old-fashioned and passé to the contemporary musicians and society. After the interview, when Richard was leaving, he left warm greetings from John. It seemed to me I had been hearing John's greetings to Alan from different people from time to time and felt his warm friendship toward Alan. But Alan didn't recognize it because of his own isolation and resentment toward the *avant-garde* music movement at that time.

On October 6, 1991, Alan's Eightieth Birthday Gala Celebration Concert opened at Carnegie Hall. It was the idea of Archbishop Mesrob Ashijian, Archbishop of the Prelacy of the

Armenian Apostolic Church of America and was produced by him and solely funded by his church. After the concert, Alan and I were at his church for a reception, and there I saw John Cage on the street through the window. That was the first time I had ever seen him in person. Without any hesitation, I went out and greeted him and said, "I am Alan's wife." He looked at me with such a warm expression, and I knew then he accepted me unconditionally. After that, Joni, my daughter, who was a graphic designer in New York, wanted to meet him, so I introduced Joni to him, and all this came so naturally, so I knew what I felt about John was right. He always liked Alan and had good thoughts toward him regardless of their musical differences.

On January 26, 1992, the day after the concert of John Cage and Lou Harrison at the Cornish College of the Arts in Seattle, Alan and I got a call from John. He wanted to drop in at our house before catching the airplane to New York since our house was near the airport. He came with the percussionist who was driving him during his stay for the concert. We were barely ready for his morning visit because we were "night owls." Come to think of it, John was a morning person. In an earlier time in New York, John came to Alan's apartment in the morning, but Alan was sleeping and told him to "Go home!" Alan used to compose all night long and went to sleep in the morning.

So that morning, just as before, we were not prepared to receive him, nor did we have anything to offer him except Washington apples. So we shared apples and tea with them. It was nice and just right for that morning because John was a vegetarian, like a Buddhist priest. John was truly happy and content to find Alan doing very well. He had known Alan for a long time and knew his difficult life; now Alan had a comfortable house and most of all, he was with me, a "Japanese wife." John knew very well that was important to Alan, and he was very pleased with me. I could tell by his expression, without so many words. I found something about him very spiritual. A thought came over me and I said to him spontaneously, "Thank you very much for helping Alan with money a long time ago."

Then he said modestly, "Yes, we all needed money then." He remembered what I was referring to. Years ago, Alan was in New York, struggling to survive as a composer. One day, John and he bumped into each other on the street. John looked at Alan and said, "You may need money," and handed some money to Alan. Alan told me this story, but he added, "Of course, I paid back the money."

Then my mother came into our house to see John; being a contemporary painter, she could not miss the opportunity to meet a famous *avant-garde* composer. I took a picture of John and my mother together. That was the last time we saw him. He died shortly after, back in New York.

I met him only a few times, yet it was as if I had known him always. My memory of him is profound and I think of him as a philosopher and his music was his philosophy.

In 2001, the year after Alan died; I presented Alan's Memorial Concert at New York's Lincoln Center on my own. There was just one financial contribution which came from the Foundation for Contemporary Performance Arts, Inc., a John Cage foundation.

Alan's Eightieth Birthday Concert at Carnegie Hall

♪

In early 1991, Alan got a call from Archbishop Mesrob Ashjian, Archbishop of the Prelacy of the Apostolic Church of America in New York City. He wanted to organize a concert to celebrate Alan's eightieth birthday.

Previously, in 1989, he had invited Alan to "The Glory of Ani" Concert in the Metropolitan Museum, and Alan had conducted his Wind Symphony No. 23 "Ani." We did not meet him at that concert because he had been called to be in Armenia, even though the event was his idea and project.

For that concert, Alan had appointed Larry Sobol to be the contractor for the wind orchestra. Larry was the clarinetist and conductor who had commissioned a piece for his high school symphonic band in 1972. It happened to be that composition was the Wind Symphony No. 23 "Ani," was the same one selected by the archbishop for this occasion.

On the night of the event at the Metropolitan Museum was a long, drawn-out program with many speeches and picture showing. Finally, we got to the "Ani" performance. Afterward, a priest came on the stage, and I assumed he was taking the place of Archbishop Ashjian, and he started to make a speech in Armenian. I did not understand anything, but it sounded like a pep talk with howling and yelling. Alan had told me that Armenians are a very talkative people, and their speech gets fanatically wild. I understood then what he had been telling me.

The orchestra was seated throughout the speech; then one of them stood up and left, then another. The musicians were hired to perform the music, but not to sit through a speech. Then Alan, who was the conductor, came out from the wings onto the stage, walked all the way to the conductor's podium, picked up his score, and exited. Alan's unexpected gesture expressed what we were all thinking.

That was then. But this time, Archbishop Ashjian was planning to have Alan's eightieth birthday celebration in Carnegie Hall. At Alan's recommendation, the archbishop again appointed Larry Sobol as the artistic advisor, along with Iris Papazian, who was working for the archbishop. On February 11, 1991, Alan signed the contract for his birthday concert; in addition to the concert, he got a commission to write a symphony to be premiered at the concert.

It was the most grand and expensive concert Alan had ever had, at least when I was with him. Why did the archbishop do it for Alan? I think most of all, he liked Alan's music and respected him; but moreover, Alan was a hero in his mother country of Armenia. Alan being a famous Armenian composer in America was important to a small country like Armenia. Although, Alan was only half-Armenian. So this time, it was essential for Archbishop Ashjian to have the honor of celebrating Alan's eightieth birthday in America since Alan's seventy-fifth birthday had been celebrated by the other church: Archbishop Manoogian's Diocese of the Armenian Church.

Alan told me about the issue of the sensitive relationship between the two Armenian churches. The Armenian Christian Church had two denominations. At one time, the archbishop of one church visited New York and was assassinated by fanatics of the other church. Since then, they had been secretly resenting each other.

On September 25, we left for New York. The prelacy church put us in the Southgate Tower Hotel in Times Square. We stayed there for the two weeks of rehearsal, the concert, and related activities. Our hotel room had a small kitchen unit, so I cooked breakfast for Alan; for dinner, I went next door to a Korean grocery to take out hot buffet food and also cold cuts from Macy's basement food department.

So we survived well despite Alan's delicate condition. The year before in July, he had fallen from the basement stairs and broke his hip. After the physical therapy, he walked with a cane; also, since then, his health had gone downhill. In the hotel room, in the evenings after his daytime activities, his nose often bled, and I had to stop his bleeding by pushing against the upper part of his nose with my two fingers as hard as I could for fifteen minutes.

During our stay in New York, on two separate occasions, we were invited out for dinners by BMI's Ralph Jackson and also by Dr. Barbara Petersen. The dinner with her was at a French restaurant with all the production staff, including Larry and Karel Husa the composer, who was participating in the concert by conducting Alan's "Prelude and Quadruple Fugue" and also Symphony No. 2 "Mysterious Mountain." Previously, Alan had expressed to me his fondness for Husa. One time, Alan was not sure of his own compositions and was hesitating; then Husa said to him, "Oh, no! It is good," to encourage him.

But that night I did not feel Husa's warmth that Alan had spoken of, too. They never had that "composer to composer" talk, and it seemed to me that Husa kept his distance from Alan. Alan was an emotional, hot-blooded Armenian, and Husa was a reserved, pale Czech. But why was Husa conducting Alan's music? It was a mystery to me.

During our stay in New York, my daughter Joni came to see us every day. She was a freelance graphic designer then; she had gotten a scholarship to study at Cooper Union, the well-known art school in New York, and she had graduated in 1982. She was talented and smart, and on top of that, she was the most beautiful girl you had ever seen. At least Alan and I thought so. But she had been living for a decade with Sal, an Italian man much older than her. He was so possessive and jealous that she could not get a job because he did not want her to see any men at her work. When she was visiting us in Seattle she had to call him to report her locations many times a day, to let him know she was not seeing a man, but he still gave her hell every time she called, because of his jealousy. She was screaming and crying on the telephone. Alan could not stand to watch her that way, so he grabbed the telephone from her and said to him, "I will kill you!"

Anyway, during our stay in New York for Alan's birthday concert, Joni was seriously thinking of leaving him and wanted to come back to Seattle with us. The day of the concert, she called me frantically and said that Sal might have found out that she was planning to leave him and was behaving weirdly, and she was not sure what he was planning to do.

I realized the danger since Alan would be on the stage, conducting, he was the perfect target. I had to think of something quickly, without telling Alan, because it was the most important day for him and should not be disturbed. I thought of the fruit knife belonging to the hotel room kitchen, a six-inch long, black handled one. It was very cute but very sharp. I practiced throwing it at the hotel room couch over and over. The knife went through the couch every time. My plan was to watch Sal's every move during the performance, and if I noticed him taking out a gun to shoot Alan on the stage, I would stab him with my fruit knife before he could shoot.

The day of the concert, I hid the fruit knife in my purse and went to the concert hall where I was seated next to the archbishop in the center front row of the balcony, which was the best seat in the house. Joni and Sal were seated in the same row near me. Suddenly, up above, higher in the balcony, there was a commotion. Marvin Rosen, the pianist, and his wife, Beata, were waving their hands and calling for me to come and sit with them. Marvin had always been Alan's faithful fan and showed up at Alan's concerts on the East Coast. But how could I leave my seat, sitting side by side with the archbishop?

Alan's Eightieth Birthday Gala Celebration Concert opened with Alan conducting "Armenian Rhapsody No. 1," then "Prelude and Quadruple Fugue," and "Mysterious Mountain," conducted by Karel Husa. It was not as grand as I had heard at the rehearsal but maybe because those pieces were written for strings, so they lost their grandeur in the large expanse of Carnegie Hall, packed with the audience. Then Richie Havens narrated and sang three songs of his own. I did not know why he was on the program, and it seemed to me he was out of place. Alan and I did not know him at all, even though he was a well-known musician and singer in New York. It must have been Larry's idea, and maybe he knew Havens or he thought having him in the concert would help fill the concert hall.

Then Alan came onstage, majestically walking with his cane, and conducted his twenty-five-minute-long Symphony No. 65 "Artstakh," the symphony that had been commissioned for the concert. It was like Alan himself, majestic and had a unique rhythmic pattern I had never heard before. Larry noticed it and complimented it, too!

The concert ended safely without incident, and I did not have to use my knife, and after the concert I brought it home and have been using it ever since. Alan had difficulty during this period, and I had to help him, but, come to think of it, he did well for being in his eighties. He did conduct his own symphony in front of a full house at Carnegie Hall. He was a giant in every way, and he was one man in a million.

After the concert, a crowd of people formed a line to meet him, all the way from the main hall, upstairs, and to Alan's backstage room. Security was controlling the crowd as if Alan were a movie star, which he was. He was the most popular contemporary composer of the 20th century. Whoever came to the concert and saw Alan, the living composer, it was an unforgettable experience. I know that more than anybody else.

Dining at Ivar's (Clam Chowder Symphony)

♪

Dan called me and told me he was coming for our session on Saturday instead of Friday, the day we usually met, because his wife would be out of town, so he could go to dinner with me after the session. He was our old musician friend; after Alan died, he had been editing my writings, and at the same time teaching me English. Not only that, but he helped me with whatever he could, even carpentry.

Even though he was much younger than me, I had avoided going out with him in public because you never knew what people would think, so every time we went out, I took a girl friend with me. But in order to do this, I had to do the driving for them because they were getting old and were not driving anymore. "Is it worth it, just for one meal? Do I have to drive all over the countryside?"

After Dan's telephone call, I took his request seriously. I thought it seemed to me that every time I took him out for dinner the food was bad, so I should make it up to him sometime. I started to look for restaurants, then I remembered that I had been getting invitations from Ivar's restaurant for Alan's and my birthdays. Every year they sent us cards to treat us to a free dinner, even though Alan had been gone for nearly five years.

Ivar's is a well-known restaurant in Seattle. Ivar Johan Haglund, the founder of "Ivar's," was born in 1905 to Swedish and Norwegian parents. He started out with a fish-and-chips counter in the aquarium and then expanded into three restaurants and over twenty-five seafood bars throughout the Northwest. Every year, he treated people on the Fourth of July to fireworks over Elliott Bay, continuing for thirty-eight years. He was especially protective of the senior citizens like himself in his late years. He gave them discount cards and invited them for a dinner at his restaurants for their birthdays.

It was the year 1973, shortly after I had met Alan at a Northwest Composer's concert in North Seattle Community College. After the concerts, he wanted to see me, but I thought it was not proper to see him alone, because I was married and had three children, and he was obviously attracted to me. But I did not want to let go of my exciting experience. After all, I was a singer; to meet a famous, living composer was a once-in-a-lifetime experience! And it also happened that I liked his music! His music was very original yet not like any other contemporary composer's music I had heard; it was something I could connect with. His music had that beautiful melodic line and the emotion that all my favorite composers from the past had.

I decided to invite him to dinner with my family, Peter, my husband at that time, and my children, and I also invited Dora and Larry Mason. Dora, a soprano, was my former voice teacher. She was actually the one who had introduced me to Alan's music for the first time; at one of her vocal recitals, she sang "O Lady Moon," with clarinet and piano. I liked his music and was surprised to know that such a good composer existed in our time. She seemed to know a lot, both about him and his music, so I thought she would be interested in meeting him in person.

We picked up the composer at the bottom of Queen Anne Hill. He showed up with a gray cap and gray jacket and worn-out looking pants, carrying a heavy briefcase. Just looking at him, who would have ever thought of him as a famous composer? But we knew who he was and were all excited to meet him. We took him to the "Captain's Table," one of Ivar's restaurants on the waterfront.

We all sat at a table overlooking the waters of Elliott Bay. I wanted to treat him to something special; after all, Ivar's was well known for fish. But he did not show any interest in food and ordered a tuna sandwich.

I was sitting among the people, enjoying being with the composer and pretending not to know of his interest in me. I thought our get-together went successfully, but, when we went out to the parking lot, he came straight toward me and said to me that he wanted to see me and help my singing. He had gone through that masquerade party, but his intention, under the mask, never did sway and, now, he made his point without any hesitation; he was only interested in me, not anybody else! After that, he met me whenever he could, while he was in town, and helped me with my singing.

By 1974, Alan and I were very much in love with each other. During my mother's visit, I took her to my singing practice with Alan. I told my mother about our affair; she was very unhappy about what she heard, but she came along with me that day anyway.

After the practice, I asked my mother to take a picture of us at the church parking lot, even though Alan looked terrible that day. He was wearing his usual beat-up pants and jacket and carrying his worn-out brown briefcase. It had all his composing equipment and it looked more like a suitcase. But we were so much in love; we could not take our eyes off of each other.

From there I drove to Magnolia and my mother took three pictures of us under the eucalyptus trees beside the sea. After that, we had dinner at Ivar's restaurant on the waterfront at Pier 54. We all had fish dinners, but my impression was nothing special.

Later that day, my mother told me she felt strong eye contact between Alan and me all throughout the day. (We could not do anything but look at each other's eyes because she was with us.)

Where the Eucalyptus Trees Grow

Under the glory of sun
Where the eucalyptus trees grow
Edge of the seaside—we stood.

Our love young and strong then.
I can grasp it, in the photo.

But your mortal image—forever lost
And your resemblance remains only in the photo.
Can I ever find consolation equal to my comprehensive emptiness?

By February of 1987, Alan and I had been married for ten years. By that time, my mother, who had been living alone all those years in New York, had gotten old, and my sister Sunako in Japan was worried about her living all by herself. She asked me to find a place for her near us. So my son and his family all went out together and looked for a place for my mother. It happened at that time, the house next door to us was for sale. It was Alan's idea for my mother to live next to us. I never would have thought of my mother at seventy-nine years old living in a big house all by herself, but she liked the idea. Immediately, she came to Seattle and liked the house and bought it with her savings and help from my sister. She lived there until her death in 1996.

We went out together whenever we could, like the three musketeers. We went to many good restaurants, but my mother's favorite place was Ivar's seafood bar. After our grocery shopping, we dropped into Ivar's in Burien. It was a small, flat building at the corner of 1st Avenue. She liked fish and chips, and Alan always had clam chowder. His Symphony No. 40, the third movement, was inspired by Ivar's clam chowder. He used "clam chowder" as a simple original theme (subject) and developed it into a fugue and strict canon. We three sat around the small table and ate. It was our usual pastime. My mother was in her eighties, and by that time, our differences and difficulties were all resolved and replaced with acceptance and love for each other. Alan, who was three years younger than her, was getting old and was enjoying simple pleasures with me. I was twenty-one years younger than him, but I was well blended with them both. It was my simple happiness, and I wanted it to continue.

Finally, Dan and I were in Ivar's Salmon House in the University District—it was Dan's choosing. I was seated by a view window overlooking the Space Needle across Lake Washington. This was the place where Alan and I used to go often, after my singing lesson. The large, open dining room was built in native Indian style, and their specialty was salmon.

Dan and I ate salmon, and after the dinner, the waitress brought a bowl of dessert with a lighted candle in the center. Suddenly, a large baritone voice filled the hall. That was Dan, sitting in front of me, singing "Happy Birthday" to me. Soon, everybody in the room joined him in singing and then they applauded.

Alan often spoke of the founder of Ivar's restaurants, whose pictures are all over the restaurant walls. His business successors have kept his "will" well, to treat senior citizens well.

By now, Alan and my mother are meeting Ivar in the new place (or, their place of origin), thanking him for his generosity.

(But his singing clam chowder song on the TV commercial with his guitar was not up to Alan's professional standards.)

On Her 100th Birthday Year (My Mother, Jun Fujihara)

♪

"Why am I so depressed?" I have been asking myself this question.

I have nearly finished writing my husband's story, which I started seven and a half years ago. After he died, it was the only way I could cope with my unbearable pain of losing him; it became my daily routine.

And now, to realize it is coming to an end, is like losing him all over again. But then an idea came to me, if I still have the time, I could translate my mother's memoir into English. It was written in Japanese; I remember she had been writing it for a decade in New York when she was in her seventies.

So, since I have nearly completed Alan's story, my mother must have been thinking that this is her turn and demanding that I act on my words. Now it is clear where my depression is coming from, so I have to move on.

Her stories started with her memories of her childhood in old Korea, the time when spirits and witches were real. One night, she went to the waterfront and saw a pile of logs burning where the dark night and white sand met. The flames were flickering from the wind, and it was oh, so bright in her eyes. In front of the fire, a medium stood, her arms were stretched out to the sea, calling a spirit. My mother witnessed the enchanting, mystic world we have long lost.

In her teens, while she was teaching at a mission school, she got a scholarship from a Japanese bank to study in Japan. There she attended a women's school called *Sensin Jogakko* (Jr. High–Sr. High). She went to a Japanese women's college. During her college years, she met my father, who was studying to be a medical doctor in *handi* (Osaka University) but had contracted tuberculosis and had dropped out of college.

At that time in Japan, many young people were affected by this incurable disease and died. But throughout Japanese history, there had been propaganda against old age (I think it was a necessity because of their poor economic condition) and the people worshipped youth. So in their thinking, dying young were regretful yet beautiful and they romanticized it, like short-lived, falling cherry blossom petals.

One of their favorite love stories I read when I was young was called "Fu Jo Ki," the story of Takeo, a young naval officer, and his beautiful wife, Namiko, who dies from tuberculosis. Many tears were shed over this story.

My mother married my father despite his incurable disease, and he died a few years later, leaving her and his two children, Sunako and me. I was only two years old and Sunako was one.

My mother raised us all by herself, yet she never regretted her decision to marry him; instead, it was her pride and she idealized it. In the past, Japanese marriages were arranged; moreover, for my father to marry a Korean despite his family's opposition, it was unthinkable!

He was the love of her life, and she continued to love him for the rest of her life. In 1995, the year before she died, she was reading his love letters (sent to her during their separation when she was in Tokyo studying at college) and was seeing him clearly in her dreams. She said to me, "After all, he has been with us all these years, watching over us."

In 1986, she left New York and moved next door to us. Around that time, one of her short stories was published in a Japanese magazine called *Shufu No Tomo*, a magazine for ordinary housewives. She got an idea that they might publish her complete memoir. So she went to Japan but came home empty-handed. She could not publish her memoir, not because of her writing, but opposition from her own family, my sisters Sunako and Ahiko.

Sunako was a well-known knitting dress designer in Tokyo. She was afraid that if her mother's memoir was published, it would have exposed her as the daughter of a Korean and it would hinder her career. Even my younger sister, Ahiko, who was just a housewife who lived with her husband and two sons in the countryside near Kyoto, had kept her secret from her husband that she was half Korean.

At this time, I have to explain the relationship between Japan and Korea. The Japanese were openly prejudiced against the Koreans (not so much to other Orientals). Even though Japan and Korea have had a good relationship in the past, when Japan was still in a savage state, Korea was already a civilized country, and many skilled people went to Japan to teach.

In Ikeda, the town I lived in when I was a child, there were two shrines at both ends of the town, one on the hill and the other on the lowlands. When their festival (*omatsuri*) seasons came, everybody in the town participated. There were many temporary shops that formed on both sides of the street, all the way to the upper shrine (*ue no miya*). I never missed these festivals. I wore a summer kimono and stopped at each store, zig-zagging the street, side to side, eating candy, all the way to the *ue no miya* at the top of the hill. One of the shops I stopped at, a man was making candies in front of an audience. He mixed the candy dough and put it on sticks, one by one, shaped them into animals and birds, and painted them with a brush, red, green, and yellow. I was fascinated by it.

Ironically, everybody in town knew the shrines were a memorial for two Korean sisters. They had come to Japan to teach weaving, and after they died, the townspeople built shrines for them because they had been their teachers, even like gods.

Yet the Japanese, in general, ignored the past history of their relationship with Korea and degraded Koreans to a great extent. Even my father's understanding of Korean people was that "they were like animals" because once he saw a Korean man digging through a garbage dump, looking for something to eat. But when he met my mother, he was surprised to see an educated Korean woman and realized that his concept of Koreans had been influenced by Japanese prejudice.

My mother told me about what the Japanese did to Koreans, according to her own personal experience. They came to Korea and, little by little, took over the well-to-do and useful sections of the land. My mother told me that, every time she went home, their family had been pushed away to a different location, becoming poorer and poorer. She said, "The Japanese have a characteristic of invading others."

While growing up, I had difficulty at school, even though I was the prettiest girl and one of the top students in the class. One boy who was the most popular found out my mother came from Korea and tried to expose it to everybody. It was the most humiliating thing, to my young mind, and I could not admit it, so I denied it. But that made it worse; my denial excited him, and he became even more inquisitive. All this was happening to me, but my mother had never taught me to be honest and to say, "Yes, my mother is Korean, so what?"

(Japanese and Korean people are from the same Asian background. They look alike; therefore, it created suspicion toward the Koreans, like a "witch hunt.")

Obviously, my mother was a target of this prejudice. On top of that, she was a widow, which in Japanese writing "*mi bo jin*" means "person of no future." This word, in Japanese, clearly shows their concept of women; men owned women like possessions. It was figuratively like what the ancient Egyptians did when a husband died; the wife was buried alive in his tomb, with his dead body, along with his other belongings. Despite this injustice, she raised us by managing a sewing shop, dress making, and even teaching sewing, during the war time, because during war time, sewing notions and materials were no longer available and she did not have any way to earn money.

My mother must have had great financial difficulties, especially in the beginning, when we were very young. I remember one summer day we were riding in a bus, going to the country. It was supposedly a fun trip, but actually, we went there not for the vacation, but to escape from the money collectors.

Another time, we went for a walk. We were sensing something was not right and we asked my mother, "Where are we going?" She said, "We are going to a pond, to throw ourselves in." We were so scared and begged her not to do it and brought her home.

When I think of those days, I feel so grateful we survived and I appreciate what she did for us; that is why it is so important for my mother's memoir to come out, if not in Japan, by all means, in America.

At the same time, I express my gratitude (my mother joins me) to the United States of America, the country of all races, which gave me the freedom to say, "My mother was Korean!" without shame.

THE UNITED STATES OF AMERICA

No. 8558424

CERTIFICATE OF NATURALIZATION

Petition No. 57907

·ORIGINAL·

Personal description of holder as of date of naturalization: Date of birth March 28, 1932; sex Female; complexion Medium; color of eyes Brown; color of hair Black; height 5 feet 3 inches; weight 96 pounds; visible distinctive marks None

Marital status Married; Country of former nationality Japan

I certify that the description above given is true, and that the photograph affixed hereto is a likeness of me.

Hinako Fujihara Holst.
(Complete and true signature of holder)

United States of America
Western District of Washington } ss:

Be it known, that at a term of the U. S. District Court of Western District of Washington, Northern Division, held pursuant to law at Seattle, Washington on March 23, 1964 the Court having found that HINAKO FUJIHARA HOLST then residing at 804 S. W. 118th Street, Seattle, Washington intends to reside permanently in the United States (when so required by the Naturalization Laws of the United States), had in all other respects complied with the applicable provisions of such naturalization laws, and was entitled to be admitted to citizenship, thereupon ordered that such person be and (s)he was admitted as a citizen of the United States of America.

In testimony whereof the seal of the court is hereunto affixed this 23rd day of March in the year of our Lord nineteen hundred and sixty-four

Seal

It is a violation of the U.S. Code (and punishable as such) to copy, print, photograph, or otherwise illegally use this certificate.

HAROLD W. ANDERSON
Clerk of the UNITED STATES DISTRICT Court.
By [signature] Deputy Clerk.

DEPARTMENT OF JUSTICE

Hinako Holst's certificate of naturalization

Mother's Day, 1994

Mother's Day is coming, the day after tomorrow…

My mother is in the air.

One Mother's Day I will never forget was in 1994.

Alan had just finished composing two choral pieces commissioned by Bellevue Chamber Chorus, and they were going to be performed on Mother's Day. "Pastime With Good Company" op. 432 no. 1, was based on Henry VIII's poem, for flute, drum, timpani, and chorus, and "The Baby's Dance" op. 432 no. 2, was based on a poem by Ann Taylor, for flute, harp, and chorus.

We sat all the way through the first part of the concert, and finally at the end was Alan's piece. His piece was the only one we enjoyed that day; it was like a delicious dessert after an ordinary meal. After that, they changed the theme to something entirely different, old-style popular music ("Begin the Beguine," etc.), so we had to leave the theatre without going backstage, as usual, to meet the performers.

We had parked the car at a Bellevue Square parking garage and crossed the sky bridge to get to the shopping center. I was going to take my mother to shop to buy her some lipstick so she could choose her own favorite color, but halfway on the sky bridge, my mother put the brakes on her feet and said she couldn't walk anymore, she didn't care to shop, and she wanted to eat. My plan was to take her to a coffee shop after the shopping and then we would drive to a Japanese restaurant on Capitol Hill for dinner, but I had to drive her to the Japanese restaurant in mid-afternoon.

I was grumbling, but my mother was insisting, so what was Alan to do? He was swaying whatever direction the wind was blowing. Finally, we got to the restaurant and a young Japanese waitress showed up at our table. Immediately, my mother started ordering her dinner and told the waitress what to do in Japanese, in the manner of a tyrant. She could have done it in such a manner in old Japan, but not nowadays, especially in America. Her dinner was bad, she was upset, and she complained in the same manner of a tyrant.

My plan for Mother's Day for her had entirely failed. How about my Mother's Day?

But funny, now my mother is gone, and even Alan is gone…

I have forgotten any other sweet, happy Mother's Days, but this Mother's Day, 1994, is towering among all the other Mother's Day memories.

Sea of Unko

Unko is a Japanese word, the first word anybody would pick up. It means "feces" in English. My son's family and Alan and I openly used this word because it was very convenient. In America, nobody knew what we were saying, so we felt very safe.

When Bill was very young, we lived on top of a hill. There was a large Japanese-Hawaiian family who lived down the hill, and one of their boys was in Bill's class. The first time Bill visited him in his home, Bill came home and said, "Mom, Orientals are bad, they were saying '*unko*.'" I noticed he was smiling; he himself was half Japanese, so it was a happy surprise to him to find children who spoke such a bad word so freely.

Alan and Bill often used "that word" with certain smiles on their faces. Alan and I used it, too, every day; after all, it is a very necessary word.

Alan told me a funny story. One night, he was writing concert program notes for his music. In the notes, he was going to write "sea of unconsciousness," but he didn't know the exact spelling at that moment. He meant to look it up later in the dictionary but forgot, so he proceeded to complete his writing and sent it out the next morning.

On the day of the concert, he was seated in the audience; then he opened the program and saw what he had written. To his horror, his program notes said, "Sea of Unco." Then he realized he had never completed the word "unconsciousness." He looked around to see if any Japanese audience were there because they would know the meaning of the word.

That story became our family favorite. Obviously, Alan was enjoying telling his story, knowing we were the one sympathetic and appreciative audience.

Just the other day, I was talking to my son Bill on the telephone; he expressed himself as to why this word is so freely used by us, because it sounds very friendly; "unko," compared to English or German sh… They sound terrible, and we could not speak of it. That is true; I never thought of it that way, but he has a point. Using that word doesn't give us a dirty, obscene feeling; instead, it sounds cute and gives us a feeling of intimate closeness.

What is the matter with me? I am supposed to write an important letter to a record company. Instead, I got an inspiration from "*unko*."

Baby's Dance

Coleen, my son's wife, was going to have her fourth baby. The night of the delivery, Alan and I were invited to the hospital to witness the baby's birth.

To my way of thinking, inviting people to the delivery was unthinkable. The arrival of the baby is a very important event, but in my time, it was kept private, even from your own husband. I will summarize an ancient Japanese story I knew from childhood that expresses how we felt about birthing.

There were two brothers who lived at a place between the mountains and the ocean. Every morning the elder brother went to sea to catch fish and the younger brother went to the mountain to hunt. But one day, the younger brother wanted to switch their positions, so they did, but at the end of the day, the elder brother who had gone to the mountains came home empty-handed. Also, the younger brother returned without catching any fish. On top of that, he lost his brother's fishhook. To calm his brother's anger, he made hundreds of fishhooks, but his brother only wanted the one he had lost.

So the younger brother had to go back to the sea to find his brother's fishhook. When he got to the bottom of the sea, there was a palace where the Queen of the Oceans dwelled. He was welcomed and entertained by the queen and her fish maids. When he was leaving, the queen gave him back the fishhook he had lost and offered her daughter to be his wife.

Soon they were on land. They married, and the daughter, now his wife, became pregnant. Her delivery day came near, and she asked her husband to promise not to see her while she was having the baby. He promised her, but when the time came and he heard her moaning and crying, he could not help it and opened the door to her room. There he saw an alligator, writhing on the floor in agony. After the birth, she left her human baby with him and went back to her ocean palace. This story expresses the way women of my time felt about sex and baby bearing, because we were not educated openly about it like people nowadays.

Nevertheless, we were invited, and when we got there, Coleen was already on the delivery table. Bill was dressed like hospital staff, with a cap and mask. There was another person in the room, Sue, Coleen's sister. Alan thought it was not proper for him to see her giving birth, so he took their three children, Xenia, William, Jr., and Gregory, to the waiting room. Alan became the babysitter for the night. But as time went by, things got difficult for Coleen. I don't think she expected that, because she had had easy births in the past. The nurse notified the doctor, but he did not come into her room for a long time, and this made Coleen suffer. Every time she cried, Sue and I cursed the doctor; finally, when the baby was about to come on its own, the doctor came and delivered the baby.

In the meantime, back at the waiting room, Alan was watching the three kids with pen and notebook in his hand. The kid's game was climbing on a couch and jumping on the floor, especially Gregory, the youngest. He was the baby in the family, and he had been getting all the attention to himself. But now, he was noticing something was wrong. His mother had been taken away and some excitement was taking his place. He was wild, jumping down from the edge of the couch, over and over, despite Grandpa Alan's disapproval.

After all the excitement and activities were quieted down, Alan told me about his evening and said, "That Gregory—he was suiciding himself." That night, February 3, 1994, the baby girl Tracy was born, and also Alan's composition "Baby's Dance" op. 432, in the waiting room of the delivery room, inspired by the event.

Harold's Curse – Our 1994 Trip to Whistler Mountains

♪

In the summer of 1994, we planned to take a family vacation during my son Bill's vacation from his work.

Here in Washington state, there are so many places to explore, so the choices are endless: the Cascade mountain range going through the state from north to south, the Olympic mountain range over the Olympic peninsula between Puget Sound and the Pacific Ocean, Mount Rainier, the most impressive mountain in the middle of the state, and Canada is just a two-hour drive from Seattle. Alan made the choice to go to Whistler, north of Vancouver, BC.

In 1976, after our painful three-month separation, Alan had come back to me for good, and soon after that, on July 4, we drove to Canada (because Alan wanted to escape from the noise of fireworks). We drove north of Vancouver and found a small village called Squamish; this place attracted Alan very much, so we stayed there in a motel and explored the surrounding mountain countryside.

One day, we drove north and found ourselves among the endless mountains; Alan loved it. Finally, we got to the place called Whistler Mountain Resort. We saw the empty chair lift on the side of the mountains and realized we were there at the wrong time of the year; this place was for skiers in winter.

Alan remembered this place and wanted to go back for our family vacation. According to our travel agent, the place was all built up since our visit, and she persuaded us to take the trip.

With Bill and his wife Coleen and their four children in one car and my mother and Alan and me in another, we all left for the Whistler Mountains.

We drove for two and a half hours to the Canadian border, then bypassed the road to Vancouver and took route 15 to highway 1 and drove along the coastline of Horseshow Bay, a never-ending, dangerous, winding road. I very much regretted driving there; if I would have known this, I never would have taken this trip. Finally, after over three hours of driving, we got to the Whistler Resort. The place was as large as a village, located between two mountain ranges, Blackcomb and Whistler.

We stayed at Glacier Lodge; our room came with a kitchen and my mother's room was next to ours, without a kitchen. I was thinking she would just sleep there and come to our room to eat breakfast with us. Bill's room was farther away from ours; it was very spacious and private, like a large cabin. It had a kitchen and even an extra bed in a loft upstairs.

In the evening, we all went to Monk's Grill, which was recommended by the hotel, but we found it a disappointment. After we went back to our rooms and were about to go to bed, the fire alarm blasted off, so we all ran out of the building and stood outside in our nighties. We waited for a long time, but nothing happened, so we all went back to our rooms.

In the daytime, Bill's family was on their own and did whatever they wanted, and we "old folks" did things at our own pace; however, we all got together at dinner. The day following the alarm scare, even though I did not like their recommendations, I again asked the front desk about a good place to eat. This time they recommended "Thai One On" and said it was the best restaurant in the resort. (I had never eaten Thai food before, but I was going to try it—after all, it was supposed to be the best restaurant.) So off we went.

When we got to the restaurant, I could not believe what I saw: a large, life-like monkey standing in the center of the restaurant. His name was "Harold." His thing was overemphasized and exposed; how could we eat, looking at such a vulgar thing? What could we do other than leave the place? I made the waiter move the monkey and a couple of them came and carried it away. But our difficulty did not end there. The food was just as bad as their taste, too many mixtures of different kinds of foods, no continuity and no artistry (like Japanese food). We left the restaurant, having hardly eaten anything.

After Bill's family left to go to their room, we walked up the stairway to our rooms. I was beside my mother, holding her arm to support her, as always. Suddenly, without warning, she lost her balance and tipped over violently. We both were thrown through the air and my purse flew away on impact. As soon as I hit the floor, I looked for my mother and I saw her hitting the back of her head on the cement floor. I ran to rescue her; meanwhile, Alan stood there, doing nothing, as if he could not connect what was happening. That was the year before his Alzheimer's condition became apparent. Come to think of it, he may already have had that condition, but I didn't know it then. After we went back to our rooms, we debated about taking my mother to the emergency room or not, but she seemed okay, and she never had any difficulty from her fall.

The next day, the 11th, we went up the Whistler Mountain by gondola. Alan had wanted to do this all along, since 1976 when we had been there before, but my mother could not stand the height, so we had to leave her in the car. On the top of the mountain, we saw the glorious mountain ranges Blackcomb and Whistler. I took many pictures of Alan, surrounded by the mountains; a nice person saw us and took pictures of Alan and me together. When we came down from the mountain, we saw our car doors all open and found my mother very upset because we had been gone so long.

On August 12, we decided to drive to Vancouver instead of going straight home, because I wanted to treat them to good food. On the way there, we stopped at Squamish and visited August Jack Motor Inn, where Alan and I had stayed in 1976, then we went to Shannon Falls.

Finally, we got to the Bayshore Hotel in downtown Vancouver, where we had had fond memories; Conductor Andre Kostelanetz had invited us for his concert and had put us up in this hotel. There in the hotel dining room we had a formal English-style dinner, at a big, long table with a white tablecloth, all to ourselves. We had a steak dinner, and it was oh, so good. It made up for all the bad food we had eaten in the mountains and was worth driving there.

My granddaughter Xenia said that the accident my mother and I had in the mountains was caused by "Harold's curse."

Victoria, Victoria – Your Memory Breaks My Heart

♪

When I think of Victoria, my heart aches from my painful memory.

On July 31, 1995, while I was taking a bath, Alan came into the bathroom and asked politely if I was his wife. I was more upset than anything else and answered him, "No!"

Then he said, "She must have gone to Philadelphia with her family." My son Bill and his family had been living near us, just over the other side of Benson Hill, but recently he left for Philadelphia because he was about to lose his job and he had found another job there. He had to support his wife, four children, two dogs, two cats, and birds, so he did not have any choice but to go.

Now, I realize Alan must have been very much dependent on my son's family. Alan had had many marriages, but for the first time, he had a family. Since our marriage, he had seen weddings, childbirth, etc., within the family, and he was content to be their "grandpa."

There in the bathroom, I should not have said *no* to him (that I was not his wife); it may have caused his mind to snap. As far as I was concerned, I was not prepared for such nonsense; I was his wife, naturally, and for him to ask if I was his wife or not was not at all what I had expected to hear. So I gave him a sarcastic answer. If I had known his condition, I would have said, "Yes, I am your wife," and explained it to him kindly, but this was the first sudden indication of his sickness, and I was not prepared. After that, his confusion rapidly progressed.

On August 24, less than a month later, I took Alan to Port Angeles, on the Olympic Peninsula, a place we had visited many times before, from which we had many nostalgic memories. I drove through Tacoma to Bremerton, instead of taking the ferry, and crossed over Hood Canal and drove all the way to Port Angeles.

I was about thirty minutes away from Port Angeles, and Alan, who had been sitting beside me in the car, said, "I left my wife at home."

I thought, "What does he mean, I am here in the car, but he thinks I am there?" He was confused, but now, I was confused also. I was very upset, but I explained to him that I was his wife and we had left home together, but he could not believe me and wanted to drive back. But we were almost to Port Angeles, so I drove there against his will. We had an uncomfortable night in the hotel room; his condition was worse there than at home. (This often happens to a person who has Alzheimer's condition; they do better in their own familiar environment.)

Earlier that evening, at the hotel restaurant, I ordered a salad, but it was a huge amount, more than I could possibly have eaten, so I called my daughter June, who lived in Sequim, a fifteen-minute drive from us, and asked her if she would like to have my salad. She said she would, so Alan and I drove to her house, bringing the salad.

Before the trip, she was not particularly happy about us going to Port Angeles and visiting her, but we had decided to go anyway on our own, with no plan to visit her. But I was glad I called her. The next two days, she joined us for dinner at different restaurants. For some neurotic reason, her husband did not join us, but June was very happy and enjoyed eating out. Somehow, June being with us helped Alan's mind to stabilize and softened our difficulties.

The next day, the 25th, we took a ferry boat to Victoria, B.C. As soon as we got off the boat, Alan said he would get on the boat and go back because he did not want to be in a foreign country. During that period, his confusion came like a cloud, and he became a stranger to me. There we were on the Victoria waterfront, bright red geraniums planted in perfect order all over the gardens in front of the buildings, huge hanging baskets with multi-colored flowers hanging down on both sides of the light posts, all around the port, against the blue water. This striking beauty made a big contrast to my inner suffering.

I managed to find a coffee shop for Alan. I thought that would help him to feel comfortable, because he composed in a coffee shop, almost every day. I made tea for him, with honey and cream, and it did help him, but I had to give up on going to Butchart Gardens—it was out of the question. So we stayed there in Victoria, looked around the flower gardens, watched the boats come in and out of the harbor, and I took a few pictures of Alan under the hanging baskets.

On the way back on the ferry boat, I stood alone on the front edge of the deck, looking at the water. At the end of the water, I saw Port Angeles coming nearer as the boat sailed. It was the loneliest time of my life with Alan, because it was as if he had been taken away from me by somebody else. It was because of his mental condition, but it was as if I were experiencing that situation, losing Alan. Later, his sickness progressed, physically as well, and I had to work hard for him. My sympathy and concern for him turned to a deeper dimension of love and devotion.

The evening of the day we were going to leave Port Angeles, before we left, we were to have dinner with June, but I could not get her on the telephone. (Her husband must have put the brakes on her because she had been enjoying herself too much.) So instead, Alan and I had dinner at a Kentucky Fried Chicken. They had a buffet dinner and, to my surprise, it was the best we ever had. Their custard bread pudding was so good, I took some home. We were happy there because Alan was his usual self.

Through My Pain ("Rubaiyat" Performance with Alexandria Symphony)

For the last three days I have had a stomach flu-like condition with severe pain in the abdomen. After breakfast, the ordeal started and I had to be in bed, bearing the pain. It seems to me this condition comes back to me every few years. At my first attack, I was taken to the hospital in the ambulance; between the tests I threw up everything and came home with Pepto-Bismol.

One of the most unforgettable times was in 1995. Alan and I had been invited to Alexandria, VA, for a performance of his "Rubaiyat." Rita Balian, a very influential Armenian lady, invited us on behalf of the symphony. According to her, the Alexandria Symphony was the most sophisticated orchestra, more so than the National Symphony in Washington, D.C., but they chose to perform Alan's most popular piece, "Rubaiyat."

By that time, Alan's Alzheimer's condition had become apparent, but still, I kept it quiet. That trip was not an easy one, not just because of taking care of Alan, but having to watch out for him at every minute so people would not notice his condition. The day of the concert, we were invited for dinner at the Balians and for a reception after the concert. But the next morning, when I woke up and went to the bathroom, I started my ordeal. After that I was in bed with stomach pain all day, until the next day.

Two of my children, Bill from Philadelphia and Joni from Brooklyn, came to the performance, and we were looking forward to having breakfast together, but they had to go to breakfast without me, and Bill had to take my place to watch Alan.

Bill told me the story; at the restaurant dining room, he was getting food for Alan and himself at the buffet cart. In the distance, he could see Alan sitting at a table, and a waitress came up and asked Alan if he would like to have coffee. Alan was nodding his head, and just as the coffee was being poured in his cup, Bill yelled, "No!" from across the room, one finger up in the air. (He had had instructions from me not to give Alan coffee because of his stomach condition.)

After that, while I was moaning in bed, my children left, one by one. The next day, I got up from bed, just because we had to catch the airplane to go home. I could drink only water that day.

I had another attack in the year 2000, a few months after Alan died. I went to bed with stomach pain early on New Year's Eve and could not get up from bed until New Year's Day.*

Today, after I went through my agony, I understood what sick people have to go through. After Alan died, at a psychic reading, the psychic told me how happy Alan was when he died;

he was finally free from his defective body. I felt a certain jealousy when I heard that because I had tried so hard to keep him alive, yet he was happy when he left me. But now I understand what he had felt.

He had endured his discomfort for such a long time (only to please me) because he could see my effort, my desperate attempt to save him by any means, but it was very hard for him to keep up with me. Now that I look back, I feel guilty and even tortured by what I did. But if I had the chance to do it over again, would I let him go earlier? Could I let him die?

On June 4, 2000, Alan almost died in the emergency room. A young woman doctor told me to let Alan die and said, "Give him his dignity." Did she know the real meaning of her words? I think that giving up trying to cure elderly who are sick and calling it "dignity" is just an excuse, taking the easy way out and not feeling guilty.

So my answer was *no* because how could I let him die without doing anything, just watching him go? I do not have that in me.

*On November 23, 2005, Dr. Sanford diagnosed that I had gallstones and operated on December 14 of that year. It was the end of my unpredictable pain.

Peaceful Life (One Snow Day in 1996)

♪

That disastrous day in 1996…

I took you (Alan) to the emergency room, and later you were transferred to a hospital room; I stayed in the room with you that night, then the snow started. In the meantime, my mother became sick at her house next door to us, but I was snowed in at the hospital and could not get to her, so I called an ambulance for her. She was brought into the emergency room of the same hospital where you and I were staying. I knew she was seriously ill and that she needed me, so I had to be in two places at the same time. Every time I left your room to be with her, you made trouble, so the nurse had to tie you onto a post, you and the wheelchair together, so you could not hurt yourself. One elderly nurse who watched me with my difficulty couldn't help expressing herself: "I wish for your peaceful life in the future!"

Now, after you and my mother have gone, it seems I am having that peaceful life that the nurse spoke of, but I never asked for it. All my life, the one thing I could not stand was being alone or loneliness. But that is what I have and what I have to endure; I assume that for what I am and for what I have to do, I have to be alone.

You have been gone for one year and seven months. Living alone in my house is like I have gone from the world, like a "sennin."* It is as if I am living in the midst of a high mountain, looking down on civilization, thinking of you, that is my whole world. I haven't really lived since you died. Is this called a "peaceful life"?

*sennin: A mountain genie who existed in the high mountains of Japan, surviving by eating mountain mist; an unworldly person.

Fantasy on *M*A*S*H*

♪

I was watching an old rerun of *M*A*S*H* on TV last night. This is the program I started watching recently that comes on at midnight. The stage is set during the Korean War, and a group of doctors, nurses, and staff were thrown in together in a combat medical unit. The program is presented with humor and pathos. I understand and I am sympathetic to these people because of my experience of taking care of Alan for three years before he died.

Last night, the episode was about the temporary replacement of a young, tall, impressive surgeon who came to help the unit. A flood of injured soldiers was carried in while all the doctors were busy operating. Later, this young surgeon lost his mind because of overwhelming injured bodies and so much blood. Other doctors and nurses were looking at him as if they were looking at themselves—they were going through this and dealing with it in their own way.

This show reminded me of a story my mother told me about my father's experience when he was an intern. The first-time interns were brought to the dissecting room for their first demonstration of an actual dissection, where you heard the noise of bodies hitting the floor, one by one. They fainted, but they experienced this over and over and overcame their fear. On the contrary, some others never made it.

When I was taking care of Alan, after his stomach operation in 1997, I tried to make him walk again. I gave him exercise every day, first with a walker; I followed behind him with a wheelchair to catch him, in case of falling. I continued this for a long time, long after the professional health care nurse gave up.

Toward the end, his condition worsened, and I experienced unimaginable things, but it was unavoidable, like I was in combat. I had to deal with lots of bleedings and cleanings. I never knew if he might die at any time. I had to call an ambulance to take him to the hospital as often as twice a week; by that time, he could not even move his own body. But I survived and I became stronger. The doctor and I never gave up; we tried to do one more procedure to save him. He died in the midst of our attempt. It was the end.

But now, I look back and question where my strength came from. After all, was my father helping me?

In 1990, Alan broke his hip. After the operation, he came home, but he was a little confused because of the effect of the anesthesia. He said, "Hinako, I saw a young Japanese man was taking care of me when you were not around." I knew he was confused, but we came to the conclusion that it was my dead father watching over Alan.

My father, who tried to be a doctor, couldn't make it because he died from tuberculosis when he was only thirty-one years old. He had to leave his wife and two baby daughters behind. How difficult it was for him to die; he had every reason to help me and Alan. After all, my father was a doctor; to take care of the sick was his business.

Today I look back on my life as a whole and the most important thing I did was taking care of Alan when he needed me the most. I could do this because my father gave me the gift of his "doctor's genes." So, my question is, did he come through me to help Alan, or was he actually there in person? I know this, he was there. We are being watched over by spirits, the spirits of our loved ones.

Their love is in a timeless zone.

Alan's Ordeal – 1997

♪

The year 1997 started out very badly for Alan. On January 3, his blood count went down to 22.8, and he stayed overnight in the hospital for a blood transfusion. He had another two transfusions in the same month; his blood count was watched closely and tested at the doctor's office every week. The month of February was not so bad since he had only one transfusion, but on March 5, his blood count went down drastically, and he was hospitalized.

He had been losing blood from his stomach. It was not cancerous, but the blood vessels in his stomach bled. In my opinion, his condition did not start then, but it was the result of his lifetime of coffee drinking. Especially when he was on concert trips, he drank coffee non-stop, one cup after another, and this irritated his stomach.

He was in the hospital for three days, but his bleeding did not stop. Every time the tester became blue to indicate he was bleeding. On March 7, Dr. O'Neill, who was Alan's doctor, sat with me and told me that he could not help Alan this time. He thought Alan's bleeding would not stop. He would discharge him, and hospice would come to my house to help me. So I asked him, "Does that mean he will bleed to death?" and then he said, "Yes." I could not believe what I'd heard.

After that, my son Bill came to the hospital and took us home. On our way home, Alan began bleeding heavily. As soon as we got him home, Bill came in and helped me put him in the bathtub and wash him. When he saw so much blood, he was surprised and thought Alan would not live but a few days.

The next day was Alan's birthday. Bill and Coleen and their four children came to Alan's birthday party. Hospice had been calling me to come to my house for me to sign the papers to take over Alan's care from the doctor. I could not sign such a paper; it was very bad arrangement because if I would have signed it, then there would be no more doctor and no more transfusion for Alan—just sit and do nothing, watch him die. It was like a death sentence, so I told her, "Today is Alan's birthday—just leave him alone," and dismissed her.

We had an intimate family gathering. We ate together, like we always had done, but this time we were holding somber thoughts. Alan might die in a few weeks or even a few days, and this may be the last gathering.

I was very upset with Dr. O'Neill because of his decision to let Alan die without asking my wishes. He was of Scottish descent like Alan (Alan's mother was Scottish); also, he knew who Alan was and was proud to be his doctor and would try everything in his power to save him, at least that's what I had thought.

Helping the sick and hurt has been my instinct because I came from a doctor's family. Though my father could not become a doctor because of his sickness, his older and younger brothers were doctors. They had a hospital together in the country in Japan.

One night at the hospital, Alan was confused and made trouble; then the elderly nurse who had been taking care of him called me outside the room and told me I should consider letting Alan die. I was shocked and reported this to Dr. O'Neill, but to my surprise, he was not shocked. He said to me that that was the general thinking of health care people concerning the sick elderly.

Around that time, former President Nixon died and President Clinton praised Nixon publicly because Nixon had refused to take any treatments and so had died.

I thought this would be a bad influence on people, as if Clinton was setting a tone to let old people die at a certain time without prolonging their treatment. But our circumstances are all different. It happened that, in Nixon's case, he chose to die because his wife had died before him, so he had no reason to linger on without her. But Alan's case was different, and I needed and wanted him to live, even though his life was hanging by a thin thread. How about Alan's audience? With Alan being alive gave a different perspective to them, listening to the music of a living composer.

Because of our technologies and drugs, people live longer than in the past, so the number of elderly people has been increasing, and they are becoming a burden on society instead of honorable senior citizens. The pendulum has swung the other way, and people's idea is that the value of human life has declined; this has happened in over-populated countries in the past, especially towards the elderly.

In my opinion, by and by, we are losing freedom and respect for the individual by just becoming numbers. To keep them alive by any means was considered prolonging life unduly, letting them die naturally is giving them dignity. This idea helps a person or society to make a decision for the sick (to live or die) without guilt.

Help from Mr. Schwarz

By March 9, the day after Alan's birthday, my decision was very clear. I could not sit and watch Alan die. I stopped hospice (even though they were eager to come) and called Gerard Schwarz, the music director/conductor of Seattle Symphony. Up to that time, he had not been our personal friend, but he had performed Alan's "Mount St. Helens" Symphony to great success and was beginning to understand Alan's greatness. In my desperate attempt to save Alan, I had to use Alan's reputation, which was the last card I hadn't used before. I told Mr. Schwarz that Alan was dying and asked him to please find the best doctor in town for him. He called me back that evening and had found a doctor. His name was Dr. Martin Greene. Mr. Schwarz had known him through his involvement with the symphony, and his wife was a well-known cellist in town. The doctor called me the next day and thought he could help Alan.

We went to see him on March 12th, and on the 14th, he examined Alan's stomach with the scope. Miraculously, his bleeding had stopped, and his blood count stayed around thirty. According to Dr. Greene, patients like Alan who were anemic could survive with a low blood count. He also wanted Alan to see Dr. Goldberg, a young, brilliant Jewish hematologist. So we went to see him, and he gave Alan an injection to help stimulation of his blood production. He gave me the sample vials for me to give the injections at home.

April, May, and June passed more or less smoothly; then in July, Alan was hospitalized for a transfusion and test. All along, Dr. Greene had had difficulty determining exactly where Alan's bleeding was coming from, even with his wonderful scope. This instrument, which had been invented in Japan, was like a long water hose with a magnifying glass attached at the end, so the doctor could see inside the intestine, while the tube was traveling inside the body. It could even take pictures by attaching a camera to it.

In early 1990, Alan had started having this problem, and he had been with two other doctors. They, too, had never found out the source of Alan's bleedings, and they called his condition "mysterious bleedings."

Dr. Greene explained that bleeding from the stomach stops sometimes, especially during testing, so it was very difficult to catch the bleeding at the right time, and he thought Alan's bleeding must have come from the small intestine, where the scope could not go through the narrow passage. This time, even Dr. Greene could not stop Alan's bleeding, so he asked Dr. Cohen, the chief surgeon of Swedish Hospital, to operate on Alan—to cut out the bleeding part of the stomach.

Alan's Stomach Operation

On August 26, Alan was brought into a large waiting room outside of the operating rooms. I sat beside his bed. Alan was very much like his old self that day. We passionately expressed our love for each other since we knew this might be the last time we would be together.

Alan went into the operation, and I waited the longest hours, fearing I might lose him. Finally, Dr. Greene came into the room and told me the operation had finished and Alan had come through okay. I was overjoyed!

He had been put into the intensive care unit, and I slept in his room in a small space between the room full of machinery. The nurse's station was just outside the room so they could take care of Alan when he needed them. He screamed so loud from the pain, as if the end of the world were coming. I felt so guilty that I had put him through this to save his life, but at the same time, I did not want to lose him, for my sake. A week later, on September 2, we left the hospital. As soon as we got home, Alan's training started. The visiting physical therapist came to help him to walk again.

At Schwarz's Party

Three weeks later, on September 17, we were invited to a pre-concert reception at Mr. Schwarz's house. The famous pianist Van Cliburn was going to perform a concert with the symphony and Maestro Schwarz was conducting. At the opening of the concert, Alan was to receive the 1997 Art Award in recognition of outstanding leadership and dedication to the Seattle Symphony.

When we got to his house, I realized I had forgotten to bring Alan's walker. By this time, he could walk with a walker, but without it he had to be supported by me, a woman half his height. He was practically hopping up and down during the party, among Van Cliburn and all the important people. The whole evening we sat all by ourselves. We must have looked strange to the distinguished guests.

At the Concert and Dinner Party

On September 19, before the concert, Maestro Schwarz suggested that I accept Alan's award for him, so I went up on the stage, dressed in a striking purple dress, and accepted the award. From the edge of the stage, I waved to Alan, who was sitting in the first row at the opera house, to acknowledge him to the audience. After the concert, somebody mentioned I had made the evening; I cannot help that I am a "ham" actress.

After the concert, an usher transported Alan in his wheelchair, pushing him all the way to another building where the party was going on, through the pathways of Seattle Center in the night. When we got there, the large room was filled with people and a band was playing. I had never expected a party to be like this after a classical concert. We should have left right away, but we stayed. People were dancing in an area in front of the tables and food was brought in, one table at a time. We had to wait between the courses and it took the whole evening to get something to eat. The main dish of the dinner was roast pheasant with champagne cranberry glaze and pine nut stuffing, but I don't remember anything of what I ate. We left the noisy party with a feeling of loneliness.

Alan's Seizure

The next day, September 20, I put him on the toilet. He wanted to get off, but I told him to stay put; then he got upset, like a little child, and the next minute he started having a seizure. I held his body tightly so he would not fall, and after the ordeal, I called an ambulance and we both went to the hospital. Alan was unconscious for two days, and when he finally opened his eyes, I was overjoyed, and noticed the other people in the room, too, who had been watching my agonizing wait.

The day before he was going to leave the hospital, the doctor decided to put him in a rehabilitation house before going home. Alan had a choice as to which home to stay in. I drove around all day, visiting a dozen nursing homes to find the nicest place for him to stay. Finally, I found a place in Des Moines, overlooking the ocean, not far from my house. By the time I had finished filling out papers, etc., it was almost six PM and I had not eaten breakfast yet.

Jodson Park Health Center: Alan and Me Together

Alan shared a room there with another man. We were lucky, Alan's bed was near the window side, so we had more privacy. Between the two beds there was a big drapery to divide the rooms, so when the roommate was in, I closed it.

I practically lived there with Alan. I went home late at night just to sleep, after Alan had been all taken care of and I had tucked him into bed. I even brought a small TV from home. Before each meal, I selected food from the menu for him and warmed it up in a microwave oven. It seemed Alan and I were making ourselves at home, but poor Arthur, Alan's roommate, was all alone.

One evening, Alan and I had finished eating and were watching the TV. I sensed someone was there and opened the divider; there was Arthur, on his wheelchair beside the bed, all alone. Somebody had left him there, all this time.

According to the health care people, Arthur had Alzheimer's and could not walk, but he was very strong and violent. He had hurt a nursed aide in the past, so he was not popular, and it seemed everybody had been staying away from him. But I had a certain sympathy for him because I knew something about him the other people didn't.

He talked all by himself while he was asleep. "I am Arthur, my dear father and mother died…" And he spoke a woman's name; she must have been his wife. I was wondering what had happened to her since I never saw anybody visiting him, so she must have died also. In the middle of the night, he cried, "Help, help!" but nobody came. Even Alan, who had his own condition and could not talk much, noticed his fellow man was in trouble and looked at me with worried eyes.

Alan was so lucky because I was young, so I could take care of him and keep him company. But those old people, they had lost their mates and were all alone.

That ward was for the Alzheimer's patients. In the evening, after most of the workers had left, strange things began to happen. The patients were wandering around the place and were going into the rooms of those who were sleeping. One old girl came into our room to see Arthur very often when he was sleeping—she had a certain interest in him. (I guess no matter how old we get, interest in the opposite sex never goes away.) She reminded me of a kindergarten girl who was interested in a boy who was in her class.

Another patient I got to know was Mary. She was younger than the others and it seemed there was nothing wrong with her health, but she was very lost. She did speak, but nobody could understand what she was saying. Somehow I deciphered she had a daughter and, on her good days, she remembered her.

Many patients missed their old homes; to come to a nursing home was not necessarily their own choice. Sometimes a new patient came in and cried like a child, wanting to go home.

The place was much protected, but like a jail, patients could not go out by themselves. I did not see any patients going out, even with an escort, in the two weeks we were there. The nurse's station was at the front elevator entrance, and they kept their eyes on the patients at all times. The nursing home doctor came once a week, and every time he came, Alan was asleep. The doctor interpreted that he was in bad shape, so I said to him, "That is not true. You come in every time while he is sleeping. How can you tell his true condition?" He was upset at what I had said and told me I had verbally abused him. (What a weak character, abused by what I had said! Altogether, the word "abuse" is becoming a habit; it is a convenient word to put innocent people in trouble.)

In order for Alan to come home, I had to prove to this doctor that Alan was in good condition and that I would be able to take care of him at home. For that I had to demonstrate to him what I could do. I moved Alan from his sleeping position and let him sit on the edge of the bed, then lifted the bed and supported him into the wheelchair. I had been practicing this at the same time Alan was undergoing his physical therapy. But I could not please the doctor.

I desperately wanted to go home. First of all, I thought Alan would stay in the nursing home for only a few days; Medicare would pay for only two weeks stay, but I was beginning to sense they wanted to keep Alan indefinitely. I talked to a social worker and a physical therapist, but they were all working for the nursing home. Only one nurse, Sue, was sympathetic to me.

I thought Alan was doing well with his physical therapy, even though he had not walked yet. I thought the physical therapists were on my side, but they weren't. Finally, they all came to our house with Alan to see how he could get along at home. While we were home, I played Alan's music so they could understand how important it was for him to hear his music and see the mountains. But I could not impress them.

The next day, we all sat in a conference room with the doctor, social workers, physical therapists, and nurses; all of them against Alan going home. They said his condition was progressive, so I would not be able to take care of him. And if I took him home against their opinion, the doctor would not give any prescriptions for Alan's medicine. That was blackmail; they all ganged up on one woman (me) to keep Alan there. Just as I thought, they had no intention of letting him go. (I think it was for the money, for they charged patients $5,000 a month, $60,000 for a year, at that time in 1997.)

I cried because it had been very difficult for me to be there to take care of Alan, but if I did not stay with him, he would not get adequate care. I knew that by watching Arthur.

Every day I put Alan on the commode, with the help of a male worker, so he was always clean. But just one morning, before I got there, he must have made a mess. I noticed he was very dirty, so I did major cleaning for him with hot water and soap. After that, I looked for the young black nurse's aide who had been very nice to Alan and was fond of him. That's what I thought, but that morning I could not even find her. I looked all over the place and finally found her. She had been hiding from me. Just one big mess Alan had made and she could not take it and ran away; therefore, she could not face me.

How could I leave Alan in this kind of care? Come to think of it, since he came there, I had been taking care of him by myself; and besides, I could do it much better at my own home. Why did he have to stay in the nursing home? I didn't know the nursing home had such power. I had heard of social workers taking children from their own parents, but I didn't know they could take my old husband from me, too.

I thought I might call a lawyer to fight for me. Then I thought of calling Dr. Greene, Alan's doctor. He was the one who had sent Alan to the nursing home to start with, even though he had told me it was a rehabilitation center for a short time only. I told him that if I were to bring Alan home against the nursing home doctor's orders, he would not give Alan the medicine he would need. Then, to my surprise, Dr. Greene said to bring Alan home. He said that the final decision was mine, and he would give him the medicine. So I brought him home.

When I was just about to leave the place, I had to say goodbye to Mary. I felt sorry for her, so I gave her a flower, a flower somebody had given to Alan. Then she took it and said, "It is not even pretty!" I thought so too! It did not compensate for her feeling of unfairness. I was leaving, but she had to stay.

Life with Alan at Home

Dr. Greene was so kind, he arranged for a visiting nurse to come to our home, and I took Alan to the hospital for transfusions whenever he needed one. Toward the end of Alan's sickness, Sue, my Japanese friend, came to live at my mother's house next door to help me.

Every day, I put him in the wheelchair and brought him into the dining room for his breakfast. I played his music for him while he was enjoying his food and the view of the mountains. I took care of him at home for over three years, until his death in June of 2000.

"Dearest, Most Beloved Hinako"

One day, I was under Alan's piano, where he kept his personal possessions like his books and notebooks, piles and piles of them on top of each other. Even though I had kept them all these years the way he had left them, I thought that maybe I should organize them. In the midst of doing this, a cranberry-colored paper fell out and it was Alan's writing to me. I burst into tears.

I remember exactly when he wrote this, that terrible day, June 17, 1997, the day of our twentieth wedding anniversary, just before Alan's terrible operation, when his mental condition was very much deteriorating. It was a nice day… I think I took some pictures of Alan and flowers in our yard earlier that day. My plan was to go to the library that was about four blocks away from our house to look for some books and later we would go to a nice restaurant to celebrate. We were not doing anything special, but I wanted to have a nice private night together. After all, a twentieth wedding anniversary doesn't come every day.

We drove to the library, and as soon as we got there, Alan said to me, "I left my wife at home." By that time, I was aware of Alan's mental condition, so I tried patiently to explain to him, "I am your wife, we just locked the door of our house and came here together; we are going out to have a good time…" I thought I had convinced him very well, and he went back to compose at the library table while I was looking at the books on the shelves; but then, when I came back to the table, I couldn't find him anywhere—he was gone. I was very upset, but I knew that he went back home by foot to look for his wife.

I drove back home and found him standing outside the front door. I was so upset, I unlocked the door to the house to let him in and drove away. I couldn't control myself anymore. I needed love and sympathy for myself…after all, this was our twentieth anniversary, and it was very important to me.

I was driving around Southcenter Shopping Center and saw a poster on the front of a movie theater, Julia Robert's *Runaway Bride*. I thought I might see that movie to pass the time, but it was just an advertisement of an upcoming movie, so it was not on yet. I don't know what I did after that, but I killed a couple of hours and went back home.

The house door was not locked—with no Alan in sight. Then shortly after, Alan came into the house, escorted by Natansee, my beautician, and her husband. Alan's face was bleeding all over. According to what they told me, Alan had fallen on the sidewalk near the library and a neighbor happened to drive by, saw the episode, and called Medic One. Alan was being treated on the spot when my two friends who were in the crowd at the scene recognized him and brought him home. On the way out the door, she handed me a letter Alan had written while I was gone. This is the letter I found that day. I didn't pay attention to this letter that night, because I was very upset.

But today, four years later, this letter made me cry…

He was very confused on the surface, but he truly loved me and looked for me in the dark night of his confused mind.

His letter to me:

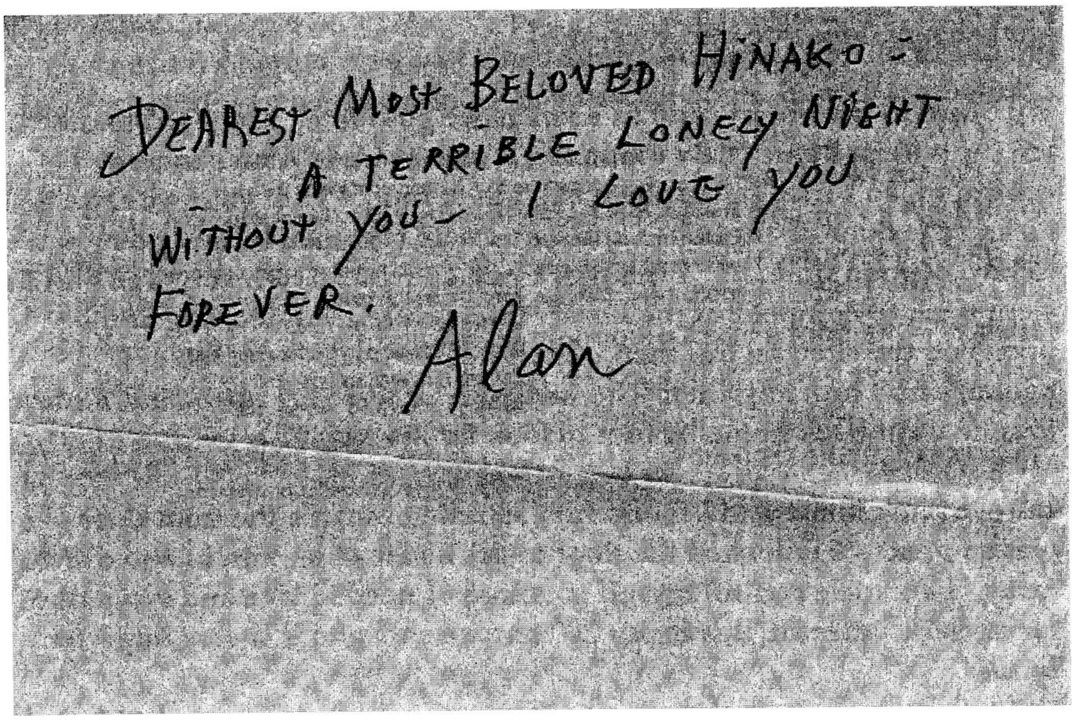

DEAREST MOST BELOVED HINAKO –
A TERRIBLE LONELY NIGHT
WITHOUT YOU – I LOVE YOU
FOREVER.
Alan

Alan's writing to Hinako

Cello Concerto
Premiered on March 18, 1999

♪

Alan composed this cello concerto in 1936 when he was only twenty-five years old. The concerto was published in 1939 by Whitney Blake Music, his first publisher. Their office was located in Broadway, NY, over a prize fighters' office, so Alan bumped into prize fighters from time to time when he visited his publisher. Alan was very tall and thin, and those prize fighters were shorter and physically fit, so Alan must have felt intimidated by them.

In the late 1990s, I approached Maestro Schwarz, the Seattle Symphony conductor, and expressed my wish to have the cello concerto performed. I wanted to have a flashy premiere with a well-known cellist to perform because I thought this masterpiece deserved a big splashy start. I suggested Yo Yo Ma, the very well-known Chinese cellist to be the soloist, but Maestro Schwarz thought that he would be very expensive; besides his fee, we might have had to wait for a long time because of the long list on his performance schedule. Then he told me later that Janos Starker, the very prestigious cellist, was interested in premiering Alan's concerto.

On March 18, 1999, Starker premiered the concerto at Benaroya Hall with the Seattle Symphony under the baton of Dennis Russell Davies. It was supposedly the official premiere of the concerto, but Alan had performed it in 1975 at Western Washington State College in Bellingham, WA. At that time, Alan's cellist friend Barton Frank was the conductor of the student orchestra at the college; he invited Alan to conduct a concert, so Alan took this opportunity to perform the cello concerto. He used the orchestra parts he had in his own possession without reporting to his publisher, C.F. Peters, who owned the music. That is why this premiere was not considered official. It seems to me he was doing whatever it took to get the concerto performed.

At that time in 1975, Alan and I had not married yet. He wanted me to be at his concert in Bellingham. On January 27, the day of the concert, I headed up to Bellingham, a northern city in Washington state, very close to the Canadian border, about a two-hour drive from downtown Seattle. I drove from the south of Seattle, so it took a good two and a half hours to drive. I was excited, like a teenager; he always gave me this excitement every time I drove to meet him.

When I got to the Leopold Hotel where Alan was staying, he came to meet me in the hotel lobby and then he took me up to his hotel room. Then what he said to me was, "You drove all the way here for sex, didn't you?" I was shocked and insulted. I don't know why he said that, but that remark was not like the Alan I knew. I am hurt even now, while I am writing about this. I was simply in love with him, and I didn't separate love and sex. I could have turned around and gone home, but I didn't.

After the concert, the audience was leaving the hall. Alan showed up on the edge of the stage, still in his tails, looking for me. As soon as he spotted me, he came down from the stage to meet me, like a young kid all excited, his eyes fixed on me. I thought he was so cute and loveable. After that, we were invited to Barton Frank's house for the formal party. Barton and his young wife, Jan, were the hosts. Alan and Barton were still in their tails. Barton made a toast with champagne. I remember Alan and I were eating caviar. That night in the hotel room, we had the most passionate sex; Alan always got extra sexy after his concerts.

That was in 1975, but in 1999, twenty-four years later, we had been married for twenty-three years and he was eighty-eight years old and had been ill for the last two years. The day before the premiere of his cello concerto, he was hospitalized for a blood transfusion. During that time, he had been getting transfusions as often as once every two weeks. He did not speak and could not move his body by himself; he was completely under my care. I put him in the wheelchair, and with my friend Sue's help, we put him in the car and took him to the hospital.

That day, March 17, Father O'Neill, the Chicago priest, arrived at my house for the concert the next day, but we were at the hospital. Sue helped him get situated in our house, and in the early evening, I came home for a few hours to prepare dinner for him. Sue and I joined him at dinner.

The next day we were lucky that the doctor discharged Alan with just enough time to get to the concert that evening. Sue and I frantically got Alan ready for the concert along with everything else, and in just a few minutes, we changed our working clothes into dress-up clothes for the big occasion, and off we went! My son Bill, who had come from Arizona for the occasion, joined us. That night I had two men to help me, Father O'Neill and Bill. Father O'Neill pushed Alan's wheelchair through the concert hall and put Alan in his seat.

The performance was superb! I stood up for Alan for his acknowledgement by the conductor from the stage. What more could I have asked for? A performance from an excellent conductor and the solo played by a world-renowned cellist. After Alan's sixty-three long years of waiting, he finally could hear it! After the performance of Alan's piece, Maestro Schwarz expressed to me that he wished somehow Alan had heard his own music. He was aware of Alan's real mental condition, which not too many people knew about. At the intermission, we all went backstage. In the hallway, Davies, the conductor, his wife, and Janos Starker came out and greeted us. I think Alan was aware of what was happening that night. He used those kingly manners he always had in the public.

We did not stay for the second part of the concert because I was afraid Alan might get tired, and I had to feed him soon. We pushed Alan in the wheelchair through downtown Seattle streets to get to Leo Melina Restorante, the restaurant recommended by the symphony.

Bill, Sue, Father O'Neill, Seattle composer Greg Short, and Don Gillespie from C.F. Peters joined us. After changing rooms a few times, I finally approved the room and we sat down. I was worried Alan had not eaten for so long, so I immediately ordered soup for him and fed him before anything else. The food was excellent, and my son, who was particular like me and was seldom pleased with restaurant food, agreed with me.

After the dinner, Bill drove my car to the front of the restaurant for Alan. Then Greg Short bent his big body over to say goodbye to Alan, who was sitting in the front seat of the car. I told Greg to kiss Alan and he did. That became his last goodbye to Alan, for Greg died shortly after that. He had a heart attack in his sixties. He passionately adored Alan. We had met him on many occasions like concerts and meals.

Now, as I am listening to the concerto, after Alan has been gone for four years and my tears have still not dried, I deeply sense the frustration of a young man. In his early life, he had lost his mother when he was nineteen years old, which was too young to lose one's mother. Then a few years later, he married a girl older than himself, practically the first girl he knew. That marriage was obviously her idea, but Alan went along, I think, because in his subconscious mind, she was a replacement for his mother whom he missed so much. In no time at all, a baby came, but he was not ready. He was a born composer, so when overwhelming music came to him, he had to write it down. But as of yet, he had not achieved anything with it, and he was a frustrated young man with genius inside of him.

The cello concerto was recorded the day after the premiere, on March 19, 1999, at Benaroya Hall. In 2003, Naxos released that recording with Alan's Symphony No. 22 "City of Light," recorded in May of 1992 at the Seattle Opera House and conducted by Alan; I chose my mother's painting *Milky Way* for the cover of the CD.

"Habakkuk," Alan's Last Composition

♪

In June 2001, Dr. John Ogasapian wrote to me. John was a professor of music history at the University of Massachusetts and has been an organist and choirmaster of St. Ann's Church for forty years. He was looking for Alan's two organ sonatas and also some of Alan's other organ pieces, which were not published but still in manuscript form. I made copies of Alan's three organ sonatas and sent them to him from my company Fujihara Music Co., Inc. He also asked for Alan's last piece "Habakkuk" op. 434 for organ.

This organ piece was commissioned by the organist Marijim Thoene; specifically, she wanted this composition to be Alan's interpretation of the last chapter of the Old Testament book *Habakkuk*. I told Dr. Ogasapian that this piece was Alan's last piece, and the commissioner Marijim Thoenewas was not happy with it. When she premiered it, the audience liked it very much and she was surprised.

I asked Dr. Ogasapian for his opinion of this piece. He wrote to me:

> I came home the night before last from California and found the copy of Habakkuk in the mail. I spent a good bit of time with it yesterday and must say I think it's a superb piece, and I intend to play it this fall in recital. It's clearly a mature and introspective piece, and I believe that each section of it—and by section I mean wherever the texture changes—has to be thought through very carefully for shape and subtle changes in tempo. But there is no doubt that it is an impressive work of art, and that he knew EXACTLY what he wanted.
>
> The only issue, if it can be called that, is the range he calls for in the left hand. It goes beyond the compass of the organ keyboard. Clearly he knew that—he had played the organ himself, after all—and I can only assume that he purposely notated the part that way to suggest the kind of color and effect he wanted the performer to aim for, whether by using 16′ manual stops or by taking the notes in question in the pedal.
>
> Although my sense of his style in the works I know is that he was always pretty precise on the sort of instrumental color he wanted, I wonder if here, like Bare November Day, he thought of the piece as playable on the piano OR the organ—in which case, the notes he calls for ARE on the keyboard. That, of course, is consistent with the last 2-1/2 pages, where he doubles the left-hand with pedal. The section is easily playable at that tempo on the piano with the left hand in octaves. Did he say anything to you about that? *Also, how did he happen to choose the title "Habakkuk?"
>
> – excerpt from personal letter dated August 18, 2001

Enclosed is a program of the recital last evening at the University…

> You will also be interested in the reaction of the students, which was enthusiastic (as you can see, I ended with *Habakkuk;* I did not do any encores, by the way). But you may be more interested in the reactions of my colleagues who were at the recital. As it turned out, both the Co-Ordinator of Choral Activities (who conducts the touring choir, among other things) and the conductor of the University orchestra were there, superb musicians, and both were bowled over by the piece, just as I was when I first saw and played it. So my reaction to it is not the only one. I have no idea why she didn't care for it; I CERTAINLY have no idea why the dedicatee wasn't happy with it. I know I am.
>
> – excerpt from personal letter dated Sept. 19, 2001

> Enclosed is another program. The response to *Habakkuk* was again very strong. One person (himself a published composer) was deeply moved by it, and observed that in spite of his knowing better, he could not help relating it as a profound 'elegy' for the events of September 11th. He was especially hit (as I was when I first read through the piece) by the strength of the big dissonant chord passages that frame the first section, and by the sharp dramatic contrast between the two sections (which also is a stroke of genius).
>
> – excerpt from personal letter dated Sept. 28, 2001

What can I say; I have a deep secret from the world regarding this piece and two other compositions. By the time Alan was composing "Habakkuk," his health and mental condition had very much deteriorated. I usually took care of the contracts for the commissions for him, but at that time, I had great doubts about his capability to compose. I asked him, with hesitation, if he could, and Alan was enthusiastic, as always. All these years, he "devoured" all his commissions; as soon as he got one, even before, he got tremendous inspirations and always completed the composition well before the completion date. So his instinct was there, but I didn't know his ability at that time, but what could I do? I could not make the decision, with my judgment of him not to compose. I always respected his professionalism, and who was I to say *no* to his wish?

The commission was confirmed on January 31, 1995, by Alan's accepting letter, but by the completion date of July, he was not yet finished. He didn't know what to do with it, and he just stared at his sketch book.

Finally, I had an idea. I asked Alan to play his recent sketch for the organ for me on his piano, which he did; then, I selected and put it in order, led by my inspiration. He made a transition between each section to connect and complete it. This is a very painful secret of how his last composition came about. I could not dare tell anybody, but the truth should be written, and I believe mysteries should not be left unsolved.

Text of the music "Habakkuk."

Habakkuk, Chapter Three

17. Even though the fig trees are all destroyed, and there is neither blossom left nor fruit; and though the olive crops all fail, and the fields lie barren; even if the flocks die in the fields and the cattle barns are empty.
18. Yet I will rejoice in the Lord; I will be happy in the God of my salvation.
19. The Lord God is my Strength, and He will give me the speed of a deer and bring me safely over the mountains.

* The reason for Alan's scoring of this particular passage is due to the commissioner Marijim Thoene's infirmity, an inability to play left-hand octaves.

Alan and His Guitar Concertos

How Alan started to compose for guitar…

In February of 1978, when Alan and I were performing in Berkeley, California, his daughter Jean Nandi, who was a harpsichordist, introduced us to a guitarist called Michael Lorimer. He came to see Alan and demonstrated the guitar to him. Alan was a pianist, but as a composer he understood theoretically all the orchestral instruments and how to get the sound he wanted, but the guitar is not an "orchestral instrument," so Lorimer's instruction was helpful to Alan.

Since Alan met Lorimer, whenever he composed for the guitar, he sent the music to Lorimer and got his comments, and then dedicated them to him. Later, Lorimer wanted to publish them with his own series of guitar publications; he sent legal documents, written by his lawyer father for Alan to sign. Alan realized what was happening. If he were to sign the documents, he would lose all his rights for the pieces. So he did not sign, and that was the end of his relationship with Lorimer.

Today, as I was looking at his catalog, I realized he had written for guitar long before Lorimer. In 1974, he composed "The Way of Jesus," a 100-minute-long oratorio premiered in New York. Alan used guitar for the first time at the beginning of the oratorio "Behold the Lamb of God" for Baritone and Chorus, accompanied by three guitars. The same theme repeats throughout the oratorio. By that time, guitar music had come into the churches. It was a tool to invite young people into the churches—and they were vitally important to their survival. As usual, Alan sensed the new movement in sound and put it into his oratorio.

In 1978, Alan composed the Symphony No. 39 for guitar and orchestra, commissioned by Michael Long, a guitarist from Phoenix, Arizona. According to Long, he called Alan sometime in June hoping he would compose a guitar concerto for him. Alan said *yes* to him in his usual gracious manner. Then six weeks later, a mailman delivered Mr. Long a package. It was from Alan; it had the score of his Symphony No 39. Long was surprised because he was expecting Alan to take a year or two to complete the concerto. This story is so much like Alan. I remember he used to start to compose spontaneously like the wind, as soon as a commission came in by telephone. He didn't even wait for a written contract.

But why a symphony and not a concerto?

Around that time, he heard about the composer Havergal Brian, an English composer of the early 20th century who had written numerous symphonies. Alan got a silly idea to compete with him, so he called many of his compositions "symphonies," even though they were not written in strict symphonic form. His symphonies' authenticity was debated by Melinda Bargreen, the *Seattle Times* music critic in a concert review. But he kept on producing his so-called "symphonies."

One example is that he composed a piece for baritone horn for Henry Charles Smith, the Assistant Conductor of the Minnesota Symphony Orchestra and also a baritone horn player. Alan called it Symphony No. 29 for Baritone Horn and Orchestra, and he did not call it a concerto.

After Alan composed the guitar symphony for Long, strangely enough, we did not hear from him, even though he paid the commission fee and gave Alan the copies of the orchestral parts that had been made by Long's copyist. Then unexpectedly in 1981, when Alan and I were in Walla Walla for the premiere of his Symphony No. 47 "Walla Walla," we saw the announcement that Long would be premiering Alan's Symphony No. 39 with the Spokane Symphony. Later, he recorded the symphony in Seoul, Korea, with the KBS Symphony, and it was included in the CD "Alan Hovhaness," which was released by Koch International.

In 1978, Javier Calderon, a young guitarist, came to see Alan in the condominium where we lived for a short time. He was born in Bolivia and was short and black-haired, with a nicely-tanned, boyish-looking face and a likeable personality. He wanted Alan to compose a guitar concerto for him, and after a brief correspondence, his commission came from SRO Production Performing Artist Management in conjunction with the Minnesota Orchestra for the premiere.

Alan and Javier Calderon

Alan signed the commission on July 10, 1978, and completed the work on January 21, 1979 (at 2:15 AM). The concerto is sixty pages long, with a performance time of thirty minutes. After Calderon's premiere of this concerto with the Minnesota Orchestra, conducted by Leonard Slatkin, he sent a performance tape to Alan, and that was the last time he heard from Calderon.

In 1991, we were in New York for Alan's Eightieth Birthday Concert in Carnegie Hall. During that time, Ralph Jackson from BMI, the head of the Classical Department, wanted to introduce his guitarist friend David Leisner to Alan.

He invited us to dinner at a small exclusive restaurant. It was unlike the high-priced restaurants designed for tourists but was instead for the sophisticated New Yorker who knew where to go. The dinner started with wine, and Alan and I could not drink wine, but were impressed by the food. There we met David for the first time and found him friendly and easy to talk to. After we came home to Seattle, we received a cassette from him, playing his guitar, with a note saying, "Enjoy!"

In late October of 2001, one year after Alan's death, and just after September 11, my son and I were in New York for Alan's Memorial Concert held on November 1 at Alice Tully Hall in Lincoln Center. Again, Jackson invited us to dinner with me, my son, and Larry Sobol, who was Alan's musician friend and was helping me with the concert. Jackson brought David with him, and we met at a Chinese restaurant. It was large and more like a nightclub; the center of the restaurant had wide stairs going upstairs. We all went up and were seated around a large circular table. It was just before Halloween, so all the waiters and waitresses were in costume; then, a towering waitress appeared and stood in front of us. She was so huge but had all the ingredients for a woman, so we (Bill, Larry, and I) were wondering whether she was a woman or a man. Anyway, she served us exquisite Chinese food.

Bill (Hinako's son) outside of Alice Tully Hall Lincoln Center at Alan's Memorial Concert in October 2001

David wanted to see Alan's two concerto scores—one written for Calderon and a second concerto for Spanish guitarist Narciso Yepes.* I was reluctant to send them to him; besides, I did not have the orchestra parts for either of them. Calderon had the parts copied by his own copyist and never gave Alan copies of them. Finally, in 2006, I obtained the concerto parts from the Minnesota Orchestra (who premiered the work) thanks to the kind help of their music librarian Paul Gunther. Yepes premiered the concerto in the Granada Festival in Spain, but he never sent copies of the parts to Alan, and then he died!

So in order for anybody to perform them, I had to make the parts, but due to David's strong persuasion, I finally sent them to him. By that time, I learned he was not just a guitarist, but also a composer. He composed for the guitar and said to me that he would not necessarily perform the pieces unless he liked them. He came back to me and said he liked both of them and would make the premiere recording of both of them. (As if he had exclusive rights without asking me.)

After all, David was a very professional guitarist; he had made a recording of Alan's "Spirit of Trees" for harp and guitar, with Yolanda Kondonassis in her all-Hovhaness harp CD. This piece was a great success. Also, I was obligated to Mr. Jackson, who had introduced David, so I sent the two concerto scores to David. What David wanted to do with them was to show them to Robert Spano, conductor of the Atlanta Symphony, where he had just finished performing. The conductor was pleased with David's playing, so he thought Spano might be interested in Alan's concerto for his next recording (with David playing on it). But he did not hear from Spano for a long time.

In the meantime, I had established a production to record Alan's music in Berlin, Germany, through Gerard Schwarz, the conductor of the Seattle Symphony. I was paying for the Berlin Radio Orchestra to record Alan's music and broadcast it by radio over Germany and other European countries; then I would get a master to make CDs in the U.S. One of the repertoires was Alan's first guitar concerto, the one written for Calderon. I thought that since he had not communicated with us for so long and he never gave copies of the orchestra parts (written in the contract), it was about time I should give David a chance, and so I did, and he was thrilled by such an excellent opportunity.

The recording date was set for July 6–8, 2005, and David was supposedly practicing the concerto beforehand. One day, he told me the concerto was altogether too long and needed the cuts, especially the optional cadenza. He called it "inferior" and wanted to talk to the conductor about it.

I was shocked! I mentioned this to Mr. Schwarz, and he had one thing to say to this, "He is a joke!" Later he told me to tell David "to study all the cadenzas and after the recording at the time of editing we will decide which one to cut." David was unhappy and said to me, "If I were to play it, my heart would not be in it." I was beginning to get suspicious about his persistent remarks and thought, "He may not be able to play the cadenzas and is blaming Alan's music instead."

At about that same time, another guitarist named Dr. Alexander Dunn, who was also interested in Alan's concertos from Vancouver, BC, called me. I told him that David was going to do the premiere recording; then, he said he had read an article by David saying that he had injured his hand and could not play the guitar like he used to, but he had found a method to compensate for his handicap. But Dunn still had doubts about David's ability.

So I called David and asked him about what I had heard, but my question was never answered. Instead it became an open fight between the two guitarists. It ended up with David saying to me that what Dunn had said to me was morally and ethically wrong.

By that time I was regretting that I had asked David to play the premiere recording of the concerto. It was written when Alan was at the height of his composing power and was extremely romantic. I thought David was rude and stuck up. Was he the right one to do this?

I had always thought performers were like mediums that came between the composer and the audience, delivering the music as truthfully as they could, just the way the composer had written it. My voice teacher Leon Lishner taught me to sing songs to the audience with conviction, as if you really meant it, even though some songs were not to your taste.

Then I thought of Javier Calderon, who had commissioned the concerto, it was written for him. He had such a different spirit. He respected Alan's music so much that he performed all the cadenzas, even the optional one. I had a strong impulse to talk to him. Since Alan's death, I had become fanatically loyal to Alan and his music, and I needed someone to support me in what I felt about David. I knew Calderon would understand my feelings more than anybody else, so I called his agent, got his telephone number, and left a message for him. He called me that night and we talked.

He was so surprised at what David had said about Alan's optional cadenza and said, "Who is he to say 'inferior' to Mr. Hovhaness's music?" And he was regretful that he would not be the one to record the concerto. He asked me to let him do it instead of David, even though the recording session was coming in just one month. I felt sorry for him, but I could not do that, so I had an idea—I would let him perform the premiere recording of Guitar Concerto No. 2, composed for Yepes, for my next recording project. I promised him I would do this. A few days later, I received his heartfelt e-mail. **

On July 6, 2005, the day of the recording, I went into the sanctuary, the recording room at Jesus-Christ Kirch in Dahlem, Berlin. The musicians were not there yet, and I put my stuff on the pew in the front row. David was at the left side of the conductor's podium and came to me and said I could not sit there because my presence disturbed him. I was surprised about his sensitivity and thought, "How could he be a performer with such a touchy attitude?"

Then the conductor came in and told me to sit at the right side of him in the front pew. Then David complained to him that he did not want to play the optional cadenza because it was inferior. (He said it again!) Then the conductor said to him, "Play it anyway!"

The recording lasted three days, and afterward David confessed that it was his first time recording with an orchestra. I had not known that! I think he played accurately, that much I can say.

Why did David criticize Alan's music so bluntly? If Alan had been there, how could he have said such a thing to him? And why am I so sensitive to what he said? Since Alan died, I have become so protective of his music. It has become so personal to me, as if I were Alan himself.

Now I am looking forward to the day his second concerto will be recorded by the musician who loves and respects his music, and then the magic will happen!

As Alan once said, "Composer and performer unite in beautiful cooperation for altruism of a better civilization. The composer, as in China, joins heaven and earth and threads of sound... and the world receives the benediction."

* More information about Narciso Yepes' "Guitar Concerto No. 2" can be found in "Spirit of Trees," February 26, 2005.

** Letter from Javier Calderon, May 24, 2005

The idea and commission of the Concerto for Guitar and Orchestra was mine. I have always loved and respected the music of your husband, Alan Hovhaness, so since I was young I wished that there was music written for the guitar by him so I could have the opportunity to perform it so I approached him to write a concerto. I still have the hand written letters that he wrote to me when we were collaborating on this project and also the photographs that you took of us together at that time. When he finished he wrote at the top of the score dedicated to Javier Calderon.

... Though I have much talent for music and performing and I am now a seasoned world-renowned concert guitarist and a music professor at a major university, I have no talent for self-promotion and have failed after all these years to bring my dream of recording this concerto to reality.

You Were the Luckiest Man (I Am That Little Monkey)

♪

I saw a TV program, *The Practice*, a court drama. A doctor on the program was accused by a cancer patient's husband of helping his wife to terminate her own life. The prosecutor and defense lawyer both were emotional about this case because of their own personal experiences. The doctor's defense lawyer told a story about a cancer patient who was no longer recognizing her husband, and her husband wanted to stop her suffering by stopping the respirator. But he could not do it, so his son stopped his mother's respirator. The defense lawyer said that if they had had a doctor like his defendant, they wouldn't have had to go through this by themselves. In other words, the defense lawyer portrayed the defendant doctor's action as a mercy killing; in other words, he had helped to end the terminal patient's suffering.

Then the prosecutor who was accusing the doctor also told her story about an elderly woman (actually, the woman was her grandmother) who said she would like to die because she was afraid of the hardship to her family and whoever would take care of her, even though she might want to live one more day. The prosecutor said that if the defense would win, that would set a standard, so she, the prosecutor, could not let that happen because of her experience with her grandmother (whatever that experience was). She won the case; I am glad.

In this day and age, people are so busy, it seems the value of human beings is only as long as they are moving and earning money. If doctors should get the power of making the decision of when one is to die, it has the danger of not taking care of the old and the sick altogether. It could happen easily. Even when I was taking care of Alan, I experienced this prejudice from doctors and nurses. I had to be strong to protect Alan by finding a doctor who would honor my wishes.

I cried as I watched the TV show because I was reliving my experience with Alan when he was very ill. It was very hard, especially in the beginning when his mind was confused because of the bleeding from his stomach and his major operation. But I gradually learned to take care of him better. The last two years of his life he was completely helpless, and I became a professional nurse plus!

I took care of him at home. Every day I cleaned him and transported him from the bed to the wheelchair. I sat him on the edge of the bed and raised the bed to the same level as the wheelchair; then I lifted him up with my arms around his waist and swung him to the wheelchair. Then I went to his back and stood on the chair and hoisted him up to put him in position. (I was too short to do this in one step.) Then I took him to the bathroom and cleaned his face and mouth, and finally to the dining room (by this time over an hour had passed), the beautiful view room, to feed him. First I gave him pills, one at a time with juice. Toward the end of his time, he could not swallow pills, so I got the liquid form of the pills or crushed them and mixed them with applesauce. It took all of the morning hours for his breakfast, but those hours were the most precious time we had, and I knew it; we talked and listened to music together.

The second time he woke up, in the evening, I sat him on the bed to feed his dinner to him. I went to sleep after I completely finished taking care of him. I could not change his schedule, so *I* followed *his* schedule. I usually went to bed anywhere from five to seven AM. This was our everyday routine, other than going to the hospital.

I took him to the hospital in my car, whether somebody else was helping me to put him in the car or by ambulance. At the hospital, he usually got a blood transfusion or procedure, but otherwise, it was like a vacation. I didn't have to cook. I ordered food from the hospital menu, like a restaurant; they brought food for us in our room like room service in a hotel. I fed him and we ate together. We always had enjoyed eating together very much, in the past, so what was the difference? Hotel or hospital room, we made the best of it, the time we had together.

Now I realize how lucky Alan was, because he was loved by me, and I wanted to have him. I didn't want to lose him, so I fought not to lose him; I did everything to keep him. I was not perfect in dealing with his troubles, especially early in his sickness. I tried to put him in the wheelchair and dropped him on the floor, and I had to get help to lift him from the floor, and it took many hours to hoist him up on the bed from the floor without help. By all means, I was not perfect, but I worked very hard for him. I knew he was trying to help me, too, and finally, I safely put him on the wheelchair. We both laughed: "It was hard work."

After he died, I felt I was guilty because I thought I could have done better, but tonight, I think he was the luckiest man because he was so loved and wanted, in spite of his condition. I was determined to push through our needs and to insist on the medical professionals helping Alan; otherwise, he never would have been allowed to live as long as he did. If Alan had been a composer in a small country like France or Finland, I think their government would have done everything to help him because he was an important national treasure, but in America, the principle is that everyone should be treated equally.

I saw on another TV program a young, paralyzed man was sitting on a complicated machinery chair and a little trained monkey was taking care of him. She had an electric belt around her middle, and when she didn't do the right thing for the young man, she got an electric shock from the belt, but when she did right, she got a reward on a tray. This little monkey was working for the young man. She was so good and did many things for him, and she was so cute. I cried, watching her; she reminded me of myself when I was taking care of Alan. Alan was a tall man, and I am a small Japanese, like this little monkey. After all, I was the monkey.

The next film clips were a recent picture of both of them. The young man was much heavier and older and so was the monkey. The man said she was getting older, and her motion was slowing down. The TV reporter asked, "What are you going to do with her when she gets very old and cannot do her duty?" Then the man answered, "My family will be sure to take care of her until the end. I will make sure of it!"

I am that little monkey. Like that young man said on TV, and my old age is being taken care of by Alan. He made it so, by his royalties from his music.

Alan and Hinako in their home

To Live for One Who You Love

♪

It was on the TV news the other day, a woman whose husband had died was expressing her appreciation to the doctors who had given him a heart transplant operation, even though he lived for only six months after the operation. Then I saw a photo of them together, in their happier times. I could not help but think of Alan and me.

When Alan was very ill, I knew I might lose him at any time, but I tried to beat the odds and watched him closely, so death couldn't creep in to take him away. My neighbor Cindy, a professional nurse and nursing home owner, said to me, "You know he is dying." Obviously, everybody is bound to die sometime, but she thinks that way because the old folks in her house are dying practically every day. To her, Alan was another statistic. I was defiant to that idea and knew I would fight back until the day Alan died. If he would die, at least he would die in an attempt to live. How serious my love became because of the danger of losing Alan and our life together, and I knew how painful our separation would be. I became a warrior with one thought: to make him well.

Doctors often told me, "Let him go." Months before Alan died, one night in the emergency room, a woman doctor told me how she let her father die in order to not let him suffer anymore; it sounded sweet and thoughtful, but, in other words, what she was saying was not to do anything for Alan to help him live. But the truth is, to let him live or die was dependent on what your degree of love was for him. How far can you go? To help the sick and save the dying is our instinct, but this does require one's effort, so the practicality is, where to draw the line? How much do you love him, how long can you take care of him? My answer was, "Love never gives up."

Alan lived three years after the first doctor gave up on him. Alan always wanted to live, to live for me. Whenever the doctor asked him, "Do you want to live," his answer was always "Yes!" He intuitively knew what I wanted. He didn't have pain, but his life was uncomfortable and with suffering, I am sure. But he chose to live with me in a suffering life, instead of death, heavenly peace of no more pain and suffering.

During his sickness, I didn't think of the future, but only of today.

Living meant "now." I sat with him in the room with the mountain view and fed him. I knew our time was limited, so I tried to grasp the time, to not let it slip away.

One morning, after Alan's blood transfusion at the hospital, he was sitting on the bed. The urologist, who hadn't seen Alan for a few years, came in and was shocked by Alan's condition.

Then he said to me, "He doesn't even know you—what is the difference who takes care of him—put him in a nursing home and do something for yourself." What was he saying? He didn't know me at all!

Most of all, Alan needed me desperately. He could not express it himself, but I was his necessity and life—without me, he could not live. My life was to be with him, to share everything good or bad; life and marriage is not just good times, as my mother said. Put him in a nursing home, forget about him, and live normally? Where did that idea come from? Is that the way people think nowadays?

To that doctor's eyes, Alan was an extremely thin, speechless man, but to me, I never lost my fondness of his looks. I saw pure essence of beauty in his face, most trim line of face, large, innocent animal-like eyes. In fact, I loved his face; that face will haunt me all the rest of my life. Alan was always tall and thin, yet before he died, he was extremely thin. His narrow shoulders were just bones, but I saw his body with sympathy and affection as I touched every part of his body with my caring hands.

How we fought to stay together, how we resisted being apart. The power of love, how precious and victorious! The test comes with our great suffering. The beautiful early spring of romance that was the beginning was only a prelude to the real love to come, with our conviction and effort.

The Day Charles Let Alan Fall from the Wheelchair

♪

Today is Easter Sunday, and Alan died almost one year ago. Alan's Memorial Concert is coming soon, and I am presenting it as his public funeral. For the concert, I invited everybody from the hospital, such as doctors, nurses, and even parking-lot attendants. For the last three years of Alan's life, he was in and out of the hospital for blood transfusions. We became regular visitors there, and I became his personal nurse and worked with the hospital staff, so I got to know them and admired those dedicated people. But I hate to think about one person: Charles the transporter. How can I forgive him for what he did to Alan?

It was on April 13, 2000…

I had taken Alan to the hospital as usual. His blood count was 25.8, which was low enough to have a transfusion. I took him to the hospital and at the front I stopped the car and waited for a transporter to come for us. The transporter usually put Alan in a wheelchair and then transported him to the patient room for me. Charles came that day, and he always treated Alan with respect. He said he was a drummer and knew who Alan was. Charles was short but was well-fit with a prize fighter's physique. He transferred Alan smoothly into the wheelchair, and then I got a wide cloth from the trunk of the car, which I used to tie Alan into the wheelchair. Then Charles said it was not necessary to tie him, so I explained to him that Alan did not have any control over his body, so if he was not tied in, he would fall in a matter of a split second. But Charles dismissed what I said. He said to me with full confidence that he would lift the front of the wheelchair so that Alan would not fall forward. In spite of my repeated pleas, he dismissed me and pushed Alan away in the wheelchair.

I parked my car in the garage underneath the hospital and went up to Alan's room. When I got there, Alan had already settled in the bed. The good nurse Nancy must have taken care of him. I sat on his left side of the bed. Then Bubba, a black male nurse, came in and shouted, "What happened to him?" I looked at Alan. The right side of his forehead had a big bump, one and a half inches in diameter. Then I realized that Alan must have fallen and hit his head on the floor; despite my warnings, Charles had dropped him. After my inquiry, I found somebody who had actually seen Charles drop Alan on the hospital floor.

I did not complain to the hospital at that time, but after that accident, Alan's health declined. The next week he was hospitalized for another transfusion. This time I told the hospital about the incident and told them at least to test Alan to see if damage had been done by the fall. The result of the CAT scan did not show any bleeding in his head, but his grim condition continued.

On May 31, Alan went through a procedure to put a tube in his stomach so he could be fed directly to his stomach. It was my desperate attempt to get Alan's condition to improve. I took care of him like a professional nurse. I fed him through the tube every so many hours, in addition to his regular meals. He regained his strength for a while, but it did not save him. He died on June 21.

The doctor could not tell for sure the cause of Alan's death. The exact cause could only be found by autopsy, and my answer to that was a definite "No!"

I suspected Alan's fall could have been the cause of his death, and I blamed Charles for that. But I never complained to the hospital, because they had taken care of Alan all these years, and he had gotten more care than most people. I could not repay them with hostility instead of my appreciation for their good deeds.

How about Charles? It is very difficult to take care of old patients; they are fragile, like breakable porcelain. Accidents do happen. Suppose I had dropped Alan, I could not blame anybody but myself. Charles must have suffered from what he had done, as I would have, and he could not dare face me to tell me about it.

Ten months have passed since Alan died. We all should be forgiven for our shortcomings and be remembered by our good intentions and love. I should forgive Charles, and he should be at Alan's Memorial Concert and join us in celebrating Alan's life.

Death with Dignity –
A national election is coming soon....

♪

The TV is flooded with political advertising with one of the initiatives, I-1000, which bothers me. It allows the doctors the right to give lethal drugs to sick old people in order to terminate their lives. A woman for this initiative is speaking on TV about her husband who had a terminal illness (brain tumor) and died. She says he suffered terribly at the end and "lost his total dignity," so she promised him she would change the law and help others like him. To kill themselves or put them to sleep like we do to animals. She says that, if she could change it, her husband would be very happy.

It is fine with me to have the choice of whether to live or die, but this law could open the door further to discriminating against the sick and old, and it could give people the idea that all the sick old people who are not productive anymore should die.

By the way, that has happened in old Japan. It was written in the story *Oba-Ste-Yama* (The Mountain to Throw away Old Women To). A long time ago, in one small village in Japan, there was a law. When a woman got to be a certain age, her family had to bring her to the mountain and leave her there to die. This law was for their necessity because they were very poor farmers and had difficulty taking care of their aging mothers or grandmothers who needed care and were no longer helpful to the family. Because this law was mandatory, people could get rid of old, so-called useless people without guilt.

The story goes; regardless of the law, a young farmer was daily bringing food to the cave where his old mother had been left to die. One day, one of the village governors was hunting and saw the young man going into the cave; then he found out what the man was doing. The governor was so moved by what the young man was doing that, instead of punishing him, he was influenced to change the law of that region so that people could take care of old people with respect and honor.

But most of all, I am offended by the woman's words on TV, which were "total loss of dignity." Besides, I have to hear her over and over, many times a day, every day, and I have become more than upset. I hate her guts! So I have to say what I have to say.

I look at old and sick people from a different view; it is the natural process God intended it to be. All living things on the earth get old and wilt and die. The Buddhists put it this way: "returning to our source—to become united with nature."

We take care of babies, and we also have the duty to take care of the old and sick who have come a long way, like tired warriors. I respect them for what they were.

I saw my husband, my mother, and my dog grow old and die. I took care of them, like a mother and a nurse. When I look back on those days, I feel humbled that I had the privilege to serve them in the twilight of their days and, on behalf of their birth mother who had delivered them into the world, and I was to send them safely back to their Maker. I am honored that I could go through that difficult and suffering time with them; moreover, during my husband's last stage of terminal illness, I never gave up on him. Even at his last moment, I wanted him to live, even though he was in a useless condition "without dignity," as this TV woman put it. Without that experience we would never have found the true meaning of love, to love and be loved, and suffering is very much a part of it. But if you skip this process, you never learn the real meaning of life and have to come back over and over again, until you will face God's Law, face to face.

My dog Koko reminded me this morning…

He was my family dog, who I lost in 1981, and I was his mother. He was born in 1967 and lived for fourteen years. He was mostly Pekinese; he lost one eye in 1968, the other in 1969, and became totally blind. We loved him dearly, and he lived for us without his sight for the rest of his life. If we had put him to sleep when he became blind, as most people would have done, we would never have known the most precious thing, which was our deepest love for each other.

The Day I Almost Lost Him – June 4, 2000 – My One Wish

♪

On June 4, two days after Alan came back from having a transfusion at the hospital, he became gravely ill. I called the ambulance, and they took him back to the hospital. While I was getting ready and was about to leave for the hospital, a telephone call came. It was from the emergency room doctor. She said, "Alan may not make it."

I drove frantically, practically flew in my car to get to the hospital, only one thing on my mind, praying to God, "Please don't let him die before I get there!" In Japan there is a saying that the most disloyal thing to do for your parents is not to be with them on their deathbed. So, in my opinion, not to be with my husband (the most important person in my life) when he was dying, was the worst thing I could do.

When I got to the hospital, the emergency room was desolate on the Sunday evening. It seemed nobody was around to help me, so I walked into the patients' rooms, looking in each one to find Alan. In one room, as I passed by, I thought I saw an old, gray-haired woman curled up in a blanket. But something bothered me and, as I came back to look again, it was Alan, my husband. I called his name, and he heard me. I was overjoyed that he was not dead! Soon he opened his eyes and smiled at me. He had gotten a transfusion right after he had come to the emergency room, and that had saved him!

Shortly afterward, my son called from Iowa, and I told him of the good news that Alan had revived. Alan had scared the family so many times before, being near death, that my son had become immune to his episodes and had gotten the idea that Alan would never die. I gave the telephone to Alan, and he said to Bill, "Hello, Bill," adoringly, as always. That was a great relief to everybody.

What a wonderful miracle day it was that I almost lost him, but he came back to me. Today I don't have him anymore, but come to think of it, God did grant my wish. When Alan died seventeen days later, on June 21, I was in the hospital room with him.

The Last Days of Alan – Year 2000

♪

On June 20, after Deborah, the usual visiting nurse, had left, the nutritionist from Swedish hospital came. We were in the dining room discussing how to improve Alan's tube feeding.

Ever since April 13, when Charles dropped Alan on the floor, Alan's condition had drastically declined. For my last attempt to save him, I asked the doctor to put a feeding tube into his stomach so I could put food and medicine directly into his stomach so he could get the adequate nutrition he needed. This was in addition to food taken through his mouth.

Dr. Murakami, a Japanese woman doctor, did the procedure on May 31. I don't know why Dr. Greene, Alan's regular doctor, did not do this. I fed Alan through the tube four times a day, adding medicine and vitamins, etc., into the liquid food. His condition had improved for a while but became bad again. That was why I had asked the nutritionist to help me find a way to help Alan. While we were talking, a call came from the laboratory and told me Alan's blood count was 13.4, which was drastically low.

Immediately, I called an ambulance, and he was taken to the hospital. He got four units of blood in a transfusion, one after another, all night long. I slept in a portable chair-bed beside him. The next morning, I expected him to wake up, refreshed as usual the day after a transfusion, but I noticed his face looked dull, so I knew something was wrong.

That morning, as usual, I fed him his favorite meal for breakfast, orange juice, scrambled eggs, soft fruit, and cream of wheat with milk and honey. He did eat for me; when I look back, how could he eat? He was dying then. He ate because he didn't want to disappoint me. He knew how hard I had been trying to get him well; in order to get well, he had to eat.

Earlier, while I was putting on my makeup, my lipstick brush broke off just at the brush head. I didn't think very much at the time, but it was a premonition of the disaster to come.

It became more apparent that Alan was not doing well. Doctor Sanford, the gastrointestinal specialist who was in charge for the patients that day, thought we should determine where Alan's bleeding was coming from. I had a certain worry about the feeding tube just recently put into Alan's stomach; it might have been bleeding from there.

Immediately, Alan was put on a gurney and carried downstairs to the procedure room. We waited in a hallway outside. Alan was awake all that time and looked at me. I knew then what he was saying: "Please help me—I cannot go through this!" He was pleading to me, so I told the transporter, "Please take him upstairs—he cannot go through this." Without hesitation, he followed my command and quickly pushed Alan upstairs to his room.

When two nurse's aides put Alan back in his bed, I heard Alan's crying noise, complaining of his discomfort.

After that, the room became quiet. I sat beside Alan. He was awake, and I looked into his eyes and talked to him, explaining that if he died, we would never see each other again. It would be the most terrible thing happening to us. My eyes filled with tears, and I begged him not to leave me, over and over. His empty eyes looked at me, helplessly, without a word.

Then Alan's doctor, Dr. Goldberg, came into the room. I explained Alan's condition; then he said he would give him one more shot. He was going to put Alan into the intensive care unit and give him some procedure to save him. I was overjoyed that he was not giving up, so neither would I! I started to put our belongings together to take Alan upstairs to the intensive care; then a male nurse's aide came into the room and helped me. I was filled with energy and hoped the doctor could help Alan once more so I might be able to keep him. Then I looked back to see Alan and I noticed he was not breathing; his eyes were closed and he was quiet. I shouted, "Alan is not breathing!" I rushed to him, but he was not breathing anymore.

The nurse's aide left the room swiftly and never came back. Soon, nurses came in and Alan was pronounced dead at 2:55 PM, but his actual death was 2:45 PM. I sat at Alan's bedside and talked to him, but I could not wake him. I sat there for I don't know how long. An elderly woman with a Mexican accent came in. I had never seen this woman before, but she was supposed to clean Alan's body. I sensed she was indifferent to Alan's body, like some object. I was upset and said to her, "Go out! I don't want you to clean my husband!"

After that, I picked up the telephone and called the tenth floor where Alan used to stay—everybody on that floor knew us. Mary, the good nurse, answered, and I told her Alan had died. I wanted somebody to help me clean him, but not just anybody, somebody who cared about him. She understood and said she would send somebody for me. She sent Mohammed, a big nurse's aide. He was not my best choice, but he was a familiar face. I cleaned Alan's body; it was very important for me to clean him for the last time, as important as washing a newborn. Mohammed helped me. I thanked him and gave him some money. I thought it was the proper thing to do at such a special time.

I sat there for a long time. I could not leave Alan there. I had been with him all the time since we were married. The day was getting dark, and a nurse came in and told me soon somebody would come and put him in a body bag. They did not want family to see this and wanted me to leave. I stayed there until somebody with the body bag came in and then I left.

When I got home, the telephone had been ringing non-stop. People already knew Alan had died. They had heard it over the TV and radio news because, right after Alan died, I had called the Seattle Symphony and also Melinda Bargreen, the music critic of the *Seattle Times*, to inform them about Alan's death. I was on the telephone all night, even talking with people I hadn't heard from for a long time. It was very nice of them to call me; otherwise, how could I have spent that night without Alan after I had lost him?

In Japan, after a person dies, they do not take the dead away right away like we do here in this country. Instead, their family and close friends gather around the dead person's body and stay up all night to keep him company until the morning. They call this *otsuya*, "through the night." Now I realize it is a beautiful custom; it is very necessary to do this for both parties, the dead and the living, because they are both in shock. Even the dead have difficulty adjusting to their new situation, so it is not good to separate them so soon.

On June 24, three days after Alan had died, we had Alan's last viewing at a nearby funeral home. My son Bill came from Iowa and my daughter Joni came from New York. I thought this personal goodbye to Alan should be limited to our immediate family; for the public, I would give a memorial concert at a later date. Melinda Bargreen wrote a big article about Alan in the newspaper, but I did not give her the information about his funeral. Still, a few friends called and insisted on seeing Alan for the last time. I could not stop them from coming. Those who came were: Michael Ter-Minasian and Hamlet Ayvazian from Los Angeles, young producers of an Armenian magazine; Rodney A. Reed, our CPA, and his wife Jenny; Al Swanson, Seattle Symphony recording engineer; our Japanese friend Toshikazu Osako; Sue Hagard, Bill's sister-in-law.

Joni and I had gone to the funeral home earlier to take care of Alan for the viewing. When we got there, Alan had been placed on a stand sitting at the head of the room, his head facing to the left side of the room. I noticed his face was showing the fatigue, so I looked at the other side of his face. It was better, so I told the funeral director to change his position. He turned the stand so the good side of Alan's face was facing right. He looked not bad, but I put a little color onto his face. He was dressed in a white shirt and necktie, brownish-purple with a design, the necktie I had given him for his birthday, plus a pinkish, wine-colored sweater over it, the sweater he had worn under his jacket many times at his public appearances. Alan always had worn a jacket, but I thought that since he was lying, a sweater would be more comfortable. While Joni and I were taking care of him, I smelled a certain scent; it must have been put on by the caretaker to cover up the odor of the body. The day he died was the day I usually cleaned him, but because he had to go to the hospital by emergency, I could not clean him. That is why he smelled, and that scent lingered on me for a long time.

The time came when everybody came into the room. They all hesitated and stayed at the far end of the room, so I told them, "Please come forward to see Alan, and you can touch him," to encourage them. Then the people came forward, one by one, to see Alan. Michael, the young Armenian who had an outgoing personality, unexpectedly broke down into tears, then suddenly something remarkable happened, we heard priest-like voices, embracing their tradition Hamlet and Michael began to pray in Armenian language, their voices resonating like those of ancient priests captivating everyone in a profound spiritual presence. The prayer spoken in Armenian was *Our Father, Hayr Mer*.

During Alan's viewing, back in Chicago, Father O'Neill, a Catholic priest, was giving a Mass for Alan. He had called me earlier to coordinate the timing so he could give the Mass at the same time, while Alan's last viewing was taking place.

After the viewing, everybody gathered at my home and, one by one, they left. I took Bill and Joni to a nearby Japanese restaurant. Rodney and Jenny Reed came along with us. The whole evening, I talked about Alan.

A couple of days later, I had a telephone call from Brenda, my friend Sue's daughter. She also had lost her husband earlier that year. She told me she had visited her husband many times before his cremation. I was overjoyed; I didn't know I could see Alan again.

I went to see him on Wednesday, June 28, the day of his cremation. I drove up to Capitol Hill, where the main Bonney-Watson funeral home was located. When I got to their driveway, I saw a large van had stopped in front of my car, and I knew it was carrying Alan's body. Two men came out of the van and carried a big box with Alan in it into the building.

I followed them to a private room. Alan had been placed on a stand where he was lying in front of me, like a wounded warrior, pale, but as if sleeping. He had been ill for so long, I was used to seeing him sleeping, so I could not believe he was dead.

I looked at his hand. It was so white, and the fingers were straight, not contracted, like I was used to seeing during the last part of his sickness. I was painfully remembering his long fingers. Those fingers that had written so much music and had played the piano so vigorously. His hands were helplessly empty.

I tried to put a pillow under his head since his neck was loose, like a Raggedy Ann doll. Then I felt something inside his socks, it was heel pads. The nurse had put them there and he was still wearing them. I cried, "So uncomfortable!" Tom, the kindly funeral director, heard me and came to help in taking the pads off from Alan's feet and putting the socks back on.

My tears fell all over Alan's body. Then a sudden desperate inspiration came over me. I cut a lock of my long hair and put it in his white shirt pocket, close to his heart. "I will go with you, so you won't be alone."

I followed him to the cremation room and watched him going in, that was the last time I saw Alan. Later, I found his song, written for me:

> Long Black Hair
>
> In thy long black hair let my soul, my soul be buried there,
> In one long sigh, let me die.
>
> To Hinako, St. Valentine's Day
> February 14, 1975, from Alan

It is all over—the great composer is dead. He was my dearest husband and my whole world.

The next morning, I woke up and opened the sundeck door. My eyes, withered from so much crying, were squinting in the dazzling sunlight, and everything looked white. Then I saw something purple in the vegetable garden.

Purple Flower
June 30, 2000, 3:30 PM

What a miracle.
I found purple flowers, all blossomed, in my vegetable garden.
They weren't there yesterday or the day before.
I don't know this flower—I never saw if before in my life.
I know it's you—your color is purple.
You are giving me a beautiful message.

"What a Lovely Flower!"

Sat., Apr. 23, 2016, 11:55 AM

On a beautiful April day…

This year spring came early. The cherry blossoms, *Yoshino, Kanzan, Mt. Fuji*, came one by one, and already their petals are wilted and falling. But flowers covered the ground, exploding with their colors – among them a burning red-colored Azalea, hanging over the rockery, taking over the show.

I showed it to Chris, my company helper, and said, "Look at this flower!" Then he pointed to the Azalea next to it and said, "I like this one" – one with white and pink in the center (it was slightly past its peak).

Then I led him to another location and showed him the three little purple violets I had just planted – then he pointed to a small, white, weed-like flower and said, "I like this one better." I was shocked!

I was hurt, so I called my son Bill in Arizona and told him what Chris had said; then Bill said that he often calls India to discuss his project with an Indian engineer who works for the same company. His opinion to Bill is initially "no," to be "on top of him" (in order to be in control), even though he may actually agree with him. But Chris's case was not intentional – just his spontaneous reaction.

But I like a "Gentleman," like Alan my husband, old-fashioned gentleman that he was. He loved flowers, all flowers – that is why my yard is covered with flowers.

He often said that roses were (his master) Francis Bacon's flower. So what is Alan's flower? His favorite color is purple, so he would like my small purple flowers I have just planted; and I know what he would say –

"What a lovely flower!"

5/20/2016 *Hinako Fujihara Hovhaness*

Writing from Hinako about Alan

Tanabata
Story of Stars

♪

When I was writing the introduction of my mother's art book entitled "My Mother and Her Paintings," I mentioned my favorite painting of her, *Milky Way*. Then I remembered "Milky Way" in Japanese is *Amano Kawa*, which means "Heaven's River." I also remembered the beautiful legend surrounding "Heaven's River"—*Tanabata*. When I told this story to Dan, the editor of my writings, he said to me, "Why don't you write the story down?"

Yesterday I called my sister in Japan and talked with her about *Milky Way* and asked her if she knew the story of *Tanabata*. Today I found a three-page fax from her, all she could find out about the *Tanabata* story.

The story originally came to Japan from China in the *Nara* Period, 711–794 AD; and in the *Edo* Period, 1698–1838, it became the Festival of Stars among the Japanese people. It is the story of the stars, Vega and Altair, overlooking each other across the river, the Milky Way.

In ancient China, Vega (*Tanabata*), the Lady of Weaving, who was the weaver of the emperor's garments, and Altair, the Man Who Leads Cows, fell in love with each other and she became tardy with her weaving. The emperor was displeased with her and punished her by not letting her see her lover. However, she could see him once a year, in a clear night; otherwise, they could not see each other. The lovers were parted by the river between them, so the story goes.

In my childhood memory, in Japan, July 7 was the Day of *Tanabata*. Everybody dressed in a summer kimono (*yukata*) and walked to the stream carrying young bamboo tree shoots cut from the bottom and decorated like a Christmas tree with ornaments of colored paper (*origami*) and a poem written on them to the *Tanabata-Sama*. We all gathered on the riverbed and placed the bamboo shoots on the water to flow downstream, and we wished the two lovers could meet, and we hoped our wish could reach them. In the summer evenings, I sat and watched the beautifully decorated bamboo shoots carried away on the stream, and I could see the fireflies, one by one, lighting the hillside along the stream as the night approached.

Early this year, I had a psychic reading with Christina; she was seeing "stars" while we were communicating with Alan, who had died in 2000. At that time, I didn't know what the significance of the star was, but I realized how important the stars were to Alan. He wrote numerous pieces inspired by stars and planets.

His interest in astronomy started at a young age. He said in his own words, "At the age of four, I made my first attempt at composing on the eleven staff. My mother, who had a small harmonium organ, could not play it, so I gave up composing for astronomy—until the age of seven." Alan told me that, as a child, he built an observatory, by himself, in between two trees and watched the stars.

The story of *Tanabata* affected me deeply, maybe because the story reminds me of Alan and me, helpless lovers separated from each other, under the restriction of the rules of the universe.

Comic Strips

Since Alan died, I have had two readings with a Chicago psychic; during those readings, she told me that I am not alone, that Alan is right beside me. Recently, I received a comic strip "The Family Circus" from her, along with a letter in which she said, "Imagine my delight as I stumbled across the enclosed comic on Sunday while glancing through the newspaper"—something I rarely do, as it depresses me—"Alan is trying to deliver the proof—recognize it, my dear."

In the cartoon, a white-haired old lady is listening to the wedding song "I Love You, Truly" on the radio, crying and missing her husband. Her husband, who is on the clouds up in heaven hears his familiar song from below, so he decides to come down and dance with her, with the music "I Love You, Truly," and at the end of the dance, he kisses her and says, "Thank you for the dance," and she says, "It was heavenly."

I was hurt. I never expected my behavior. I never could accept my husband's death, and I tried to find him, even through psychics. I would be put in such a humor. I don't think Alan would like it either. I was disappointed in her and realized each of us interprets others on their own level.

Then I remembered exactly the same feeling I had when I was in the third grade, about nine years old, in Japan. I lived in a town called Ikeda. Ikeda was about forty-five minutes from Osaka by train. The town was divided into different sections by the train track. One side was the residential section; all the well-to-do people lived in custom-built houses. I lived on the other side of the track, which was the business section, and my mother had a sewing shop "*Acacia*" there. One block from our section, there were poor people who lived in run-down, traditional Japanese houses, and there was a candy store for the poor kids. We, Sunako and I, were attracted by their cheap candies, but we were not allowed to go there; my mother bought candies from Kogetsu (moon fragrance), the best candy store in town.

My mother was not rich; she was a working single mother raising Sunako and me, but she raised us as upper-class children; also, she believed in education, for she herself had gone to the women's college in old Japan and had put me in a very honorable state-built school for exceptional students, with uniforms and badges and all.

In my town, on the main road that ran parallel to the railroad tracks, was a small, shabby variety shop in a tent on the sidewalk where the ordinary public school kids hung out. I was attracted to this shop, so after school, I changed my uniform and crawled into the tent secretly from my mother. I remember that shop looked like an unkept den, but it had the junk, including the cheap candy *dagashi*, etc., every child wanted to have. I watched a man flipping *choboyaki*, which was like pancakes but not sweet, that they had diced Japanese pickles *takuwan* in them.

One day I was in a hurry and crawled into the den without changing my uniform; then the owner of the store with the cook and everything else was surprised to see me with the uniform and realized I was a student of the state-built school. He said, "Oh! You go to Fuzoku school." I was so ashamed that that was my last time. I never went back to the den.

Just as the candy store owner judged me based on my clothing, the psychic assumed that since I was older that I could easily accept Alan's death.

Even though I was offended by that cartoon, one picture caught my attention. On the cloud it is supposed to be heaven, and everybody is wearing white robes; some of them have wings, some of them are in the center of the cloud, but a few of them are on the edge of the cloud and looking down, still missing the earth. It made me cry; it is so true to life.

But one thing I am sure of is that if I look like this old lady, then Alan will never bother to visit me.

President's Name

All this started just because I turned on the TV one night. There was the presidential debate on the air, and it was just at the tail end of it, but I could still get to hear John McCain's talk. In the past I had felt uncomfortable looking at his face, because during the Vietnam War, he was a prisoner of war. He survived, but his body and face were disfigured from mistreatment and torture by his captors during his four years of captivity. But this time I heard him, and the genuine goodness in his voice, beyond his appearance.

When this presidential campaign started, I was not interested in any candidates, Republican or Democrat, even though I have voted for Republicans all this time like Eisenhower, Nixon, Reagan. Well, except the time of Bush, Jr. and Gore, I really could not vote for either; and also, at the next presidential election, I voted for Kerry the Democrat.

This time my intuition told me to vote for McCain, even though he was not doing well at the time. I had that same intuition for Reagan, and he became one of the great presidents of the 20th century.

So I have been following the activities of the candidates on TV and found out my sister Sunako over in Japan was doing this also. She explained to me that the Japanese economy is very much affected by the U.S. economy, so who will become the next U.S. president is of interest to the Japanese also.

During our conversation, she could not say the name of any of the candidates, even though the debate was translated into Japanese, but the funny thing was that I could not think of their names either except for Hillary Clinton. So I looked at the voter's pamphlet and realized how confusing their names were: Mitt Romney, Mike Huckabee, John McCain with so many m's. Besides, none of the names are fit for the President of the United States of America! In the past, the presidents had such great names like George Washington, Thomas Jefferson, Abraham Lincoln, Dwight D. Eisenhower. I knew those names even when I was a child in Japan.

I think the name is important because it represents the individual. Speaking of names, one name comes to my mind—Alan Hovhaness, my husband's name. When I heard it the first time, I liked it, and also, it sounded like "hosanna." I was right; his name was fit for a king. And he is the king.

Alan's Lifetime of Exposure to Different Religions, Including the Occult

What is God? It is the one who created the universe and everything in it, the one who holds the key to the mystery of life and death, the questions our mortal minds cannot decipher.

What is religion? It is to help us to live, but so many religions in the world claim their God is the only genuine one. Their narrowness and prejudice to others are behind our many wars.

To me, the different religions are like many gates, you eventually get to the same place, but you choose the gate most fitting for you to find God. We are like the story of the blind men trying to describe an elephant, but each one touching a different part of the body and describing it differently, but we are all touching the same animal. Alan believed people who live in this dimension are all in different states of development. Some are in animal states, so they have to reincarnate many times to learn to achieve their higher rank. Very few, like Jesus Christ and Buddha, had achieved mastery and reached heights in life that many cannot, and due to that, they don't have to come back to this earth and reincarnate.

My Religious Background

Before I talk about Alan's religious path, I would like to explore my own religious background.

My father was the second son of a rich country family. He studied to be a medical doctor, but at the time my mother met him, he had contracted tuberculosis and was recuperating from this disease that affected many young people in Japan at that time. I don't know what his religious belief was, but his family was Buddhist, which was the common religion of Japan.

My mother was born in Korea. Before she came to Japan, she was teaching in a mission school; then she got a scholarship from a Japanese bank to study in Japan. She attended "Senshin" Women's High School and eventually made it to Japan Women's College "Josidi." At that time in Japan, Japanese women were not educated, and they were even discouraged from pursuing a higher education. I had often heard, "A man does not want to marry a woman who has too much education." I think it was men's propaganda against women so they could control them.

So my mother was one of the very few highly educated women in Japan. When she was in college, Communism came to Japan and became fashionable among the progressive students, but later, they were expelled from school. My mother was one of them, but she confronted the school principal and insisted upon staying in school. Her argument was, just because she had been reading Karl Marx's modern social theories and had attended a few of their meetings did not make her a Communist. The principal was convinced and kept her in school, under one condition: to study Buddhism. So she did.

My mother was not religious, even though she understood religion theoretically. Her attitude towards it was sarcastic; she thought religion was for the uneducated and naïve people and it was good for them if it helped them.

But she believed in education. She sent my sister and me to Christian kindergarten, where children of rich, modern Japanese families attended, even though she did not have the money because my father died when I was only two years old and she had been raising us all by herself.

When I look back, my relationship with God (Jesus) was natural from the start. I talked to Him directly, praying every night before I went to sleep, even though my prayers were shopping lists of all the things I wanted to have. I grew up without a father, so in my young mind, Jesus became a father figure. In my understanding, all the men in my life, such as my uncle Onichan, my stepfather Otosan, my former husband Peter, and especially my husband Alan, were sent by God to fill my father's place.

Catholic

By the time I was in junior high school, boys and girls were separated. The boys went to a different school and passed by us on the street on the way to school. At the girls' school, there was a thing called "S" (sister)—an intimate relationship between two girls, usually an older girl chose a younger girl. I think this lesbian-like relationship was the result of separating boys and girls.

At that time, two older girls handed me letters because they wanted me to be their "S." But I liked boys and did not understand such a relationship and did not react in the way they expected. I must have been a big disappointment to them.

One of those girls who was kind of homely-looking was Catholic and took me to her church. It happened to be the building I passed every day on the way to school, but I had not known what it was. It was unlike other Japanese houses with the same black roof with grayish siding. It was a beautiful, bright, beige-colored building with an orange-brown-colored roof, and I was attracted by it.

She took me to her church and introduced me to the Father of the church. I was not familiar with Catholics and had many questions for him. One of them was: why was he, as a priest, not married? His answer was that if he were married, his baby's diapers would be drying on the line all around the church grounds and would not be proper. Another question was: why did he claim his religion was the only true religion? Then he pointed across the street. There was a bright, orange-colored, arched bridge leading to a garden. He said it was a shrine for the fox; people were actually worshipping the fox. He said that his God was Jesus Christ, the Son of God, and that it was very important to worship the true God. He also said that he was helping educate people; otherwise, people might be praying to a dry fish head (*mezasino atama*).

He was right—there were many superstitious religions in Japan. My sister and I found a small shrine in the middle of a farming field. Inside of it we saw an artificial coiled snake placed in the center. The farmers believed that snake was sacred and was a protector of their farming.

I attended the Father's catechism class, but I thought their catechism book was obviously man-made and was lacking the freedom of spiritual inspiration, so I quit going to the class.

Alan's Religious Background – Christianity

His mother's ancestors, the Pugsleys, came from Scotland and settled in New England. According to Alan, they were stubborn troublemakers who, at one time, challenged the American government. His grandfather, Walter Scott, was a Baptist minister who, at the time Alan knew him, was married to his second wife, who was much younger than him. Alan remembered one scene where his grandfather was, as usual, carrying on with his sermon-like talk to his company of guests. Then his wife said to him, "Eat your dinner, or else…" to shut him up. He was often mistaken for Sir Walter Scott, the famous Scottish writer, and he was proud of that. Alan read one of his grandfather's poems to me, and it went something like:

> "I sit on my easy chair, my cat on my lap.
> "Why can't the world get along with each other
> "Like my cat and I?"

I thought he was too naïve.

Alan's mother was a very serious Christian. She taught Sunday school, so he had to go to church with her every Sunday. While she was teaching the class, she often cried from her overwhelming religious inspiration. Young Alan felt ashamed, but he himself inherited her tears. By the time Alan came home, he was wild, having been confined in church for so long. His father, who had stayed home, said to Alan's mother, "Madeline—you brought a devil from the church."

Alan's mother was so rigid, even movies were evil, and she did not allow Alan to attend young people's gatherings. The one Christian girl who his mother approved of Alan found her "not interesting." Instead, he was interested in the prettiest girl in the school, and it was obvious to her, so what she did was tell everybody in school, "He has a crush on…" the homeliest girl in the school, in order to ridicule him. That was his first experience with a girl.

Alan was not interested in the religion set up for him by his mother. Instead, he was interested in psychics, and he asked his mother about them. Her answer was that they were all "scammers." They sent out "runners" to find out about people before the readings. And so she dismissed Alan's question.

His mother died when he was only nineteen years old. He must have missed her very much and hoped at least she was in the spirit world. I think his desperate need became his belief and religion.

Psychiatry

Shortly after his mother's death, he met Patt at a young people's gathering. That night he was playing the piano, entertaining the crowd; then his librettist requested Alan to play Mozart's aria "Là Ci Darem La Mano" (Give Me Thy Hand, Oh fairest, Whisper a Gentle Yes) from the opera "Don Giovanni." It was the librettist's intention to propose to Patt, but there was a twist, she thought that the music was Alan's proposal to her instead of his librettist's. As a result, Alan was married to the first girl he had ever been acquainted with, getting into the marriage before knowing anything about girls.

She was older than Alan and from a rich family. In fact, at one time, her father ran for the United States presidency. She had sisters and they were all lesbians, including Patt. At that time she was under the care of a psychiatrist to correct her lesbianism, and to do this, he thought she should marry a man. Alan was a good candidate to be her husband because he did not know girls, so he could take her the way she was and not freak out.

During their marriage, in the evening, she was smoking away, talking about Dr. Adler and psychology; that was her religion and answer to everything.

Rajah Hoydn, the Magic Ruler – Spiritualism

After his divorce from Patt, he lived for the next decade in a one-room apartment with Rajah the cat. This cat played a very important role in Alan's life. He even tried to save Alan's life by jumping into a river but was saved by Alan instead.

During that time, Alan became organist in the Watertown church to support himself. He played organ every Sunday, accompanied the choir, and also played for weddings and funerals. He wanted to make it as a composer, but at that time in Boston he was known as "composer of no performance." So in order for his music to be heard, he had to do it himself. He organized an amateur orchestra to perform his own compositions; he was the conductor and pianist for his concertos.

Often, his faithful violinist Grace Deeran came to his apartment to practice music with Alan. One

Alan and Rajah Hoydn

evening, they were practicing Beethoven's "Kreutzer" Sonata; suddenly, Rajah jumped up on the piano bench and played the piano wildly with his paw, looking at them both with most serious eyes. He was moved by one particular serious passage in it, and he did this every time they played this sonata. After Rajah's death, Alan became more deeply interested in Spiritualism and desperately looked for Rajah's spirit. His spirit came through many times, in many ways. Often, Alan saw his black fur out of the corner of his eye.

Alan called Rajah "Magic Ruler" and believed he was taking care of dead animals, who were entering the spirit world, including dogs! Every memorial day, Alan would put milk in a saucer on the table for Rajah.

Hermon di Giovanno, Alan's Spiritual Teacher

In 1942, Alan got a scholarship to study at Tanglewood. There his music was criticized and ridiculed by the powerful composers who were the heads of the school. Alan left the school the next day. After that incident, he seemed to have lost confidence in his composing and destroyed hundreds of pieces of music he had composed up to that time.

Shortly thereafter, Alan met the psychic Hermon di Giavonno. One night, Alan and his painter friend Hyman Bloom went to a Greek restaurant where Hermon worked and he waited on them that night. Even though he was a waiter, Hermon wanted to be an opera singer, so he changed his Greek name to di Giovanno, thinking an Italian name would help him to become an opera singer. That night, Hermon gave Alan a drawing of an Armenian king; this painting came to him psychically before his meeting with Alan. According to him, this king was Alan in his past incarnation.

One of Alan's medium paintings

Since that night, the three of them, composer, painter, and psychic, became inseparable friends, and that shabby Greek restaurant became their regular hang-out. Hermon used to dump table salt over the table and involuntarily move his hands in the salt to make a psychic image. Hyman was the one who persuaded Hermon to use paper instead of salt. Thanks to him, and because of his advice, Alan was able to keep many of Hermon's paintings.

Alan called Hermon his spiritual teacher. He gave Alan spiritual guidance and helped him find his new direction in composing. His advice was to disregard the fad of the contemporary music movement of that time, and he encouraged Alan to go back to his roots. So Alan went deeply into ancient Armenian music. "Prayer of St. Gregory" was one of his masterpieces composed during that period, and it has been the inspiration of many people.

Spiritual Experiment with a Dumb Witch

In 1947, Alan married Serafina, a young Italian girl who called herself an actress and a psychic. According to Alan, she was a so-called "dumb witch"; she could not help herself at all. The only power she had was negative power, and her anger caused damage to people around her.

During that period, Alan was interested in psychic phenomena and was hooked on the Ouija board, spending many nights playing it with Serafina and his regulars. He took Ouija messages and stories seriously and recorded every one of them in his notebooks. Among them, many of the stories were supposedly from Alan's past incarnations. The funny thing was, Serafina showed up in every one of them, as if she cut into Alan's life to make herself important.

Alan could not stand living with her, not because of her being a witch, but because of the chaotic life with her. While he was teaching at school, she was at a theatre, sweeping the floor, hoping to get into acting. The only thing she could offer him was coffee. Alan had always been thin, but during that time, he was most undernourished and sickly. Alan said, "When my body was weak, I became spiritual." He wrote "Mysterious Mountain," his most godly piece, during that period. He also said, "In my most depressed time, I wrote cheerful music."

Finally, he had to divorce Serafina.

India and Hinduism

In 1960, Alan married Elizabeth, a pianist. She was unlike Serafina because she was smart, intellectual, and honest. That was what Alan thought because he had the idea that musicians were honest.

During that time, many Indian musicians came to New York. Alan got to know them and spent many nights with them, listening to their music. They also brought their religions, which became a fad among the New Yorkers. Hyman was one who was interested in their religions, and he even visited India and encouraged Alan to get to know it. When Alan got a Fulbright Research Scholarship to study music in a foreign country, he chose India.

Alan took Elizabeth with him to India. Just before the airplane was landing, he saw a purplish smoke rising from the ground. Knowing India was a very religious county, he thought it was a "holy smoke." But it happened to be the smoke from burning cow droppings, which the Indians used for fuel.

Alan and Elizabeth had just been married, but India was not at all the place to go for a honeymoon; it was so dirty that she could not find a place to lie down. Their foods were so contaminated that most Americans who visited there suffered diarrhea because they were not immune to India's bacteria.

So Alan had to hire a servant to cook their meals for them.

On top of that gloom, he had to play the Ouija board with her every night. According to Alan, the Ouija guide who came through was a very low-grade spirit and not as Alan had experienced in the past who would criticize Alan's previous wife Serafina in low language over and over. That was about all of it; Elizabeth became ecstatic about the whole thing, but Alan disliked it very much. There was something neurotic about it all, and I think that the messages were not from a spirit, but came from Elizabeth.

Prior to that trip, in New York, she had a confrontation with Serafina, a peasant-like Italian woman. Serafina said she was still married to Alan because he had gone to some obscure state to get the divorce, so it was not legal; in other words, Elizabeth was not Alan's legal wife. So Elizabeth had to get even with her by influencing Alan to dislike her. She knew Alan had divorced Serafina not because he did not like her but because he could not live with her. Moreover, Elizabeth wanted to cut off Serafina's alimony that Alan had been giving. Elizabeth, being clever, must have memorized the position of the letters on the Ouija board and was spelling out words to manipulate Alan, becoming more and more excited as she progressed.

In conclusion, in India, Alan's basic need was not met, and he must have found out their religions were not for him but for strong Indians. But he was influenced by the original Indian music and added it to the vocabulary of his music languages.

Togi Matutaro and Shintoism

On the way back home from India, they stopped in Japan, which was like a paradise to Alan. At the airport, they got a hero's welcome from the Japanese; among them was a *yakuza* (gangster). Alan and Elizabeth stayed at the Sanbancho Hotel in Tokyo. Every morning they walked to a nearby restaurant and had a good breakfast. Alan was fascinated by Japan and their theatre: *No* (Japanese medieval lyric drama with very limited instruments and body movements), *Kabuki* (the most lavish and extravagant musical play, accompanied by *samisen* and other instruments), *Joruri* (recited ballad drama with *samisen* accompaniment), and *Bunraku* (puppet theatre). And Japanese girls! Alan thought they looked so young and were the most beautiful women in the world.

There he met Matutaro Togi, a Shinto priest and *gagaku* musician. *Gagaku* is ancient Japanese music used for Shinto ceremonies. Togisan taught Alan and Elizabeth their instruments. Alan chose the *hichiriki* (seven-and-a-half-inch-long pipe that looks like a piccolo and makes a sharp, piercing sound); Elizabeth chose the *sho* (mouth organ). There Alan was exposed to Shintoism and called Togisan his teacher. Much later, in 1977, when Alan and I were married, Alan asked Togisan to give us the Shinto marriage ceremony, but Alan's letter was never answered. I think Alan was a scandal, according to the Japanese moral standard. He was a divorced man. As long as he was married to an American (one of his own kind), that was not their business. But marrying a Japanese (one of their own kind), that was too personal to them.

Francis Bacon, Alan's Master

The 1960s, during Alan's marriage to Elizabeth, was his most intellectual period. He did not have an intimate relationship with her, but she influenced him intellectually.

During that time, Alan's interest was Francis Bacon, and both he and Elizabeth joined the Francis Bacon Society. I don't know which one of them was interested in it at first, but through this subject, Elizabeth found a mutual ground with Alan.

The Bacon Society was a secret society like the Free Masons, and it was based on the idea that Bacon was Shakespeare and also that he was the illegitimate son of Queen Elizabeth. The so-called "Virgin Queen" was not a virgin; in fact, she was married secretly to the Earl of Leicester and had, not one, but two sons. Bacon was the author of all of Shakespeare's plays and more. At that time in England, freedom of speech and writing was not permitted, so he disguised himself under his pen name to avoid possible prosecution. Moreover, the secrets of the queen had to be sealed, so he invented ciphers (secret codes). The secret of him being the son of Queen Elizabeth and other secrets were hidden in the Shakespearean plays in ciphers. The Bacon society has been researching and deciphering his codes to find the truth and prove Bacon was Shakespeare.

Alan had been interested in Bacon's ciphers, and so was Elizabeth, but that interest backfired on her. Alan applied Bacon's method (ciphers) to conceal his secrets from her. At the time I met him, Alan had that double personality and was rather fond of his cleverness. I think it was his solution to compensate for his unhappy marriage.

Christian Church Soloist

During the early 1970s, I was married and the mother of my three children. When I came to America, I found out from a local voice teacher that I had a coloratura voice (high soprano) and should not sing popular songs like I had been used to in Japan, and the only place I could sing was in church, so I joined a church choir in order to get to sing occasional solos. Every Sunday, I sang in the choir and my family came to church along with me—it was our routine.

Peter, my husband at that time, was born a Christian, and I was comfortable with his religion. After all, I had been exposed to Christianity before, and Jesus Christ was not a stranger to me. Then Alan came into my life, like the mysterious Flying Dutchman; he was a well-known composer and gave me his exclusive attention.

Divine Prophecy

One day, on Alan's birthday, he called me and said that his music was being broadcast over the radio, so I turned it on, and it was Alan's Symphony No. 4. While I was listening to it, I heard a voice, and the next minute I was on the floor thanking God. The voice came inside my head and told me I had been given two men in my life. I did not know the exact meaning of it at first, but I interpreted it to mean that Alan had come to me to fulfill my father's place, and he was the one to help me with my singing. After that event, strangely, I fell in love with Alan; that's all we needed for our love exploded.

The Devil Is Among Us

I later confessed to Peter about our affair, and that was a very difficult time for everybody. One night, Peter took me to his church. The minister of the church told me that the devil was not an imaginary being, but real, and he was among us and was working on us. He made it seem as if Alan was a devil, and I was scared. His intention was to help Peter and to scare me away from Alan, but I found that Alan was not a devil but was a loveable man. His weakness was that he could not control his emotion; moreover, he thought I was his true love, the one he had been destined to meet and the one he had been waiting for all that time, as was prophesied by a psychic a long time ago.

All my life I had been afraid of the devil, but now that I think about it, it is a convenient word invented by fanatical religions. Anybody who breaks their rules or practices religions other than theirs is called a "devil." It is a scary word. They prosecute people using that name, even innocents, and our wars have been fought over their religious differences. We call each other "devil," and it is happening right now.

Alan's Guilt

In early 1975, I separated from Peter and lived with Alan in a small apartment near the airport. At that time, he was not completely committed to me, for he was going back and forth between Elizabeth and me. He was torn between two women. Even though he did not have a physical attachment to Elizabeth, he was obligated to her because she had been loyal to him, helping him out by making recordings of his music, which took most of his income. *Sasano Yuki* (snow on bamboo), a stray cat, found by them on Queen Anne Hill and became like their son; Elizabeth thought he had been sent to them to save their marriage. Alan loved that cat.

Alan also felt guilty for taking me away from my family. He had grown fond of Peter, my three children, and Koko, my dog, and he knew he should not live with me in such an uncertain way. He had to make a decision whether to leave me or divorce Elizabeth.

Psychic Reading with Crown

When Alan was in New York, he went to Boston to meet Jean Crown, a psychic and wife of Alan's old friend Jack Crown. He had been telling Alan that his wife was a psychic and that he should get a reading from her. Alan visited her out of his frustration, hoping she could help him make a decision.

The reading took an hour and a half and was recorded. She sounded intelligent and spoke in a highly educated language. She talked non-stop for an hour all by herself; her words supposedly came to her psychically. She called Alan "master" and spoke to him as if he were in the same rank as the master composers of the past. She spoke of Alan's music and its future, etc., on and on, and I heard Alan kept on interrupting to put her on the right track, the subject he wanted to hear, the real reason for his visit. But she never paid any attention to him, so Alan finally gave up.

She spoke of Elizabeth and symbolized her as a bird. She kept on telling him to let Elizabeth fly; in other words, give her a divorce. Meanwhile, Alan was desperately trying to correct her, not Elizabeth, but Alan was the one who wanted to leave! But the psychic didn't pay any attention to him and told him, "Even though she will fly, she will never go away from your life completely." That part was true, because she got a large portion of Alan's income for the rest of her lifetime.

Then she told him about his daughter who had grown up without him and her unfortunate physical condition—that part had really come true. Later she developed a Parkinson's Disease-like condition and was in a wheelchair. The last time I saw her she could not sit anymore and was lying on a bed-like cart, but she was going everywhere on it. This subject made Alan worried, and he kept on asking her if this person was his daughter or his friend, and he was talking about me.

An hour passed and, by that time, Alan's anticipation had reached its highest. Then she finally asked, "Do you have any questions?" After a moment, he spoke, telling her he had a Japanese friend and was helping her with her singing by playing the piano with accompaniment for her. Then Jean said, "She is a sweet person, child-like—she always worships you in the right way. She is a lady I respect—don't reject her." Alan was so happy because that was what he wanted to hear and to have somebody to agree with him. He was relieved, even though he did not get a definite direction as to what he should do with me. Then she said, "I see a butterfly, the symbol of new light in life—you cannot get rid of her. As to Elizabeth, she will leave you anyway—let her fly."

At the end of the reading, Alan mentioned the invitations from Japan and Beirut, Lebanon. She strongly objected to him going to Lebanon and persuaded him to go to Japan.

Buddhism in Japan

He called me from New York and told me about the invitation from Monbusho, the Japanese Ministry of Education, and he wanted to take me to Japan with him. I got busy getting ready for the trip by getting a passport, etc. When he came back, we left for Japan together.

There I reunited with *Onii chan* (brother), my old friend. On one of the days he took us to a Buddhist temple. He was the kind of Japanese who was very knowledgeable and talkative and charming. Alan also was a talkative Armenian, but he could not speak Japanese, so he did not say much that day. *Onii chan* educated me about Buddhism; I thought their concept of religion was unlike Christianity and was theoretical and cold. One example was a Buddhist's death means "nothingness," dissolve into dirt and become one with the earth, not like the Christian idea of resurrection, eternal life.

In the temple, we sat on a bare floor. The building was wide open to nature with no doors or windows and filled with the early spring air. We felt the coldness to our bones, which was especially difficult for Alan.

Buddhism had been Alan's long-time interest, but at that time he must have found out he could not stand it physically. But he did not lose his fondness for the religion. He kept in communication with Shokagakai, one of the Buddhist denominations, for the rest of his life.

Sibaba, God's Helper

On one of those days when Alan was in and out of our apartment, he went to California. There he met one of Sibaba's disciples; according to that disciple, Sibaba was one of the Indian "gurus" and was supposed to be a reincarnation of another guru. He said Sibaba was like a magician; people prayed to him for help. He knew their needs; all they had to do was think of him.

Also, Alan had gotten a book of Sibaba's teachings from him and brought it back to me for my protection. I kept it with me, and whenever I was in trouble, I called on him. He was like a friendly helper of God. He looked Indian, and his hair was a kinky afro-style. He said his looks were "intended to be in tune with the people nowadays."

It was early in 1976, the last time Alan left me. Actually, he had disappeared, and I didn't know where he was. When he had gone back to Elizabeth, she took him to Canada so he could not communicate with me. But a month later, on my birthday, I saw him at a violin recital of Yehudi Menuhin at the Opera House. This was not by accident, but it had been arranged by Menuhin's sister Hephzibah in order for me to get to see Alan. They knew our situation and took my side.

The next day, Alan and Elizabeth and a friend of theirs came to my apartment to let me know Alan was not coming back to me. According to them, he had made the decision to remain in his marriage to Elizabeth. I could not believe that was Alan's intention, because he was so in love with me, to the extent that he got excited by my slightest touch. I am sure that this visit was Elizabeth's desperate attempt to cut off our relationship for good.

Before their arrival, I asked Sibaba to help me to get Alan back to me, using his magic. Shortly after their arrival and our brief conversation, Alan and I went into our bedroom and talked. What could he do? He could not hide his feelings for me and knew he was my husband and promised to come back. I know Sibaba was working for me that day, and at the end of our meeting, Elizabeth's intention to end our love affair was completely reversed.

After that day, Alan's painful journey without me continued. Elizabeth's plan was to keep us separated and as far apart as she could. He was taken to European countries by her, like a prisoner. He was watched by her every minute. He got into this situation because of his sympathy for her. She took him to France and Switzerland to establish his music career there, and so they could live there. But Alan's heart was not there. In his confinement, he wrote many letters to me. Those were his desperate attempts to keep me waiting for him in our apartment.

Psychic Reading at the Francis Bacon Society

Toward the end of their trip, they stopped in England. There, Elizabeth took Alan to the Francis Bacon Society and they set up a psychic reading for him. It was obviously intended by Elizabeth to influence Alan by using his master, Bacon. At the beginning of the meeting, Alan's music "Prayer of St. Gregory" was played, in order to arouse his spiritual inspiration and make him realize his higher calling and to forget about me. He cried, but it was because he missed me. Then a psychic was brought in and started the reading. Francis Bacon came through and gave a profound message to Alan about his music and its importance. At one point, Elizabeth asked the psychic about her future with Alan, starting with the question, "Why is he not touching me?" Her answer was, "He is confused," and her general answer to Elizabeth was that her future with Alan was not favorable to her. As far as I was concerned, the psychic said, "If he marries her, he will be tortured by her." Overall, that psychic reading did not go well for Elizabeth.

Conclusion

Finally, on June 20, 1976, he came home, his life-long journey was over. Later, in 1984, we found a house that Alan really liked, and he called it "Mountain View House." Here he lived with me for the rest of his life. Every morning he woke up to the view of Mount Rainier and the surrounding Cascade mountain range, as seen from the east side of our windows. His appreciation of nature became his adoration of the God who had created them.

Now, Alan is gone. Without him, the only thing that keeps me going is to believe in his belief. He said to me, "I will be with you in spirit."

In spirit, I will see him again; that is my salvation and hope.

History of Alan's Medicine

Last night I watched the movie *Awakening*, a movie about a doctor who tries to wake patients who have no memory and no function as a normal person. This doctor uses drugs to experiment, and at one point a miracle happens, everybody wakes up from their sleeping state. But soon they start having bad side effects and finally go back to their original condition.

This very dedicated and humanistic doctor learns from this about the limitation of medicine or drugs and that a cure is not the only answer for the sick, but it is also important to care for them with love and to accept God's intention for their condition, even though we are limited and do not wholly understand it.

This story brought me back to my own experience with a history of Alan's medicine...

Stewart Robertson, the conductor of the San José Youth Symphony, had invited us to come to California for the performance of Alan's Symphony No. 7 "Nanga Parvat." Our hotel was at the bottom of a hill, and every morning we had to go up the hill to get to a restaurant for breakfast. Alan used to go up and down Queen Anne Hill, where he used to live in Seattle, but this time, for the first time, he complained about chest pain.

After the trip, he went to see a cardiologist, whose finding was that Alan's heart valve was leaking and for this he gave him Lanoxin. Much later, in the 1990s, when Alan was hospitalized, I gave him one Lanoxin pill in the morning, as usual; later, the nurse unknowingly gave another one to him. Then I learned from the nurse that Lanoxin is very toxic and that is why the pill is very small. This could have killed him, being given two of them. Then I realized that the side effects of some drugs are deadly; from that time on, I stopped giving him Lanoxin.

In 1990, we were just about to leave home one day for my singing lesson. Alan fell from the stairs and landed on the basement floor. He broke his hip and was taken to the hospital by ambulance. The next day, he had an operation; he was under anesthesia and his memories were confused for many days. Come to think of it, it was a premonition of things to come.

Alan was bleeding from the stomach; it was not cancer but a broken vein in his stomach. For that, the doctor gave him Premarin, a female hormone, to stop his bleeding. According to the doctor, this was a new finding. Also, at that time in the 1990s, doctors were heavily influenced by the big drug companies and were giving many of these drugs to their patients.

Alan's bleeding stomach worsened. In 1997, he had an operation to cut out the bleeding part of the stomach. That was the only way to stop the bleeding. A few days after the operation, the doctor gave him Aricept, a new drug that was supposed to stop the progress of Alzheimer's. Two weeks later, after he had started this drug, he had a seizure and was unconscious for a few days. After he woke up, the doctor gave him another drug, Dilantin, to stop the seizure, so Alan was completely drugged. During this time, under these drugs, he had a funny, involuntary movement in his hands; the doctor said he had Parkinson's Disease.

A year later, I had to talk to the Alzheimer's Association and learned that there are cases of seizures reported from Aricept. I took him off the drug right away, but the doctor was not convinced the cause of Alan's seizure was from Aricept. He insisted on Alan continuing to take Dilantin to prevent the possibility of seizures.

Finally, one night he was so ill, I thought he would die. He couldn't even swallow the Dilantin; he spit it out and went to sleep. He woke up the next day and was fine, and for the first time, he was free from the drugs. I discontinued Dilantin altogether without the doctor's permission. After that, his involuntary body movements stopped and his seizures never came back, but, by that time, it was too late—he had been damaged by the drugs.

This movie reminded me of our situation at that time, and I cried for forgiveness. My husband was damaged by drugs and lived in such discomfort, and now I know for sure. The doctor's and my intention was to improve his condition and make him well, but Alan had to suffer. When he had his involuntary body movement, I watched him painfully, but what he felt, what suffering he went through, I will never know.

Tonight I suffer so much because our good intentions hurt him. We try everything to help those who are sick, but do not necessarily give them comfort but misery instead. Progress is obtained by trying even though it may fail, but there should be salvation for one's effort and concern for others.

If I could have the chance to do it again, I would not give him any drugs, even though he might not live as long as he did. At least he would have lived naturally. But it is easier said than done. How could I not have given him those miracle drugs? To give him a transfusion was essential because of his bleeding condition.

This painful memory has surfaced because I watched the movie *Awakening*. Whatever I did wrong to Alan was all in the name of love. I hope all is forgiven and only greater love will remain.

Alan's Photo

When I was looking for my daughter Joni's photo, I saw a picture of Alan and Joni together. I burst into tears. It was taken the year before Alan died when she was visiting us from New York. I am so surprised to see that Alan looked so bad. For three years he was so ill, and toward the end he could not even move his body by himself. I moved him and carried him in a wheelchair. I didn't realize he looked so bad then, maybe because then I was with him all the time and was used to the way he looked.

Just last night I was upset with all my family and even Alan. I was remembering the time he was unkind to me. I went to bed not liking him, but this picture made me forget everything bad about him and I was sorry and cried out for his forgiveness.

During his sickness, a journalist from Oregon wanted to see Alan because the symphony orchestra was going to perform Alan's music and he was to write about it in an article. Even though Alan was a well-known composer, this writer didn't know very much about his music. He needed to know more, and since we lived within driving distance, about a two-hour drive from his house in Portland, he wanted to come to see Alan. I told him Alan was very ill and could not even talk, but he insisted on coming and interviewing me on Alan's behalf, regardless of my inconvenience. He came and brought his wife with him. My friend Sue, who was living next door at that time, helped me dress Alan, put him on the wheelchair, and bring him to meet them. It was a big effort for us. We had Greek-style baklava, which his wife had baked and brought to us, along with tea. After that we had the interview, and I thought it went well.

After they had gone, Sue told me the journalist's wife had asked her, "Isn't Mr. Hovhaness unhappy living in such a condition?" I was astounded at what she had said. What a question that she did not see what we meant to each other and how precious our togetherness was, especially since Alan's condition was so fragile and we might be parted at any moment.

But regardless of his condition, we graciously shared our time with them. The value of life is different in different circumstances, but she did not have an understanding of that. After that, I didn't have anything to do with them.

During the same period, when Alan was very ill, Larry Sobol, a clarinetist that Alan knew because he had commissioned, performed, and recorded Alan's music, came to pay his respects to him. We had such a wonderful evening together, even though Alan could not speak like he used to. Sue and I prepared food for them. On such short notice, we didn't have enough food for everybody, so I shared my food with Alan and him. How admiringly Larry talked to Alan and kissed him so passionately at the good-byes. That was his last time with Alan. He always talked about how fortunate he was to get to see Alan for the last time.

A priest from Chicago, Father O'Neill, came to see Alan. He was a long-time admirer of Alan's music; he told me that the first time he heard "Prayer of St. Gregory," he had fallen in love with it. Ever since, he had been communicating with Alan, and finally, twenty years later, for the first time, he got to see him. But Alan was very ill and could not talk.

That evening I prepared food and we three ate together. Alan had not actually spoken in quite some time. Father O'Neill asked if he could feed Alan during dinner. After dinner, I was in the kitchen, cleaning the dishes, and Father O'Neill came in and asked for a washcloth. I was wondering and asked him, "What for?" He said he needed it to clean Alan's saliva from his mouth. Father O'Neill returned to wipe Alan's face, as I followed him into the dining room from the kitchen and sat down. I expressed my frustration and sadness that I was not sure if Alan recognized or knew who I was any more. I asked Alan, "Do you know who I am?" Alan responded very clearly, "You are my beloved wife." I could not stop the tears from streaming down my face. Strangely, Alan's saliva stopped after Father O'Neill cleaned it from his face. I think Father O'Neill's hand healed Alan when he touched his face because, Alan had faith that he would be healed through Father O'Neill.

How different were our views regarding the value of life. Some people believed that I should just allow Alan to die in peace, but others, like myself believe that it is a precious spiritual experience to preserve his life. Father O'Neill returned to Chicago and shared this story with his congregation during a Sunday service.

For three years I took care of Alan. It was a very painful time, yet such a wonderful experience and teaching from above for both of us, Alan and me.

He lived in such a bad condition for three years, but it was intended to be. We both needed that time to say goodbye, and I am thankful for the time given to us, and I am glad I took Alan's picture when he was very ill.

My Visit to the Emergency Room

Just because I had pressure on my chest, I went to the emergency room. I was confined in a hospital bed for four hours and hooked up with tubes on my arms. I turned on the TV placed high up on the wall, but it was such bad quality I had to turn it off. I asked the nurse, "Free me—otherwise, I will be sick! For the results of the test, I will come back tomorrow." But he said, "You cannot go because you are in Emergency."

Finally I got free, and all the tests came back fine. It was about eight PM and I hadn't eaten or drunk anything. So I dropped in to a Taco Time to get one taco and it was oh, so good!

Today I thought of my ordeal, how uncomfortable it was. Then I remembered when Alan was helplessly ill for three years and could not even move himself and I had to take him to the hospital often, and towards the end of his life, twice a week.

Shortly after he died, a psychic told me he was happy to be free when he died. When I heard that, I was upset. I thought I had tried so hard to save him, but he was happy when he left me. Just before he died, I begged him not to leave me; he looked at me with empty eyes, as if he was saying, "I cannot keep up with you anymore." Now, for the first time, after I went through my own ordeal, I understand how difficult it was for him, to be confined in his own body, not being able to do anything, even though he was sleeping most of the time.

One of those times when we were in the hospital room, a doctor who was on call for that day came in the door and saw Alan. He said to me, "Why are you keeping him alive in that condition? If he was my wife, I would let her die." I was shocked! He was a doctor; he should be saving the sick instead of letting them die. I hated him, but today I understand why he said that. He had been seeing sick people all day long for so many years; he felt their discomfort and suffering more personally.

So now, after this, would I try again to save Alan as I did, or let him die without trying?

I cannot answer that question.

Epilogue

by Tracy Holst

I am Tracy Holst. My husband Brandon Boik and I cared for my grandmother in her final days. My family moved to Seattle from Arizona to live with my grandmother. I took care of her full-time every single day while homeschooling my two children. I ensured that she had her basic life and hygiene requirements met as well as helping her accomplish basic life needs, such as paying bills and getting to doctor's appointments. Growing up I did not talk much to my grandmother, but I really got to know what kind of person she was during the last year of her life. She was a very strong-willed and stubborn person who didn't like being told what to do. Unfortunately, a hard fall made her life change drastically, and it was hard for her to accept that.

Alan passed away in the year 2000, and the many years after were extremely lonely for her. She would fill her void in life with writing poetry and stories. Bookcases are filled with the poetry she would write and occupy her time with. It is obvious that her love for Alan never faded. One thing I remember as a child was one time my grandmother offered me a chocolate, and I said, "Yes, I would like one." So I picked one that was in the shape of a crown, and she told me, "No, that one is for Alan," even though he had passed away a few years prior. She also never stopped signing his name with hers on all Christmas or birthday cards we received.

Within the first few days of coming out to take care of my grandmother, it was Alan's birthday. We celebrated it with cheesecake and tea while he sat with us on the dinner table, as he always did, in ash form along with an old portrait. She enjoyed reading to the family out loud the many stories she wrote out of this book. My grandmother would tell me that Alan would come to her in her dreams and tell her to hurry up and finish this book and get it published. I knew it was the one thing she needed to do before she died.

Then almost exactly a year after her first fall, my grandmother found herself back at the hospital from another bad fall in the bathroom. Her back was fractured, and despite being released from the hospital, she was unable to get up to go home. My family and I were the only ones able to visit her in the hospital, and she was embarrassed to be seen in such a state. Unable to turn to face us, we had to go around the bed to be seen. Up to her final day, she was requesting things from home and planning on getting us food on the way back from the hospital for the trouble we were being put through. She simply stopped eating, and with no reasons holding her here, I think she finally made the decision to let go and be with Alan. I was told by the nurse that she passed away in the very early morning. Her last word to the nurse on duty was "sayonara."

As I write this with tears falling to the keyboard, I am reminded of the phoenix, immortal but never stagnant. When it is very old, it erupts into flames and is devoured until only ashes remain from which a new baby emerges. I know that the ashes that my loved ones become are a symbol of their spirit being free once more and also that it is a necessary process to go through, just like the phoenix. The day after my grandmother passed away, my husband opened the front door to find a small bird sitting on the doorstep. Thinking it was injured or sick, he reached out and stroked its head a few times. The bird's little eyes opened sleepily and looked up at the giant that was petting it and instantly awakened and flew off. Earlier in the year, a good friend had died in a tragic accident, and the very next day a woodpecker burst into the house through the open door and began trying to get out the window and hitting it fiercely many times. I had to catch it to release the scared bird outside once more and was immediately reminded of our friend's passing. There were red feathers from its head stuck to the window, and our friend had red hair.

Tracy and Brandon at Grandma Hinako's funeral

The signs from beyond that our loved ones live on are numerous, and it is our duty to carry their memories to the future generations so they can be remembered for the moments they walked the earth. A dream of Grandma comes to mind where she was ecstatic that she could be seen and heard finally. She said, "Everyone has been pretending like I am not there, but now you can finally hear me! I have been trying to get everyone's attention by making the flowers bloom." Who knows what comes after this life; it is a mystery at this time, and perhaps that is the way it is meant to always be. I do know that what matters in life is the effect our actions have on others and what we do right now. Material things have no place after we leave. If we take nothing with us, then we must leave things behind. Material goods fade away, but the memories and love we leave behind are what will carry on.

My grandmother's life was honored with a beautiful service at the Bonny Watson funeral home. Many were gathered together and shared their most memorable experiences and memories of her impact on their lives. Now I feel like it was destined all along to be my duty to bring about my grandma's wishes she had while she was alive. In the month before her death, she would express her desire that this book be published, but not only that, but for the family to bring about Alan's full potential by sharing his legacy with the world. Alan had dreamed of a thousand harps playing his music in symphonies. I, too, share this vision and would love to bring forth such majestic performances. My grandmother was very elderly in the two decades after Alan passed away, and she had much trouble keeping up with the times. Business and interest would go unanswered and unacknowledged for months sometimes due to her declining health and ability to function like she had in her prime. I find myself in Alan's home surrounded by his life's works and I know that this is where their spirits are urging me forward to bring forth all of our destinies to the world. The music of Alan Hovhaness has a fresh new energy and is only getting started. The next chapter of this Shakespearean play of life goes on, and Alan and Hinako will certainly play a major role in all of our lives. Thank you for reading this beautiful book and getting a glimpse into the past as well as the mind of the world's greatest composer.

Epilogue

by Bill Holst

I was unexpectedly awakened from a deep sleep by the penetrating ringing of my cell phone in the dark, unlit room. I turned over to look at my alarm clock to check the time: 3:30 AM. Still in a slumber state, I questioned myself: "Who would be calling at this time?" Past experiences told me that a phone call at this hour could only mean bad news. It was just three days before Christmas, and I had been enjoying my vacation from work. I stumbled in the darkness to reach my glowing cell phone on the desk. I answered the phone to hear a very impatient woman's voice with restless activity in the background. She said, "This is the nurse at Valley General, we just checked on your mother and she is not responding. Would you like us to try and revive her?" I quickly responded, "What? Yes, of course." The nurse acknowledged my response and said she would call back. By this time, my wife, Coleen, had turned on the bedroom lights as we stood there frozen in our sleep attire. We could not comprehend what had just happened. The night before, the doctor had reported to us that my mother was doing well and that they planned to release her to go home for Christmas. Coleen and I quickly got dressed and paced the room for another twenty minutes, awaiting the return phone call. When the phone call finally came, the nurse told us that my mother could not be revived.

My mother's bogus journey started around the beginning of summer 2021. I would call my mother every night at 6:30 PM after her late afternoon nap. Since she was nearing ninety years old, I thought that I should check on her daily, considering I lived in Oklahoma and she in Seattle. My sister and her husband lived next door, but they had their own medical issues to concern themselves with. As summer turned to fall, I found that my mother would not always answer the phone at our set time. She claimed that she would oversleep, and I became aware that she would forget recent conversations. In early December, I noticed that she was getting much worse. She rarely answered my phone calls and would return my calls much later in the evening. Then, one morning in mid-December, I got a phone call from Mark, my sister's husband. He told me that my mother left the previous afternoon to shop at Costco. Later in the afternoon, Mark entered my mother's house to perform some phone, internet, and electrical repairs. Late in the evening, he was concerned that my mother was still not home from her shopping. He went out to the garage to see if her car was there, and he discovered my mother face down on the garage floor; she had been there in that state for over six hours. He quickly helped her up and took her to bed to rest for the night. When I heard his story, I told Mark to immediately call 911 and have her transported to the hospital.

This was during the height of the COVID-19 pandemic, and my mother was admitted to a special room for testing. That evening, the doctor called me and stated that my mother was stable, but she needed to remain in the hospital for observation. The next day the doctor called again and told me that my mother had too much calcium in her system, which may have caused her to pass out for the long period of time, and that she had several fractured vertebrae. He also stated that she would need to be submitted to a rehabilitation facility before returning home.

Coleen and I remained in Oklahoma, looking for a suitable rehabilitation center for her. After approximately one week, the hospital staff moved my mother to a large open area with many patients, separated with temporary room dividers. There was no longer a television or phone available, and the food was miserable. My mother spent day and night with no entertainment. When I called my mother, the nurse carried a cell phone to her bed, and my mother complained bitterly.

Due to the COVID-19 pandemic, none of the rehabilitation facilities could admit any additional patients, and my mother wanted out of the hospital now, if not sooner. The hospital would not release my mother unless one of her immediate family members checked her out of the hospital. My sister and her husband could not take on that responsibility; therefore, Coleen and I instantly booked a flight to Seattle.

When we got to the hospital and the nurse wheeled my mother out in a wheelchair, I was amazed that she looked so much older and fragile since the last time I saw her just six months before. Once she saw us, she appeared to be very happy and grateful, as if being released from the dungeon. We took her home; Coleen made her a home-cooked meal and we discussed our new plans.

I still worked as a systems engineer in Oklahoma on a highly visible military project; I could work remote temporarily, but not indefinitely. Coleen remained in Seattle and cared for my mother for the next six months while I split my time between Oklahoma and Seattle. We talked to our daughter Tracy to see if we could work out a six-months-on and six-months-off schedule to care for my mother, since twenty-four-hour care for someone can also impact the caregiver's health. My mother became quite comfortable with Coleen's care, so it took a considerable amount of persuasion to work Tracy into the schedule. By this time, my mother was very much stronger and had to be reminded to use her walker.

In late December of 2022, my mother fell in the bathroom, and Tracy called 911 and had her rushed to the hospital by ambulance. The doctor reported that her vitals and blood work were doing well. My mother did complain about back pain when trying to walk, but this was expected as the fractures had not completely healed. The doctor planned to release her within the week, just before Christmas.

After high school, I moved out with a couple friends—that rental agreement ended quickly and horribly. At that time, I moved in with my mother and Alan on a temporary basis.

Alan and I earned each other's trust and became very good friends. Every evening while my mother made dinner, Alan would tell me about his younger life adventures. Although Alan's life was centered around music and my life around baseball, we had many basic similarities. After dinner, I would sit on the couch and listen as Alan would play the piano. I had several conversations with Alan about what his music meant to him. He always said that his music was not written to make money, rather he wanted everyone to have the opportunity to listen and enjoy his music. At one point, Alan wanted to adopt me as his son. Unfortunately, out of respect for my father, I had to refuse the generous offer. Alan fully understood, and this seemed to create a greater appreciation for me.

My mother, Alan, and I shared many good times together. We all enjoyed good food and talking about past experiences. There were a couple of instances where Alan and my mother had disagreements. On one occasion, at the peak of the battle, Alan decided he was leaving for Tibet to become a Buddhist monk, and my mother planned to become a nun. Suddenly Alan was out the door (and heading for Tibet?). I spent the night driving around the neighborhood looking for Alan. When I found him, I was able to convince him to come back home. The next morning, things went on as usual as if nothing abnormal had occurred the night before.

Coleen and I were married on February 14, 1984. Alan played the music he had composed for the wedding, and my mother sang. After the wedding, they gave us a honeymoon trip to San José and Carmel, California as a gift. It just so happened that this trip would also be the premier performance of Alan's Symphony No. 50, "Mount St. Helens" Symphony in San José. The premier was performed on my birthday, March 2nd, and was a complete success. Our honeymoon in Carmel-by-the-sea was incredible and will never be forgotten.

Coleen and I had four children; although Alan had a daughter, he was very nervous around children. Initially, Alan and my mother built special precautions into their house for when Coleen and I visited with the children. Alan and my mother gradually became more comfortable with the children, and Alan very much became attached to the children. The children enjoyed Alan and my mother's company, and Alan seemed to be very content with his role of being a grandfather.

After Alan passed away in 2000, my mother started documenting the many adventures she and Alan had during their years together. She recorded these adventures into short stories and wanted everyone to know the personal side of Alan, not just as a composer. Her ultimate goal was to publish this book before she died. Unfortunately, the fall in the garage created a roadblock for her to complete that goal. This very important purpose now lies in the hands of my family, to share these valuable memories of Alan and Hinako Hovhaness's life events.

My mother and I always had our differences; she had a very strong, overpowering personality, and she was always the center of attention. My father was a very calm, consistent, and silent contributor. Although my mother and father were no longer married, they still had a very close friendship; whenever my mother needed help or advice, my father was there. I have been told that my personality weighs heavily on my father's side. When my father passed away in 2014, I became the person to provide her support. Even though my mother and I had quarrels, we always had a mother-son bond and had a certain dedication to each other. I recall during the final months that Coleen and I cared for my mother, we would help her to bed and kiss her good night, and she would always say, "You are my good son."

I got up early this morning to renew my driver's license. I arrived at the Department of Motor Vehicles fifteen minutes before they opened, expecting to be the first in line. To my amazement, there was a line of people standing and waiting to get in, and several more rushing to get in line. As I stood there in the Seattle drizzling rain, I observed the people in line and realized that each person had a very important story to tell about their journey. Each and every decision that they make has an impact on their families and the people around them, ultimately having some effect on the framework of the universe.

Alan has made a great contribution to the world through his music, and my mother's ambition was to provide that gift to as many people as possible. However, that mission is still not complete. Alan's ambition was to share his God-given creative beauty with others. I consider my commitment to Alan is to now carry that torch. As I grow older, I ponder the future and seek to fulfill the initial question that I very much sense will be asked at judgement: "What was your contribution to humanity?"

Bill and Coleen Holst at the Hovhaness home

Author's Family History

♪

Jun Bokuhuku was born on April 5, 1909, in Kunsun, Korea (South Korea). She attended the primary school and Merry Bowellton Junior High School (American missionary school) in Kunsun, Korea. She then went on to study at Senshin High School for Women (Buddhist School of Shingon-sect, connected with Koyasan) in Osaka, Japan. After graduating from high school, she attended Japan Women's College in Tokyo, where she majored in Home Economics. In that time period, it was extremely out of the ordinary for a woman to attend college, and even more so for a Korean woman in a Japanese college, due to the prejudices between the Japanese and Koreans.

While attending college she met Katsuji Fujihara, a Japanese surgeon and sculptor. He was attracted to Jun's beauty and her determination. Although Katsuji's middle-class (Samuri) family did not approve of his relationship with a Korean woman, the relationship continued, which eventually led to marriage. Jun and Katsuji had two children, Hinako (March 28, 1932) and Sunako (October 31, 1933). Unfortunately, Katsuji was diagnosed with tuberculosis and died just ten months after the birth of Sunako. With little or no support from Katsuji's family, Jun was tasked with raising two young girls without the help of a father.

In Japan at that time, a widowed woman with children was considered a doomed woman. No man would think of establishing a relationship with a woman in this situation; therefore, it was up to Jun alone to provide for her daughters. Jun started to sew for a living to support the family using the little knowledge of dressmaking she learned from college. During World War II there was a massive food shortage, and the Japanese government allowed communities to harvest the mountain potato fields. Jun and Sunako would get up early to walk an hour to the fields (carrying hoes and wearing straw sandals) to dig potatoes most of the day, just to bring home the necessary food to survive. Hinako would occasionally participate (mainly during sweet potato season) but would remain at home and write poetry and practice her singing.

The family was very poor, and during wartime, there were occasional air bombing alarms, and everyone would need to scramble to their assigned shelters. There were many daily obstacles that added to the difficult life; however, the two girls still did very well in school. Both girls attended school at Minoh Jiyu Gakuen, Minoujugakuen Elementary School, and Baika Jogakuin High School. Hinako was the more sociable of the two daughters, whereas Sunako was the more intelligent. These traits would very much contribute to their success in the future.

Jun did eventually remarry and had another daughter, Ahiko. Jun's first two daughters would refer to their stepfather as "Otosan" (respectful and affectionate term for father). Hinako remembered that after school, she (carrying baby Ahiko on her back) and Sunako would go and buy "street vendor" treats (considered poor children's junk food); they very much craved these cheap delicacies.

The three went through very rough times during World War II, but their lives would gradually change due to their dedication, education, and love for art.

Jun Fujihara

Jun Fujihara

While her two daughters were very young, Jun supported her single-parent family by dressmaking. This eventually transitioned into owning her own sewing shop named "Acacia," which is an exotic European tree with fragrant yellow flowers. Prior to her husband, Katsuji's, death, he told Jun that she should have something of her own. He knew she wanted to paint and encouraged her to do so. When her daughters were still children, she would take them to art exhibitions, and they grew up amongst her artist friends and art galleries.

After Jun's daughter Hinako married, moved to Seattle, and had her first child, she visited Seattle and entered her paintings into competition. She won first prize at the exhibition of Bellevue Arts with her painting *Birds Waiting for the Night* and Honorable Mention at the Puyallup State Art Fair with her painting *Dark Stream*.

One of the leading artists in Seattle at that time was Mark Tobey, and Seattle art was tending towards oriental artwork. Several of her paintings during this time frame took on the oriental style of painting. Later in 1959, she arranged a one-woman show at the Otto Seligman Gallery in Seattle. On opening night, Mark Tobey attended the show and bought one of her oriental-style paintings.

In 1961, Jun moved to New York City and resided there until 1987. While living in New York she began painting the city skylines in separate series called *Memorial of Time*, *Skyline*, and *Windows*. These paintings captured the skyline, integrating colors, shapes, angles, and textures.

In 1987, Jun moved to Seattle next door to her daughter Hinako. Her artwork again transitioned into another phase; this time she began painting vibrantly colored flowers. Some believe that these paintings were her masterpieces. There she spent her remaining years experiencing adventures with Hinako and Alan, her grandchildren and great-grandchildren.

Jun Fujihara's exhibitions and awards are too extensive to display here; however, here are a few important events:

- 1955: One-Woman Show at Saegusa Gallery, Tokyo
- 1957: One-Woman Show at Cultural Center of America in Yokohama, Takashimaya Galleries, in Tokyo and Osaka
- 1961: Exhibition of Contemporary Japanese Painting by Japan Society in New York

- 1962: Five Painters' Show at Nippon Gallery in New York
- 1965: The 29th Biennial Exhibition of Contemporary American Painter at Corcoran Gallery, Washington, D.C.
- 1976: One-Woman Show at Korean Center in New York
- 1977: Painting Exhibition by Jun Fujihara at the National Museum of Modern Art

Hinako Hovhaness

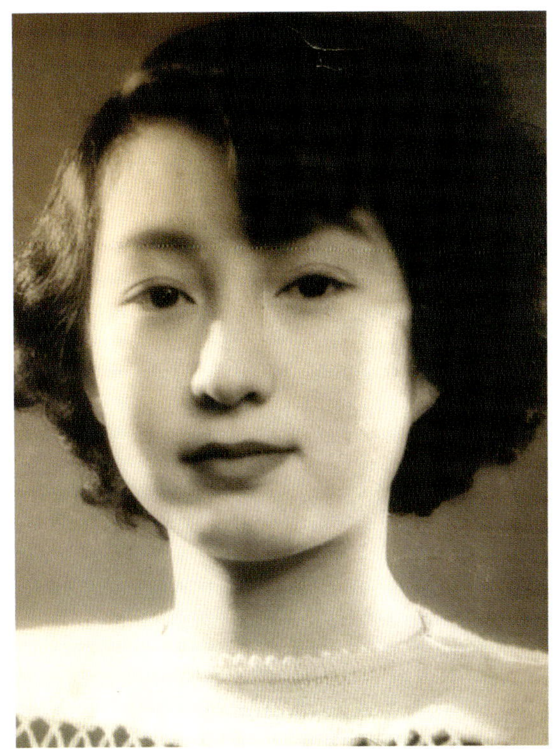
Hinako Hovhaness

When Hinako was seventeen, her many interests included koto (traditional Japanese string instrument), Japanese dance, ballet, vocal music, and piano. Otosan (her stepfather) worked at the Daiei Film Company in Kyoto. Otosan noticed that Hinako had an interest in singing and acting, and he was able to obtain an apprenticeship for her at the studio. Every morning Hinako would get up early and walk to the train station in Osaka, which would take her to Kyoto, where she would walk to the movie studio. The days and commute were long, but her hard work paid off. Hinako appeared in several Japanese advertisements, and she also played a role in the movie *The Tale of Genji*. This experience and dedication to her talents exposed her to new avenues. Although Hinako had been dedicated to acting, her career took a turn; during the Korean war she established herself in the *Tony and Joni Show*, where she starred as a singer performing in a club for American soldiers. She met the conservative club manager Peter Holst, where his restraint for the indulgences intrigued her. Hinako left an opportunity for the two to meet, which eventually led to a long relationship. The two were married in Osaka. Peter secured an honorable discharge from the army, and in 1956 they moved to America to start their family. They initially had a brief stay in San Francisco, but when Peter was offered a job at Boeing, they moved to Seattle. Hinako and Peter remained in Seattle and raised three children (June, Joni, and Bill).

Hinako continued her studies as a singer and was known for her beautiful coloratura soprano voice. She performed in the Seattle Opera auxiliary chorus and performed in numerous concerts and as a church soloist. During a piano recital in 1974, she met the world-renowned composer, Alan Hovhaness. After both went through divorces, they eventually married in 1977 (Alan twenty-one years her senior). Hinako continued her singing career and took over the role of Alan's manager so that Alan could concentrate on composing. They created Fujihara Record Company, later changed to Hovhaness-Fujihara Music Company.

Due to Alan's music popularity, they traveled to many countries and throughout the United States and had many music and personal related adventures. Alan wrote many pieces tailored to Hinako's voice and several were performed and recorded. As Alan grew older and his composing slowed due to health issues, Hinako had a major issue confronting her. She decided to give up her career as a singer to care for Alan and operate the Hovhaness-Fujihara Music Company. After Alan's death in 2000, Hinako continued to successfully manage Alan's works and keep his legacy alive, until her passing on December 22, 2022.

Hinako Hovhaness's list of achievements

- Seattle Opera auxiliary chorus
- 1984 KCTS Television Documentary
- Coloratura Soprano 38th Symphony
- Coloratura Soprano 47th Symphony
- Hovhaness Treasures CD, Coloratura Soprano
- President of Hovhaness-Fujihara Music Company, Inc.

Sunako Hata

Sunako Hata

About the time Sunako graduated from Kobe College, her mother, Jun Fujihara, moved to New York to follow her career, and her sister, Hinako, had already married and relocated to Seattle. Sunako felt somewhat alone since her mother was her best friend and art-awareness mentor.

Sunako met Makiko Hata (Women's Integrated Art Organization) during her college days and found that Makiko was working on original, radical designs in color and knitwear fashion. After graduating from college, Sunako went to Tokyo and became Makiko's assistant. Meeting Makiko changed the course of Sunako's life, and soon she became Makiko's adopted daughter.

When Sunako first saw Makiko's collection, she felt as if she had seen color for the first time. For the next eight years Sunako grew an interest in the color design. During a trip to Paris, Makiko presented her collection to top haute couturiers; her collection was a great success and was labeled as "Poet of Knitwear." During that trip influential colorists from France, Italy, and Switzerland were meeting to organize an International Commission for Fashion and Textile Colors and Japan needed to be represented, based on the magnitude of this collection. In 1963 Japan joined the association and Makiko was named as a board member of the Japan Fashion Color Association.

Makiko never tried to influence Sunako to be a designer or ask her to become her successor. Regrettably, toward the end of 1964, Makiko was diagnosed with cancer, and ten months later in October 1965 she passed away. The staff was in disarray and was not sure of the path of the company. Sunako had to make a serious assessment and realized that she must take on this challenge as a colorist. She needed to find a way to express her designs through color.

When Sunako took over the company, knitwear designers were low on the fashion design scale, so she had to challenge the position of knitwear in the fashion world. She started with plain stitch and believed that the value was not dependent on the complexity represented by the knitted plane, rather how it was used in the design. Sunako knew the different techniques to knitting and how to choose type of yarn and gage, but she did not know how to knit. "Designing is the representation of an idea in a single instant, and knitting is the process; they are different in nature. Designing requires a greater variety of factors to be considered: color, yarn type, texture, and shape. This requires the proper combination of these elements."

Six months after Makiko's death, Sunako introduced her first collection, *The Creation of Color*. She had to produce an entirely new collection in six months; however, she enjoyed designing knitwear and accumulated the experience and knowledge, so she felt very comfortable. The 1968 Paris Student Demonstration changed her way of thinking. She realized that Paris was no longer the center; cultures of all regions are equal.

Sunako has continued her successful knitwear career with evolving designs, producing yearly profiles. She has partially retired, generously giving her business to the company staff, and she is currently active in presenting design seminars.

"I express myself, my feelings, and ideas in design; design is simply a means of expression. Its possibilities and its limitations are part of the totality that includes an environment, models, a mise-en-scene, lighting, sound, printed matter, and so on. My knitwear is part of this totality."

Sunako Hata's accomplishments:

- 1965: Chairman of the White South Wind Company of the foundation corporation and educating "Fashion and Color"
- 1970: 14th "Japan Fashion – Editors Club – Award (FEC Award)"
- 1992: Received the seventh "Wada Sanzo Colors Award"
- 1994: 8th CS Design Award Experiment Division Gold Prize Winner
- 1995: Sold as a representative of Japan to the Gwangju Biennale International Art Costume Exhibition

Awards

The composer Alan Hovhanness earned
the following awards and accolades.

1997 Seattle Symphony Arts Award, Japanese and Armenian Awards

1985/1986 National Academy of Television Arts and Sciences Award,
Key to Dade County, Florida, and Armenian Award

1992 State of Nevada Governor's Proclamation and Key to Las Vegas

HARVARD UNIVERSITY AWARD
1993

HARVARD
UNIVERSITY

The President
of Harvard College presents
this certificate to

Alan Hovhaness

in grateful recognition of his service as
Visiting Artist during 1992–93
and of his contribution to the Arts.
Given at Cambridge, Massachusetts in
the Year of Our Lord, nineteen hundred
and ninety-three and of Harvard College
the three hundred and fifty-seventh.

Neil Rudenstine

PRESIDENT

1993 Recognition of Service as Visiting Artist from Harvard University

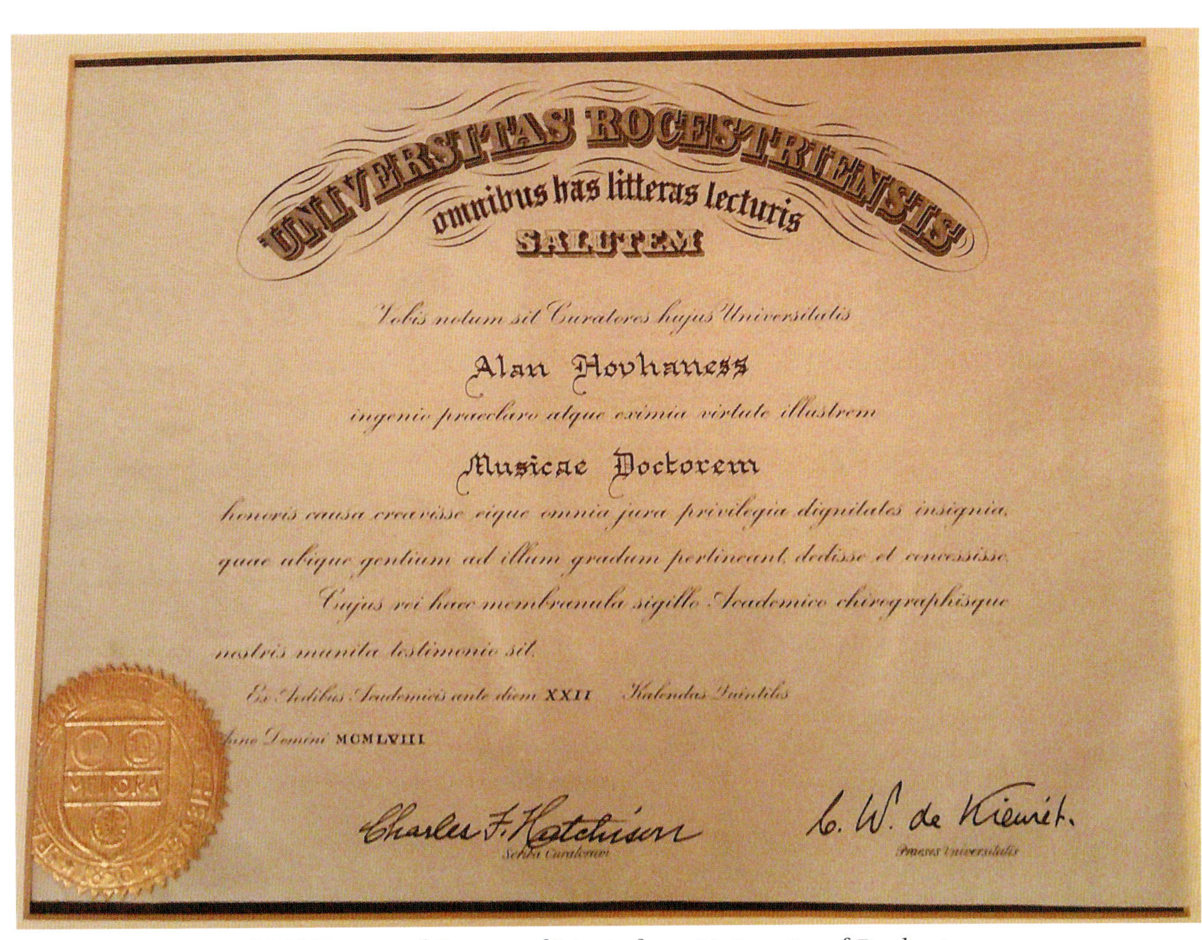
UNIVERSITAS ROCESTRIENSIS
omnibus has litteras lecturis
SALUTEM

Vobis notum sit Curatores hujus Universitatis

Alan Hovhaness

ingenio praeclaro atque eximia virtute illustrem

Musicae Doctorem

honoris causa creavisse eique omnia jura privilegia dignitates insignia, quae ubique gentium ad illum gradum pertineant, dedisse et concessisse.

Cujus rei haec membranula sigillo Academico chirographisque nostris munita testimonio sit.

Ex Aedibus Academicis ante diem XXII Kalendas Quintilis

Anno Domini MCMLVIII

Charles F. Hutchison
Scriba Curatorum

C. W. de Kiewiet
Praeses Universitatis

1958 Degree of Doctor of Music from University of Rochester

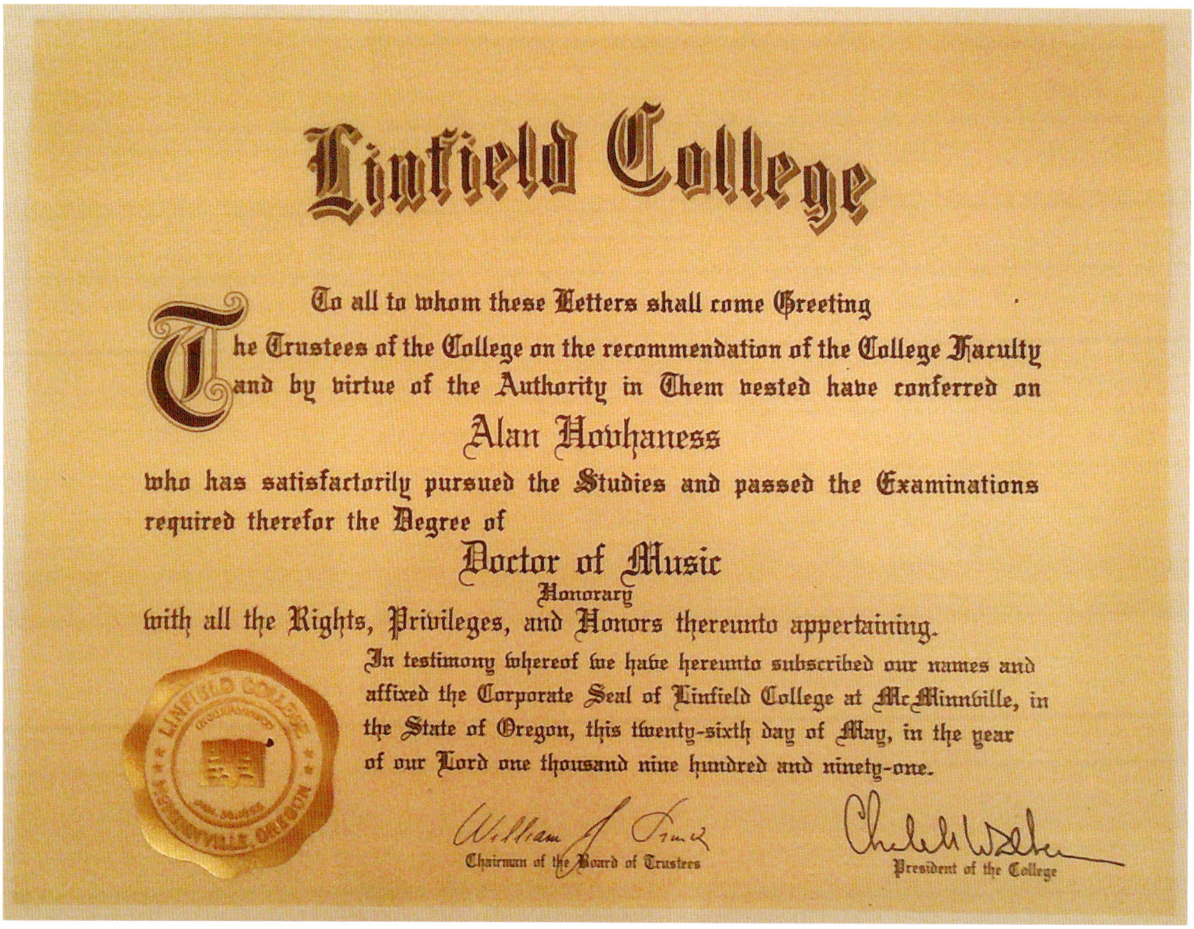

Linfield College

To all to whom these Letters shall come Greeting

The Trustees of the College on the recommendation of the College Faculty and by virtue of the Authority in Them vested have conferred on

Alan Hovhaness

who has satisfactorily pursued the Studies and passed the Examinations required therefor the Degree of

Doctor of Music
Honorary

with all the Rights, Privileges, and Honors thereunto appertaining.

In testimony whereof we have hereunto subscribed our names and affixed the Corporate Seal of Linfield College at McMinnville, in the State of Oregon, this twenty-sixth day of May, in the year of our Lord one thousand nine hundred and ninety-one.

Chairman of the Board of Trustees

President of the College

1991 Degree of Doctor of Music from Linfield College

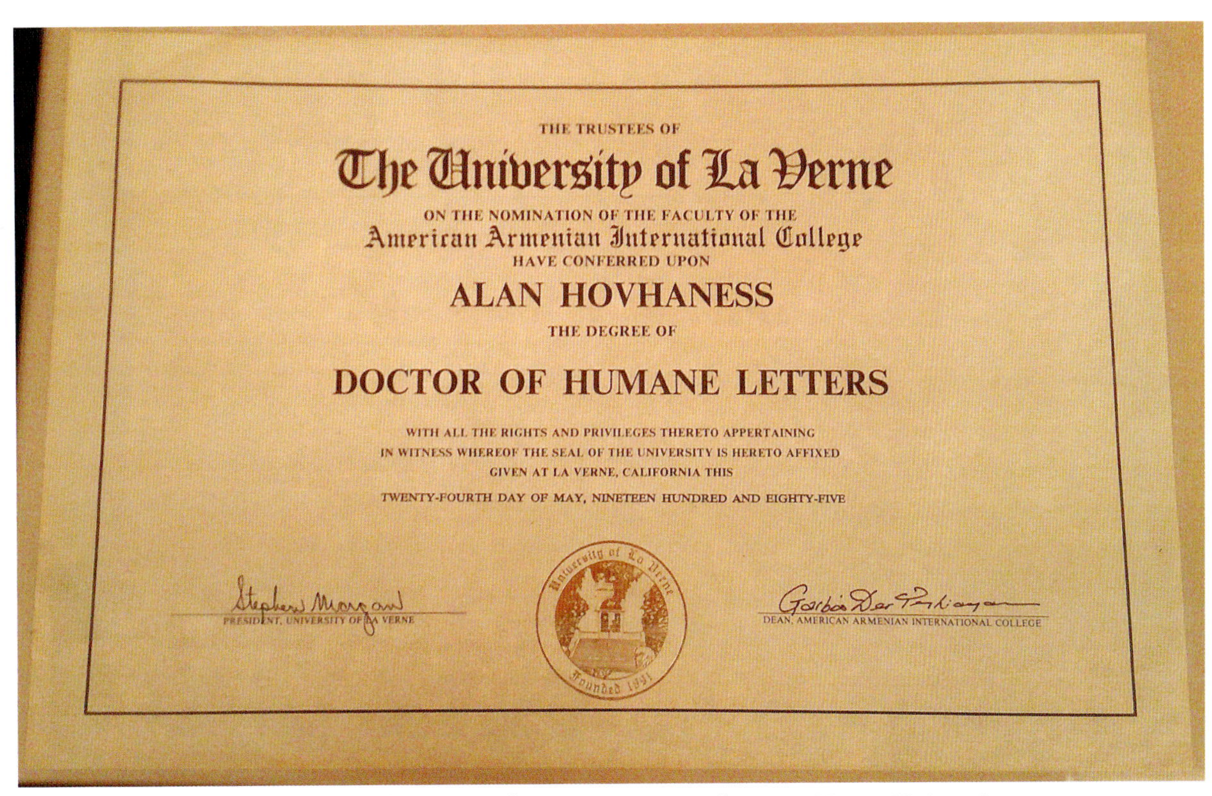

THE TRUSTEES OF

The University of La Verne

ON THE NOMINATION OF THE FACULTY OF THE

American Armenian International College

HAVE CONFERRED UPON

ALAN HOVHANESS

THE DEGREE OF

DOCTOR OF HUMANE LETTERS

WITH ALL THE RIGHTS AND PRIVILEGES THERETO APPERTAINING
IN WITNESS WHEREOF THE SEAL OF THE UNIVERSITY IS HERETO AFFIXED
GIVEN AT LA VERNE, CALIFORNIA THIS
TWENTY-FOURTH DAY OF MAY, NINETEEN HUNDRED AND EIGHTY-FIVE

PRESIDENT, UNIVERSITY OF LA VERNE

DEAN, AMERICAN ARMENIAN INTERNATIONAL COLLEGE

1985 Degree of Doctor of Humane Letters from La Verne University

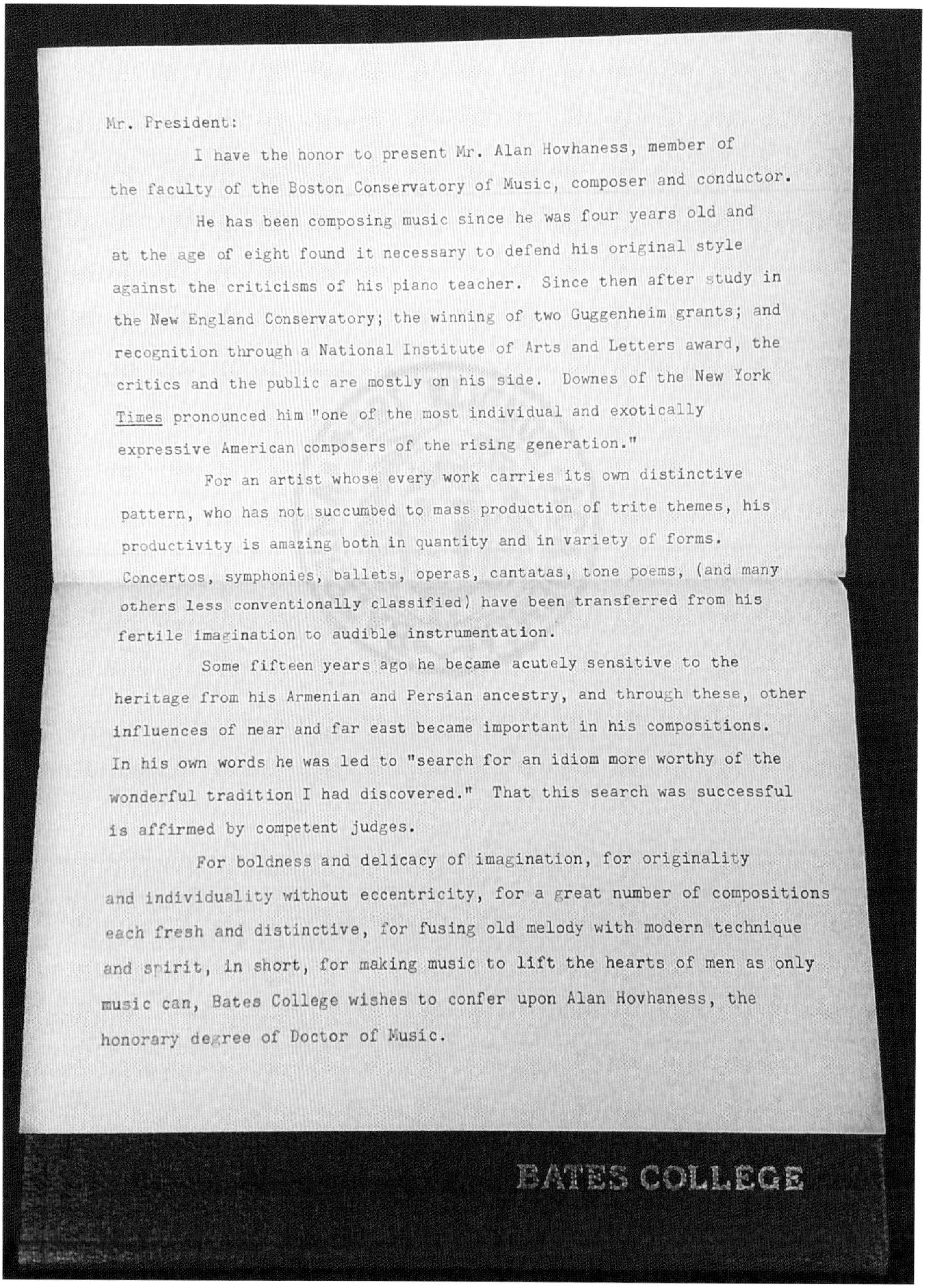

Mr. President:

I have the honor to present Mr. Alan Hovhaness, member of the faculty of the Boston Conservatory of Music, composer and conductor.

He has been composing music since he was four years old and at the age of eight found it necessary to defend his original style against the criticisms of his piano teacher. Since then after study in the New England Conservatory; the winning of two Guggenheim grants; and recognition through a National Institute of Arts and Letters award, the critics and the public are mostly on his side. Downes of the New York Times pronounced him "one of the most individual and exotically expressive American composers of the rising generation."

For an artist whose every work carries its own distinctive pattern, who has not succumbed to mass production of trite themes, his productivity is amazing both in quantity and in variety of forms. Concertos, symphonies, ballets, operas, cantatas, tone poems, (and many others less conventionally classified) have been transferred from his fertile imagination to audible instrumentation.

Some fifteen years ago he became acutely sensitive to the heritage from his Armenian and Persian ancestry, and through these, other influences of near and far east became important in his compositions. In his own words he was led to "search for an idiom more worthy of the wonderful tradition I had discovered." That this search was successful is affirmed by competent judges.

For boldness and delicacy of imagination, for originality and individuality without eccentricity, for a great number of compositions each fresh and distinctive, for fusing old melody with modern technique and spirit, in short, for making music to lift the hearts of men as only music can, Bates College wishes to confer upon Alan Hovhaness, the honorary degree of Doctor of Music.

BATES COLLEGE

Honorary Degree of Doctor of Music from Bates College

pizz

Pizz